More Praise for *High Noon*

"Though Frankel began this sumptuous history long before the latest election, he ends up reminding us that 2016 was far from the first time politicians trafficked in lies and fear, and showing us how, nonetheless, people of integrity came together to do exemplary work." —*The Washington Post*

"Mixing elements of biography, social history and film analysis, author Glenn Frankel uncovers drama and tragedy not usually found in discussions of moviemaking. His detailed narrative is a primer for those who don't understand how the blacklist era endangered free speech and other constitutional values." —Associated Press

"Frankel reviews the now familiar history of the blacklist with grace and accuracy; his descriptions of witness testimony are particularly vivid . . . Fascinating." —*Los Angeles Times*

"Frankel paints a devastating picture of a powerful force crumbling under oppression—a cautionary tale in borrowed cowboy hats . . . *High Noon* is a sharp social history that reminds us just how common for a broken system to abuse its power and cause deep human damage—the worst is coming, any second—but also that a little cynicism can be useful. Kane defends a worthless city; Kane wins. There are no clean endings, except in the movies." —NPR.org

"So much has been written about the blacklist's perpetrators and victims that you might be forgiven for thinking you know all there is worth knowing, but Frankel offers new details and fresh insights. His portrait of Gary Cooper's life and career is equally incisive . . . It will almost surely stand as the definitive document about this landmark movie. I can't wait to see what subject this skilled journalist will tackle next." —Leonard Maltin

"[A] compelling new book . . . The real strength of Frankel's account lies in its illustration, in many shades of gray, of the Hollywood blacklist and what it did, in practical terms, as it ruined or derailed many, many careers . . . The Red Scare Hollywood era is familiar nonfiction territory, but Frankel makes it vital and gets down to the roots." —*Chicago Tribune*

"Film historian Glenn Frankel profiles the times, the movie and its message in his fascinating and revealing new book *High Noon* ... Frankel—who previously uncovered the backstory of the classic John Wayne movie *The Searchers*—says the blacklist marked a uniquely grim time in American history, one with special resonance today."
—*The Christian Science Monitor*

"Glenn Frankel has endowed the term 'film historian' with a sweeping new dimension. *High Noon* is full of scholarly insight, compelling history, and wonderfully dishy moments, but like his previous book on *The Searchers*, it is also an American chronicle of real consequence. When Frankel writes about the making of a movie, he is writing about the making of a country." —Stephen Harrigan, author of *The Gates of the Alamo* and *A Friend of Mr. Lincoln*

"The blacklist has provided grist for many books, including Victor Navasky's seminal study *Naming Names*. But Frankel's book feels fresh nonetheless ... He brings out the drama and the no-win situation of everyone who was called before HUAC: throw your friends and colleagues under the bus by naming them as former or current Communists or sympathizers, or watch your life and career go up in flames." —*The Dallas Morning News*

"Film buffs and history aficionados will be delighted and riveted by Glenn Frankel's insightful and intimate look at the making of the classic 1952 western *High Noon* ... Frankel's saga presents a gripping and coherent picture of the corrupt politics, paranoia and fear mongering that drove Hollywood studio heads to capitulate to anti-Communist witch-hunters." —*Shelf Awareness*

"Glenn Frankel's *High Noon* isn't just everything you always wanted to know about an enduring classic; it's a deeply insightful portrait of the forces in postwar America and in blacklist-era Hollywood that made the film such a powerful product of such a troubled moment."
—Mark Harris, author of *Pictures at a Revolution* and *Five Came Back*

"Not far removed from a James Ellroy novel. The 1950s film industry portrayed in *High Noon* is, like Ellroy's Los Angeles, stocked with hard-core commies, idealistic fellow travelers, paranoid Red-baiters, union busters, corrupt congressmen, power-hungry gossip columnists,

secretive FBI agents and their snitches, philandering actors and eager starlets. But far from being a *Hollywood Babylon* of the Red Scare, Frankel's book is a detailed investigation of the way anti-communist persecution poisoned the atmosphere around one film, which succeeded nonetheless, and damaged the lives of the people who made it."
—*Bookforum*

"An absorbing account of how a routine 1952 western starring a has-been and an unknown became an unexpected classic . . . This story of politics, art, loyalty and conscience is more relevant than ever. And a nice bonus: Although it may impart a civics lesson, it doesn't read like one." —*Minneapolis Star Tribune*

"Glenn Frankel's *High Noon* is three splendid books in one: a moment-by-moment account of the making of the classic Western, a history of the Hollywood blacklist with much new material based on primary research, and, in the rise of Stanley Kramer Productions, the story of the independent producers who gradually supplanted conventional studio production. Even if we know how each story ends, it's never less than a continuously fascinating read." —Scott Eyman, author of *John Wayne: The Life and Legend*

HIGH NOON

The Searchers: The Making of an American Legend

Rivonia's Children: Three Families and the Cost of Conscience in White South Africa

Beyond the Promised Land: Jews and Arabs on the Hard Road to a New Israel

HIGH NOON

The Hollywood Blacklist and the Making of an American Classic

GLENN FRANKEL

BLOOMSBURY

NEW YORK · LONDON · OXFORD · NEW DELHI · SYDNEY

Bloomsbury USA
An imprint of Bloomsbury Publishing Plc

1385 Broadway   50 Bedford Square
New York   London
NY 10018   WC1B 3DP
USA   UK

www.bloomsbury.com

First published 2017
This paperback edition 2018

ISBN: HB: 978-1-62040-948-0
              PB: 978-1-62040-949-7
              ePub: 978-1-62040-950-3

LIBRARY OF CONGRESS CATALOGING-IN-PUBLICATION DATA IS AVAILABLE.

2 4 6 8 10 9 7 5 3 1

Typeset by RefineCatch Limited, Bungay, Suffolk
Printed and bound in the U.S.A. by Berryville Graphics Inc., Berryville, Virginia

To find out more about our authors and books visit
www.bloomsbury.com. Here you will find extracts, author interviews,
details of forthcoming events and the option to
sign up for our newsletters.

Bloomsbury books may be purchased for business or
promotional use. For information on bulk purchases please contact
Macmillan Corporate and Premium Sales Department at
specialmarkets@macmillan.com.

To My Parents,
Herbert and Betty Frankel,
With Love and Gratitude

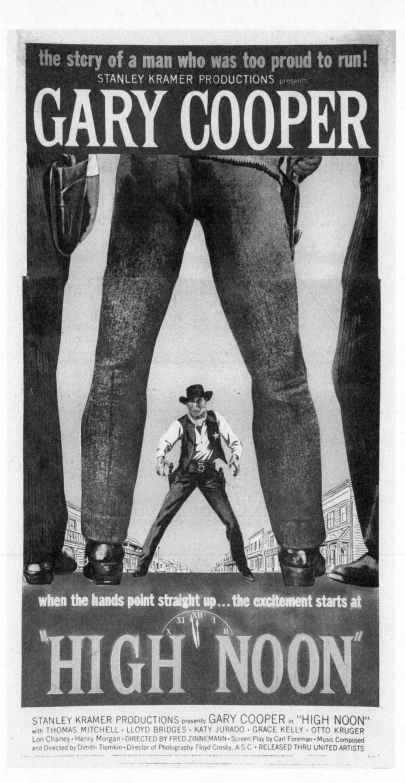

CONTENTS

INTRODUCTION

A character is defined by the kinds of challenges he cannot walk away from.
ARTHUR MILLER

It is one of Hollywood's most iconic images: one man walking down a deserted Western street toward a showdown with four armed killers. For more than sixty years, *High Noon*, starring Gary Cooper, has embedded itself in our culture and our national memory. Its title itself has become legendary, connoting a moment of truth when a good man must confront evil. It has been beloved by presidents, ordinary moviegoers, and even political movements—most notably in 1989 when Solidarity used the image as its main campaign poster in Poland's first democratic election—as a symbol of courage and determination in the face of overwhelming odds.

Shot in thirty-two days on a shoestring budget, with its famous star working for a fraction of his normal wage, *High Noon* was something of an afterthought for those who made it, a rush job to fulfill the tail end of an old contract. Yet it vaulted almost immediately to critical acclaim and box-office success. Its taut narrative, powerful performances, evocative theme song, and climactic shootout made it an instant classic. It won four Academy Awards, including best actor for Cooper. Even today it is considered one of the most enduringly popular films of Hollywood's golden age, on a short list with *Gone With the Wind*, *The Wizard of Oz*, *Casablanca*, *Citizen Kane*, *Singin' in the Rain*, and a handful of others.

Each generation has read into the film its own politics and values. Yet what has largely been forgotten is that *High Noon*'s original creator set out with a very specific meaning in mind. In the brief moment of good feeling that followed the Allied victory over Germany and Japan in World War Two, screenwriter Carl Foreman wanted to make a Western about a gang of violent criminals and the lawman who brings them to justice. Inspired by the promise of the newly formed United Nations, it was to be Foreman's parable about the need for international law and order to defeat aggression and defend democracy.

But by the time Foreman sat down to write a draft a few years later, the sunny optimism was gone, replaced by a new age of anxiety. The spirit of international cooperation had given way to a Cold War between the United States and the Soviet Union, a brutal conflict on the Korean peninsula, and a nuclear arms race that would last nearly half a century. At home, the progressive coalition that had ruled the United States for more than a decade under President Franklin Roosevelt was unraveling under his successor, Harry Truman. It was challenged by conservatives who had resisted the growth of the federal government in the New Deal era and who now joined forces with embittered working-class populists who felt excluded from their share of prosperity, and self-styled Americanists who believed that outsiders had taken control of the nation's civil institutions and culture and were plotting to subvert its security and values. Together they forged a classic backlash movement, as angry and self-righteous as the right-wing crusaders of the modern era. Usurpers—liberals, Jews, and Communists in those days; gays, Muslims, and undocumented immigrants today—had stolen their country, and the self-appointed guardians of American values were determined to claw it back.

For many Americans, Communism posed an existential threat even more alarming than that posed by Islamic extremists in the modern era. Communists, after all, could be anyone—neighbors, relatives, close friends. They looked and sounded exactly like us, yet they were agents of a ruthless foreign power whose declared goal was to destroy the American way of life. They were the enemy within—the "masters of deceit," in J. Edgar Hoover's chilling characterization.

"What is a Communist?" asked Karl Baarslag, staff member of the National Americanism Commission of the American Legion in 1948. "A Communist is a completely transformed, unrecognizable, and dedicated man. While he may retain the physical characteristics of the rest of us as far as natural functions are concerned, his mental and psychic processes might as well be from another planet. A Communist . . . is completely emancipated from all moral inhibitions and is therefore above law, ethics, or morality."

It was not just the far right that spoke of Communists as if they were brainwashed zombies. J. Howard McGrath, attorney general under President Truman, said each Communist Party member "carries in himself the germ of death for our society." Adlai Stevenson called Communism worse "than cancer, tuberculosis, and heart disease combined."

Although exaggerated, these fears were not groundless. The Soviet Union under Joseph Stalin was one of history's most brutal dictatorships, responsible for killing or imprisoning millions. The American Communist Party was a secret political organization that faithfully honored directives from Moscow as if they were commandments, and many members defended the regime even after its crimes were exposed and documented. But most American Communists saw themselves as responding to the inequities and deprivation of the Great Depression by working to create a fairer and more egalitarian society through peaceful means, not violent revolution.

Still, when faced with what they perceive to be an existential threat to their security, Western democracies have often responded by repressing human rights with alarming energy and self-righteous rhetoric, and the early 1950s was no exception. A powerful coalition of investigative agencies, legislative panels, citizens' groups, private corporations, and influential journalists banded together to expose and root out the evils of Communism, its true believers, and fellow travelers.

In truth, Hollywood was a mere sideshow in the larger struggle. No atomic secrets were sold or stolen in Beverly Hills. No acts of sabotage or espionage were alleged to have taken place. No large amounts of people or money were involved. But the symbolic power of Hollywood, its extraordinary high profile, and its abiding role in our national culture and fantasies made it an irresistible battleground. The very features that drew the leaders of the American Communist Party to set up shop in Hollywood in the 1930s attracted its antagonists a decade later to come hunt them down.

The House Committee on Un-American Activities was at the vanguard of this crusade. Created a decade earlier, HUAC first held public hearings into alleged Communist infiltration of the motion picture industry in 1947. The sessions had ended in stalemate: eleven current or former Communist Party members had been called to the stand, ten of whom cited the First Amendment in refusing to answer questions about their political affiliations and were charged with contempt of Congress. Civil libertarians condemned the committee's methods and actions; even Hollywood's studio heads briefly resisted congressional repression, but ultimately purged the Hollywood Ten from their ranks. Four years later, when the committee returned for a second set of hearings, it faced no meaningful opposition as it issued salmon-pink subpoenas to dozens of actors, screenwriters, and other film workers.

One of those called to testify was Carl Foreman, who had come to Hollywood in 1938 from his native Chicago in the midst of the Depression and began a long apprenticeship as a screenwriter. The son of Russian Jewish immigrants, he and his wife, Estelle, soon joined the Communist Party, which they believed was the organization most dedicated to fighting racism and poverty at home and Fascism abroad. Like that of many other members, their faith in the party eroded over time and they left it permanently soon after World War Two ended.

Foreman had been a low-ranking and struggling writer during the first round of hearings in 1947—"a very unimportant little fellow," as he himself put it—and he had been overlooked by the committee, which had focused on more prominent prey. But by 1951 he had been nominated twice for an Academy Award for best screenwriting and soon would be tapped for a third time. He and Estelle and their four-year-old daughter had recently moved into a large cottage in fashionable Brentwood with a swimming pool in the backyard and a touch of Hollywood glamor in its past: the woman they had bought it from had herself purchased it from Orson Welles and Rita Hayworth, who had lived there during the early days of their ill-fated marriage.

And so he was not surprised when a pink slip of paper arrived at his office at Motion Picture Center Studios in Hollywood early on the afternoon of June 13, 1951. "BY THE AUTHORITY OF THE HOUSE OF REPRESENTATIVES OF THE CONGRESS OF THE UNITED STATES OF AMERICA," it solemnly began, and went on in its convoluted way to command him to appear before the Committee on Un-American Activities, "or subcommittee thereof," on Thursday, September 6, at ten A.M., "then and there to testify touching matters of inquiry committed to said Committee; and he is not to depart without leave of said Committee."

It was an invitation to an inquisition. Witnesses who were willing to cooperate underwent a ritual of humiliation and purification. They were required to confess to and renounce their membership in the Communist Party and praise the committee for its devotion in combating the scourge. And finally, to prove the sincerity of their conversion, they had to name the names of other participants in the Red plot to destroy America. The committee already knew almost all the names—its own investigators had membership lists supplied by Hoover's Federal Bureau of Investigation and had collected secret testimony. No matter. The naming of names was considered a defining part of the process.

The alternative was to invoke the Fifth Amendment against self-incrimination and refuse to answer questions. This meant appearing like a criminal who had something to hide and would ensure that you would lose your job within hours or days, because the major Hollywood studios had all adopted a policy of blacklisting anyone who refused to cooperate. Few would acquit themselves well. Not the committee, which far exceeded the constitutional limits of its powers and acted as judge, jury, and executioner; nor the studios, which caved out of fear of losing profits and prestige; nor political liberals, who were trapped between a bullying committee and its dogmatic Communist targets and wound up enabling the blacklist purge; nor journalists, some of whom cheered on the committee from the sidelines and almost all of whom failed to hold a critical spotlight to the process of repression. Nor did Hollywood's powerful Jewish community, which by and large failed to defend the civil liberties of its most targeted members.

For Carl Foreman it all came down to this: either sell out his friends or lose the job and the career he had worked so hard to achieve. As he pondered what to do, he began to rethink his screenplay for *High Noon* and turn it into an allegory about the Red Scare and the blacklist. The marshal was now Carl himself, the gunmen coming to kill him were the members of HUAC, and the hypocritical and cowardly citizens of Hadleyville were the denizens of Hollywood who stood by passively or betrayed him as the forces of repression bore down.

"As I was writing the screenplay, it became insane, because life was mirroring art and art was mirroring life," he would recall. "There was no difference. It was all happening at the same time. I became that guy. I became the Gary Cooper character."

ON A GLOBAL STAGE, the Cold War was an epic clash of empires and opposing ideologies. But in Hollywood the struggle played out in far more intimate terms. People lost their jobs, business partnerships unraveled, friendships were destroyed, and families turned against each other. And the bitterest conflicts often were not between political enemies but among former allies and friends.

At the time he began writing *High Noon*, Carl Foreman was part of a small but agile independent film production company led by Stanley Kramer, a colleague and close friend. Together they had made three critically successful and socially relevant films in a row, two of which had also been substantial box office hits. The Stanley Kramer Company was, in our modern vernacular, a nimble and creative start-up that was making movies better, faster, and more cheaply than the older, more bloated, slower-moving traditional studios. It attracted talented filmmakers like director Fred Zinnemann and music composer Dimitri Tiomkin and was gaining popular attention and respect. Some of Hollywood's most gifted young actors took pay cuts to work with the company—including Kirk Douglas, Marlon Brando, Teresa Wright, José Ferrer, and an as-yet unknown actress named Grace Kelly.

High Noon was supposed to be a Western, that most quintessentially American of genres. But Carl Foreman was the son and Stanley Kramer the grandson of Russian Jews, and Fred Zinnemann was a Jewish émigré from Vienna whose parents had both perished in the Holocaust. None of them had ever made a Western before, and together with a talented cast and crew they created a most unusual one. It was a gritty, low-budget, black-and-white drama with no beautiful vistas, no cattle drives or stampedes, no gun violence until its final showdown, a morally corrupt community, a frightened, vulnerable hero, and a political message that quietly defied the reactionary spirit of the times. The great cowboy star John Wayne hated it—an arch-conservative, he smelled out the left-wing politics lurking in its soul—while some distinguished critics said it wasn't a Western at all but a modern social drama artificially grafted onto an Old West setting. Still, whatever its provenance, *High Noon* succeeded in becoming, in the words of critic Leonard Maltin, "a morality play that just happened to be universal."

Its unexpected success led to bitter disputes among its makers over who was ultimately responsible for its brilliance. While *High Noon*'s creators have all passed away, the conflicts have continued to this day among their families and supporters. A documentary film in 2002 made by a devoted friend of Carl Foreman alleged that Carl had been denied his proper credit as producer of the picture and betrayed by Stanley Kramer. These allegations were heatedly contested by Kramer's widow. She and her family used the centennial of Kramer's birth in 2013 to reassert their claim that he was the creative genius behind the film. Several myths have arisen over the years, most notably the claim that *High Noon* was a botched project that was rescued at the last minute by skillful editing.

There are widely conflicting claims over who deserves credit for the powerful storytelling, the stark visual beauty, the suspenseful use of real time, the evocative music, and the superb acting. All of those conflicts were rubbed more raw by the toxic politics of the blacklist era.

This book tells the story of the making of a classic movie against the backdrop of a tumultuous era of American history whose meaning and lessons remain unresolved. No one was put up against a wall and shot during the blacklist. Yet it was a time of paranoia and persecution, and there are many echoes of its public anxieties, ritual humiliations, and moral corruption in our own troubled era. I can't pretend to answer all of the questions still surrounding the blacklist. But I have had the advantage of access to HUAC's investigative files and executive session transcripts that have only been made public in recent years. At the same time, I have been able to uncover previously unpublished interviews with Carl Foreman, Stanley Kramer, and others involved in the making of *High Noon* that have enabled me to present a more authoritative account of who was most responsible for the creation of this American classic. And despite the reservations of some distinguished critics, this book makes the case that *High Noon* is indeed one of the greatest American movies and the most significant triumph of its legendary star.

Ultimately this book is about a small group of highly talented people who came together to achieve compelling creative work and what happened when they came up against the machinery of political repression. It asks the question that history demands of each of us: if we were confronted with the same terrible choice that these people faced—in this case, between betraying our principles or losing our livelihoods—what would we do?

THROUGHOUT ITS COLORFUL FIRST century, Hollywood has been characterized as many things: a dream factory, a state of mind, a place of crass commerce, grandiose calculations, and broken hopes. It is surely all of these, but it's also a destination; most of the people who end up there have come from somewhere else. This was true for Carl Foreman, Stanley Kramer, Fred Zinnemann, and most of the gifted craftsmen responsible for creating *High Noon*, and it was also true for Gary Cooper, who arrived there in November 1924 at the age of twenty-three from his hometown of Helena, Montana, a small state capital some 1,250 miles away.

He could not have presented more of a contrast to Foreman and Kramer, the men who would hire him to star in *High Noon* twenty-seven years later. They were fast-talking urban intellectuals from the Jewish ghettos of Chicago and New York, whereas he was a tall, elegant, and reticent Anglo-Saxon Protestant from the rural West. They were politically radical or liberal, while he was a conservative Republican and staunch anti-Communist. They were self-styled iconoclasts who were contemptuous of the slowly decaying studio system, while he was well-established cinematic aristocracy and the ultimate product of that system. They were young, enthusiastic, and on their way up, while he was fifty years old and burdened with increasingly poor health, self-doubt, a troubled marriage, and a career that was beginning to fade after two decades as one of Hollywood's biggest stars.

But Cooper offered them something that for all their robust talent they couldn't accomplish on their own. He didn't just look and sound like an authentic Man of the West, he actually *was* one. It was, after all, the land where he had been born and bred, and where he first acquired his own set of myths and dreams; and it is a fitting place to begin the story of the making of *High Noon*.

1.

The Natural

Whatever happened to Gary Cooper? The strong, silent type? That was
an American. He wasn't in touch with his feelings. He just did what he
had to do.
TONY SOPRANO TO DR. MELFI IN *THE SOPRANOS*, EPISODE I

In 1914, when Frank Cooper was thirteen years old, his father took
him to the state capitol building in Helena, Montana, to see a
stunning new mural created by Charles M. Russell, one of the great
artist-mythmakers of the Old West. Mounted on the wall behind the
desk of the Speaker of the House of Representatives, *Lewis and Clark*
Meeting Indians at Ross' Hole is a twelve-foot-high and twenty-six-
foot-wide highly stylized depiction of the historic encounter in
September 1805 between the legendary explorers and a hunting party of
one of the region's fiercest Native American tribes. Flathead Indians
dominate the canvas, their ponies pivoting wildly in the tall prairie
grass while the majestic, snowcapped Bitterroot Mountains hover in the
distance. Lewis and Clark and their fellow explorers stand passively to
the side, overshadowed by the drama playing out before them.

This was Indian Country, bursting with motion and myth—just the
kind of evocative, outsize drama that Russell, a former ranch hand who
worked out of a log cabin in Great Falls ninety miles away, believed in
and made his fortune from. Some of what it depicted might have been
true, but that didn't really matter. It *felt* true, and it evoked feelings of
excitement and longing for a time and a place and a way of life that had
long passed—and it inflamed young Frank's imagination and ambition.
"I was stopped, really nailed in my tracks," he would recall four decades

later. "All I knew then . . . was that I'd give anything to be able to paint like that."

From the beginning of his life, Frank Cooper was captivated by the power and beauty of the vast wilderness he had been born into. His parents were immigrants from England, strangers in a strange, half-tamed land that they grew to both adore and fear. Each passed on to their son their sense of awe at the vast, rugged spaces of their adopted home. And he in turn was moved in ways he could barely articulate by this evocative and challenging landscape.

Frank's father, Charles, had left his native Bedfordshire, forty miles north of London, in 1883 and headed to America, following his older brother Arthur. The Cooper men were drawn to the Montana territory by economic opportunity—first gold, then silver, and finally copper helped power successive financial booms—but also by the romance of Indians and cavalrymen and gunfighters and pioneers. It was, after all, less than a decade since George Armstrong Custer and his men had faced death before an overwhelming force of Sioux and Cheyenne Indians at the Little Bighorn in the southeastern corner of the territory. Charles wound up settling in the small town that became Montana's capital, which had recently changed its name from Last Chance Gulch to Helena. He got a job as an engineer for the Northern Pacific Railway during the day while studying law at night. Then he opened a law practice and dabbled in Republican Party politics, leading to his eventual appointment by President Theodore Roosevelt as U.S. attorney for the newly established state. Prosperity bred respectability, but Helena still honored its frontier past. As late as 1895 the town sent out printed invitations to public hangings in the main square.

Another young Englishman, Alfred Brazier, who had arrived in Helena at around the same time, sent for his younger sister Alice to come join him. She lacked her brother's uncritical affection for the new territory: as soon as she got to Helena, Alice deposited enough money in a local bank account to cover her return fare to England. When the panic of 1893 ripped the floor out from under the price of silver and Helena's banks collapsed, Alice consulted Charles Cooper as to how to retrieve her money. But instead of fleeing back to England, she married the young lawyer. A year later she gave birth to a boy they named Arthur, and six years after that, on May 7, 1901, they added a second son—Frank James Cooper—born in a bedroom on the second floor of a modest but comfortable Victorian at the corner of Eleventh Avenue and Raleigh Street.

Cowboys, Indians, wolf hunters, and women of uncertain virtue still walked the streets of Helena in 1901, but Charles Russell's Old West was already more fable than reality. The Coopers lived in a succession of houses just south of the state capitol building for a decade, while Charles built a legal and political career that eventually led to a seat on the state Supreme Court. They spent part of the year on a ranch fifty miles north of town on six hundred acres that Charles bought from the Northern Pacific in 1906. The 7 Bar 9 Ranch was located on the banks of the Missouri River in the foothills of the Big Belt Mountains parallel to the Rockies, an area named "the Gates of the Mountains" by Meriwether Lewis. He and William Clark and the thirty-two-member Corps of Discovery had camped a mile upriver on July 17, 1805, and one hundred years later young Frank Cooper could still explore the same sites and observe the same wildlife as Lewis and Clark: steep volcanic canyons and soaring rock formations, home to bear, deer, elk, mountain lions, bobcats, mountain goats, coyotes, grouse quail, geese, duck, and beaver. Frank would later recall his proper English mother shearing sheep, branding cattle, shoveling manure before dawn, and "swinging an ax at twenty below zero to break open bales of frozen hay."

Then there was the chinook, the warm wind that raced through the valley in early spring, melting the deep snow and creating a wall of water that barreled down the river gorge and swept away soil and seed, leaving the Cooper ranch stripped to its bedrock.

Alice Cooper never quite overcame her mixed feelings about this wild country and feared its coarse impact on her two sons, and she convinced Charles to take them to her native Kent for a proper English education. They deposited the boys for three years at Dunstable, a boarding school that sanded their rougher edges and subjected them to the rigors of Latin, French, and higher mathematics. It was there that Frank Cooper learned to speak French, solve an equation, wear a top hat, and bow from the waist.

He returned to Montana in 1913, grew six inches in two years, and began filling in his handsome, narrow face, with its sparkling blue eyes and long lashes. He learned to ride a horse with skill and precision, clean and shoot a rifle, hunt game with a bow and arrow, and spend hours alone in the silent landscape, sketching the wilderness in charcoal and pencil. Early in his teenage years, his friend Harvey Markham crashed the family Model T, throwing Frank from the passenger seat. Limping and in pain, he was told it was just torn ligaments, but many years later he found out his hip had been broken and never properly healed. The injury cost him two years of schooling. He entered Grinnell College in Iowa at age twenty, lasted three years, charmed teachers and fellow students with his easy manner and crooked grin, but never graduated. By then his father had left the bench for a lucrative private law practice. A complex real estate case brought Charles and Alice to Los Angeles for an extended period that became permanent. Frank, still hoping to become a commercial artist, came to visit at Thanksgiving 1924. He never left.

At first he looked for a job as a newspaper cartoonist but got nowhere. He drew display ads on commission but sold none. For a few weeks he went door-to-door seeking in vain to convince residents to pay to have their family photos taken, then spent three weeks as a theatrical scene painter. He was living at home with free rent and food—important for a young man who was now six foot three and harbored an endless affection for a square meal any time of the day or night. But his goal of saving up the funds to attend a private art school in Chicago seemed to recede from his grasp.

One day on Vine Street in Hollywood he ran into two pals from back home. They told him that Slim Talbot, a Montana rodeo star, was hiring riders to work as stuntmen in the thriving motion picture business. It was hard work but paid ten dollars a day—exactly ten dollars more than Frank Cooper was making in his artistic pursuits. Tom Mix, Hoot Gibson, and dozens of imitators were riding the cinematic range, churning out cheap Westerns that relied on stunts, horseback riding, showmanship, and outsize cowboy costumes filmed on a variety of ranches and open-air studio lots on the outskirts of town. Frank had seen few movies, read no fan magazines, knew nothing about how pictures were made or who was making them. But he was a capable and fearless rider who could fall off a horse convincingly upon command, and the camera seemed to love his chiseled face with its thin lips and sculpted cheeks.

Soon he was getting bit parts beyond stunt work. He felt awkward in this strange new line of work. "My wrists were too long, my knees were too pointed, and my shirt looked as though it was draped over a wire coat hanger," he would recall. "Leading ladies resented playing scenes with me, complaining they had to stand on tiptoe and crane their necks to unladylike angles."

None of that mattered. His father arranged an introduction to a client, actress-producer Marilyn Mills, who along with her husband was making two-reel Westerns. Frank Cooper was just what they were looking for. She got him a role as a villain in a film called *Tricks*. Frank liked the work—and the money—enough to resolve to devote the next year to seeing if he could launch a successful career in movies. By now, thanks again to his father's connections, he had acquired an agent. Her name was Nan Collins and she got him small parts in more than a dozen films. But her most important contribution was to inform him that there were already two other Frank Coopers in the motion picture business and to suggest that he take the name of her hometown in northern Indiana instead.

From now on he would be called "Gary Cooper."

IN LATER ACCOUNTS, Gary Cooper would portray himself as a reluctant film idol who accidently and inadvertently fell into stardom. In fact, he plunged into the craft of movie acting with energy and commitment. He started going to the movies every day, studied Rudolph Valentino's smooth, fluid movements, and observed how the great British actor Ronald Colman used minimal gestures—a faintly raised eyebrow, a slight pursing of the lips—rather than the broad over-emoting of many stage-trained performers. According to Cooper, Colman realized "his audience was no farther away than the camera lens."

Cooper bought his own makeup kit, which he tried out at home. He would pile on chalk-white face powder, heavy lipstick, and coal-black mascara, then adjourn to the backyard where his mother, an amateur photographer, would take snapshots and develop them immediately. Remember, Marilyn Mills had told him, "you don't go by how it looks to your mirror. The only judge of how you look is the camera." Looking at the photos his mother took, Cooper noticed something peculiar: "The more ferociously I scowled, the funnier I looked. On the other hand, if I just looked at the camera impassively, and thought to myself, *You treacherous little box, if you don't make this one good, I'm going to tear you apart with my two hands* . . . the picture of me would come out looking so mean I'd be shocked."

He also invested sixty-five dollars—a major sum—for his own screen test. He rented a horse and a motion picture camera, hired a cameraman, and set them up in a vacant lot at the corner of Third Street and La Brea. He charged the camera on horseback, made a flying dismount, swept off his hat, and gave what he called "a ghastly grin." Then he took the reel to the Goldwyn studio, where he had the good fortune to run into a director named Henry King, who liked the graceful riding and easy manner, and cast him in a small part in Ronald Colman's new picture, *The Winning of Barbara Worth* (1926). When the actor who was supposed to play Colman's rival for the love of a young woman had to bow out suddenly, King decided that his lanky Montana boy could do the job. Cooper's character died in Colman's arms. "Easy does it, old boy," the star actor advised him before the camera whirled. Women wept. When he saw the rushes, Cooper said he nearly cried himself.

He was good enough that Paramount Pictures signed him to a contract for $150 a week. The studio's leading young star, Clara Bow, was entranced by Cooper's good looks and physique and insisted he be given a bit part in *It* (1927), her next movie. The Brooklyn-born actress, one of the sexiest and most uninhibited celebrities of the era, had a long list of lovers and paramours, ranging from the dashing director Victor Fleming, to actors Buddy Rogers, Richard Arlen, Fredric March, Eddie Cantor, and John Gilbert, to various and sundry members of the UCLA football team. Cooper for a brief time served as her newest companion and was rewarded with the co-starring role in her next film, *Children of Divorce* (1927). He also got the male lead in *Arizona Bound* (1927), his first starring role and his first Western, in which he convincingly wore an oversize cowboy hat and did his own stunt work.

But his biggest break came when director William Wellman, at Bow's urging, cast him in a small role in the aviation epic *Wings*. It was a tiny part: he played Cadet White, a doomed flight instructor whom two cadet flyers, played by Rogers and Arlen, meet when they first arrive at flight training camp.

His only scene ran just 105 seconds. Cadet White wakes from a nap, climbs out of his cot, pushes his mussed hair off his face, tucks in his shirt, pulls on an overcoat, produces a chocolate bar from the pocket and offers it to his new tent-mates, then heads for the tent door. When the new boys wish him good luck, his face suddenly turns serious. "Luck or no luck, when your time comes, you're going to get it!" he tells them. Then he gives them a two-fingered salute and a toothy grin and heads off to his destiny—a fatal midair collision.

It required only one take, Wellman would recall. Seventy years later, actor Tom Hanks, one of Cooper's spiritual heirs as an ingratiating and naturalistic performer, paid tribute. Cooper "does something mysterious with his eyes and shoulders that is much more 'being' than 'acting,'" wrote Hanks. "In this one scene, Cooper somehow crosses a bridge from the artifice of acting to the manner of behavior via a process that eludes most other performers."

Wings, which won the first Academy Award for Best Picture, helped launch Cooper as a star. His scene was "the most valuable of my life," he would recall.

His fling with Clara Bow was the first of many in Cooper's early days in Hollywood, with a list of actresses that included Evelyn Brent, Marlene Dietrich, and Tallulah Bankhead (who once famously told reporters, "I've come to Hollywood to fuck Gary Cooper." Asked later how it had gone, she replied: "Mission accomplished."). His most serious entanglement was a tempestuous two-year affair with Lupe Vélez, a passionate, self-destructive starlet whose disastrous taste in men would lead her to commit suicide a decade later. Cooper's mother took credit publicly for helping break up the romance.

Despite the wave of praise for *Wings* and other successful early roles, Cooper constantly worried about his lack of acting skills. Unlike many of his peers, he had no prior experience on the stage or in drama school. He described himself as suffering "an agony of self-consciousness . . . Other actors had had their rough edges smoothed off in dramatic classes or amateur production. I was having mine sledge-hammered off in huge painful chunks, right in front of the finest professional talent in Hollywood."

TALENT AND BEAUTY ARE important ingredients for an actor's success. But it never hurts to be lucky, and Gary Cooper's luck was impeccable. He was nearing stardom just as the studios were beginning the treacherous pivot from silents to talkies, a moment of maximum collective anxiety that launched a frantic search for new faces and, just as crucially, natural voices.

Producer Samuel Goldwyn's wife, Frances, captured the moment of realization among the Hollywood elite in December 1927 when the first talkie, *The Jazz Singer*, had its West Coast premiere at the Warner Theatre on Hollywood Boulevard. She saw the "terror in all their faces . . . the game they had been playing for years was finally done."

Which meant a new one was about to begin. The advent of talkies changed the very nature of screen acting. Vanished were the exaggerated gestures and overwrought theatrical style of the silent screen, where emotions had to be physically expressed without benefit of dialogue. They were replaced by a more subtle, naturalistic, and intimate approach, one that was perfect for a "non-actor" like the young Gary Cooper.

Suddenly, actors had voices and voices had to be part of the craft and magic of screen acting. Some performers were quickly and cruelly cast aside. Clara Bow was uncomfortable with microphones and disliked the sound of her own voice, while many stage-trained actors sounded phony and artificial. But Cooper's slow, emphatic tenor was easy on the ears and quintessentially American in its timbre and tone.

He got his first opportunity to use it as the title character in *The Virginian* (1929), the third filming of Owen Wister's classic Western novel. Cooper played a taciturn man of honor from the Old South who had reinvented himself as a cowhand in the West. Although the novel was published in 1902, Wister seemed as if he had Cooper in mind when he described his iconic hero: "a slim young giant, more beautiful than pictures . . . He had plainly come many miles from somewhere across the vast horizon, as the dust upon him showed . . . The weather-beaten bloom of his face shone through it duskily, as the ripe peaches look upon their trees in a dry season. But no dinginess of travel or shabbiness of attire could tarnish the splendor that radiated from his youth and strength."

Cooper not only looked the part, he sounded it as well. When Trampas, the evil cattle thief played by veteran actor Walter Huston, insults him during a poker game, the Virginian growls back menacingly, "If you want to call me that, smile!"

Before his climactic shoot-out with Trampas, the Virginian must first confront Molly, his schoolteacher lover, who pleads with him to leave town with her rather than risk his life. "We can go away—I'll go with you—anywhere," she tells him.

"You mean run away?" he replies. "Where could a man go? You can't run away from yourself."

Molly accuses him of succumbing to pride "because you've got some idea about your personal honor."

The Virginian can't explain his feelings, but he knows what he must do. "I don't know what you call it, but it's something in the feelings of a man—deep down inside. Something a man can't go back on."

The exchange sums up one of the key characteristics of the archetypal Western hero: a sense of honor that he cannot articulate yet must obey. There is a standard of behavior for a man that a woman simply cannot understand or intuit. This is the essence of American masculinity as defined by three generations of Western movie heroes. We will hear those same sentiments, in the same inarticulate language, more than two decades later in *High Noon*.

Cooper, a son of the modern West, seemed to effortlessly embody the mythic, make-believe past. He made nine Westerns in his first five years at Paramount, which was eager to exploit his talent at projecting authenticity. He had a shrewd taste for publicity. He jumped at the opportunity to be the first movie star to appear on the cover of the *Saturday Evening Post*, in a May 1930 Norman Rockwell portrait entitled *Gary Cooper as the Texan*, referring to the name of his latest film release. He spent three days at Rockwell's studio, posing in full cowboy outfit with leather vest, chaps, spurs on his boots, red bandanna, and pearl-handled revolver, sitting atop a saddle while a makeup man applied lipstick to his mouth.

By that spring, Gary Cooper was a full-fledged star, his name above the title of every movie he made. He starred in seven films that year, often working days on one picture and nights on another. While he ate like a horse, his thin frame could not endure this punishing schedule. He passed out from jaundice and exhaustion and wound up overnight in the hospital. He finished *I Take This Woman* in May 1931 and then vanished for several months. He was spotted in Europe, at the Lido in Venice, where he sunned himself in relative obscurity. He was not just physically exhausted, but emotionally spent as well, and troubled by his own insecurities as an actor in an industry that puzzled and vexed him. "I began to wonder who I was . . . ," he later recalled. "Was I a star simply because I happened to screen well? Was I the figment of a director's imagination or did I have some stuff of my own? Looking at the question honestly, the answer seemed to favor the directors. Very depressing."

He was in no hurry to return home. Instead, he traveled to Rome, where he was introduced to Dorothy Taylor, an American heiress and socialite who had married an elderly Italian aristocrat and was using her husband's connections and his majestic villa to entertain herself and an ever-shifting collection of celebrities, friends, and parasites. The Countess di Frasso, as she called herself, fell helplessly in love with the handsome young actor thirteen years her junior. She turned him into a project, introducing him to good food, fine wine, careful tailoring, great art, and other expensive pastimes, re-molding him as a gentleman of continental tastes without tampering with the innate cowboy sensibility she found both quaint and erotic. She introduced him to friends who invited him to their horse ranch in Tanganyika. There he showed off his Montana-bred skills on a luxury safari in the foothills of Mount Kenya. He could ride and shoot and often seemed more comfortable around animals than human beings. After they bagged an obscene amount of big game, the countess invited her dashing paramour and the rest of the party to relocate to the Riviera. There were sightings in the European press in Monte Carlo, Nice, Cannes, and the Antibes. He heard that Paramount had lost patience with him and had signed a new dashing young man, Cary Grant. "Cary, huh, instead of Gary," thought Cooper, "and with my initials reversed." He had also heard that the Depression-conscious studios were cutting back on actors.

Having finally run low on money and nerve, he decided it was time to return to Hollywood and a reckoning with his employer. "Outwardly, I was playing my new role, a poised man of the world," he would recall. "Inwardly, I was a scared young man. Paramount had shown no signs of wanting me back."

To his great surprise, they did indeed want him back. Facing economic hard times, the studio heads believed stars were more important than ever, and virtually all of Cooper's films had made money. He was as close as they could get to a sure thing, and they were willing to pay handsomely for his services. While many other attractive young actors were struggling to get by—John Wayne, for one, spent nearly a decade making cheap B Westerns for "Poverty Row" studios—Cooper led a charmed career. By 1933, he was earning six thousand dollars a week, sleeping with starlets again, and running out of luxury goods worth buying. "I bought a Duesenberg so lengthy I had to start turning corners in the middle of the block," he wrote. Its color was chartreuse.

As a rising star he sat at the golden apex of a lucrative and well-oiled money-making machine. Having moved indoors and built expensive sound stages to handle the demands of the new technology, Hollywood was rapidly evolving into a quasi-factory system. Paramount was completing a feature-length motion picture every week and developing the bureaucracy to service this process.

"There were departments for everything," writes film historian Jeanine Basinger of the evolving studio system. "An administrative department . . . the story department . . . the art direction department, the makeup department, the cinematography and lighting departments, the sound department, the music department, the casting, publicity, costume, library and research, special effects, legal, purchasing, payroll . . ."

It was the beginning of Hollywood's golden age—a three-decade period when the eight biggest studios thrived and dominated, when there were more movie theaters in America than banks, when more than fifty million people went to the movies every week and avid customers lined up for blocks to see the latest hits. Paramount and several of the other major studios had created a classic integrated vertical monopoly: they controlled the production, distribution, and exhibition of their products. Paramount alone owned more than 1,200 theaters across the country. It dictated what those theaters showed, compelling them to buy packages of movies that included the best and worst of its pictures, and mandating schedules and ticket prices. Each of the major studios had a different personality, reflecting the values and sensibility of its leaders and most senior producers and the distinctive attributes of its various stars. Warner Bros. was known for its gritty urban dramas, while Metro-Goldwyn-Mayer (MGM) specialized in glossy, star-driven stories and lavish musicals, and Paramount emphasized sophisticated comedies. Even during the height of the Great Depression, customers flocked to movie houses to escape their troubles and watch beautiful people in evening dress sail through penthouse apartments with cigarette holders and martini glasses in their hands.

Yet while Hollywood was thriving economically, its culture was complex and contradictory—creativity and inspiration uneasily mixed with coarseness and corruption. Novelist Christopher Isherwood, who arrived in Los Angeles not long after Cooper did and remained there until his death more than forty years later, saw the film studios as sixteenth-century palace societies. "There one sees what Shakespeare saw," he wrote in his novel *Prater Violet*, "the absolute power of the tyrant, the courtiers, the flatterers, the jesters, the cunningly ambitious intriguers. There are fantastically beautiful women, there are incompetent favorites. There are great men who are suddenly disgraced. There is the most insane extravagance, and unexpected parsimony over a few pence. There is enormous splendor which is a sham; and also horrible squalor hidden behind the scenery. There are vast schemes abandoned because of some caprice. There are secrets which everybody knows but no one speaks of."

Hortense Powdermaker, a social anthropologist, came to Hollywood after World War Two to study its society employing the same field techniques she had used to study South Sea aborigines. Her report, published in the book *Hollywood: The Dream Factory*, reads like a psychiatric evaluation of a prosperous madhouse.

On the surface, Powdermaker writes, the denizens of Hollywood treated each other with "warm words of endearment and great cordiality." But "underneath is hostility, amounting frequently to hatred, and even more important, a lack of respect for each other's work . . . People are property in no uncertain terms . . . and everyone has his price . . . Human relationships are regarded as basically manipulative and are lacking in all dignity." Friendships and love affairs were superficial and impermanent. Even the sex was grim—plentiful and much-discussed but used more as a means of advancement than for enjoyment. "Pretty young girls . . . are prepared and ready to use sex as a means of getting ahead . . . This attitude seems more common than the Bohemian one of sex for fun or pleasure."

Because the movie business was relatively young and was the first popular art form to be turned into an industry, the rules were unclear and the people making them never felt secure, no matter how successful they were nor how much they were paid. "Most people give the impression of Cinderella at the ball, just before the clock strikes midnight," writes Powdermaker. Status was transitory; because everything they had could be snatched away in an instant, studio heads were obsessed with being in control and quick to suspect subordinates of stupidity, ingratitude, and, worst of all, disloyalty. "Almost no one trusts anyone else, and the executives, particularly, trust no one, not even themselves," she writes. After all, "trust is impossible to men whose major drive is to exploit and manipulate other human beings."

Stars, no matter what their status, were no exception to Hollywood's psychosis. They were seen as pampered, stupid, oversexed, and overpaid, and were treated with a combination of envy and contempt. "Instead of being admired, they are looked down upon as a kind of subhuman species," she writes. "No one respects them. The cliché that there are three kinds of people—men, women, and actors—is heard over and over again. They are often described as children . . . immature, irresponsible, completely self-centered, egotistical, exhibitionistic, nitwits, and utterly stupid . . . Hollywood attitudes towards actors range from pitying condescension to contempt, hostility, and hatred."

Powdermaker believed the studios were vulnerable in part because their owners didn't really understand what made a successful motion picture. Still, they treated themselves like gods. Screenwriter Ring Lardner Jr. recalled that Darryl F. Zanuck, head of Twentieth Century-Fox, would conduct a major story conference for each movie-to-be that would include the associate producer, director, writer, and anyone else with responsibility. All were invited to speak freely and fully, while a stenographer took it all down. The next day each participant would receive a transcript of Zanuck's remarks, "not a word of anyone else's."

Even the most astute of the studio heads understood that they were playing a con game. Sometimes you have to fake it, says Monroe Stahr, in F. Scott Fitzgerald's novel *The Love of the Last Tycoon*, a character based on the brilliant young MGM production chief, Irving Thalberg. "You have to say 'It's got to be like this—no other way'—even if you're not sure. A dozen times a week that happens to me. Situations where there is no real reason for anything, you pretend there is."

But there was one key reason for their vulnerability that the astute Dr. Powdermaker completely overlooked in her analysis of "The Men Who Play God," her term for the studio bosses: that the men who founded and operated the country's most quintessential institution of American popular culture were themselves Eastern European Jews who were for the most part recently arrived immigrants—strangers in the country they now called home.

Cultural historian Neal Gabler notes in his landmark study *An Empire of Their Own* that Jewish writers, talent agencies, and lawyers dominated Hollywood, while Jewish exhibitors operated the nation's movie palaces. And at the top of the pyramid Jews ran nearly every major studio and produced the movies these studios made. According to one 1936 study, fifty-three of eighty-six film producers were Jewish.

Together they built "a never-never land, a construct," said playwright Arthur Miller. "These immigrants, these Jews from Eastern Europe, had developed this dream that had blond hair, blue eyes, and a straight nose. It all had to be beautiful. It was a fairy tale, because they were immigrants who saw this country as a fairy tale. It was incredible; it captured the whole country."

The Jewish studio heads were by and large self-styled patriots who wanted nothing more than to assimilate into American society. Laemmle, Zukor, Schulberg, Lasky, Fox, Mayer, Warner, Loew, Cohn, Schenck, Goldwyn, Selznick, Thalberg—by and large these were cunning and brilliant men, yet they were men without a past whose families had fled a forgotten land and who had reinvented themselves as wise, brave, and powerful. Their aspirations were similar to those of generations of immigrants who came to America seeking economic opportunities and social redemption. But the Jews who ran Hollywood had a special position from which to express and achieve those aspirations. They were indeed uniquely powerful, and yet uniquely vulnerable at the same time to the attacks of anti-Semites who accused them of using the movies to undermine traditional American values. As early as 1921, Henry Ford's *Dearborn Independent* was editorializing against Jewish ownership of the major studios: "As soon as the Jews gained control of the 'movies,' we had a movie problem, the consequences of which are not yet visible. It is the genius of that race to create problems of a moral character in whatever business they achieve a majority."

Alongside Ford's virulent hatred of Jews was a more generalized public antipathy that peaked in the 1930s, a time of economic hardship and global instability that many Americans blamed at least in part on Jews. American Jews were banned from or heavily restricted in enrolling in many colleges and universities and entering professions such as medicine and law or joining social clubs and living in certain residential neighborhoods. Public opinion surveys indicated these discriminatory practices had strong popular support. A majority of Americans felt Jews were greedy and dishonest, and a substantial minority believed they had too much power.

These attitudes colored and infected many peoples' views of Hollywood. When Joseph P. Kennedy, father of the future president, took control of one of the smaller studios, Film Booking Offices of America, in the mid-1920s, he depicted himself as a white knight who would rescue Hollywood from immoral foreigners. "There was," writes film historian Garth Jowett, "a basic resentment that this 'art of the people' should be in the hands of 'Jewish ex-clothing merchants' who sold their product like so many cheap garments."

Jews were "a rotten bunch of vile people with no responsibility for anything beyond making money," Joseph Breen, administrator of the Motion Picture Production Code, Hollywood's board of censors, wrote to a fellow Catholic in 1932. "Here [in Hollywood] we have Paganism rampant and in its most virulent form," added Breen, a powerful official whose paycheck came directly from the very people he despised. "Drunkenness and debauchery are commonplace. Sexual perversion is rampant . . . Any number of our directors and stars are perverts. Ninety-five percent are Jews of Eastern European lineage. They are, probably, the scum of the earth."

Given these attitudes, the studio heads felt compelled to tread carefully on what was for them still foreign soil. They tended to vote Republican, clung to what they considered conservative values, and had an almost visceral aversion to their fellow Jews on the political left, whose radicalism they saw as threatening their own stature and security. And most of them ignored or buried deep the fact of their Jewishness both in their private lives and in the content of the movies they made.

SO FAR AS THE studio system was concerned, stars were made, not born. When the studios' army of talent scouts rounded up and shipped to Hollywood young people with potential, they were screen-tested and dressed, coiffed by hairdressers and remade by makeup artists. Ronald

Reagan in his memoirs recalls that on his first day on the job at Warner Bros. a hair stylist examined him "the way a paleontologist might examine a newly discovered but as yet unidentified fossil plucked from a prehistoric riverbed." She reconfigured Reagan's "Harold Teen" haircut—short and parted down the middle—into the genial pompadour he wore for the rest of his life. The Warners makeover team also decided his head and neck were too small and his shoulders too big, and they dispatched him to the same tailor used by James Cagney, who supposedly suffered from a similar affliction, for custom-made shirts to conceal this grievous physical defect.

The newcomers also got lessons in acting, singing, and dancing. If they made it to the next level, their names would be changed (Reagan got to keep his only after convincing the studio that his previous career as a sports broadcaster made him a known name in the Midwest) and fake biographies created. Photographs of all kinds were taken, favorable stories were planted, and introductions were made to every publicist in town. Some studios even occasionally arranged marriages to give their young stars backstories of respectability.

"We did everything for them," said legendary publicist Howard Strickling, who headed public relations at MGM from the late 1920s to the early 1950s. "There were no agents, personal press agents, business managers, or answering services in those days. All these services were furnished by the MGM publicity department."

Stardom was a strange existence—one that often felt more like a glamorous form of imprisonment than a well-paid aristocracy. A big part of the reason why was the seven-year option contract, which gave the studio total control over an actor's livelihood and fate. Under the contract, every six months the studio would review the performer's progress and decide whether to renew his or her option. Every contract also had a morals clause that allowed the studio to cancel if the performer in question engaged in any activity—sexual, political, moral—that damaged the reputation or economic well-being of the studio.

The option contract didn't just tie the performer to the studio. "It had restrictive clauses that gave the studio total control over the star's image and services," writes film historian Tino Balio. "It required an actor 'to act, sing, pose, speak, or perform in such roles as the producer may designate'; it gave the studio the right to change the name of the actor at its own discretion and to control the performer's face and likeness in advertising and publicity; and it required the actor to comply with rules covering interviews and public appearances." If the aspiring star refused an assignment, the "studio could sue for damages and extend the contract to make up for the stoppage."

The main reason for these sweatshop-style controls was economic: stars were at the heart of the Hollywood business model. They were the most tangible and identifiable indicator of the quality and market value of any particular motion picture. The major studios offered their pictures to exhibitors a season in advance of actual production. At the same time, although the big studios owned many of the theater chains, their ownership tended to be regional: Paramount, for example, was the biggest theater owner by far but its holdings were concentrated in the Midwest. Each studio had to entice theater chains in other parts of the country to rent its pictures. And the maximum rentals inevitably went to the pictures with the biggest stars.

From his earliest days in Hollywood, Gary Cooper seemed to thoroughly understand his role in this vast commercial machinery, its value, and the potential financial rewards he could reap from it. But he also harbored no illusions about the pitfalls of stardom and the damage it could inflict upon his personal life, destroying his privacy while rendering him a manufactured persona rather than an actual human being.

"It's an odd sort of responsibility that has been loaded on the film actor," he told a newspaper interviewer in 1929, just three years after entering the business. "Perhaps no other people in the world are permitted to have so little life of their own. It's natural, I suppose, for the fans to want to know all about us—what we do, what we like, what we don't like. But it does give you a rather goldfishy sensation, and if you stop to think about it, it is a big responsibility.

"You see, we actors are just a commodity that the studios have for sale. If we do anything that decreases our value, we'll be replaced by another line of goods."

He realized early on that he had few friends and no one he could trust. "Kid, stay out of Hollywood," he warned his nephew Howard in a letter. "It's a dirty place . . . Nobody in Hollywood is normal. Absolutely nobody. And they have such a vicious attitude toward each other . . . and nobody has any real friends."

THE TRANSITION TO TALKING pictures had transformed the movie business. It greatly increased the expense of making films. It vanquished a generation of actors and directors who could not adjust to the new needs and sensibilities. The studios embarked on a search for acting talent, raiding Broadway and theater circuits throughout the country for attractive young men and women who not only looked beautiful but sounded good, too. Sound created more intimacy on the screen, removing the distance between the star and the audience. And thousands of young people descended on Hollywood hoping for a break.

But it wasn't just young actors who were in demand. The call also went out for writers who could produce snappy, realistic, and entertaining dialogue. Even before the first talking pictures, screenwriter Herman Mankiewicz had sent a telegram to his pal Ben Hecht, a Chicago newspaperman and novelist, beckoning him to Hollywood. "Millions are to be grabbed out here," Mankiewicz told Hecht, "and your only competition is idiots. Don't let this get around."

Many famous and accomplished novelists and playwrights headed west seeking fat paychecks and sunny weather, among them William Faulkner, Robert Sherwood, Aldous Huxley, Dorothy Parker, Elmer Rice, Nathanael West, and F. Scott Fitzgerald. But many others were aspiring young, unknown writers with short résumés and unproven talents, bursting out of America's Depression-ridden cities and trekking west in search of their big break and a piece of the new, celluloid American dream.

2.

The Elephant Man

There is no avoiding the fact that the very nature . . . of every writer, is revealed in his writing. What you are as a human being shows up in your work.

LILLIAN ROSS

In February 1934—the heart of an angry Chicago winter in the midst of the Great Depression—one of those aspiring young writers loaded his bags into a secondhand Plymouth and began the long, punishing drive to Southern California. Carl Foreman was just nineteen and due to start his senior year at the University of Illinois. He told his parents he was taking a leave of absence, but in truth he had no intention of returning to school. Instead he was hoping to launch a career as a screenwriter, relying on the promises made to him by his mother's sister Florence, who had married a prosperous furniture dealer and invited Carl to come stay with them in Hollywood, where she could help him meet influential people in the movie business. The car wasn't his; he was supposed to shepherd it to an automobile dealer on the West Coast. He had signed on three passengers to help fund the journey but their impecuniosity turned out to exceed even his own. The car was not quite as advertised—it guzzled gas and oil and broke down with alarming regularity—and neither were Carl's skills as a motorist. Heading south to escape the cold on pre-Interstate, narrow country roads, he hit a cow and overturned a lettuce truck near Joplin, Missouri. Two of the passengers quickly peeled off, and he and his sole remaining travel companion, a Greek fry cook named Nick, abandoned the vehicle, black smoke pouring ominously from the hood, outside Odessa, Texas. Carl bought a bus ticket with borrowed money and took a Greyhound to the West Coast with a small sack of clothes and a portable typewriter.

He arrived in Los Angeles with fifty-seven cents in his pocket, only to discover that Aunt Florence's situation was also not quite as advertised. She had divorced the furniture dealer, married a doctor, and divorced him as well. Now she was broke, hungry, unemployed, and living in a friend's apartment. There was, of course, no room for Carl.

He left his typewriter with her and wandered the streets looking for work. For a while he had a job as a janitor in a rooming house, eating peanuts from the shell for breakfast, lunch, and dinner because they were cheap and filling, and sleeping in public parks and in the hallway or on the roof of an apartment building managed by his cousin Lou. Then he got temporary work as a freelance public relations manager for a new musical and for nine evenings as a silent torch carrier in Max Reinhardt's production of *A Midsummer Night's Dream* at the Hollywood Bowl. But he missed his family and his college girlfriend, Estelle. He never even got past the gates of a film studio, let alone got the chance to try to write for one. After a year of fairly consistent misery, he fled back to Chicago, bowed but not broken—a far different introduction to Hollywood than Gary Cooper had experienced eight years earlier.

It was an inauspicious beginning for an ambitious son of Russian Jewish immigrants. Carl's father, Isidore, had come from the town of Chudnov in the Ukraine, while his mother, Fanny, was from the Crimea. They met in Chicago and got married in 1913. When Carl was born a year later, they were living in a long, chaotic railroad flat presided over by his maternal grandmother. His father worked long hours as a pants cutter at Hart Schaffner and Marx, while his mother worked at a millinery factory. When they saved up enough money they opened their own store on Division Street, the colorful thoroughfare connecting east and west Chicago and serving as a hub for immigrants. Foreman's Millinery had a hopeful motto: "Exclusive But Not Expensive."

His parents bounced from poverty to modest success to poverty again. For a while they opened several shops in different parts of Chicago, but the Depression forced them to sell all of the stores as well as the small, two-story house they had bought. With its heavy reliance on manufacturing, the city was one of the hardest hit in America. Unemployment peaked at nearly 50 percent, thousands of jobless workers staged frequent demonstrations, and bread lines of forlorn men, women, and children were regular sights. Even Al Capone opened a soup kitchen to feed the hungry. Evictions were so common "you couldn't walk three doors without walking into people's furniture," a resident told Studs Terkel. Carl was so shaken by what he saw that later in life, according to his son, Jonathan, he kept small bank accounts in five or six countries as a hedge against another economic collapse.

While it wrecked the Foremans' dreams of prosperity, the Depression also affirmed their radical politics. Isidore Foreman was a Zionist, socialist, and trade union activist, while Fanny and her older brother Joe both belonged to a Young Communists group.

Carl's own earliest exposure to radicalism occurred at the corner of Division Street and Washtenaw Avenue near Humboldt Park when he was twelve or thirteen. A street-corner political meeting to protest the rising toll of joblessness and poverty was disrupted when two police wagons drove straight into the gathering crowd. The cops arrested the speakers, then turned their attention to the onlookers. One of them grabbed Carl, kicked him all the way across Division Street, and threatened to do much worse if he ever saw Carl again. Angered by the bullying tactics, Carl lingered for the neighborhood dance that followed. There were tea and biscuits and Russian folk songs, and a very pretty older girl who danced with him. "When I went home at two in the morning I was a Communist," he recalled.

Early on he wanted to be a lawyer, modeling himself after Clarence Darrow, the legendary Chicago defender of the underdog. At age ten he memorized big chunks of Darrow's passionate and successful twelve-hour appeal to the court to spare the lives of Nathan Leopold and Richard Loeb, the coldly calculating young killers of a local schoolboy in what was then the trial of the century. "I am pleading for the future," young Carl would proclaim to his parents' dinner guests, tears streaming down his face. "I am pleading for a time when hatred and cruelty will not control the hearts of man, when we can learn by reason and judgment and understanding and faith that all life is worth saving, and that mercy is the highest attribute of man." The performance was a cleverly calculated marriage of idealism and melodrama—a forerunner of Carl's career as a screenwriter.

The movies were another source of melodrama and fantasy. Carl's parents opened a drapery shop on Lawrence Avenue, where there were three movie theaters within a six-block radius. He was smitten by the beautiful women he watched on the screen—Joan Crawford, Merle Oberon, Madeleine Carroll, Eleanor Powell, Gladys Swarthout, Maureen O'Sullivan—and by Estelle Barr, a pretty, brown-haired girl he met at Theodore Roosevelt High School during his sophomore year. He loved dramas and musicals, and most especially Westerns, particularly those of William S. Hart, the first great cowboy movie hero, who always played the outsider: the noble outlaw, or the cowhand who got framed and took justice into his own hands, or the sheriff under attack by narrow-minded citizens for doing his job without fear nor favor—"in short," as Carl later put it, "the individual in conflict with himself and his frontier environment." Hart's characters lived by a personal code; they treated women with respect, were kind to animals and small children, always kept their word, and fought their enemies honorably—they never drew first. Carl was less enamored of the gentleman cowboys who replaced Hart in popularity as the silent era came to a close. Tom Mix, Hoot Gibson, Ken Maynard, and Tim McCoy had no inner conflicts and no complexity—they were just handsome, heavily powdered leading men in dry-cleaned, well-pressed costumes. Carl longed for grit and authenticity.

He was a string bean in those days, five foot ten and underfed, with dark brown hair, bottle-thick glasses over warm blue eyes, and pale, pitted skin that gave him the countenance of a Russian Jewish intellectual who spent too much time in basement coffee shops. Later on, even as his hair thinned and his waistline thickened, he never lost that nerdy, intelligent look nor the sardonic and intuitive skepticism that went with it.

He graduated high school early and at age seventeen headed to the University of Illinois, where he majored in English, minored in journalism, and wrote for several student publications. Storytelling quickly emerged as his special gift. And he was immediately drawn to Hollywood, the promised land for storytellers. "The movies are the great mass art of our times, the people's art . . . a theater that knows no boundaries," he passionately declared. Still, after the debacle of his first trip to the West Coast, he was wary of venturing there again.

For a time he managed the Nickelodeon in downtown Chicago, then ran the John Hicks Show on State Street at the tawdry southern end of the Loop. There were all-women wrestling matches and dancing girls and faked prize fights. The lead attraction was Michaeline of the Waters—"The Most Beautiful Girl in the World." She and her friend Marie would dance seductively in their bathing suits and wrestle each other while the male customers cheered. He made forty dollars a week, took a room downtown, and went home early Sunday mornings to sleep in and see his parents.

Around 1937 he hooked up with a traveling carnival, playing the West Coast: Vancouver, Washington, and Oregon. He served as the barker, enticing people to enter the tent—good experience, no doubt, for a future career in Hollywood. Carnival life was an endless mix of adventures and temptations—drinking, gambling, and women. The rummy and poker games went on all afternoon, then by six he'd open up the show; he would talk himself hoarse until one or two A.M., and then seek out a woman to take to his cot. He'd exhaust himself to the point where he needed Benzedrine to stay awake and alcohol to go to sleep. There'd be times during the evening when he couldn't sit down for fear of not being able to get up again.

Carl loved the rude, grotesque intimacy of the freaks: the human pincushion who sewed buttons on his naked chest and had an icepick implanted in his cheeks; Beasy and Billy, the pinhead twins from Africa whose skulls came to a point; the frog-faced boy; and the beautiful black woman who could pick silver dollars off a table with her vagina.

But he still dreamed of Hollywood—and of Estelle. In early October 1938 he made his inglorious return to Los Angeles in a circus train loaded with elephants. The beasts stood tightly packed in freight cars all day, noisily eating, moaning, urinating, and defecating in vast quantities, and the smell was beyond suffocating. "The second coming of Foreman to Hollywood was with the elephants," he would later boast. A few weeks later Estelle joined him there and they were married.

If his first trip to Hollywood had been an unmitigated disaster, this one didn't start out much better. He enrolled in the Federal Writers' Project of the Works Progress Administration, a New Deal program, which paid him eighty-five dollars per month to write guidebooks (he was, by his own reckoning, terrible at it), while Estelle worked weekends at a shoe store downtown. Her parents, who thought Carl was a dubious match for their attractive and talented daughter, pleaded with the newlyweds to return to Chicago, but they resisted. They got a one-room apartment on Gregory Way with a tiny kitchenette and a pull-down bed for thirty dollars a month on the ground floor next to the parking lot. "You could hear the cars as they pulled in and the impetuous fellow who kept hitting the side of the building," Carl would recall.

There were no film schools in those days where an aspiring screenwriter could study and hone his craft. But the League of American Writers, a professional writers' organization founded by the Communist Party in 1935, set up a night school for writers in Hollywood. Students could study screenwriting with such respected luminaries as Paul

Jarrico, John Howard Lawson, Irwin Shaw, and Donald Ogden Stewart, the league's president and author of *The Philadelphia Story*'s Oscar-winning screenplay. Carl got a scholarship to attend. He took a screenwriting course with Lester Cole and Robert Rossen, both of them—like Stewart—members of Hollywood's small but hyperactive branch of the party. His next course was with Dore Schary, a New Jersey–born former actor in the New York theater circuit who was establishing himself as a top screenwriter and producer at MGM.

Schary's first homework assignment was to write a synopsis for a story to be workshopped in class. Two sessions after Carl turned in his treatment, Schary asked the class, "Now which of you is Carl Foreman?" Carl raised his hand with trepidation. Schary told him, "Mr. Foreman, you're a writer." Carl was stunned and ecstatic. It was the first time that anyone of stature had taken notice of his work.

After that, Schary kept an eye out for him. When Carl failed to qualify for another eighteen-dollar scholarship to continue his studies, Schary paid the tuition out of his own pocket. "He was one of the most important people in my life," Carl would recall. "He was my father out here when I needed a father."

The League of American Writers combined professional development and left-wing politics at a time when communists, socialists, and liberals mixed somewhat uneasily in a broad "Popular Front" coalition that shared a commitment to social justice and an abhorrence of Fascism. Schary was a liberal who believed that movies could combine hard-hitting social relevance and entertainment. But he also had a robust skepticism about Communism and its acolytes. He had no use for Carl's radicalism, but their disagreement was largely good-natured. When the younger man gave Schary a large salami that his father had sent from Chicago wrapped in a copy of a Communist newspaper, Schary thanked him, saying, "I ate the salami and I read the baloney."

THE PROFESSIONAL WRITERS WHO flocked to the West Coast studios during the golden age of the studio system brought along their politics as well as their typewriters, as did the writer-émigrés who fled the growing chaos and dangers of Europe in the 1930s and set up shop in Hollywood. A disproportionate number of these newcomers were Jews, eager for the fresh start and egalitarian opportunities that Hollywood seemed to promise those with the talent and skills to compete. Like Carl and Estelle Foreman, many of their tribal and cultural loyalties were on the left: families, friends, neighbors, teachers, and instincts all skewed to liberalism, socialism, or beyond, just as Gary Cooper's in Montana had naturally skewed to the conservative right.

For its first few decades, Hollywood was a monopoly-capitalist's dream. The large studios owned everything from the offices where the producers and screenwriters gave birth to movie ideas, to the soundstages where those ideas became pictures, to the theaters where they were exhibited. The studio bosses also owned the people who populated every step of the process. They created a tame company union in 1927, the Academy of Motion Picture Arts and Sciences, to encompass producers, directors, actors, writers, and other professionals. There were fledgling unions for skilled and semiskilled craftsmen, technicians, decorators, and manual laborers who built and tore down film sets and moved equipment, but no independent guilds for the artisans, whether performers, directors, or writers. Nothing about Hollywood seemed like it would be fertile ground for preaching class struggle. But by the time Carl first arrived, the landscape was rapidly changing.

The first attempt to organize artisans was launched in 1933 with the founding of the Screen Writers Guild. In January of that year Paramount and RKO declared their lucrative theater chains bankrupt. Ticket sales were down and economic control of the industry was rapidly migrating from its original entrepreneurial owners to the East Coast bankers and investors who financed them. On March 8, most of the studios announced they were unable to meet their payrolls. The next day—the same day that Franklin Roosevelt declared a bank moratorium—the major studios collectively imposed a wage cut of 50 percent for all employees for a two-month "emergency" period. The move brought home to thousands of artisans their utter powerlessness before the men who owned the companies they worked for.

Ten prominent screenwriters had gotten together at the Hollywood Knickerbocker Hotel a few weeks earlier to discuss forming a guild. Now they decided to seek an alliance with other organizations of authors, playwrights, and journalists throughout the country to demand a share of the profits from their work. More than two hundred writers left the Motion Picture Academy in April to join the Screen Writers Guild and elected John Howard Lawson, a former New York playwright and proud, prickly, self-acknowledged Communist, as their president. Over the next two years, the directors, cameramen, and actors formed similar organizations.

The studio bosses, frightened by the specter of independent unions for their most skilled workers, vehemently resisted. Irving Thalberg, the genteel head of production for MGM and perhaps the most respected of the studio executives, declared that "unions are for laborers, not dignified people like writers." William Randolph Hearst's rabidly right-wing *Los Angeles Examiner* denounced the guild as "a device of Communist radicals."

For a time, the studios supported a breakaway organization of conservative writers who called themselves the Screen Playwrights Inc. But in June 1938 the Guild won a commanding victory of 267 to 57 in a federally supervised election, and two months later the National Labor Relations Board formally certified the Guild as the sole representative of Hollywood's screenwriters. Still, it took three more years for the Guild and the studios to forge their first contract. Under the threat of a writers' strike, negotiating committees for the two sides finally got together one evening at the Brown Derby restaurant. The Guild left its fire-breathing radicals like Lawson and sharp-tongued columnist Dorothy Parker at home, sending over milder-mannered liberals like Charles Brackett, Sheridan Gibney, and Carl's good friend Dore Schary. After dinner and drinks the writers made a proposal for a temporary minimum wage and recognition of the Guild as the sole bargaining agent for all screenwriters and final arbiter of writers' credits.

"Is that all you want?" Harry Warner of Warner Bros. asked mildly.

Schary wondered if they'd sold themselves too cheaply. But then Warner exploded.

"That's all you want, you goddamned Communist bastards? You dirty sons of bitches. All you'll get from me is shit!"

Warner stormed out of the room. The writers eventually got their contract on their terms. But the depth of anger and bitterness among Hollywood's old guard was clear. Red-baiting, even of liberal anti-Communists like Schary, from now on would be an accepted weapon in the arsenal of the producers and their allies.

Communist organizers came to Hollywood for the same reason that their enemies in the House Un-American Activities Committee ventured there later—for the prestige and the publicity, and to make their mark on an industry that had become the effective overseer of American popular culture. The party wanted to attract celebrities and intellectuals and raise money. It also wanted to get at least a toehold in the craft unions whose work was essential to the industry. The Hollywood branch reported direct to national headquarters at 235 West Twenty-Third Street in New York City. Its members were treated with kid gloves by the national party because of their prestige, wealth, and ability to draw crowds to large public events and causes. Its numbers were small: at the zenith there were probably no more than 350 active party members in Hollywood in an industry that employed nearly thirty thousand. Screenwriters were estimated to make up nearly half of that small number. There were "fractions" in which artisans in the same field—writers, directors, performers—gathered to discuss the issues of the day, talk strategy, and organize. And there were study groups in which the gospel of Karl Marx, as seen through the special lens of Joseph Stalin, was preached and practiced.

Despite its egalitarian ideology, the party was riddled with gender and class divisions. "The men were always working in a group in the Beverly Hills area, and the wives were sent out to the San Fernando Valley with the dentists' and doctors' wives," recalled screenwriter Jean Rouverol Butler, a party member married to fellow writer Hugo Butler. "Within the studios, the most important writers were in the elite group, and the rest of us were in a hodgepodge with all the nonprofessionals, the script readers and so forth."

Carl and Estelle Foreman had arrived in Hollywood around the time of the Munich Pact in September 1938, when the Western powers acquiesced to Hitler's territorial amputation of Czechoslovakia in a vain effort to prevent another world war. Many of their early friends in Los Angeles were party members. While the Foremans admired Franklin Roosevelt and voted mostly as Democrats, they saw the Communist Party as the only political organization wholeheartedly committed to supporting the cause of anti-Fascism and the rights of blacks, Jews, immigrants, and trade unionists, and they saw the Great Depression as the ultimate judgment of capitalism's failure. For them the party clearly seemed to be the most courageous political organization in the country. "The people we met were very bright," Carl would recall, ". . . alive and friendly and warm, and in no time at all . . . I was so imbued with the idea of joining in what seemed to me to be a crusade for a better America that I went to my friend X and literally pleaded to be allowed to join."

As much as half the party's membership consisted of Jews. This was partly for reasons of culture and ideology: as with Carl's family, many of the Jews who came from Russia and Eastern Europe brought their socialist politics along with their baggage, and passed on those beliefs to their children. But it was also a matter of identity. The passage to America was not just a physical transition but an emotional and psychological one as well. Many who came retained their traditional beliefs and their Jewish heritage, but others sought to trade those vestiges of the Old World for a modern new identity in the new one. It's too simple to say they gave up being Jews to become Communists, although some did exactly that. For many more—including Carl and Estelle—these identities coexisted in complicated ways. As Irving Howe wrote in *World of Our Fathers*, his landmark study of the coming of Eastern European Jews to America, "The greatest contribution of the left-wing immigrant Jews to the Communist movement was, finally, neither their time, nor money, nor minds; it was their children."

Carl and Estelle joined the Communist Party at the height of the Popular Front era. The party, which early on had preached world revolution, had toned down its rhetoric and its tactics by the mid-thirties, and repackaged itself as a Jeffersonian force for progressivism and nonviolent social change. Communism, declared its moderate new general secretary, Earl Browder, "is the Americanism of the twentieth century."

The party's official policy was to join forces with other progressive groups to form organizations like the Hollywood Anti-Nazi League, the Motion Picture Democratic Committee, and the Motion Picture Artists Committee to Aid Republican Spain. These groups often consisted of liberal Democrats, a sprinkling of socialists and Communists, and even some moderate Republicans. Liberals like Dore Schary, Edward G. Robinson, Melvyn Douglas, and Fredric March joined forces with conservative Republicans like Bruce Cabot, Joan Bennett, John Ford, and Dick Powell in the Anti-Nazi League to organize massive rallies against Hitler's alarming success in Germany and growing attacks on Jews and other minorities. Communist Party members often played the role of good partners in these groups, sharing their expertise and their commitment.

"The activities I was engaged in until the time I left were not disloyal to the United States," recalled screenwriter Richard J. Collins, one of the most active party members, who later turned informer. "They may have been misguided, but disloyal they were not . . . In other words, the people who became Communists, at least in my time, didn't join because the Communists were going to overthrow our form of government by force and violence."

Collins recalled an atmosphere of idealism and mutual support among his fellow Communists. "When I joined the party, I was handed ready-made friends, a cause, a faith, and a viewpoint on all phenomena."

"The Communist Party was for years the best social club in Hollywood," recalled screenwriter and director Abraham Polonsky, one of the most committed intellectuals among party members. "You'd meet a lot of interesting people, there were parties, and it created a nice social atmosphere."

Screenwriter Philip Dunne, a dedicated liberal who was president of the Hollywood Democratic Committee, said one of his favorite young colleagues at Twentieth Century-Fox told him she had joined the party "because she was new in Hollywood and hadn't been able to make many friends. To her, the Communist Party was a sort of glamorous Lonely Hearts Club."

For Norma Barzman, a writer who joined the party after marrying her fellow screenwriter Ben, the party became part of the fabric of their commitment to each other. "It sounds silly and maybe that's why no one mentions it," she writes in her memoir. "Hollywood Communist couples had a romantic notion of themselves as the ideal young man and young woman surging forward with the Red flag, the logo of Artkino [Soviet films] . . . To be together in this enterprise of making the world better brought with it a chest-bursting pride, a heady elation, a belief in the gloriousness of life."

In its earliest days, the party's artists and performers had focused on appealing to a limited audience of fellow radicals. But as time went on, according to historian Michael Kazin, the growth of mass culture, coupled with the more general shift in public opinion to the left, created opportunities for left-wing artists to reach a much broader cross-section of the population. The party's influence stretched far beyond its small membership. Party members were responsible for songs like "Strange Fruit," and "This Land Is Your Land," novels like *Native Son*, plays like *The Little Foxes*, and films like *Mr. Smith Goes to Washington*. Fellow travelers with leftist sympathies created *Citizen Kane*, *Death of a Salesman*, *For Whom the Bell Tolls*, *Yertle the Turtle*, the screenplay for *Casablanca*, and the lyrics for *The Wizard of Oz*.

"We knew who we were," said Dorothy Healey, one of the most respected leaders of the California party. "We weren't subject to any doubts or hesitations. Not only would we triumph, we would triumph soon."

There were two serious and lingering problems, however, that made many liberals anxious about working with Communists. For one thing, the party was a clandestine organization that did not hold open meetings nor make public its membership, and while some members were open about their involvement, most adhered to a strict code of secrecy. All were subject to party discipline, and many were prepared to lie about their involvement. Party leaders argued that the secrecy was necessary to protect members from harassment by the FBI and local "Red Squads" such as the Los Angeles Police Department's Public Disorder Intelligence Division. But it gave the party a conspiratorial aura that severely limited its ability to attract a larger following and gain the trust of non-party members.

The other problem was the party's close ties to Moscow. The Communist International, or Comintern, set up by Lenin in 1919, became the clearinghouse and overseer of organizations abroad, including the American party. The gradual release of secret files following the fall of the Soviet Union in the early 1990s has revealed the extent to which the Comintern transmitted orders on policies and practices from the Kremlin to the American party's New York headquarters and to which those orders were strictly obeyed. The first loyalty of the party's leadership clearly belonged to the world's one Communist nation—"the motherland," as playwright Lillian Hellman once solemnly called the Soviet Union. At a time when capitalism seemed to be collapsing across the globe, members saw socialist Russia as a lonely beacon of hope and idealism. Many members believed in the infallibility of Joseph Stalin with the same certitude with which staunch Catholics believed in the pope. Dissent was condemned as deviationism. Trotskyism became a hated epithet. Philosopher John Dewey's investigation of the Moscow show trials in 1936–37 was publicly denounced by loyal Communists. The trials' defendants had "resorted to duplicity and conspiracy and allied themselves with longstanding enemies of the Soviet Union," read a chillingly delusional statement in *New Masses*, the Communist weekly, signed by such luminaries as movie star John Garfield and authors Dashiell Hammett, Lillian Hellman, Langston Hughes, and Dorothy Parker.

As historian Kazin points out, the Moscow connection gave American Communists influence and impact. They weren't just members of a tiny radical splinter group but were part of a worldwide movement. But it was also a fatal flaw. How could a political organization that claimed to believe in the ideals of human rights, economic justice, racial tolerance, and world peace justify taking orders from one of the most bloodstained, repressive, and antidemocratic regimes in history? People could claim not to have known in earlier days about the crimes against humanity of Lenin and Stalin, but by the late 1930s there was little doubt or moral justification for the blind loyalty of American Communists to the Soviet Union.

"The Party tried very hard to present Communist or Socialist ideas as an advance in America's development that was in fact rooted in American traditions," recalled film director Jules Dassin, a loyal party member. "Well, they failed in this. The American people couldn't buy it. The association with the Soviet Union was too powerful."

Steve Nelson, a Spanish Civil War veteran and senior party organizer, conceded ruefully in his memoirs that "We treated the Soviet Union as the single pivot in the world around which everything else was centered. Nothing else mattered . . . We had the mentality that the Soviet Union was always right and that its interests were paramount."

Occasionally word of dissent within the party would leak through its shell of secrecy—as when local party leader Lawson sought to rein in young Budd Schulberg, whose Hollywood novel, *What Makes Sammy Run?*, was deemed anti-Semitic by the party elders because of its acidic portrait of the studio heads, their morals, and their lackeys. One of Schulberg's younger friends within the party, Charles Glenn, wrote a glowing review of the book for the *Daily Worker* and *Daily People's World*, calling it "the best work done on Hollywood." Lawson then summoned Glenn to his office for a dressing down. When Glenn suggested that Lawson write a letter to the editor criticizing the review and launching a dialogue, Lawson told him that no such dialogue was necessary, that Glenn just needed to write a new review retracting his earlier one. Thoroughly bullied, Glenn did what he was told, and said later he had always regretted it. Furious at what he saw as the party's hidebound orthodoxy, Schulberg quit and later named names of party members in testimony before the House Un-American Activities Committee.

Similarly, when *New Masses* published "What Shall We Ask of Writers?," a thoughtful piece by screenwriter Albert Maltz arguing that artists should be free to pursue their creative instincts outside the boundaries of orthodox Communist ideology, he was hounded, excoriated, and humiliated until he felt compelled to retract his apostasy in print.

The question of the party's honesty and true loyalties came to a sudden head on August 24, 1939, when Moscow and Berlin announced the signing of the Molotov-Ribbentrop nonaggression pact. Overnight, the party's position on war and peace swiveled 180 degrees from relentlessly promoting the fight against Fascism to denouncing the corporate warmongers who were purportedly pushing the United States into another world war. The pact caused thousands of members to drop out of the party and shattered any sense of trust between liberals and Communists. Without taking a vote of its membership, the leaders of the Anti-Nazi League changed its name to the Hollywood League for Democratic Action. Its New Year's card for 1940 denounced "the war to lead America to war." Its new motto: "The Yanks are not coming." Many of the organizations that had comprised the Popular Front simply collapsed, marking the end of that phase of left-wing and liberal solidarity.

Rueful liberals got the message. More former sympathizers were shocked and disgusted when the Soviets invaded Poland at the same time as the Nazis. Melvyn Douglas and Philip Dunne resigned from the Motion Picture Democratic Committee after it refused to consider a motion condemning the Soviet invasion of Finland and instead passed a resolution demanding that the United States remain neutral in the war between Nazi Germany and Britain and France. Control of other Popular Front organizations was seized "in similar fashion by the same wrecking crew, as all over town the industrious Communist tail wagged the lazy liberal dog," recalled Dunne.

Dore Schary was stunned when Lawson, a leader of the League of American Writers, submitted a petition condemning Franklin Roosevelt's foreign policy in Latin America. Schary was advised to sign or at least keep quiet in order to avoid friction between the league's factions. Instead, he quit.

"A Communist was no longer just a Communist . . ." said Roger Baldwin, founder of the American Civil Liberties Union, an organization that had previously welcomed Communists to its ranks. From then on, "a Communist was an agent of the Soviet Union."

Carl Foreman would later say that the American Communist Party effectively committed political suicide by supporting the Moscow-Berlin pact. But despite their gnawing doubts, he and Estelle hung on to their party membership. They accepted the leadership's claim that Stalin had had no choice but to sign with the devil because of the cowardice and weakness of France and Britain in failing to oppose Hitler's designs. Staying with the party, Carl later said, had been "an act of faith" on his and Estelle's part, based upon wishful thinking rather than hard facts. Even so, their reservations were growing. The subsequent invasion of Finland was even harder to swallow. And the elitism of the Hollywood party, which Carl began to see was ruled by a clique of prestigious writers, began to eat at him.

Still, the party was the center of Carl and Estelle's professional and social life. They had made friends with other young writers, attended the party's writing workshops, drew on moral support and encouragement. "If you left the party you were leaving the friends you had," he recalled.

For Carl and many other American Communists, the German invasion of the Soviet Union in June 1941 was a blessing in disguise. While it put Russia in huge jeopardy, it helped to paper over the rifts on the left and revived the concept and spirit of the Popular Front. "It was one of the happiest nights of my life," recalled Donald Ogden Stewart, with more than a little sense of irony.

CARL'S SCREENWRITING CAREER WAS proceeding in fits and starts. He learned from fellow writer Charles Marion that Monogram, one of the smaller "Poverty Row" studios, was looking for a script that would combine its two biggest attractions: the Bowery Boys and the aging Hungarian actor Bela Lugosi of *Dracula* fame. Charlie and Carl knocked out *Spooks Run Wild* in two feverish weeks, splitting the grand sum of $425. Carl was bitterly unhappy with the pay, and even more so with their second Bowery Boys assignment, which paid only three hundred. He could see that things were moving in exactly the wrong direction: pretty soon, he quipped, they'd be paying the studio for assignments.

Still, Carl would recall the sale of that first screenplay as "probably the most excruciatingly exciting thing that has ever happened to me," although he understood just how low writers like himself stood on the ladder of importance. "I was a flunky, a hack, the lowest of the low, a joke, despised, barely tolerated, underestimated, undervalued, and underpaid," he recalled. "My scripts, like those of every other writer—regardless of stature—were at the mercy of the whims, neuroses, foibles, ulcers, stupidities, and blind spots of the producers, directors, and actors who worked with them. I fought hard . . . and they fought back with confidence because they knew the truth . . . To make matters worse, I didn't even have the comfort of believing that I was a good screenwriter in those days."

It was only a slight improvement when they landed a gig as gag writers for the Charlie Ruggles radio program (entitled *A Barrel of Fun* because the sponsor was a brewery) at $250 each per show. Carl quickly graduated to writing jokes for Eddie Cantor's radio show, a step up both in professionalism and pay. But it still was a long way from his dream of writing original film scripts. He went back to Dore Schary, his friend and mentor, and pleaded for a job. All Schary could offer him was a temporary spot at MGM as a script doctor for $150 a week—less than half what he was earning with Cantor. The pay didn't matter; Carl eagerly grabbed the opportunity. Cantor was shocked to lose him. But Carl stayed at MGM for fourteen months until a bigger and more demanding employer came along: the United States Army.

THE JAPANESE ATTACK ON Pearl Harbor and Nazi Germany's subsequent declaration of war on the United States definitively ended the bitter domestic debate over whether America should enter World War Two. It also unambiguously established the United States and the Soviet Union as allies in the war against Fascism. For now, at least, both countries were committed to military collaboration to defeat their common enemy.

Many of Hollywood's most talented filmmakers enlisted in the war effort. Darryl F. Zanuck, head of production at Twentieth Century-Fox, became a colonel in the Army Signal Corps, while acclaimed director John Ford headed up the Navy's newly formed Field Photo Unit. He and fellow directors William Wyler, John Huston, and George Stevens took their cameras into combat zones, putting themselves in harm's way to create an enduring collection of memorable battlefield documentaries.

After Pearl Harbor, Carl tried to enlist in the U.S. Navy but his nearsightedness was so bad he was rejected. He was eventually drafted by the Army, and he applied to and was accepted by the Army Signal Corps's film unit, under the command of Frank Capra. The legendary movie director was compiling an impressive collection of producers, writers, and editors to create a series of indoctrination films called *Why We Fight* that attempted to explain to newly minted American soldiers the context and meaning of the war against the Axis powers. Carl almost lost the assignment. The Army had a dossier from the FBI that recorded his attendance at Communist Party events in Hollywood, and Capra was inclined to shun anyone who might be considered a security risk. But screenwriter Leonard Spigelgass, a close friend of Dore Schary, intervened on Carl's behalf.

He worked for nine months as a writer and researcher on a twenty-minute documentary called *Know Your Enemy: Japan*, under the supervision of a Dutch-born socialist filmmaker named Joris Ivens. Capra's superiors eventually scrapped the film as too radical, then assigned Carl and Irving Wallace, the future bestselling novelist, to write an entirely new version.

Carl's next assignment took him to New York—it was his first trip on an airplane—where he reported to Anatole Litvak. The Ukrainian-born film director had been promoted to major and put in charge of a movie, reportedly a personal pet project of President Roosevelt, explaining and extolling Russian-American cooperation in the fight against Hitler. Litvak was an annoying boss—Carl found him pompous, demanding, and lazy—and nothing ever seemed to get done. After Roosevelt's death in April 1945 the Army quickly shelved the project.

BEYOND CONTRIBUTING SOME OF its finest filmmakers to create military documentaries, Hollywood made dozens of films that were designed to support the war effort. They ranged from gung-ho combat movies like *Wake Island* and *Back to Bataan* to entertaining fantasies like *Casablanca*. And with the encouragement of the Roosevelt administration, the studios also made several pictures that were designed to convince audiences that the Soviet Union was a worthy ally. Samuel Goldwyn produced and RKO distributed *The North Star* (1943), written by Lillian Hellman, who had been a Communist Party member in the late 1930s, which celebrated the heroic resistance of Ukrainian partisans against Nazi invaders. MGM, under Louis B. Mayer, a conservative Republican, produced *Song of Russia* (1944), in which the dashing Robert Taylor plays an American orchestra conductor who falls in love with a beautiful young Russian pianist and tractor driver. The film was written by Richard J. Collins and Paul Jarrico, two of Hollywood's most successful and influential Communist Party members.

But the most blatant and disturbing ode to the Kremlin was *Mission to Moscow* (1943), written by Howard Koch and directed by Michael Curtiz, two non-Communist Hollywood veterans, for Warners. The movie was based on the bestselling memoir of Joseph E. Davies, a former ambassador to Moscow, and chronicles his gradual conversion from skeptic to passionate advocate for Joseph Stalin's regime. "No leaders of a nation have been so misrepresented and misunderstood as those in the Soviet government," intones Davies himself in a filmed preface to the story. The picture defends the Hitler-Stalin Pact and the Soviet invasion of Finland, depicts the defendants in the Moscow show trials as pro-Nazi fifth columnists, and celebrates their subsequent conviction and execution. "Based on twenty years as a trial lawyer, I'd be inclined to believe these confessions," declares the Davies character, played by Walter Huston, oblivious to the torture that Stalin's thugs had used to extract those admissions.

Jack Warner later defended the picture before the House Un-American Activities Committee, saying his studio had made the movie out of patriotic duty. "That picture was made when our country was fighting for its existence," he told the committee. ". . . If making *Mission to Moscow* in 1942 was a subversive activity, then the American Liberty ships which carried food and guns to Russian allies and the American naval vessels which convoyed them were likewise engaged in subversive activities. The picture was made only to help a desperate war effort and not for posterity."

Although Carl Foreman felt suffocated by the slow and super-cautious Army bureaucracy, he was acquiring valuable experience during his time in New York. Working out of the Astoria film studio just across the East River from Manhattan, he was exposed for the first time to the craft of modern filmmaking—lighting, camera work, film editing, film-set construction. He met a wide range of filmmakers and writers, including playwright Herbert Baker, who became a lifelong friend; screenwriter Theodor Geisel, who later gained fame as author of the Dr. Seuss children's books; and Ukrainian-born composer Dimitri Tiomkin. And one evening at the Manhattan apartment of Dore Schary's sister Lillian, he met an intense young film editor named Stanley Kramer.

Stanley was just a year older than Carl, but he had toiled for almost a decade in a variety of frustrating, low-paying jobs at several film companies, and he seemed keenly knowledgeable about the way things worked in Hollywood. Now he was a lieutenant working out of the Astoria studio. Carl generally didn't trust officers, but Stanley's charismatic intensity and his withering critique of the studio establishment impressed Carl. They talked late into the evening, took the subway home together, and began to see each other regularly, comparing notes and venting their frustrations. "He had a brooding aura of fighting injustice about him . . ." Carl would recall of his new friend. "I liked him a lot."

3.

The Icon

Charisma, the kind of natural power that a great movie actor exerts by doing nothing, is scary because it's outside the performer's control: it comes by the grace of God, and can vanish just as mysteriously.

RICHARD BRODY

During the years when Carl Foreman was literally eating peanuts and counting pennies as he struggled to find a foothold as a writer in Hollywood, Gary Cooper was thriving. Contracted to Paramount, one of the best-established of the major studios, he worked with some of the most talented directors of the era, including Josef von Sternberg, Rouben Mamoulian, Frank Borzage, and Ernst Lubitsch. They helped expand his range and repertoire; whereas early in his career he mostly played brooding cowboys and gallant soldiers, now he added society dandies, sexy artistes, and smart-mouthed but affable ladies' men. He looked as comfortable in top hat and tails as he did in buckskins and blue jeans. In *Morocco* (1930), dressed in a tight-fitting French Foreign Legion jacket and knee-high boots, he reduced Marlene Dietrich's sensual cabaret singer to a compliant mound of desert sand.

His social life was about to be transformed as well. At age thirty, he was considered one of the sexiest and most eligible leading men in Hollywood. There were hints of androgyny and rumors of a two-year affair with a devoted male friend. Celebrity photographer Cecil Beaton was said to have slept with him. But women were always on the menu. Author Budd Schulberg recalled that his father, one of the top executives at the studio, "was quick to notice that none of the Paramount stars stirred the hearts of the front-office secretaries—and other parts of their anatomy—like Gary Cooper."

"All typing stopped, all eyes turned to devour what Father's main secretary described as 'the most beautiful hunk of man who ever walked down this hall!'" wrote Schulberg. "My father's second secretary, the pleasingly plump, happy-dispositioned Jean Baer, carried on a semi-secret affair with Gary for years. He was never a flamboyant swordsman like Errol Flynn or Freddie March. But for all his quiet speech and diffident ways, Coop might have been the Babe Ruth of the Hollywood boudoir league. It was whispered down the studio corridors that he had the endowments of Hercules and the staying powers of Job."

"Gary kisses the way Charles Boyer looks like he kisses . . ." recalled Laraine Day, one of his female costars. "Well! It was like holding a hand grenade and not being able to get rid of it. I was left breathless."

But after sampling a substantial portion of the charms Hollywood had to offer, Cooper declared himself ready for something different. Her name was Veronica Balfe—known to friends as "Rocky." A New York socialite, she was only nineteen. Her father was a prominent banker, and her uncle, Cedric Gibbons, was the famed set designer who gave MGM's pictures their distinctively elegant look for three decades. Like Cooper, she was slim and athletic. Once he got past the hurdle of persuading her parents that he was something more than just an uncouth and philandering movie star, they were married in New York in December 1933 in a small private ceremony.

Rocky Balfe was a jagged mix of timid and outspoken, painfully honest with herself and others yet anxious and insecure. She had left Miss Bennett's School for Girls before completing the program and she never graduated high school nor attended college. She didn't think she was smart and never thought she was beautiful, although many admirers genuinely believed she was both. "She was almost two different personalities," her daughter, Maria Cooper Janis, recalls. "Yes, indeed, she was extremely shy but she was very determined to overcome her own insecurities, which were tremendous." When the couple was at their best, she filled the gaps in Cooper's personality and experience. She had the metabolism of a hyperactive cruise director, always insisting on going new places and doing new things, forcing him to meet new people; take up tennis, skiing, and scuba diving; visit an art museum. But their greatest joint project was their only child, Maria, born in 1937, the one female whom Cooper eternally and unconditionally loved.

They eventually bought a three-acre mock-Tudor estate on Chaparral

Street in affluent Brentwood near Sunset Boulevard, where he built a gun room and a carpentry shop. It was a short drive to the ocean in one of the many fine cars he kept parked out back. Hunting wild game, driving fast cars, eating good food whether from a four-star restaurant in Paris or a campfire in Montana, skiing at Sun Valley in Idaho or at Mont Blanc in the Alps—these were some of Cooper's fondest pastimes when he wasn't working. Along the way, he became friends with Ernest Hemingway, another twentieth-century American icon, who had Cooper in mind when he created the character of Robert Jordan, the American volunteer who sacrifices his life in the Spanish Civil War, for the bestselling novel *For Whom the Bell Tolls*.

After he returned from Europe in 1932, Cooper's name was above the title of every picture he made. His career, already well established, skyrocketed in 1936 with *Mr. Deeds Goes to Town*, his first film directed by Frank Capra, and Cecil B. DeMille's *The Plainsman*. Those two pictures set the character of a masculine, iconic hero, whether on the untamed streets of New York or the high plains of the Wild West. Then in 1939 he began an unprecedented run of critical and box office hits, beginning with *Beau Geste* (1939) and continuing with *The Westerner* (1940), *North West Mounted Police* (1940), *Meet John Doe* (1941), *Sergeant York* (1941), *Ball of Fire* (1941), *The Pride of the Yankees* (1942), and finally, the film version of *For Whom the Bell Tolls* (1943).

Some of these pictures still endure as classics, while others seem stale and faintly ridiculous in retrospect (Hemingway, for one, confessed he was repelled by the perfectly tailored fashion-wear and carefully coiffed, blond-tinted hairstyles of Cooper and his costar, Ingrid Bergman, in *For Whom the Bell Tolls*, as they purportedly endured the hardships of waging guerrilla warfare in full makeup in the Spanish mountains). But Cooper was always the hero and center of gravity, whether in a snappy Billy Wilder–written comedy like *Ball of Fire* or a sappy tearjerker in which the handsome young hero dies, like *The Pride of the Yankees* and *For Whom the Bell Tolls*. Each one did well at the box office, and Gary Cooper did well, too.

"There is not an actor alive who would not give his all to have just one of these films as a credit," writes Tom Hanks.

Mr. Deeds and *John Doe*, two of Capra's populist fantasies, endure as Cooper's finest films prior to *High Noon*. As Longfellow Deeds, a hick poet from Mandrake Falls, Vermont, who goes to New York City after inheriting twenty million dollars, Cooper charms the common folk— and the hard-bitten female newspaper reporter, played by Jean Arthur, who sets out to expose him but falls for him instead. He starts to give away his fortune to unemployed urban-dwellers willing to move to the countryside and start small farms. Then he vanquishes the greedy and corrupt bankers and lawyers who seek to thwart his plans by having him declared insane. He has some great comic moments: after kissing the reporter on her doorstep, he crashes into a garbage can, bangs into an unwary pedestrian, and careens his way around a street corner, giddy with romantic passion. His defense of his own sanity at the climactic court hearing is winningly powerful and persuasive—and proves that Cooper could memorize and perform large chunks of dialogue when he worked at it.

Capra loved his leading man. "Every line in his face spelled honesty," the master director writes in his autobiography. "So innate was his integrity he could be cast in phony parts, but never looked phony himself."

Four years later, Capra created a darker, more despairing portrait of America with *Meet John Doe*. Cooper plays Long John Willoughby, a washed-up former professional baseball player. He impersonates an anonymous letter writer who has announced in the local newspaper that he's going to commit suicide on Christmas Eve to protest the misery and hypocrisy of American life. The letter has actually been written by a newspaper columnist, played by Barbara Stanwyck, who proceeds to write more articles and speeches that bring "John Doe" to life. "John Doe Clubs" take hold across the land, and Stanwyck's boss, a fat-cat newspaper publisher, seeks to exploit this new grassroots network to run for president with its support. But Willoughby exposes the fraud, gets the girl, and saves the day. "There you are, Norton, the people," he tells the corrupt publisher. "Try and lick that!"

There are many reasons for the greatness of these two films: Capra's deft direction, with its skillful blend of comedy, drama, and sentimentality; the astute scripts by Robert Riskin; and the brilliant performances of Arthur and Stanwyck, two of Hollywood's most gifted comedians. But Cooper's work is equally crucial. He manages to play both the comic and melodramatic sides of his characters without falling into pathos. He is never boring, always believable, and he displays great chemistry not just with his two talented female leads, but also with Lionel Stander and Walter Brennan, who play his sidekicks. Cooper emerges, writes *New York Times* film critic Bosley Crowther, as "the honest and forthright fellow—confused, inconsistent, but always sincere—who believes in the basic goodness of people and has the courage to fight hard for principles." He helps infuse these films with a bristling and infectious populism—a kinder, gentler version of "We're mad and we're not going to take it anymore."

EVEN AFTER THE ARRIVAL of Rocky Cooper, Gary Cooper's multitudinous love life continued, if usually more discreetly. Ingrid Bergman, one of his more memorable conquests, wrote that she had been unimpressed with Cooper at first as an actor and a man. But when she saw the rushes of his work in *For Whom the Bell Tolls*, she was smitten both professionally and personally. "The personality of this man was so enormous, so overpowering—and that expression in his eyes and his face, it was so delicate and so underplayed," she recalled. "You just didn't notice it until you saw it on the screen." Cooper, wise by now to the fleeting fascinations of Hollywood beauties, took in all the praise with a certain cynicism. After completing a second movie with Bergman he remarked, "Ingrid loved me more than any woman in my life loved me. The day after *Saratoga Trunk* ended, I couldn't get her on the phone."

He was a fashion icon as well as a movie star. When Irving Berlin revised the lyrics to "Puttin' on the Ritz" in 1946, he added an homage to America's most stylish leading man:

> *Dressed up like a million-dollar trouper,*
> *Tryin' hard to look like Gary Cooper,*
> *Super duper.*

"His clothing is handsome and not too highly organized, beautifully groomed without being too polished," reported a correspondent for *Flair* magazine who got a peek at the famous man's clothes closet. "Not 200 suits, more like twenty-five outfits, where friendly jeans jostle the casually draped double-breasted suits that Eddie Schmidt of LA cuts for him . . . Loose-fitting simple sport coats, white silk shirt and moccasin-type shoes specially designed for him by Farkas and Kovacs. Silk striped ties, sportswear from Kerr's, shoes from Peal of London, generalities from Brooks Brothers and F.R. Tripler." On his dressing table were three silver-topped brushes. On the shelf, Indian-style moccasins hand-sewn by Cooper himself and soft as butter.

He could afford a less-than-modest wardrobe. In 1941, the Associated Press reported that Cooper, "with a paycheck of $482,820, out-earned the Nation's industrial bigwigs and the motion picture colony's as well, in a compilation of 1939 corporation salaries made public today by the Treasury." The money reflected his value to the film industry: between 1936 and 1959, his name appeared every year on the list of Top Twenty performers in the Quigley Poll, a record exceeded only by John Wayne.

For an amateur actor with no formal training, Cooper had considerable range. He could do drama, adventure, action, and romantic comedy. "It's astonishing to review his filmography and see how often he played a sly con artist who could talk himself out of any jam or a character who articulates the most important issues of a film," writes film scholar Jeanine Basinger. "Cooper had impeccable comic timing as well as the capacity to convey deeply felt pain. He could play a real hick—sly and clumsy—or the ultimate sophisticate. He could act cowardly as well as heroic . . . Unquestionably one of Hollywood's sexiest men on-screen, but he could make himself believable as a guy who had no idea what to do around a woman."

"Whatever he did," concluded director André de Toth, "Gary Cooper was the truth."

Cooper knew his strengths and weaknesses, but he seemed to find a way to rise above them. His smoldering good looks, his innate sense of timing, and his overall professionalism always seemed to pull him through. The mechanics of filmmaking didn't distract him; the hurry-up-and-wait process may have annoyed him at times, but he developed coping mechanisms to deal with it. He whittled, he played cards, and he learned to take naps. While Carl Foreman crawled his way forward in Hollywood one foxhole at a time, Gary Cooper soared like a high-flying eagle.

He understood better than anyone the nature of his film persona and was intensely alert for false notes in the dialogue written for him. "Words had to fit him like his own clothes," recalled screenwriter Jesse L. Lasky Jr. He recalls laboring intensely over two speeches in a scene for *Unconquered* (1947), until he thought he had captured Cooper's style. But Cooper took the page of dialogue that Lasky had written and wrote a line through each of the speeches. Opposite one he scrawled "Yep." Next to the other one he scrawled "Nope." Lasky thought at first that these were Cooper's commentary on the lines he'd been given. In fact, they were his rewrites. "He'd reduced his entire dialogue in the scene to those two terse words," recalled Lasky. "Yep" and "Nope" became his self-mocking calling card when he appeared as a guest on radio shows or in movie cameos.

He had an almost mystical relationship with his own character.

Sometimes he talked as if the two—the man and the persona—were in constant communication. He turned down the role of Rhett Butler in *Gone With the Wind* because he believed the character known as Gary Cooper lacked the cynicism and insouciance that the role required. "My screen character saw himself emerging from the film as a dashing-type fellow. But I said no. I didn't see myself as quite that dashing." And Clark Gable—who played Butler with just the right mix of sophistication and brio—proved Cooper was right.

In *Casanova Brown* (1944), a rather lame comedy, Cooper and screenwriter Nunnally Johnson dreamt up a hilarious sequence in which he lights a cigarette, has to hide it, and burns his coat, a sofa cushion, and the entire house. But Cooper said his persona had vetoed the scene, and "my screen character was right. The public just wouldn't believe it. The character they knew as Gary Cooper would never be that dumb."

Movie-star personas can be tricky things. John Wayne built his piece by piece during the 1930s—the slow-motion, pigeon-toed walk, the hesitant line readings that broke short sentences into two, the lethal smile that preceded a punch in the nose. Humphrey Bogart took a decade to find his own, and the tough-guy-with-a-heart-of-gold roles to go with it. But Cooper seemed to slide into his character almost effortlessly, making the unnatural act of performing before a camera seem like the most natural thing in the world.

"I was always conscious of the influence of the character I was playing. Whether the character was real or fictional, I would read everything I could about his life and times." For his Western parts, he added, "I have read just about everything on the West that's worth reading, fact or fiction . . . By the time I get before the camera, Cooper has less to say about the way he acts than the character he has become."

"As a persona he's just a perfect American idea," says Jeanine Basinger. "John Wayne is a powerful American presence and he's male and he's action. But Gary Cooper has the side of ourselves where we're self-deprecating and we joke and say we don't like money, don't like fame, we're just down to earth. Yet he's one of the best-dressed men in Hollywood, living in one of the most beautifully designed homes and married to a society woman—not who we think we are. But there was something about him, I do think he's harder to define and pin down."

He drifted away from Westerns in the 1930s when the genre fell out of favor due in part to the high production costs of filming on location with larger cameras and extensive sound equipment. Still, he never totally lost touch; by one rough count twenty-five of his ninety-two feature-length films were Westerns, and in another twenty-seven he played soldiers, sailors, or other action heroes. In all of these, he seemed to be a man of the past—"the American Democrat, Nature's Nobleman as he was defined in our nineteenth-century literature," writes film critic Richard Schickel. Even in his cowboy outfit, John Wayne was a modern figure, gruff, angry, and alienated, "fuming his frustration with the intractable world he never made and would never much like." Cooper, by contrast, was Thomas Jefferson's natural man, a reassuring presence who looked comfortable and graceful riding the open range, "bestirring himself reluctantly to action only when his patience and suppleness went unrewarded or scorned." And when Westerns made their comeback in the 1940s, and most especially in the 1950s, Cooper was there despite the obvious physical toll of age and illness, still looking authentic astride a horse.

While his acting range was broad, Cooper knew his limits. There was no point stretching to play an unlikeable character, and Cooper— unlike Wayne—never did. Niven Busch, a story editor at the Goldwyn Company, says Cooper once stopped by while Busch was wrestling with a story outline. "Well, Niven," Cooper told him, "seems to me if you make me the hero it usually comes out right."

He was wary of playing a living person, worried that his manufactured movie-star persona couldn't match up to the real thing. He tried to avoid playing Sergeant Alvin York, the real-life World War One hero. York insisted that Cooper was the only actor who could play him authentically, and Cooper traveled to Tennessee to meet with him. Still, Cooper remained reluctant, almost superstitiously so. "I felt I couldn't do justice to him," Cooper recalled. "He was too big for me, he covered too much territory."

In the end, he relented. One of the attractions was working with his good friend Howard Hawks, one of Hollywood's finest directors. It was a smooth, easygoing partnership, and Cooper wound up winning his first Academy Award for best actor for *Sergeant York*. The following year, he played Lou Gehrig, another American legend, in *The Pride of the Yankees*. In both films, Cooper was able to capture the extraordinary skill and courage of real-life heroes, yet at the same time project their vulnerability and anxieties. He had become more than just an actor: his persona captured something powerful and attractive about America's character, confirming our self-portrait as a moral and honorable nation, reluctant to anger yet unstoppable when provoked, at a time when the country was entering the dangerous passage into another world war.

Even if he didn't quite understand it, he intuitively grasped how iconic a figure he had become. He was too old to be drafted into World War Two. But in October 1943 he flew across the Pacific to Port Moresby, New Guinea, for the first leg of a U.S. Navy tour that covered 24,000 miles and more than a dozen stops throughout the South Pacific, along with actresses Una Merkel and Phyllis Brooks and accordionist Andy Arcari. Cooper couldn't sing or dance, so he packed a pile of Jack Benny scripts and sought to provide some comic relief. To his surprise, the troops were eager for anything, even his dumb, awkwardly delivered jokes. "I went over great, and that was a real shock to me. Those boys weren't just starved for entertainment; they were plumb out of their minds."

One night there was a thunderstorm and massive downpour, and Cooper figured the show would be canceled. He was dozing in his tent when an officer came to tell him that some 15,000 men had gathered on a muddy slope in the rain waiting for the show to begin. The performers trekked to the water-logged stage.

They were working their way through their hour-long act when a soldier called out, "Hey Coop, how about Lou Gehrig's farewell speech?"

The men began to chant in unison for the speech. Cooper had not prepared for this, but he was game. "Give me a minute to get it straight," he told them. "I don't want to leave out anything."

The two sexy female stars took over the show while he sat to one side and wrote out the words. "The rain was falling onto the tarps and every now and then a pole would slip and I'd get a gallon of water down my neck," he later recalled. But he finally got it all down—the last public words of a celebrity athlete who knew he was dying. The raucous crowd fell silent.

"I've been walking on ball fields for sixteen years," he began, "and I've never received anything but kindness and encouragement from you fans." The speech went on to praise the championship players he had played with, as well as "my friends the sports writers" and "the two greatest managers of all time—Miller Huggins and Joe McCarthy.

"I have a mother and father who fought to give me health and a solid background in my youth. I have a wife—a companion for life—who has shown me more courage than I ever knew." And the conclusion: "People all say that I've had a bad break, but—today—today I consider myself the luckiest man on the face of the earth."

The audience burst into prolonged applause.

Afterward, Cooper reported, at every camp he visited the troops demanded the Gehrig speech. Young men facing death wanted to hear a movie star speak the words of a famous doomed athlete, and Cooper accepted that it was his duty to oblige them. In his depiction of a man seeking to summon up the courage to meet his fate, the boundary between the real person and the icon seemed to disappear, washed away in an emotional downpour of pathos, heroism, and self-sacrifice. For those few moments, Gary Cooper *became* Lou Gehrig.

HE RETURNED FROM THAT marathon USO tour, invigorated but exhausted, to a country that on the surface was strongly united in the campaign to defeat Germany and Japan. The mainstream political parties passionately supported the war effort, as did the small American Communist Party. It suspended its efforts to gain influence in the trade union movement, declared a moratorium on strike actions, and ordered that Communists who entered the military resign from the party so that there could be no confusion over dual loyalties. Then it went one step farther in spring 1944 and put itself out of business for the duration of the war. In its place the party's leadership established the Communist Political Association, a supposedly nonpartisan institution whose sole purpose was to work for an Allied victory.

But a right-wing backlash was building that would tear the fabric of national unity to shreds. Its components would include conservative elements of both major political parties, big business, citizens' groups like the American Legion and Knights of Columbus, the right-wing press, J. Edgar Hoover's FBI, the House Committee on Un-American Activities, and, in Hollywood, some of the established studios, anti-Communist trade union leaders, and a handful of conservative film directors, screenwriters, and actors—Gary Cooper among them.

The backlash had its origins in the America First movement before the war began. Longtime isolationists like senators Burton Wheeler of Montana, Cooper's home state, and Gerald Nye of neighboring North Dakota proclaimed that powerful forces—including Hollywood's purportedly Jewish-dominated studios—were secretly working to drive the country into war. In 1940, Wheeler, chairman of the Senate Interstate Commerce Committee, launched an investigation into the movie industry's role in encouraging the United States to abandon neutrality. Its first witness was Nye, who accused the film industry of producing pro-British and anti-German propaganda. He refused to name the perpetrators, he said, because most of them sounded Jewish. "Those primarily responsible for the propaganda pictures are born abroad," he testified. "They came to our land and took citizenship here, entertaining violent animosities toward certain causes abroad."

In the House of Representatives, Martin Dies, a right-wing Democratic congressman from Texas, operated his own parallel investigation as chairman of the newly formed Special Committee on Un-American Activities. He and his panel made three abortive attempts to investigate Hollywood beginning in 1938, and in 1940 the committee compelled celebrities like Humphrey Bogart, James Cagney, Fredric March, and Franchot Tone—all of them staunch FDR supporters—to appear in executive session to deny they were Communists.

Dies got little lasting traction as a Red- and Jew-baiter, and he retired in poor health in 1944. But John Rankin of Mississippi moved that the Dies committee be made a standing committee of the House of Representatives in early 1945. Edward Hart of New Jersey became chairman but Rankin set the committee's agenda and rekindled Dies's ugly, Jew-baiting tone. He called New York gossip columnist Walter Winchell a "slime mongering kike." As for a delegation of women who opposed one of his bills: "If I am any judge, they are communists, pure and simple. They looked like foreigners to me. I never saw such a wilderness of noses in my life."

Jack B. Tenney, a flamboyant California state senator, led his own inquisition as chairman of the Joint Fact-Finding Committee on Un-American Activities in Sacramento. The panel subpoenaed witnesses and issued exhaustive annual reports, beginning in 1943, tracing the supposed web of conspiracy among alleged Communists and their front organizations. Tenney's credibility was dubious at best—one of his closest allies was the Reverend Gerald L. K. Smith, a notorious anti-Semite and conspiracy monger—but the panel's reports helped lay the groundwork for the Red Scare to come.

The war effort temporarily sidetracked these forces of reaction as Americans of all ideologies banded together against a formidable enemy. But gradually the backlash regained momentum, regrouped, and reasserted their power across America.

In Hollywood its newest and most visible manifestation was the Motion Picture Alliance for the Preservation of American Ideals, a citizens' movement that was born during a series of evening meetings beginning in late 1943 at the leafy Rexford Drive home of James K. McGuinness in Beverly Hills. McGuinness was a senior writer and motion picture executive at MGM who had tried to sabotage the founding of the Screen Writers Guild a decade earlier because he believed Communists were secretly steering its policies. Dore Schary, who worked with him at MGM, described McGuinness as among the "hard-nosed Red-baiters and reckless wielders of verbal shotgun attacks." He could have added Jew-baiting: McGuinness disparagingly referred to the writers in Schary's unit at MGM as "the Yeshiva." Producer David O. Selznick, Louis B. Mayer's son-in-law and a major prince of the realm, called McGuinness "the biggest anti-Semite in Hollywood" and accused him of organizing "the Hundred Haters" group at the Lakeside Golf Club where he was president. McGuinness was a smart, articulate, and mean-spirited foe. "In this world, some people will ride and some people will walk," he had once declared. "I'm gonna be one who rides."

McGuinness brought together his disaffected friends and colleagues on the political right, including actors Adolphe Menjou, Robert Taylor, and Ward Bond, and directors Sam Wood and Leo McCarey. Wood was reputed to carry around a pocket-size notepad in which he jotted down the names of purported subversives. He was a warm and charming man, according to his daughter Jeane, except when *It*—the Communist conspiracy—came up. "'It' invariably transformed Dad into a snarling, unreasoning brute," she recalled. "We used to leave the dinner table with our guts tangled and churning from the experience." Screenwriter Borden Chase, another passionate anti-Communist, was also a charter member in the alliance. "For ten years I've been sitting back, watching them take over one local after another; one industry after another; one school after another," he wrote in a local newspaper. "I've listened to my own kids mouthing the ABCs of the Communist doctrine as I helped them with their homework. And now, as God is my judge, I'm watching it happen to the motion picture industry . . .

"They've moved into our guilds; into our studios, into our production units, and into our pictures . . . Once you have bucked that party line, you can smell it at a mile."

The alliance held its first public meeting in the Grand Ballroom of the Beverly Wilshire Hotel on February 4, 1944, where Sam Wood was elected president and Walt Disney vice president. It was a small but star-studded event. Barbara Stanwyck, Clark Gable, Ginger Rogers, and Robert Montgomery were there, along with leading directors Cecil B. DeMille, John Ford, Victor Fleming, and King Vidor. Gary Cooper, who was close to many of the founders, was one of the charter members.

The Left took notice of the alliance's claims and responded with a statement of condemnation from seventeen Hollywood guilds and unions that branded the alliance as "a subversive and dangerous organization, which comforts the enemy." In other words, they grandly and disdainfully accused the alliance of the same crime that its members leveled at Communists: treason.

THE MOTION PICTURE ALLIANCE eschewed the dime-store anti-Semitism of the rabid right. Instead, it equated Communism with Fascism and warned that Red ideology was seeping into mainstream American movies, due to the machinations of "Communists, radicals, and crack-pots."

"Motion pictures are inescapably one of the world's great forces for influencing public thought and opinion, both at home and abroad," read the alliance's inaugural statement of principles. "In this fact lies solemn obligation. We refuse to permit the effort of Communist, Fascist, and other totalitarian-minded groups to pervert this powerful medium into an instrument for the dissemination of un-American ideas and beliefs."

Matinee idol Robert Taylor, who succeeded Sam Wood as president of the alliance, noted that at the time of its founding, more than twenty organizations containing the words *Hollywood* or *Motion Picture* in their titles had been listed by the U.S. attorney general, the House Un-American Activities Committee, or Jack Tenney's Joint Fact-Finding Committee as either Communist-dominated or -infiltrated. "Whenever any of us stepped down from our own ivory tower and traveled elsewhere in the land," said Taylor, "we were confronted instantly with one question: '*Why is Hollywood so Red?*'"

Most of the big studios stayed away from the alliance, with the exception of Louis B. Mayer's rabidly Republican MGM and Walt Disney. One FBI report estimated that the vast majority of the alliance's first two hundred members worked for MGM.

The right-wing press quickly endorsed the alliance's goals and methods. Gossip columnist Hedda Hopper was an early supporter, as was Louella Parsons, her main rival. Parsons' boss, newspaper magnate William Randolph Hearst, also weighed in, bemoaning the alleged influence of Communists and fellow travelers on the content of American movies. In an editorial headlined "Americanize the Movies," Hearst's *Los Angeles Examiner* singled out "the subversive minority

[that] has connived and contrived to produce A LONG SUCCESSION OF INSIDIOUS AND EVIL MOTION PICTURES TO THE DISCREDIT OF THE INDUSTRY AND TO THE DETRIMENT OF THE COUNTRY. It has made pictures disparaging American history and American heroes and American institutions and traditions . . . [and] glorifying Communist Russia."

But the journalist who had the most impact in attacking the alleged Red influence on the movie industry was one of the least well-known outside the city limits of Hollywood and Beverly Hills. W. R. "Billy" Wilkerson was editor and publisher of the *Hollywood Reporter*, a daily news and gossip tabloid he had launched in 1930. Wilkerson was one of the town's most colorful and rapacious characters. He sported a waxed mustache, hand-tailored suits, and gray spats; was married six times; owned a custom-built Cadillac and five other cars; and claimed to have discovered blonde bombshell Lana Turner at a luncheonette near his office (her real name was Julia Jean Mildred Frances Turner, her real hair color brunette). He also reputedly had the original idea for the Flamingo resort hotel in a seedy desert oasis known as Las Vegas, long before gangster Benjamin "Bugsy" Siegel and his friends muscled their way in and pushed Billy Wilkerson aside.

A fawning "Dear Irving" letter written in the early 1930s from Wilkerson to legendary MGM studio boss Irving Thalberg shows how Billy walked a fine line between flattery and extortion. Wilkerson tells Thalberg he needs five thousand dollars in cash to buy a small engraving plant for the *Hollywood Reporter*. Wilkerson writes that he can't ask other friends for the money because he's "afraid they will ask me to do things that will neither help them, my paper, or myself. With you I KNOW it will be different . . . I am safe with you and believe me, you will be safe with me."

But just to be sure, Wilkerson concludes, "Nobody will ever know this letter is written and certainly no one will ever know of the transaction if it goes through. It would be bad for both of us." One rarely sees such a naked statement in print of the potential pitfalls of wooing the rich and powerful in Hollywood.

Most of the studio bosses hated Wilkerson: Winfield Sheehan, head of production at Twentieth Century-Fox, instructed mailroom staff to gather up each morning's entire delivery of *Hollywood Reporters* as they reached the studio, pile them in a heap on the street outside his office, and set them on fire. "Winnie liked to look out his window and see the wisps of smoke rising," reported Marcia Borie, one of Wilkerson's most loyal longtime employees. Still, his tabloid was a must-read for anyone who had a stake in the industry, as was "Tradeviews," the front-page column that he knocked out in fifteen or twenty minutes every afternoon while binge-drinking Coca-Colas.

Wilkerson launched his Red-baiting campaign in a July 29, 1946, "Tradeviews" column headlined "A Vote for Joe Stalin." It named Dalton Trumbo, Howard Koch, and nine other screenwriters as "Communist sympathizers," and accused them of using the Screen Writers Guild to try to suppress the views of anti-Communist writers. It was the first shot fired in what became the blacklist wars.

Wilkerson had been in combat with the more radical members of the Screen Writers Guild ever since the organization's formation in the early 1930s. But his real targets, according to his son, W. R. Wilkerson III, were the studio heads who had scorned him and sought to drive him out of business. In a column later in 1946 he accused them of "not only employing but actually pampering 'Commies' in their studios, particularly those writers who are out-and-out party members, party-liners, or fellow travelers. They are entrusting to those writers the creation of their scripts, knowing that those babies will do ANYTHING at ANY TIME to put over a point in their creations to further the cause of Moscow . . ."

On October 17, 1946, Wilkerson wrote that the FBI would soon be delivering a report to the U.S. attorney general documenting the clandestine role of Communist subversives in Hollywood. "We know that Hollywood is tabbed as the second most important center of subversive activity in this country," wrote Wilkerson. Hollywood deserved to be singled out for investigation "because of the big names connected with the party here, their big cash donations and the enthusiasm with which the press of the country will grab at this shakedown of Communist activity because it's Hollywood."

In fact, the FBI's Los Angeles bureau had been collecting intelligence on the party's activities throughout the 1940s, part of a fourteen-year investigation it conducted under the code name COMPIC. The bureau's enduring theme was that the slow accretion of leftists in Hollywood was no accident but rather part of a premeditated conspiracy hatched in Moscow to seize control of the movie business "for the production of pictures which will serve the interests of the foreign policy of the Soviet Union." Communist activities in Hollywood were designed to capture the trade union organizations of both the skilled and unskilled workers, technicians and artisans—actors, writers, and directors. These moves "form part of a gigantic world-wide conspiracy of control which has its origin and direction in the Communist Party of the Soviet Union." By 1943 the FBI claimed that Communists controlled half of the industry's thirty-nine labor unions.

The bureau internally issued and distributed regular reports of "Communist Infiltration of the MPI (Motion Picture Industry)." An FBI memo in October 1944 claimed there were fifty-six known Communist Party members among the screenwriters employed by various studios. A December 12, 1945, report was filled with alarming commentary, including the claim that "the strength of Communist influence . . . is much greater than was supposed heretofore." Frank Sinatra, it contended, was then "a full-fledged follower of the party line." A year later a new report citing an anonymous informant known as "Source A" claimed that top producers like David O. Selznick, Samuel Goldwyn, and Walter Wanger "not only employed known Communists . . . but also protected them whenever their names and reputations have been exposed to public notice." The Screen Writers Guild, the informant added, was "completely dominated by Communists and sympathizers who to a large extent determine who works when and where." The same source also claimed that Dore Schary "in all respects has been a follower of the Communist Party line for many years."

But the FBI went far beyond collecting gossip from willing informants and issuing internal reports for Hoover's edification. Between 1943 and 1947, bureau records reveal, the FBI staged at least eight illegal break-ins of the Los Angeles branch of the Communist Party to photograph membership records and wiretapped alleged members of the L.A. branch. The bureau found no evidence of espionage or conspiracy to overthrow the government, but the materials it gathered would later come in handy when congressional investigators—who, unlike the FBI, didn't need evidence that would stand up in court before making allegations—began to focus on Hollywood.

THE TRADE UNION MOVEMENT was the third leg of the anti-Communist stool. Roy M. Brewer, who became one of the leaders of the Motion Picture Alliance, was the international representative in Hollywood of the International Alliance of Theatrical Stage Employees, a coalition of craft unions with some fifteen thousand members—cameramen, soundmen, and stagehands—that was generally supported by the big studios. A chunky, combative man from Grand Island,

Nebraska, Brewer had worked his way up from a ten-dollar-a-week janitor's job to projectionist at a local movie theater to president of the state Federation of Labor. He fought purported mobsters and Commies and made a reputation as a tough-talking, hard-headed bruiser. After a stint with the wartime Office of Labor Production in Washington, D.C., Brewer was hired to help IATSE consolidate its power in Hollywood.

Brewer's trade union coalition was locked in a struggle with the Conference of Studio Unions, which had roughly nine thousand members—among them painters, machinists, electrical workers, and plumbers—led by a former boxer named Herbert Sorrell. The two organizations had honored an uneasy truce during World War Two, when neither wanted to be seen as undermining the war effort by violating their no-strike pledge. But in March 1945 set decorators in the CSU walked out at the major studios. The studios summarily fired the strikers, setting off an eight-month work stoppage. In October Sorrell decided to concentrate his forces at Warner Bros., supposedly the most liberal of the big studios. The result was the most violent set of clashes in Hollywood's labor history. Burbank police and studio security guards wielding nightsticks and fire hoses beat back CSU picketers, who overturned and torched studio cars and used their own makeshift arsenal of blackjacks, chains, and clubs. IATSE thugs joined in the battle with clubs, rubber hoses, and metal cables.

Actor Kirk Douglas, who had just arrived from New York to make his first film, *The Strange Love of Martha Ivers*, recalls being driven up to the gates of Paramount studios past angry CSU picketers for his first day of shooting. His driver pointed out a man with a protest sign and said, "That's Bob Rossen"—the movie's screenwriter. Once inside, Douglas couldn't find Lewis Milestone, his director, because Milestone had refused to cross the picket line and instead was spending the day at a restaurant across the street. The picture's producer, Hal Wallis, insisted that Douglas sleep at the studio for several nights to avoid being locked out until the strike was settled.

The battle went on for weeks until the CSU won a federal labor ruling. But a second CSU strike in 1946 led to more violence and a crushing defeat for Sorrell's organization. Brewer was determined and skillful at making allies and Red-baiting his opponents, whereas Sorrell was clumsy and belligerent. Brewer managed to portray the labor unrest as part of a Communist plot to seize control of the entire motion picture industry. He used as evidence the fact that known leftists like

John Howard Lawson, Rossen, and actors Larry Parks and Lee J. Cobb were seen on the picket lines. One of Brewer's earliest allies was actor Ronald Reagan, who as president of the Screen Actors Guild supported Brewer's union coalition and convinced his members to cross the CSU picket lines. Reagan took to carrying a handgun after his life was threatened.

"The Communists had created an impression that I was a Fascist, you know, because I was tough . . ." recalled Brewer, who considered himself a liberal Democrat—as did Reagan in those days. "There was no namby-pamby with me when I was fighting with the Communists, because that's how you get murdered . . . You think you can reason with the Communists. You can't. They have their own rules and they're going to play by it."

Although he was the product of conservative Republican stock, Gary Cooper had generally kept a low profile when it came to politics. But there had been moments when he flirted with right-wing extremists. In 1935 he had joined with author Arthur Guy Empey, a World War One veteran, to form the Hollywood Hussars, a paramilitary polo club that drilled in their spare time at the Hollywood Athletic Club under the supervision of retired army officers and active-duty police officers. The Hussars declared themselves devoted "to the advancement of American ideals," but some critics detected an aroma of Fascism. The Hussars were "armed to the teeth," according to the *Motion Picture Herald*, "and ready to gallop within an hour to cope with any emergency menacing the safety of the community—fights or strikes, floods or earthquakes, wars, Japanese 'invasions,' Communistic 'revolutions,' or whatnot." Cooper associated the organization with "Americanism . . . an unfailing love of country; loyalty to its institutions and ideals; eagerness to defend it against all enemies." But he quit after just three months; after some motion picture exhibitors protested to Paramount, the studio issued a statement in his name saying he was surprised to learn "that the Hussars are not the social group I had thought but the men behind it are trying to organize a national, semi-military organization of political nature." The group quickly dissolved.

Four years later, Cooper was falsely accused by left-wing critics of displaying sympathy for Nazi Germany by traveling there with his wife, Rocky. In fact, they had accompanied Rocky's father, Paul Shields, a strong FDR supporter who was on a mission to investigate the strength of Germany's finances. Returning home, Cooper told reporters, "There's no question in my mind that those people want to have a war."

It was a carefully calibrated statement that raised alarms without revealing Cooper's views as to what the United States should do.

Still, whether home or abroad, Cooper had an instinctive disdain for Communists. Screenwriter Alvah Bessie, a party member who had fought for the Republican side against the "Nationalist" Fascists during the Spanish Civil War, recalls introducing himself to Cooper in the Warners lunchroom after the release of *For Whom the Bell Tolls*. "I'm one of those guys you played in the picture," Bessie told him. "I was in the International Brigade."

"Terrible thing, civil war," Cooper replied. "Brothers fighting each other."

Bessie slipped into lecture mode. "It wasn't really a civil war, Mr. Cooper . . . It was a war of invasion on the part of Germany and Italy— against the legal government of Spain."

"That so?" asked Cooper. "That's what's so great about this country." Bessie looked puzzled.

"What I mean—a guy like you can go and fight in a war that's none of your business."

Cooper's biggest flirtation with the Hollywood right came in March 1944 when he became a member of the executive board of the newly formed Motion Picture Alliance. He most likely joined at the invitation of Sam Wood, a close friend, who had recently directed three films in which Cooper starred: *The Pride of the Yankees*, *For Whom the Bell Tolls*, and *Casanova Brown*. Cooper spoke briefly at one of the alliance's first public meetings, where he scolded "the lukewarm Americans who dally with sedition in the guise of being liberals" and suggested that they would "benefit from careful study of the pledge of allegiance to the flag."

Later that year, Cooper took an active role in supporting Republican presidential candidate Thomas E. Dewey in his campaign against FDR, who was seeking an unprecedented fourth term in office. Cooper agreed to go on national radio at the end of the Bob Hope show two days before the election and read a five-minute statement prepared by the Republican National Committee. The next day the committee bought space in newspapers nationwide and reprinted the speech in half-page ads alongside Cooper's face. The headline: "I'VE BEEN FOR ROOSEVELT BEFORE . . . BUT NOT THIS TIME."

The speech criticized FDR for dishonesty and failure to keep his word, and for maintaining friendships with dubious people and adopting "foreign" ideas: "I disagree with the New Deal belief that the America all of us love is old and worn-out and finished—and has to borrow foreign notions that don't even seem to work any too well where they come from." It was, Cooper added, "time for a change."

One letter writer from Manhattan did not miss the strong aroma of intolerance in Cooper's seemingly ghostwritten remarks: "The great shock I received was when I heard the word *foreign* come from your mouth. For some reason or other I always felt you were a real American. Mr. Cooper, just what constitutes a 'foreigner'? Can you explain? Personally Mr. Cooper, my own parents came here from Romania more than sixty years ago. I consider myself a true and good American."

There is no record of Gary Cooper's reply.

THE AVOWED GOAL OF the right-wing press and the prominent directors, writers, and performers who supported the Motion Picture Alliance was to persuade or intimidate the Hollywood establishment into ridding itself of the Communist menace that was supposedly seeking to take control of the film industry. "Despite the evidence before their eyes, producers as a whole have played ostrich so long that their tails are sunburned," declared one pamphlet published by the alliance. ". . . Unless we clean up our own mess, we are certain to have it cleaned up for us—and outside cleaners are never as careful as members of the family."

But the net effect of the alliance's campaign was to extend an embossed invitation to the FBI and congressional investigators to come to Hollywood to root out the evil and take the credit for themselves.

It was an invitation that the House Committee on Un-American Activities was unable to resist.

4.

The Boy Wonder

There is no substitute for will.

F. SCOTT FITZGERALD

Stanley Kramer was a compact man, "trim and rugged-looking as a middle-weight boxer," according to *New York Times* critic Bosley Crowther. As he aged, he took on the pugnacious attitude and controlled aggressiveness of Spencer Tracy, his favorite actor and close friend. A fatherless child with a large chip on his shoulder, Stanley was an aggressive liberal with an ingrained suspicion of the establishment—any establishment. He worshipped the Roosevelts, most especially Eleanor after she resigned from the Daughters of the American Revolution in 1939 to protest the organization's refusal to allow black singer Marian Anderson to perform at Constitution Hall in Washington, D.C. He dated his interest in civil rights to that moment and he took deep pride in the films he later made about racism in America.

When he got to Hollywood, he became known—sometimes to his face, but often behind his back—as "the boy wonder." He could be charming and soft-spoken but he often found a way to let everyone know he was the smartest guy in the room. At the same time, he regarded himself with the same unvarnished disdain he inflicted on others. "I've never been close to doing what I wanted to do," he once confided to his friend Charles Champlin, film critic for the *Los Angeles Times*. "Even when I've been successful, I haven't been happy."

Kramer was born in Hell's Kitchen, a longtime ghetto for newly arrived immigrants on the west side of Manhattan that lived up to its unfortunate name. There were street gangs and invisible borders and no policemen in sight except the ones with their hands out. A few weeks after his birth, his father walked out on his mother, Mildred Kramer, a secretary at Paramount Studios' New York office, and she raised Stanley with help from her extended family. They lived with Mildred's immigrant parents in a dark, airless apartment at West Fifty-Ninth Street and Tenth Avenue. Stanley slept in a fenced-off area in the hallway next to her room. Family photographs show a serious young man in dark sports jacket, white shirt, and tie, surrounded by aunts and uncles and cousins who look equally well dressed and sincere.

Mildred's only child was an overachiever: Stanley won prizes for writing and speechmaking at DeWitt Clinton High School, one of New York's best; graduated two years early; and at age nineteen became one of the youngest people to graduate from New York University. Like Carl Foreman, he was enamored of Clarence Darrow and thought he wanted to be a lawyer defending the downtrodden. Instead, he was one of a half dozen graduates to win a writing fellowship with Twentieth Century-Fox in Hollywood. He spent three months on the lot earning eighty dollars a week doing odd jobs until the fellowship ended and the studio summarily fired all of the formerly promising young men.

Rather than face the embarrassment of returning home a failure, Stanley stayed on in Hollywood, hooking on to any job he could get. He worked as a swing gang laborer building and breaking down movie sets for eighteen dollars a week, and an assistant film cutter at MGM for thirty-six. He wrote B films for Columbia and Republic, and ad copy and short subjects for United Artists, Fox, and MGM. His mother's brother Earl ran his own talent agency and helped Stanley move from job to job. By the time the war broke out, Stanley was already fed up and cynical about the studio system. When his draft number came up, he enlisted preemptively in the hope of getting assigned to a film unit. He spent four years in the Army Signal Corps, first as a photographer but later as a producer of some of the training films that the unit churned out for new soldiers about to be dispatched overseas.

After meeting Stanley on military assignment in New York, Carl Foreman quickly came to admire his intellect and his energy. Carl also admired the fact that for all his self-assured volubility, Stanley was a surprisingly good listener. He would lie on the couch, eyes closed, and remain silent while Carl pitched a story idea. And he always seemed supportive. The friendship quickly deepened. "Neither of us had ever had a brother," recalled Carl, "and I think we always had searched for one."

Stanley was more reserved about his new friend. In retrospect, he would claim to have had reservations about Carl's reticent personality and leftist politics from the beginning. "He was a quiet, hard-working writer who seemed to keep to himself pretty much," Stanley recalled. "While cordial, he had a wall of reserve that I was never able to penetrate. Neither of us was the sort to make great friends easily, so I can't say we were ever close, but we were friendly." Coming from a fenced-in, emotionally cautious man like Stanley, it sounds like a warm endorsement.

The two men, both approaching thirty, had long talks about the movie business and discovered they had a lot in common. Neither of them cared for the smug, sclerotic nature of the industry they had committed themselves to, and each was restless to make his mark. "We saw things pretty much alike on the subject of filmmaking," Stanley would recall. "Both of us could tell the world what was wrong with the film industry and what had to be done to correct it."

When the war ended, Carl went back to freelance writing assignments. He knocked out a story for Republic Pictures that was turned into a John Wayne movie called *Dakota* (1945) and he restlessly bided his time. Stanley was more entrepreneurial by nature and even less inclined to suffer the status quo. While in New York, he met a wealthy young businessman named Armand Deutsch who, like Carl, was impressed with Stanley's boundless energy and ideas. Now, with Deutsch's money and encouragement, Stanley bought the film rights to *This Side of Innocence*, a new and popular Taylor Caldwell novel. He wrote a screenplay based on the book and began shopping it around the studios. But Deutsch soon got cold feet, convinced that Stanley wasn't ready for big-time filmmaking. He and a business partner rejected the script and pushed Stanley out. They paid him forty thousand dollars to relinquish the book rights and go away (the movie never got made). Stanley's ego was bruised but his wallet was suddenly fat.

He took the money and formed a company called Screen Plays Inc. based upon the idea that "instead of relying on star names, we pinned our faith in stories that had something to say." The first person he recruited to join him was George Glass, an experienced and gifted publicist whom he had met in Los Angeles before the war.

Glass was an evangelist for the power of public relations. After graduating from Los Angeles High School, he worked for nearly twenty years for newspapers and publicity outfits in Hollywood, and he believed that for an independent film company like Stanley's to succeed financially, it would need to present itself as a valuable, high-class operation under a single charismatic leader. Although he had never gone to college, Glass read widely, loved literature, and stoutly defended the use of correct English grammar. He especially loved A. E. Housman's lecture on learning for learning's sake, both for its content and for the elegant way Housman expressed it. Glass was also a great believer in trade unionism. The modest cottage he and his wife, Harriet, shared on La Cienega Boulevard in Beverly Hills was a regular site for weekend hootenannies with a decidedly leftist tinge.

Glass was erudite, passionate, and a true believer in the talent and taste of Stanley Kramer. Stanley, in turn, constantly praised Glass as a master of the art of marketing and publicity. "George is the most brilliant publicist this business has ever had," Stanley told Charles Champlin. "He's a fighter—full of jazz, very bright, with a great concept of what you did with a film."

But Stanley knew he needed more. He gave a share of the company to a Hollywood lawyer named Sam Zagon, whose firm did Stanley's legal work for decades. But he also needed writers. He turned to screenwriter Herb Baker and to Baker's good friend from the Army, the same guy Stanley had met and befriended in New York: Carl Foreman.

Stanley didn't need Carl to invest money, which was a good thing because Carl didn't have any. What he really needed was Carl's writing talent. The idea was to make socially relevant movies that would attract the kinds of war-hardened young audiences who were tired of the slick, superficial entertainments the big Hollywood studios specialized in and hungry for something more meaningful.

It wasn't just the content that would make Screen Plays Inc.'s films unique, but the way they would make the pictures. In the traditional studio system, each person's role was well defined and strictly limited. The writer wrote the screenplay and the director directed the movie. Sometimes the two never even talked, and the writer was not invited on the film set nor allowed to meet with the actors. He was only called back when urgent rewrites were required. Once the director finished shooting the picture, the editor took over, cutting the final product with little or no input from the director or the writer. Only the producer oversaw the entire enterprise, served as go-between, and controlled the budget. It was like Henry Ford's assembly line for the Model T. Each person did a limited task and that task alone.

Stanley thought the system was creatively sterile. He wanted the writer, director, and producer to collaborate. As producer, he would still ultimately be in charge, but the writer would work closely with the others, including being present during the film shoot. Stanley said he was guided by "the theory that creative people can come together and own and do the job . . . which in those days was heresy." Hungry to collaborate, Carl loved this concept, at least at first.

"The team of Kramer and Foreman was a good one," recalled director Richard Fleischer, a friend of both men. "They were both in their mid-thirties, well-educated, fiercely socially conscious, had forceful personalities, and had put in lengthy apprenticeships in the industry . . . They were two terrific guys."

They leased offices in a large, sickly yellow, low-rent warehouse called the Motion Picture Center Studios, home to a bevy of small independent filmmakers who shared mostly a lack of liquidity. "It had been put up hastily during the war and looked as if it would fall down any minute," recalled composer Dimitri Tiomkin. "The walls were thin. You heard everything that went on. If someone in an office at one end of a corridor asked, 'What time is it?', somebody at the other end might answer, 'Half-past eleven' . . . It reminded me of the bedlam of sounds in the Saint Petersburg Conservatory when all the students practiced at once on different instruments."

Screen Plays Inc. was both a symptom and a cause of the financial and creative malaise that seized Hollywood in the postwar era. The economic decline started in 1947, when audiences began to find other outlets for their entertainment dollars and leisure time, like night baseball, bowling, and evening classes on the GI bill. People were moving to the suburbs while most of the movie palaces were still downtown. But the biggest destructive force on the horizon, coming on like an unstoppable tidal wave, was commercial television. In 1946 there were only 44,000 television sets, located in .1 percent of American households, serviced by eighteen television stations nationwide. By 1952, the number had skyrocketed to 24.3 million sets, 53 percent of households, and 225 stations.

Between 1946 and 1949 total box-office receipts for American films dropped 14 percent, while profits plunged from a record $120 million to $33.6 million—a decline of more than 70 percent. Meanwhile, average weekly attendance dropped from a record ninety million in 1946 and 1947 to just sixty million two years later.

Paramount's feature films required an average of 55.2 shooting days in 1946 and an average budget of $1.95 million per film. Faced with this kind of cost, the big studios started making cuts, reducing their employees from an overall 31,000 in January 1945 to 17,500 five years later. "In the process euphoria steadily gave way to a deepening malaise and a growing nostalgia for Hollywood's halcyon days," writes film historian Gorham Kinden.

The fact that most of the country was enjoying a postwar economic boom just made things worse. "Hollywood," lamented one major movie producer quoted by *Fortune* magazine, "is an island of depression in a sea of prosperity."

Perhaps the biggest damage was the Supreme Court's ruling in May 1948 that the movie theater chains of the major studios constituted an illegal monopoly. Actually the court's ruling involved two separate but related decisions: a decree that abolished block booking, price-fixing, and all rigged arrangements between studios and theaters; and a decree requiring that the studios divest themselves of their theater holdings. These theater chains were by far the most lucrative part of the movie business, and the Justice Department's successful lawsuit was a huge, seemingly irrevocable blow to their profits and their way of doing business.

Independents like Stanley Kramer's new company were moving into the creative and financial vacuum. Their numbers grew from thirty at the end of the war to more than one hundred within a few years. Most were set up by established and bankable talents looking for more leverage and control over their own work and paychecks, including actors Bing Crosby, Edward G. Robinson, James Stewart, and Rosalind Russell, and directors John Ford, Howard Hawks, and Leo McCarey. Some were highly successful, but many discovered that the rigors of making motion pictures could be just as onerous as working as well-paid serfs for the large companies.

But the problems facing the studio system were more than just financial. Darryl F. Zanuck, head of production at Twentieth Century-Fox, came back from his Army service to warn that the war was changing American attitudes and perceptions and that the old films—and the system that made them—would no longer be adequate. "The war is not yet over, but it soon will be," Zanuck told Fox's senior producers and directors on his first day back. "And when the boys come home from the battlefields overseas, you will find they have changed. They have learned things in Europe and the Far East. How other people live, for instance. How politics can change lives . . . They're coming back with new thoughts, new ideas, new hungers . . . We've got to start making movies that entertain but at the same time match the new climate of the times."

Gary Cooper couldn't articulate the problem with Zanuck's passion and precision, but he was experiencing it firsthand in his own career. After the success of *For Whom the Bell Tolls* in 1943, he hit a long dry run of uninspired films. Some were mildly amusing: *Along Came Jones* (1945), based on the novel *Useless Cowboy* by Alan LeMay, was a Western comedy in which Cooper played an incompetent but endearing cowhand who is saved by a weapons-proficient, reformed bad girl played by Loretta Young who shoots the bad guy on Cooper's behalf. Cooper and some Hollywood friends, including screenwriter Nunnally Johnson, formed their own independent company to produce it, but he soon lost patience with the budgets and minutiae of making his own film. His next major picture was *Unconquered*, an overcooked pre–Revolutionary War melodrama directed by Cecil B. DeMille. Despite mediocre reviews, it was the biggest box office hit of 1947, although it actually lost money because of its bloated $4.3 million budget. But while Cooper was good in these films, his stature seemed to slip a bit each year, especially when compared to his pals John Wayne and James Stewart, each of whom was moving up the ranks of male stardom while Cooper's own ranking was beginning to slip. The scripts he was being offered were predictable, the supporting casts were generally weak, and Cooper himself was increasingly frustrated and bored. He signed a lucrative deal with Warners in 1948 that committed him to one picture a year at $200,000 each (eventually rising to $295,000) plus a share of the profits, while otherwise leaving him free to work independently. Warners was required to submit to him three screenplays a year, but if he turned down all three he had to come up with his own. None of this guaranteed the kind of compelling stories and projects he had enjoyed a decade earlier.

"He was frustrated," his daughter, Maria, recalls. "They would send him these crappy scripts and at some point you have to do one of them. They expected him to carry the film, and he was furious at the quality of the material."

It was, at times, his own fault for being overly cautious. His old friend, director Howard Hawks, wanted him to play the autocratic cattle herd boss in *Red River* (1947), but he turned Hawks down, arguing that the audience would never accept Gary Cooper as such a mean and unsympathetic character. Hawks was surprised and disappointed, and turned instead to Wayne, whose powerful performance was a major career breakthrough. Gary Cooper, it seemed, was the prisoner of his own persona.

WHILE COOPER WAS STRUGGLING, the first picture to emerge from the brilliant and creative minds of Stanley Kramer and Carl Foreman was an unmitigated disaster.

So This Is New York is about a husband, his wife, and her unmarried sister who take advantage of a sizable inheritance from a dead relative to abandon Indiana and seek excitement and a worthy suitor for the sister in big, bad New York City. They meet a predictable array of colorful and eccentric characters: a philanderer who pretends to dote on the unmarried sister but actually tries to seduce the married one; an older wealthy man who wants to sleep with the younger sister but whose plan is foiled when his battle-ax wife turns up unexpectedly early from an African safari; a supposed gentleman racehorse owner who turns ugly and mean when he loses a fortune on a fixed race; and a hambone theater actor who squanders the sisters' money on a hopeless Broadway flop that he has written, directed, and starred himself in. For those who need more cardboard stereotypes, there are also avaricious hotel employees, sarcastic cab drivers, and sidewalks filled with chewing gum that sticks to the soles of Indianan shoes.

The script was based on the late Ring Lardner's comic novel, which Stanley had purchased from the Lardner family. It was an odd and unfortunate choice for a newly formed company dedicated to socially meaningful drama, but Stanley was confident it would be a crowd-pleasing hit and successfully launch their new enterprise. Carl and Herb Baker wrote the screenplay, and Stanley hired Richard Fleischer, a competent journeyman, to direct. Then to guarantee success, he spent one hundred thousand dollars to hire Henry Morgan, a dry and mournful radio show comic with a substantial national following, to play the male lead, presuming that Morgan would be hilarious and attract his adoring followers to the box office. Neither presumption turned out to be correct. The script was a collection of depressing clichés, as was Dimitri Tiomkin's flatulent musical score. The actors tried desperately but failed to bring the story to life, and Fleischer lacked the feel for comic timing to make it fizz. It was, in other words, a total and embarrassing flop. "We all rolled on the floor when we saw it, but nobody else laughed," Stanley recalled ruefully.

So This Is New York never actually opened in the city of its title. United Artists, its distributor, reluctantly offered it to a handful of theaters in the Midwest, then watched it die. It had cost six hundred thousand dollars to make—most of it financed by a wealthy retired garment manufacturer named John Stillman—and earned back less than one third that amount. Both Stanley and Carl wanted to forget it had ever existed.

Fortunately, they held an option for a second Lardner story, one much better suited to their talents and sensibility. *Champion* was the tale of a corrupt and avaricious young boxer and his climb to the top. Herb Baker was gone: he had returned to RKO and a more reliable paycheck. But this time Carl, working on his own, felt comfortable with the story line. The scenes he wrote were tighter and more dramatic, the dialogue crisper. Stanley chipped in as well; his special talent as a writer was for ending scenes on a dramatic note—"a highly charged curtain of some kind," as Carl put it—and for staging physical violence. Someone suggested hiring as director Mark Robson, a promising young filmmaker at RKO, who came cheap and brought with him a very creative art director named Rudy Sternad.

To make the whole thing work, they needed a charismatic star to play Midge Kelly, the troubled antihero. They could have gotten John Payne, a reliable, workmanlike performer, for $35,000. But someone mentioned Kirk Douglas, a promising newcomer from New York who had never played the lead role in a movie before. Douglas—like Carl and Stanley, another intensely ambitious son of Jewish immigrants—read the script and fell in love with the part. "He understood Midge Kelly . . ." Carl recalled. "The drive to conquer, to overcome, to achieve, to become somebody."

Douglas's Hollywood talent agent had gotten him the third lead behind Gregory Peck and Ava Gardner in a big-budget production of Dostoyevsky's *The Gambler* called *The Great Sinner*, a seemingly smart, conventional career move for an aspiring young star. But Douglas longed to play the antihero instead. "My agency was against it," he recalls. "They were telling me 'Kirk, who is Stanley Kramer? This is a little picture!' But I thought Carl Foreman was a great storyteller and I thought it was time for me to play something different, and I knew I could do it." When Douglas got to Stanley's office, he pulled off his shirt and flexed his muscles to show he had what it took to play the part.

Money was a problem, as always. John Stillman was willing to finance most of the picture, which Stanley estimated could be made on the cheap for $550,000. But he still needed someone to underwrite the project, guaranteeing completion in case of cost overruns, delays, accidents, or other misadventures. First Stanley tried the conventional route: he went to see Bernard Giannini at Bank of America. He told Giannini he had a great young star, Kirk Douglas ("You mean Melvyn Douglas?" Giannini inquired), a wonderful director, and an excellent screenwriter. "You seem to have a great many things, Mr. Kramer," the banker replied, "except money and a reputation." The answer was no.

Then Stanley got lucky. He met Bruce Church, a Salinas lettuce grower who had made a substantial fortune by pioneering refrigerated boxcars to haul his company's produce to the East Coast. A proud product of Salinas High School and the University of California at Berkeley, Church was a tenacious businessman, a devout Republican, a dedicated philanthropist who gave millions to local hospitals and the Girl Scouts, and a fun-loving traveler who enjoyed taking his wife on luxury cruises, eating fine food, and dancing the night away. He could always use the tax write-off that a box-office failure might provide, but he was more attracted to the fun and adventure of making movies and he hoped to make a profit. He loved Westerns and most especially he loved Gary Cooper, his favorite actor. But that love would wait for another day. *Champion* would do for starters. Church's daughter Joanne believes he met Stanley Kramer through a mutual friend, a New York businessman who shared Church's fascination with show business. The budget remained tight, but at least Stanley now had the safety net he needed to go forward.

Using Ring Lardner's short story as a launch pad, Carl hammered out a tough and remorseless screenplay. Midge Kelly is a working-class hero with talent, charm, and good looks, trying literally to fight his way to the top. He uses those closest to him—his admiring, disabled younger brother; his estranged, long-suffering wife; his devoted manager; and the various alluring women he meets along the way—but he casts each of them aside once they've served his purpose. He has only one goal: to succeed. Mobsters, parasites, and pretty women all want a piece of his soul, only Midge doesn't seem to have one.

"It's every man for himself," he tells one girlfriend. "Nice guys don't make money."

Embedded in Carl's script is a critique of the brutality of capitalism. "Aw, it's like any other business," says Midge of the fight game. "Only here, the blood shows."

Midge lies and cheats and battles his way up the ladder. He throws boxing matches to get ahead, double-crosses his business partners, and steals other people's wives. He wins the championship fight by superhuman effort, then dies of a brain hemorrhage in the locker room. Thanks to a powerful script and sharp editing—there are no dissolves or fades between scenes, just straight cuts—the film has the same raw energy as its angry protagonist. It also has a sensational performance by Douglas, who was nominated for an Academy Award for his first starring role. Carl was nominated for best screenplay. But the only

Oscar the picture won was for film editing, which went to veteran film cutter Harry Gerstad, one of the loyal professionals Kramer had recruited for the company.

There were many rave reviews and *Champion* was an immediate hit. It eventually grossed nearly eighteen million dollars, an extraordinary sum for a picture that cost $550,000 to make. Stanley himself cleared about one million dollars after taxes. And the film's success led to offers from Twentieth Century-Fox, Paramount, and MGM for picture deals—including a post-midnight meeting on winding Mulholland Drive with Howard Hughes, the mercurial new owner of RKO. But Stanley felt all of the offers came with too many strings attached. He jealously guarded the autonomy and independence of his start-up production company.

In postwar Hollywood, the producer was still king—he hired the director and the writer, cast the picture, set the budget—and Stanley loved the role of independent producer. Part of it was sheer chutzpah. Whether he was dealing with actors, film crews, or potential investors, Stanley knew how to bullshit. "Many times I would hear Stanley go off the track of what had been arranged into absolute nonsense," Carl recalled. "But the energy with which he delivered it, the dedication, the need, the urgency of it was so great that I could see people listening to him entranced."

Stanley himself explained the process of reeling in investors this way: First he needed a great idea for a picture. Then he would dangle the name of a star and a director whom he had not yet placed under contract as the bait for possible investors. "Before he is through, the independent producer must have a dozen or more such balloons floating in the air," Stanley wrote. "The trick is to grab all the strings and pull them down at the same time."

"He could be stubborn, I have no doubt about that," recalled Daniel Taradash, a friend of Stanley's from Army days who became a screenwriter and later president of the Motion Picture Academy. "But he was usually right when he was stubborn."

Bruce Church was sold, especially after Stanley took Kirk Douglas and other performers to Salinas for a movie premiere. "Well, Boy Wonder, do you want another hundred thousand?" Church asked him.

Stanley was stunned and gratified at his own luck. "Lettuce growers like that don't grow on trees," he remarked.

The next project was *Home of the Brave*, an adaptation of a 1946 Broadway play by Arthur Laurents. The story focuses on a Jewish soldier in the Pacific theater of World War Two who risks his life on a dangerous reconnaissance mission with a small group of fellow soldiers, all of them gentiles. The story is about bigotry, discrimination, and courage, and the twists and turns of camaraderie and prejudice among a small band of comrades. Peter Moss, the central character, narrowly misses being killed in a hail of Japanese bullets, but the soldier next to him—Moss's closest friend in the unit—is hit and dies in his arms. The resulting trauma leaves Moss paralyzed physically. He is nursed back to mental and physical health by an Army psychiatrist who penetrates to the roots of his anger and his feelings of vulnerability and inferiority. Moss recovers, and his fellow soldiers learn a lesson in tolerance and equality.

Stanley asked Carl to adhere as closely as possible to the play, but with one major exception: he instructed Carl to change Moss from a Jew to an African American. Stanley did this partly for commercial reasons. For all its controversy, racism was a hot topic in 1949 and Stanley knew there were three other Hollywood films with racial themes that were soon to go into production. He figured he could beat all of them to the theaters if he moved fast. He also felt that a black character would be more dramatic and compelling than a Jew. Stanley knew he was courting controversy—in fact, he welcomed it. But he insisted on total secrecy during the filming. He personally drove James Edwards, the gifted young black actor who played Moss, to the studio each day, escorting him to the sound stage through a rear exit door. Edwards would spend the entire day inside the building, lunching privately with Kramer and Foreman. Carl even invented a fake title for the screenplay and the film shoot. He borrowed the title from another story he and Carl were starting to develop. He called it *High Noon*.

With the help of his uncle Earl's talent agency and personal connections, Stanley hired a group of experienced and highly professional actors to appear with Edwards. Lloyd Bridges, a slim, handsome performer with a broad smile and a striking mane of blond hair, played Finch, the GI who dies in Moss's arms. Frank Lovejoy, one of Hollywood's most reliable character actors, played Mingo, the most experienced and philosophical member of the unit. And Jeff Corey, another familiar face in supporting roles, did a fine job as the psychiatrist who helps restore Moss's sanity and self-respect. They all came cheap at $750 each per week, and their low salaries helped Stanley bring in the picture at $365,000. Mark Robson again directed.

Carl finished the adaptation in just two weeks. He deleted large sections of dialogue from the play and added flashback scenes that explained the civilian backgrounds of each of the main characters.

By now, the Kramer method for producing low-budget, high-impact films was emerging. Stanley relied on Carl to produce a punchy, high-energy screenplay; hired talented young actors willing to work for low wages; brought in a fast, efficient director like Robson; and used in-house talents like film editor Gerstad, set designer Sternad, and composer Tiomkin. And when the project was completed, George Glass would design an advertising and publicity campaign to wring full advantage of the daring subject matter at hand.

An important and innovative part of the process was Stanley's insistence that each picture include a pre-shoot rehearsal. This allowed the actors to get comfortable with each other and with the director before a single roll of film was shot. The practice, combined with cut-rate casts and production methods, meant Kramer's company could bring in a film at roughly half the cost as the major studios. *Home of the Brave* was shot in seventeen days, half the time of the average big studio picture.

"We rehearsed for two weeks," recalled Jeff Corey, "and everybody connected with the picture was present during the rehearsals." Afterward, "everybody knew precisely where the camera was going to be, where the lights were going to be, where the action was going to go."

Stanley knew exactly what he wanted when he cast the parts, Corey added. "Kramer expressly did not want a 'slick' actor. He did not want somebody who looked like a professional man. No smoothness, no suavity."

Home of the Brave has not aged well. The Pacific island setting looks phony—a little like an exotic camping outfitter's display window—and the dialogue isn't much better. Apparently it was impossible to make a film about racism in the late 1940s without sounding preachy and condescending, at least by modern standards. And its powerful dramatic climax is marinated in clichés. Doc, the psychiatrist played by Corey, finally breaks down Moss's defenses and gets to the heart of the matter. Moss is right to resent "the hundred fifty years of slavery, of second-class citizenship, of being different," Doc tells him. "You've always felt that difference."

Doc goes on: "The very same people . . . do it because down deep underneath they need a scapegoat. So when people make cracks, you've a right to be angry, [but] you've no right to be ashamed." In essence the white psychiatrist gives the black GI permission to hate white bigots.

Moss claims he left his friend Finch to die because he knew that deep down Finch was a racist, like every white person. But Doc doesn't buy it. He says Moss is paralyzed out of guilt. It's not physical, it's psychological.

"Peter," says Doc, "every soldier in this world who sees a buddy get shot has that one moment when he's glad. I'm glad because it isn't me. Glad I'm still alive.

"You've got to realize you're the same as everybody else."

Then Doc gets tough with Moss. He orders him to stand up and walk. When Moss claims he can't, Doc baits him. "Get up and walk!" he demands. "You dirty nigger, get up and walk!"

And Moss does, then collapses in tears in Doc's arms.

At the end of the movie, Moss and Mingo pledge to open up a bar and restaurant together when the war's over. Cue the trumpets of brotherhood and racial harmony.

In writing the screenplay, Carl followed the path laid out by playwright Laurents. It doesn't read like vintage Carl Foreman—the emotions are too pat, the ending too upbeat. Unlike *Champion*, there's no sardonic sting in its tail.

Yet critics loved it. Bosley Crowther of the *New York Times* called it "a drama of force and consequence—a film of emotional impact as well as strong intellectual appeal . . . It faithfully shows the shattering damage which racial bias can do to one man."

Audiences loved it, too. While not as lucrative as *Champion*, *Home of the Brave* made a healthy profit and gave Stanley Kramer and his company a second consecutive hit.

OF COURSE STANLEY KRAMER and Carl Foreman weren't the only ones making socially conscious movies with mature subject matter in the postwar era. Others heeded Darryl F. Zanuck's warning that audiences were seeking something beyond standard Hollywood entertainment. Zanuck himself produced *Gentleman's Agreement* (1947), Elia Kazan's social drama about anti-Semitism among affluent Americans, and independent producer Samuel Goldwyn financed *The Best Years of Our Lives* (1946), William Wyler's powerful look at the troubled readjustment of American combat veterans coming home to families and a nation that didn't necessarily understand or appreciate their sacrifices. But the film that may have best crystallized this brief moment of cinematic social consciousness was *Crossfire* (1947), produced by Carl's old friend and mentor, Dore Schary, in his new job as head of RKO.

Like all of the major studio heads except for Zanuck, Schary was Jewish, but he was a decade younger than most of the others and had a much different sensibility and taste for risk-taking. Born in 1905 in Newark, New Jersey, to Russian immigrants, Schary had risen from working as a waiter in his family's run-down resort hotel to writing and acting in floor shows in the Borscht Belt and later on Broadway, He had arrived in Hollywood in 1932, and spent a few years at MGM, where he won an Oscar for best original story for *Boys Town* (1938). Louis B. Mayer, the studio's demanding but paternalistic leader, put him in charge of MGM's B movies, but Schary quit after a dispute over his authority to make the pictures he himself championed. He arrived at RKO armed with a strong independent streak and untested self-assurance that he knew what modern audiences wanted.

Whereas most of the studio heads were innately cautious about their religion and their politics, Schary was a proud Jew and a high-profile liberal. He passionately supported the new state of Israel, for example, while many of his peers kept quiet, at least in public. While he was aggressively anti-Communist, he had been quite willing to work with leftists in opposing Fascism and rounding up electoral support for Franklin Roosevelt. As head of RKO, he had insisted on making a noir-ish little film—written by John Wexley, produced by Adrian Scott, and directed by Edward Dmytryk, all three of them current or former Communist Party members—about the murder of a Jewish war veteran by an anti-Semitic soldier. Schary had gone ahead with *Crossfire* despite warnings from some of his own executives and from groups like the American Jewish Committee that the film could trigger an increase in anti-Semitism. Schary not only mocked their timidity, he made a movie trailer praising his own courage in making the film.

The trailer in many ways epitomizes the crusading self-confidence of the young men who briefly dominated postwar American cinema. Schary himself solemnly rises from behind his desk to address the "ladies and gentlemen of the motion picture–going public" about a film that RKO had just completed. He says the script "dealt with a subject that alarmed some people at the studio" and reads some of the memos that crossed his desk. "Are you sure the public will want to see something like this?" asks one. "This is very outspoken but have we got enough nerve to make it?" asks another.

But Schary says he is convinced "audiences still want to see courageous motion pictures." Those attending the previews were overwhelmingly positive. "At last Hollywood comes of age!" one viewer writes. "I and my whole family compliment you on your honesty and courage," says another. "I shall remember *Crossfire* as long as I live." And Schary closes with "I respectfully urge you to see it."

The gambit worked. Although it was a relatively small movie in terms of cost and box office impact, *Crossfire* was a critical and financial success and received five Oscar nominations. "It feels fine, hearing at last 'Jewboy' and 'Jew' and 'Jewish person' from the screen," wrote Cecilia Agar, film critic for *PM*, New York's left-leaning daily newspaper. "It's like hard rain after a long-breaking thunderstorm . . . With one clear blow, a long-festering, a sniveling, contemptible movie taboo is smashed."

But the film also triggered a backlash from those on the right who didn't like its subject matter nor its meaning. When the Motion Picture Alliance started singling out films it said denigrated American values, *Crossfire* would be high on its list.

STANLEY KRAMER'S NEXT IDEA sprung from a visit that he and Kirk Douglas had made to a veterans' hospital in the San Fernando Valley for a showing of *Champion* to the men in the paraplegic ward. Stanley came away believing there could be an important story to tell about the patients they had met.

He returned to the ward a few days later with Carl Foreman. They talked to a number of the paralyzed veterans about their fears, frustrations, and determination to put their lives back together. Within weeks Carl had written a story treatment and was launched on an original screenplay.

Next Stanley and Carl talked about who might be the best person to direct such a film. They were looking for someone who could give the picture the look and feel of a documentary but with no cheap sentimentality. Stanley mentioned a forty-something journeyman director he'd heard about who had been kicking around the MGM studio lot for more than a decade. Fred Zinnemann had developed a reputation as a cranky nonconformist. But he knew a lot about making movies and his price was low. Stanley, who had no problem working with talented mavericks, quickly closed the deal.

5.

The Committee

*The greatest dangers to liberty lurk in insidious encroachment by men of
zeal, well-meaning but without understanding.*

JUSTICE LOUIS BRANDEIS

The five congressional officials who checked into the stately Biltmore
Hotel across from Pershing Square in downtown Los Angeles in
early May 1947 had subversion on their minds. Representative John
Parnell Thomas of New Jersey, the Republican chairman of the House
Committee on Un-American Activities; fellow congressmen John
McDowell of Pennsylvania and John Wood of Georgia; and two staff
members had come to Hollywood to launch an inquiry into the evils of
Communism and its malignant and growing influence in the capital
of American popular culture. Thomas, a former insurance broker, bond
salesman, and small-town mayor, was a jowly, balding self-promoter, a
man in love with the spotlight and the grandstand. His partner in the
pursuit of dangerous left-wingers was committee chief of staff Robert
Stripling, a lean, intense Texan known as "Strip," with plastered-down
hair and white supremacist notions. Stripling's investigators had
compiled thick dossiers on the purported communistic activities of at
least seventy-five Hollywood personalities, most of them screenwriters.
He talked about these flabby, desk-bound writers as if they were
Superman's evil twin—"brilliantly trained, fanatically dedicated,
physically brave, and industrious beyond the comprehension of
Americans who wishfully insist that we are at peace with all lands."
Both he and Thomas believed that large parts of the New Deal had been
a Communist plot and that the federal government was riddled with

72

Reds. Like J. Edgar Hoover and the FBI, they drew no meaningful distinction between liberals and Communists: they viewed both species as dangerously subversive.

The committee's return to Hollywood was one marker of the tectonic shifts in American politics and culture following the death of Franklin Roosevelt and the end of World War Two. The old FDR coalition, which had remained united for a decade first by economic hardship and later by the war effort, was beginning to unravel. While the economy was booming for many Americans, it also suffered from an outbreak of strikes by trade unions seeking to make up for lost ground during the war, and from annoying shortages of consumer goods and foodstuffs as the country made the massive shift from a wartime command economy to peacetime. The glorious victory over the Axis powers had been overtaken by new fears as relations with the Soviet Union plunged from wary to hostile. Winston Churchill's "Iron Curtain" speech on March 5, 1946, in Fulton, Missouri, focused on the Soviet colonization of Eastern Europe and captured the popular mood of disappointment. "I do not believe that Soviet Russia desires war," Churchill declared. "What they desire is the fruits of war and the indefinite expansion of their power and doctrines." Those on the political right—who had opposed both the New Deal and the war against Fascism but who had been forced to lie low as America fought and won a global conflict—were now resurfacing. They wanted their country back, and they wanted the outsiders and subversives who had stolen it to be exposed and punished.

Surging after fourteen years of electoral setbacks, the Republicans in November 1946 won control of both houses of Congress for the first time since the Hoover administration almost two decades earlier. Five months later, President Truman issued executive order No. 9835 requiring that all federal employees be screened for loyalty, which led Attorney General Tom C. Clark to compile a list of organizations he deemed "totalitarian, Fascist, Communist, or subversive."

"Those who deny freedom to others cannot long retain it for themselves," Clark declared, "and under a just God they do not deserve it."

The backlash now had official sanction from Washington.

State and local governments throughout the country swiftly adopted similar disloyalty orders, in what historian Henry Steele Commager called "a revival of the Red hysteria of the early 1920's, one of the shabbiest chapters in the history of American democracy."

Screenwriters James K. McGuinness and Jack C. Moffitt, two of the founders of the Motion Picture Alliance for the Preservation of American

Ideals, kicked off the parade of friendly witnesses who visited the Biltmore to pay homage to Chairman Thomas and his Red hunters. Jack Warner, the only major studio head to appear, gave an extraordinarily emotional performance. Warner Bros. was known as the most politically liberal of the big studios and had been responsible for *Mission to Moscow*, the most blatantly pro-Stalin movie in Hollywood's history, and perhaps Warner felt especially vulnerable in the new age of the Red Scare. He blurted out the names of sixteen screenwriters whom he branded as Communists, and claimed to have fired all of them. Warner's list included a number of non-Communists, including Julius and Philip Epstein (coauthors of the screenplay for *Casablanca*), Sheridan Gibney, Emmet Lavery, and Howard Koch (who had co-written the script for *Mission to Moscow* at Warner's personal request). Warner later admitted he had "made a mistake" in naming Koch and the others. In fact, he had never fired any of the people he named. But the damage was done.

The sessions took place behind closed doors, but each day Thomas and Stripling emerged to faithfully report the testimony to waiting reporters. Matinee idol Robert Taylor told them that government officials had prevented him from entering the Navy in 1943 until he completed his role starring in *Song of Russia*—buttressing the committee's theory that secret Reds in the government had ordered up pro-Soviet propaganda pictures from willing dupes in a servile film industry. Ginger Rogers's mother, Lela, said her movie-star daughter had refused to speak the line "Share and share alike—that's democracy" in the film *Tender Comrades*, written by Dalton Trumbo, because it was obvious Marxist propaganda (in fact, Ginger did say the line). And dapper B-list actor Adolphe Menjou called Hollywood "one of the main centers of Communist activity in America."

"Communists in the film industry," Menjou added, "are so powerful that many little people in the industry—innocent people—are afraid to move or speak out against them."

After a week's worth of friendly witnesses, Chairman Thomas pronounced himself enlightened by what he had heard. He solemnly informed the press that "hundreds of very prominent film capital people have been named as Communists to us."

But the May executive sessions were a preliminary round. The main event was to be played in October with full-scale public hearings before a packed house in Washington.

In preparation, Thomas sought the help of FBI director Hoover at a meeting on June 24. "I told the Congressman that of course we wanted to be as helpful to the Committee as we could," Hoover dictated in a memo later that day, "but that the Bureau could not be publicly drawn into the investigation nor be called to appear in it in any capacity. The Congressman assured me faithfully that he understood that and would never embarrass the Bureau to that extent." A satisfied Hoover designated one of his top aides as a liaison to the committee and pledged to review the bureau's files "to see what help we might be able to be . . . insofar as submitting leads and material that might be used as a basis of interrogation."

"I do think it is long overdue," Hoover concluded, "for the Communist infiltration in Hollywood to be exposed."

In response to Thomas's request, the bureau compiled and delivered to the committee "blind memoranda" on eleven alleged Hollywood Communists providing background information, associations with front organizations, and other incriminating material. Richard Hood, the special agent-in-charge in Los Angeles, also provided photostats of party membership cards of twenty-five alleged Communists. These were materials the FBI had collected during its illegal break-ins of the party's Los Angeles office in the mid-1940s.

With Hoover's blessing, the committee hired former FBI agent H. Allen Smith to help plan its new set of public hearings by lining up "friendly witnesses" to speak about the Communist menace. Among the celebrities he interviewed privately were Ronald Reagan, president of the Screen Actors Guild, and Gary Cooper. Reagan had been an FBI informant for several years, but he told Smith that he was a New Deal liberal who did not agree with some of the members of the Motion Picture Alliance, most especially Jim McGuinness, whom Reagan called "a professional Red baiter." Reagan also said he resented the claim of Adophe Menjou that Reagan was a "reformed Leftist." Still, Smith came away recommending Reagan as a potential witness. "He has no fear of any one, is a nice talker, well-informed on the subject, and will make a splendid witness," Smith wrote.

Cooper had little factual information to offer, Smith reported. He said he had been approached in 1936 by someone who attempted to recruit him to the Communist Party because "men like Cooper, who had been around, driven buses, worked on farms, etc., were in a position to know more about the condition of the country than a star who has not done that, and accordingly they can best help the masses." But Cooper refused to name the person and Smith assured him the committee would not ask him to. Otherwise, all Cooper could offer was his "overall opinion . . . that from his experience, observation, and conversation . . . he is convinced that there are a number of people who are either Communists or followers of the Party line." Cooper again refused to name any names, but Smith didn't mind. "Mr. Cooper presents an excellent appearance, and will testify in a smooth, even, soft-spoken, unexcitable manner."

Also in June 1947, *Counterattack*, a right-wing newsletter devoted to exposing what it called "the hard cold facts about American Communists and their stooges," published its first issue. The weekly newsletter, staffed by three former FBI agents, was based in New York but focused much of its attention on Hollywood. It was the first of several publications that became an essential component of the Red-hunting machine by feeding names and allegations to the FBI and the committee and by passing on information they themselves were fed by those same institutions.

The committee subpoenaed forty-three witnesses for the October hearings, commanding them to report to the Caucus Room of the Old House Office Building just across Independence Avenue from the U.S. Capital. Opened in 1908, the ornate hall was a beaux arts masterpiece, featuring paired Corinthian pilasters and a double-high ceiling decorated with rosettes and a Greek key border. It was crammed with ninety-four reporters, four radio networks, countless microphones and newsreel cameras, and—like a visitor from the future—a lone television camera. Light bore down from four crystal chandeliers and six spotlights, rendering the room as "shadow-less as an operating theater," according to screenwriter Gordon Kahn. Hundreds of movie fans, most of them women, lined the solemn hallway for hours ahead of time hoping to get a seat inside or at least a glimpse of a movie star striding by. Chairman Thomas, sitting atop a red cushion placed over a District of Columbia telephone book, wielded his gavel like an ax. "He reminded me of an assistant director I had known who fell in love with a bullhorn," recalled director Edward Dmytryk, one of those summoned to testify. ". . . Without it he was a short, dumpy, very average human being."

As for the rest of the committee, author David Halberstam describes them as "a large number of the most unattractive men in American public life—bigots, racists, reactionaries, and sheer buffoons."

Jack Warner again led off the parade of friendly witnesses. The head of Warner Bros. was in full metaphorical mode. "Ideological hermits have burrowed into many American industries, organizations, and societies," he solemnly told the committee. "Wherever they may be, I say let us dig them out and get rid of them. My brothers and I will be happy to subscribe generously to a pest-removal fund . . . to ship to Russia people who don't like our American system of government and prefer the communistic system to ours." Warner, undeterred by his previous imprecision, rattled off more names of writers whom he had heard were Communists.

His father "went to Washington with a prepared speech, but he got nervous and fell apart," said Jack Warner Jr. "You could see the sweat running off his face. The cameras and the lights were on him, and he knew he was making a fool of himself . . . We walked out together afterward with a couple of our lawyers, and he said to me, 'I didn't do good, did I? I shouldn't have given names. I was a schmuck.'"

Warner's melodramatic testimony set the tone for many of the twenty "friendly witnesses" who followed. Over five days they painted a portrait of a Hollywood under siege by Communists and their allies. All of them agreed that the Reds had sought to create labor strife in order to seize control of the unions, tried to infect movies with their twisted ideology, and created a reverse blacklist in which Reds and their supporters got jobs while non-Communists were excluded. Many of the witnesses named names, even while affirming they lacked proof of their claims. After screenwriter Fred Niblo Jr. fingered Gordon Kahn as a Red, he added, "I cannot prove it any more than Custer can prove that the people who were massacring him were Indians."

But there were subtle distinctions among the witnesses. Warner and fellow studio boss Louis B. Mayer of MGM insisted they had successfully blocked any attempts to inject Communist ideology into their pictures by constant vigilance. Others disagreed. Former screenwriter John C. Moffitt recalled the advice he had received from John Howard Lawson, leader and purported chief ideological enforcer of the Hollywood Communist Party: "As a writer try to get five minutes of the Communist doctrine . . . in every script that you write. If you can, make the message come out of the mouth of Gary Cooper or some other important star who is unaware of what he is saying."

Moffitt outdid Warner by naming more than a dozen screenwriters he accused of being Communists. Charles Katz, one of the lawyers for the accused, rose to demand the right to cross-examine him. "You have said you want a fair hearing," he pleaded with Thomas. "Cross-examination is necessary." But the chairman gaveled Katz down. "Will you take this man out of the room, please?" Thomas ordered security guards. "Put him out of the room."

Both Warner and Mayer found themselves on the defensive over the propaganda films extolling the Soviet Union that they'd made during the war. Mayer tried to justify MGM's *Song of Russia*, insisting that the final script was "little more than a pleasant musical romance—the story of a boy and girl that, except for the music of Tchaikovsky, might just as well have taken place in Switzerland or England or any other country on the earth."

But novelist and libertarian icon Ayn Rand, the stern anti-Communist ideologist who had fled the Soviet Union in 1926, demolished Mayer's claim. "The mere presentation of that kind of happy existence in a country of slavery and horror is terrible because it is propaganda," she told the committee. "You are telling people that it is alright to live in a totalitarian state."

Robert Taylor, who starred in the film, told the committee how much he had hated it. He added that he would refuse to act with anyone who was suspected of being a Communist. "If I were even suspicious of a person being a Communist with whom I was scheduled to work, I'm afraid it would have to be him or me, because life is too short to be around people who annoy me as much as these fellow travelers and Communists." An indignant Taylor neglected to mention that his new picture, *The High Wall*, had been co-written by Lester Cole, one of the best-known party members in Hollywood.

Not all of the friendly witnesses parroted the same alarming line. Ronald Reagan denounced Communism and said he had fought its influence both in the Screen Actors Guild and in the craft unions. "I abhor their philosophy, but I detest more than that their tactics, which are those of the fifth column and are dishonest," said Reagan. Still, when a committee member asked if he would support banning the party outright, Reagan backed off. "I would hesitate to see any political party outlawed on the basis of its political ideology," he told the committee. ". . . However, if it is proven that an organization is an agent of a foreign power, or in any way not a legitimate political party . . . then that is another matter."

Reagan's careful tap dance was overshadowed that afternoon by the crown prince of ambivalence. Gary Cooper looked sharp in a double-breasted gray suit, white shirt, and light-blue tie, and hundreds of fans squealed and shouted his name as he made his way through the crowded hearing room, smiling and nodding like the guest of honor at an awards banquet.

Cooper said very little, but did so with insouciant humility, as if he had rehearsed his lines for maximum entertainment value. The performance began with his first answer. "What is your present occupation?" asked Stripling. Cooper paused, smiled, slightly lowered and then shrugged his well-padded shoulders. "An actor," he offered apologetically.

Then, after providing some autobiographical details, Cooper was asked if he'd noticed "any communistic influence in Hollywood or in the motion picture industry."

"I believed I have noticed some," he responded. There had been statements of "pinko mouthing," Cooper explained, such as "Don't you think the Constitution of the United States is about one hundred fifty years out of date?" and "Perhaps this would be a more efficient government without a Congress." The latter was received with twitters from the audience.

Cooper then allowed that he turned down quite a few scripts because they seemed "tinged with communistic ideas." But when pressed by his interrogators, he could not name a single one. He read most of the scripts at night, he explained, and if they weren't any good he didn't bother to finish them and sent them back whence they came.

Was Communism on the increase? "It is very difficult to say right now . . . because it has become unpopular and a little risky to say too much. You notice the difference. People who were quite easy to express their thoughts before begin to clam up more than they used to." It was impossible to tell whether Cooper found this change of atmosphere positive or regrettable.

It was over in fifteen minutes. Cooper had managed to be at once charming, patriotic, anti-Communist, and completely unenlightening. Most of all, unlike many of his fellow witnesses from the Motion Picture Alliance, he had named no names—neither of writers nor of scripts. It was undoubtedly his most nuanced performance of 1947. Still, he had managed to sum up a general popular feeling that Communism should not be taken seriously as a legitimate ideology because "I didn't feel it was on the level," meaning that Communists were dishonest about what their beliefs were and who they owed their loyalty to.

It's impossible to know for certain what Cooper was really thinking that day, to know how much of his behavior was premeditated and calculated and how much was ad-libbed by a man who knew his celebrity and often-avowed conservatism made him politically bulletproof. Apparently he had learned from his clumsy and unsuccessful intervention on Thomas E. Dewey's behalf against FDR. A few weeks after he testified, Cooper was quoted as saying, "I feel very strongly that actors haven't any business at all to shoot their faces off about things I know *we* know damn little about."

THE NINETEEN "UNFRIENDLY" WITNESSES subpoenaed by the committee had waited for a week to be called to testify. They had taken rooms at the Shoreham Hotel, where the FBI secretly listened in on their phone calls and recorded their conversations with their lawyers. "We were in our own capital, yet no foreign city could have been more alien and hostile," recalled screenwriter Howard Koch, one of the nineteen. "All our hotel rooms were bugged. When we . . . wanted to talk with each other or with our attorneys, we either had to keep twirling a metal key to jam the circuit or go out of doors."

The second week of testimony was supposed to begin with Eric Johnston, a former president of the U.S. Chamber of Commerce who was now leader of the Motion Picture Association of America, the Washington-based trade association representing the major studios. Johnston had met with the nineteen's lawyers and assured them that the studios would support their right to free speech and association. "Tell the boys not to worry," he told the lawyers. "There will never be a blacklist. We're not going to go totalitarian to please this committee."

The cause of free speech also had the vocal support of Hollywood's liberal establishment. Directors William Wyler and John Huston and screenwriter Philip Dunne organized the Committee for the First Amendment to oppose the committee's inquisition, gathered names and celebrity endorsements, and chartered a flight to Washington to protest the hearings. David Chasen volunteered his famous restaurant as headquarters and dozens of people met there every day to make phone calls, lick stamps, and stuff envelopes. Ava Gardner poured coffee, while Charles Einfeld, who ran the powerful publicity department at Twentieth Century-Fox, brought in his entire staff to write press releases and position papers. The delegation to Washington was led by Humphrey Bogart, Lauren Bacall, Danny Kaye, and Gene Kelly. They made stopovers in Kansas City, St. Louis, and Pittsburgh for public rallies and photo sessions, and there were lively drinking contests aboard the plane. Back in Hollywood, celebrities like Judy Garland, Robert Young, John Garfield, Edward G. Robinson, and Lucille Ball cut tapes for "Hollywood Strikes Back," a two-part ABC Radio program attacking the committee. "Who do you think they're really after?" actor Fredric March asked his national audience. "They're after you."

Meanwhile, the nineteen (with the exception of German playwright Bertolt Brecht) sought to work out a common strategy for their testimony. Their choices were limited and all were fraught with danger to themselves and their cause. They could refuse to answer the committee's questions and invoke the First Amendment's right of free political association, but that would undoubtedly earn them a citation for contempt of Congress. Or they could invoke the Fifth Amendment against self-incrimination, but that would make it appear as if they had something to hide. Liberals like Philip Dunne and Dore Schary suggested a variation of this idea: invoke the Fifth to refuse to answer questions, then hold a press conference immediately afterward and reveal that they were indeed Communists. This too was rejected. Their lawyers argued, quite correctly, that if any of the nineteen publicly admitted they were Communists, they would be inviting prosecution under the 1940 Alien Registration Act, which made it a federal crime to belong to an organization advocating overthrow of the government. Also, the committee could have issued each of them a new subpoena and required them to testify again and held them in contempt if they refused to answer. Once they admitted being present or former Communists, they would have no legal protection against answering the committee's next question: who else was a member?

In the end they chose another equally hopeless option: they decided they would answer the committee's questions but do so in their own way. They wanted to turn the tables on their interrogators by using their answers to attack and undermine the committee's legitimacy, invert the political theater, and somehow make the hearings work to their advantage.

When the session opened on Monday morning, Chairman Thomas had a surprise of his own: instead of the sober-sided Eric Johnston, he chose to call first to the stand screenwriter John Howard Lawson. It was a clever tactical move. Lawson, the leader of the Hollywood branch of the Communist Party, was an intelligent man but also the most strident and pompous-sounding of the nineteen.

Bushy-browed and dressed in a rumpled sport coat with a pencil and pen protruding from its breast pocket, Lawson looked more like an ill-tempered professor than a highly paid Hollywood screenwriter. He began by demanding to read a written statement. Thomas sounded amenable until he heard Lawson's opening sentence: "For a week this

Committee has conducted an illegal and indecent trial of American citizens . . ." Then Thomas ruled it "not pertinent to this inquiry," pounding his gavel to drown out Lawson. The session quickly deteriorated into an exchange of poorly aimed artillery fire between two loose cannons. Lawson insisted that questions about his political affiliations and membership in the Screen Writers Guild were "an invasion of the right of association under the Bill of Rights." Thomas replied, "Now you are just making a big scene for yourself and getting all het up."

Then Stripling took over and posed the cosmic HUAC question: "Are you now, or have you ever been, a member of the Communist Party of the United States?"

Lawson replied by not replying, accusing the committee of invading "the rights and privileges and immunity of American citizens" and of "using the old technique, which was used in Hitler Germany in order to create a scare here . . ."

Lawson wasn't finished. "It is unfortunate and tragic that I have to teach the committee the basic principles of American—" but the rest was cut off by the pounding of Thomas's gavel. The chairman ordered his security men to eject Lawson from the witness table.

Then Thomas called on committee investigator Louis J. Russell, a former FBI agent, who recited the information that had been secretly supplied by the FBI: Lawson's party registration card, number 47275, issued on December 10, 1944. Russell also submitted an eight-page résumé of Lawson's purported Communist activities. Meanwhile, outside the hearing room, Lawson read the rest of his opening statement to reporters, solemnly alleging that the so-called evidence against him "comes from a parade of stool pigeons, neurotics, publicity-seeking clowns, Gestapo agents, paid informers, and a few ignorant and frightened artists."

It was not a popular performance. Carl Foreman watched newsreel coverage at a Los Angeles movie theater and saw a middle-aged couple in the row in front of him react violently to Lawson's indignant fulminations. "Jack seemed sly, cunning, shady," recalled Carl, who was personally very fond of Lawson. "Suddenly the woman in front of me yelled, 'Kill him, kill him!' She thought he was a man who wouldn't tell the truth."

Having catapulted Lawson from the hearing room, Thomas finally called Eric Johnston, who offered a more measured critique of the hearings. "A damaging impression of Hollywood has spread all over the country as a result of last week's hearings," Johnston complained, adding, "It must be a great satisfaction to the Communist leadership in this country to have people believe that Hollywood Communists are astronomical in number and almost irresistible in power."

"We are tired of having irresponsible charges made again and again and never sustained," he added, speaking for the entire film industry. "If we have committed a crime we want to know it. If not, we should not be harassed and badgered by congressional committees."

After that, the committee fielded a steady parade of unfriendly witnesses, each of whom sought to answer its questions with his own special blend of anger and contempt. A few managed a touch of humor. Ring Lardner Jr. replied most famously after Thomas asked him for the fourth or fifth time if he was or had ever been a member of the party. "I could answer it," said Lardner, "but if I did I would hate myself in the morning." After each witness finished, Russell was called to the stand to describe the party card and alleged subversive activities and affiliations of the newly departed.

On the second to last day, Thomas took a break from the ongoing parade of party members and called RKO's Dore Schary to the stand.

As a liberal, Schary found himself in no-man's-land without a map to navigate the hearing's open warfare between left and right. The various Hollywood Ten witnesses—present or former Communists all—had come and gone, dispatched with fury and ridicule by Thomas and Stripling. Schary knew he himself was considered by the FBI and by Jim McGuinness and other right-wingers to be in league with the Communists.

Like a man on the high-wire, the head of production at RKO gave a cautious but balanced performance. Committee members demanded to know why Schary felt it was acceptable to hire known Communists. He replied by drawing a careful distinction between being a member of the party and advocating the overthrow of the government by violence or other means. He would not hesitate to hire the former if that person were best qualified for the job at hand; he would fire the latter. And he suggested that in any case a Supreme Court ruling prohibited him from denying employment to anyone for purely political reasons.

Schary's response infuriated Chairman Thomas. The two New Jersey natives then squared off. "I want to tell you something," Thomas lectured Schary. If Americans didn't wake up to the Communist threat, he warned, they would end up like France, Italy, Yugoslavia, and other countries facing Communist domination. "It is the Rip Van Winkle opinion that has been permitting Communism to grow through the world the way it has," said Thomas.

Schary stood up to Thomas's alarmism. He had opposed Communists all his working life, Schary said, and had helped defeat them in the Screen Writers Guild and other organizations. "I don't think Communism has anything to offer the American people, and that is why I don't think it is as dangerous as some people do," he testified. ". . . I don't think they have any weight, either in the organizations of Hollywood or in the actual things that appear on the screen."

Schary's realism clashed repeatedly with the committee's fantasy of Communists run amok. He walked a careful line, seeking to make the crucial contrast between dissent and subversion. A democratic society had to allow room for the former, no matter how hard it cracked down on the latter.

Thomas finally let him go. "Thank you very much, Mr. Schary," he concluded, "and don't forget what I said about Rip Van Winkle." The audience chuckled.

The next day was the final round of testimony with Ring Lardner Jr., Lester Cole, and the enigmatic German playwright Bertolt Brecht, soft-spoken, polite, and dedicated to Marxism, who repeatedly claimed that he had never been a member of the Communist Party and was praised by Thomas as "a good example" for his supposedly candid testimony. A few weeks later Brecht hopped a plane to Paris and made his way to East Berlin, never to return to the United States.

Eight other witnesses were scheduled to be questioned, but Thomas surprised friend and foe alike by suddenly halting the proceedings. He said the committee still had sixty-eight alleged party members to interrogate, and that the staff was also engaged in an "extensive study" of Communist propaganda in films. "We will resume the hearings as soon as possible," he pledged.

It didn't happen. Stripling later wrote that the committee had stopped because the hearings were taking on "the overtones of a broken record," and that they had heard through reliable sources that Communists from New York were planning to descend en masse and pack the hearing room with protesters. But the real reason, many believed, was that Thomas and Stripling feared their bullying tactics were creating sympathy for the unfriendly witnesses.

Thomas concluded with a final warning to the film moguls. "The industry should set about immediately to clean its own house and not wait for public opinion to force it to do so."

The Hollywood Ten returned home to cheering crowds and the support of mainstream newspaper editorial pages like the *New York Times* and *Washington Post*. Paul McNutt, counsel to the Motion Picture Association, claimed "a complete vindication of our position." But the victory was illusory. The Ten's futile efforts to out-shout and out-insult committee members clearly had backfired. They sounded like men who had something to hide. And indeed they did. The party membership cards and numbers that Russell presented were convincing evidence that all of the Ten were Communists either past or present.

The Ten have come under much criticism in the years since for their stridency and miscalculations before the committee. Some critics accused them of following orders from hardline party leaders in New York—and presumably Moscow—who were more interested in creating political martyrs than in helping the Ten avoid prison (this would become Carl Foreman's view). But there's no evidence such orders were ever given. In truth, the Hollywood Ten were the first of their kind to undergo this particular type of public inquisition. They had no established blueprint to follow, no coherent and well-tried strategy to deal with the unprecedented legal and verbal assault they faced. Under such circumstances, it's hard to imagine any strategy that could have succeeded.

Eric Johnston, sensing the winds of change and bowing to them forthwith, led the industry into full retreat. The head of the Motion Picture Association had pledged there would be no blacklist. But Johnston knew the film studios were vulnerable because of the changing economics of the industry and the changing politics of America. Even a localized boycott of certain films by the American Legion or other pressure groups, he feared, could ignite a nationwide wildfire.

Johnston wasted no time. He called for a meeting at the Waldorf-Astoria Hotel in New York for November 24. Some eighty studio executives, producers, and lawyers gathered. Johnston told them they only had two choices: retain the Hollywood Ten and issue a public statement pledging to keep all subversive material out of their movies in the future, or fire them and announce a policy of never again employing known Communists or subversives.

Johnston supported the latter alternative, citing the threat of an American Legion boycott and noting unconfirmed reports that an audience in Chapel Hill, North Carolina, had thrown rocks at the screen of a theater showing a film starring Katharine Hepburn, an outspoken critic of the committee. He also reported that RKO and

Twentieth Century-Fox had already decided to fire three of the Hollywood Ten.

Several of the studio heads supported him. But Samuel Goldwyn, an independent film producer and outspoken maverick, dissented, telling the group there was an air of unjustified panic in the room. Dore Schary noted there was no proof that any of the Ten had advocated the overthrow of the government, and since Hollywood's executives had all claimed there had been no Communist propaganda in their films, it would dishonor the industry to launch a witch hunt. But James Byrnes, a former secretary of state whom Johnston had hired as outside legal counsel, reminded the meeting that the morals clause in virtually every studio contract gave them the power to fire anyone at any time in order to protect the reputation of the industry. Johnston, who'd been slapping his hotel room key on the table as he spoke, now slammed it down harder and said he would quit unless the meeting agreed to take action.

No vote was taken; the consensus was obvious. Johnston had won. Schary allowed himself to be drafted onto the committee to write the new policy statement. "Do it, maybe they won't go crazy," Goldwyn pleaded.

The statement was a mishmash of contradictions, reflecting the lack of true agreement among those involved. The first paragraph deplored the action of the Hollywood Ten in refusing to answer the committee's questions, and the second paragraph announced their firing and pledged not to rehire any one of them "until such time as he is acquitted or has purged himself of contempt and declares under oath that he is not a Communist." It went on to pledge that the studios would not knowingly employ a Communist or any member of a group or party that advocated the overthrow of the government.

"In pursuing this policy, we are not going to be swayed by hysteria or intimidation from any source," the executives solemnly declared, although hysteria and intimidation were in fact the causes of their surrender. The statement recognized the risk of creating an atmosphere of fear. "We will guard against this danger, this risk, this fear," it concluded.

That same day, the House of Representatives voted by 347 to 17 to uphold the committee's contempt citation against Albert Maltz and 240 to 16 against Dalton Trumbo. The citations against the rest of the Ten were confirmed by voice vote, authorizing the legal proceedings that would lead to their arrest, trial, conviction, and imprisonment.

Schary, producer Walter Wanger, and MGM executive Eddie Mannix—all of whom had opposed the firings—were assigned the unenviable task of meeting with each of the three artistic guilds to explain what the studio heads had done and elicit the guilds' support. The Screen Writers Guild was the hardest audience. Seven of the Hollywood Ten were in the room to hear them out. Schary, himself a former guild member back in his screenwriting days, did most of the talking for the studio heads. "We do not ask you to condone this," he began.

But Dalton Trumbo expressed the fury he and the other members of the Ten felt. "These three men have come here to force their weasel-minded policies down the throat of this Guild," declared Trumbo. "I want to denounce them for what they are—liars, hypocrites, and thieves . . ."

"I was clobbered," Schary would recall.

THE HOLLYWOOD TEN HEARINGS of 1947 were one of those pivotal moments in American political history that helped set the direction for the country for more than a decade. They introduced a trio of aspiring young politicians to the national scene—future presidents Richard Nixon (a HUAC member) and Ronald Reagan, and future U.S. senator George Murphy, who, like Reagan, was a leader of the Screen Actors Guild. Senator Joseph McCarthy of Wisconsin, preparing to launch his own brief but incendiary career as the nation's loudest and most unprincipled Red baiter, stopped by the proceedings as well. "I just came over to watch the very excellent job you gentlemen are doing," he told Chairman Thomas.

Richard Nixon started out before the hearings as a gung-ho Red hunter. He promised the *Hollywood Reporter* that the testimony would be "sensational," exposing a "Red network" running from top to bottom of the film industry. But Nixon kept a low-key profile during the hearings themselves, asking simple, logical questions and showing sympathy for the studio heads like Louis B. Mayer, who later became one of his financial supporters. During the second week of the hearings Nixon vanished altogether. The Committee for the First Amendment had hoped to meet with him in Washington, since he was the only congressional member from California on the panel. Nixon's staff told the group he had been called home unexpectedly to Southern California. But William Wyler, who had remained in Hollywood during the hearings, couldn't find Nixon either at his office or home. "Somehow he had managed to disappear into thin air," recalled Philip Dunne. Nixon had other priorities; his glory days over the Alger Hiss case were soon to come.

The lessons were clear: that the committee was determined to conduct its anti-Communist campaign without regard to anyone's legal or constitutional rights; that the ultimate goal was to force the industry to bend to the power and will of the committee and purge itself of suspected subversives; that this was a very large category that included many liberals as well as Communists; and that the Communists' imperative of maintaining secrecy had proven self-defeating by giving the strong impression they had something to hide.

Jews too were back in the firing line. Six of the Hollywood Ten were Jewish, including John Howard Lawson (whose family name originally was Levy). Congressman John Rankin, perhaps the House of Representatives' most virulent Jew baiter, did not sit on the subcommittee that held the hearings, but he appeared before the House soon afterward to help tie a self-satisfied bow on the package. The Committee for the First Amendment was actually a Communist front organization, he told his fellow congressmen, and many of its celebrities were hiding behind stage names that concealed their true ethnic identity. Citing the committee's petition opposing the hearings, Rankin noted, "One of the names is June Havoc. We found out from the Motion Picture Almanac that her real name is June Hovick. Another one was Danny Kaye, and we found out that his real name was David Daniel Kaminsky . . . Another one is Eddie Cantor, whose real name is Edward Iskowitz. There's one who calls himself Edward Robinson. His real name is Emmanuel Goldenberg. There is another one out there who calls himself Melvyn Douglas, whose real name is Melvyn Hesselberg." Rankin never used the word *Jew*, but he couldn't have been clearer if he'd read *The Protocols of the Elders of Zion* into the Congressional Record.

Ten of the fifteen movie producers who signed the Waldorf Statement were also Jews. And the chairman of the committee that drafted the statement was Mendel Silberberg, an entertainment lawyer who was the unofficial leader of Hollywood's Jewish community. While it was easy, writes cultural historian Neal Gabler, "to view them as arrogant and stupid and reactionary . . . they were also in the grip of a deep and legitimate fear: the fear that somehow the delicate rapprochement they had established between themselves and the country would be destroyed, and with it their lives."

"They were frightened to death," screenwriter Jerome Chodorov said of the studio heads.

But the decision to pull the plug on the Hollywood Ten wasn't made by the moguls alone. The studios were increasingly dependent on New York investors. Chase Bank owned Twentieth Century-Fox, Rockefeller interests controlled MGM, Irving Bank was heavily invested in RKO, and other East Coast firms had large stakes in Warners and Columbia. Darryl Zanuck, head of Twentieth Century-Fox, told Philip Dunne that he personally had opposed the decision but had been overruled and ordered to fire Ring Lardner Jr. "He hinted that the actual decision had been made on Wall Street by the money men who bankrolled the movie companies," Dunne recalled.

Still, it was the studio executives who proceeded to summon talent agents to their offices and virtually command them to inform their clients that the studios would no longer tolerate public stances by performers on controversial issues. Even Humphrey Bogart, one of the nation's most popular and highly paid movie stars, got the message. He felt compelled to declare "I'm No Communist" in a flustered and apologetic article for *Photoplay Magazine*. In it, he recounted how his old friend, newspaper columnist and veteran Red-baiter Ed Sullivan, had warned him that after his appearance in Washington, "the public is beginning to think you're a Red! Get that through your skull, Bogie!" The article went on to assure his readers that he "despise[d] Communism," and that he had gone to Washington not to defend the infamous Hollywood Ten, but "solely in the interests of freedom of speech . . ."

"We may not have been very smart in the way we did things," the great Bogart confessed. They "may have been dopes in some people's eyes," he added, "but we were American dopes!"

At a meeting at Ira Gershwin's house, Bogart was less contrite and deeply furious with those he felt had betrayed him by persuading him to join a lost cause, shouting at Danny Kaye, "You fuckers sold me out!"

Edward G. Robinson, another celluloid tough guy, also caved, authoring a piece for the American Legion magazine headlined HOW THE REDS MADE A SUCKER OUT OF ME. Robinson sounded a pathetic note of contrition as he detailed all the ways he had been misled by people he believed were good-hearted liberals but who had turned out to be nefarious Communists. "I have changed from a trusting man to a suspicious one," wrote the rueful Little Caesar. "And I blame the Communists for that change . . . They slandered their enemies with innuendos and half-truths . . . to obscure their aim of world domination, oppression, and slavery."

As for Dore Schary, he said Adrian Scott and Edward Dmytryk—who respectively had produced and directed *Crossfire*, his most favored film—had lied to him when they denied they had ever been members of the party and he felt no sense of obligation to them even though he felt bad about their firing. Schary "seems completely aware of the situation in its fullest implications," wrote director Joseph Losey, himself a Communist Party member, to his friend Adrian Scott. "He acts dazed and looks sick."

Schary's view was that all three parties to the hearings had behaved badly. The committee had acted with malice and had flouted the civil rights of the witnesses; the Hollywood Ten had been badly advised by their lawyers and had participated unwittingly in their own legal martyrdom; and the representatives of the industry—presumably including Schary himself—had "behaved cowardly and cruelly."

Still, Schary was not about to sacrifice his gold-plated career for two recalcitrant former Communists. In his memoirs, Schary says he decided that he could do more good fighting the blacklist from within his company, RKO, than from outside. But he may have been more frank at the time when he told *New Yorker* writer Lillian Ross, "I like making pictures. I want to stay in the industry. I like it."

The Ten should have stood up and publicly declared their Communism, he told Ross. "That's all they had to do. As it is, ten men have been hurt and nobody can be happy. We haven't done any work in weeks. Now is the time for all of us to go back to the business of making pictures."

6.

The Viennese Gentleman

It is odd how one finds the story for the next picture; or perhaps it is the reverse: how a story finds the person destined to put it on film.

FRED ZINNEMANN

Carl Foreman watched the deadly serious HUAC follies in Washington in the fall of 1947 with a mixture of horror and disdain. While he admired his former comrades for their courage, he believed they had erred by refusing to answer the fundamental question of whether they belonged to the Communist Party. The party was wrong to cling to its secrecy, he believed: people could accept radicals who had the courage of their convictions but would suspect that those who remained silent must have something to hide. It felt like a straitjacket for members of the Ten to say, "I'm going to answer that question but in my own way." Better, Carl believed, to lay out the truth openly and defend it.

He felt a sense of relief that he was too small a fish to be of interest to the committee. He and Estelle had finally left the party—drifted away, as they put it, due to the press of having a baby (Kate was born that year) and coping with the full-time grind of making movies on a shoestring with Stanley Kramer and his partners. Still, he knew his name had appeared on some kind of suspected Red list as far back as 1943 when Frank Capra had recruited him to make documentaries for the Army. It had also popped up in later testimony before the Tenney Committee investigating Communists in Hollywood for the California state legislature, the local mini-version of HUAC. And it could always come up again. The sad irony was that the more successful and noteworthy Carl became as a screenwriter, the more likely it was that someone would come along sooner or later and expose him as a suspected subversive. His clock was ticking.

Meanwhile, as his friend Dore Schary had suggested, there were movies to be made. The next one on the list for Stanley Kramer and company now had a title: *The Men*. And a screenplay draft written by Carl. And it had a director: a genteel but insistent artist and craftsman named Fred Zinnemann.

Born in 1907, Fred had grown up in Vienna in an affluent Jewish home where culture and dignity reigned. His father was a dermatologist and played the viola in a string quartet, and his mother worshipped classical music and art. Fred himself had hoped to become a violinist but felt he lacked the talent. Instead, he studied at the University of Vienna for a doctorate in law, which he wound up hating out of sheer boredom. He recalled sneaking out of lectures to go to the cinema, where a world of enchantment and adventure seemed to open before him. With the wary approval of his doting parents, who stifled their horror that their oldest child had been captured by such a low form of popular entertainment, he boarded a train for Paris to study film.

His eighteen months there were a revelation. Paris was a world of great drama and color, and he wanted desperately to be part of it. He studied how to use a camera but he aspired to be something more than an efficient technician with a lens; he wanted to become a creative filmmaker. When his French visa expired, he relocated to Berlin, where one of his earliest assignments was as assistant cameraman on *People on Sunday* (1930), a full-length film featuring a cluster of young German talent, including Billy Wilder, who co-wrote it, and Robert Siodmak, who directed it. "My contribution was simply carrying the camera around and loading the film and keeping it focused as best I could," Fred recalled. But somewhere in there, he saw a possible future for himself.

Fred had grown up in a world where Jews were barely tolerated and often were subjected to discrimination and contempt, and it grated on his dignity and sense of justice. "It was always there—oppressive, often snide, sometimes hostile, seldom violent," he would recall. "A Jew was an outsider, a threat to the country's culture . . . Raised as an Austrian, he would still never truly belong." Later it would be much worse. Both his parents would be murdered in the Holocaust.

When Weimar Germany's economic collapse crippled its film industry, Fred boarded a decaying ocean liner for New York, and then rode a Greyhound bus that took seven days to cross the country to Los Angeles. While the grimy, economically battered cities of the eastern United States depressed him, he was thrilled by the wide open spaces and spectacular sunsets along the Santa Fe Trail and in the Mojave Desert. It was a stunning visual introduction to the American West for a young man from the claustrophobic confines of Western Europe. Despite being sponsored by the famous cameraman Billy Blitzer through a family connection, he failed to gain entry to the cinematographers' union in Hollywood, but he did get menial work as an extra in *All Quiet on the Western Front* (1930) before landing a job as personal assistant to Berthold Viertel, a distinguished Austrian stage and film director. Around the table of the comfortable Santa Monica home of Viertel and his wife Salka, a former actress turned hostess and gossipmonger, Zinnemann met scores of famous émigrés, including Charlie Chaplin, F. W. Murnau, Max Reinhardt, and Greta Garbo. One of the occasional guests was the legendary documentary filmmaker Robert Flaherty— another artist who, like Viertel, seemed uncomfortable with the conventions and culture of the studio system. Flaherty "didn't know the meaning of compromise," Fred wrote, "and this quality attracted me to him above everything else."

Fred signed on as Flaherty's assistant to make a documentary about the Soviet Union. The project never got made, but Fred spent six months in Berlin, where he absorbed the master's ideas, techniques, and attitudes, some of which would land him in continuous trouble once he returned to Hollywood. He kicked around a variety of jobs, including assistant to Busby Berkeley for dance routines on *The Kid from Spain* (1932). Then he took over from a friend the direction of a full-length documentary for the Mexican government on the lives of fishermen on the Gulf of Mexico coast. *The Wave* (1936) took almost a year to complete and was made under incredibly frustrating conditions: halfway through the film shoot, for example, the leading man decided his face was too hot and shaved his beard, delaying his participation in the movie for two months while it grew back. Still, the finished product helped Fred land a regular job in 1937 with MGM's short films department. He made eighteen shorts over three years, learning how to tell stories quickly and cheaply (the life and career of George Washington Carver in ten and a half minutes!), while meeting a dozen other promising young filmmakers on the MGM payroll like Jules Dassin, Joseph Losey, and Vincente Minnelli. Two of Zinnemann's short films won Academy Awards for MGM. His reward was a seven-year contract as a director.

His first feature-length film was *Kid Glove Killer* (1942), a B-movie police procedural with Van Heflin and Marsha Hunt. She would later recall how Fred had introduced himself to the entire cast and crew on the first day of the film shoot, explaining that he was a novice and inviting them to come to him with their ideas. No director had ever been so open with them before. "They were speechless," Hunt said. She glanced at Fred's personal copy of the script one day and saw that the margins on each page were black with his small, handwritten notes. "He had really done his homework."

After several less promising projects, Fred landed a larger, more complex film, *The Seventh Cross* (1944), starring Spencer Tracy, Signe Hasso, and Hume Cronyn. It tells the story of an anti-Nazi resistance fighter who escapes from a German concentration camp and must seek the help of friends and strangers to survive. It was the first of Fred's films to explore what became his most enduring theme: one person against a repressive system, driven slightly mad by his own principles yet determined to stick to them.

Fred Zinnemann was a small man with thin lips, a large nose, and a passive, thoughtful expression that made him seem a model of Old World gentility. He "was a lean and wiry mountain climber who spoke softly with a gentle Viennese accent—you might have taken him for a doctor or a psychiatrist," recalls George Stevens Jr., whose famous director father was one of Fred's closest friends. Yet Fred was also fiercely independent and intensely sensitive to anything that felt like a personal or professional slight. Although he worked inside a studio system in which producers had most of the power, Fred insisted that the director alone was the true author of a film, "the only person who has the *central*, overall vision of it from beginning to end." Actress Jane Fonda, who worked with him on *Julia* many years later, remembered him as "a gentleman and a dictator."

"My father had this courtly manner and he was always soft-spoken," recalls Tim Zinnemann, Fred's only child, "and when he got really mad he'd be even quieter. There's a common theme to his movies: the outsider sticking to his guns no matter what happens—and that's exactly how he was."

He was yanked from his next project, *The Clock* (1945), through no fault of his own. Judy Garland, the star, wanted to work with Minnelli, her new husband, and had the clout at MGM to make it happen. "I wish I could look upon this whole thing as a joke but somehow it doesn't strike me very funny," Fred wrote to his friend Minnelli in a private letter bristling with anger. "I think that this incident marks a new low in the treatment of directors, in professional ethics, tact, and consideration, which a director has a right to expect."

Then he was assigned two B movies with a six-year-old child star named Butch Jenkins, whom Fred described as "a perfectly normal, charming little boy who had no talent, could not remember his lines, and hated being in movies." Fred then turned down three scripts in a row—unheard-of behavior for a lowly director on the assembly line at the MGM dream factory. He was developing a reputation as a cranky nonconformist and managed to get himself suspended for several weeks, which meant he got no salary but was still bound to the studio.

It also meant he was free to accept the opportunity to direct *The Search* (1948), a drama set in the war-ravaged urban ruins of Germany. Swiss film producer Lazar Wechsler wanted to tell the story of displaced war orphans and chronicle the work of the United Nations Relief and Rehabilitation Administration, and he came to the United States to recruit talent. Having seen and been impressed by *The Seventh Cross*, he asked MGM for permission to borrow Fred's services. "MGM was happy to get rid of me for a year," Fred recalled. "The feeling was mutual."

He plunged into the project with great enthusiasm. Reacting sharply to the smug complacency and ignorance of his adopted country, Fred said, "In America there was no clear awareness of what had happened to countless human beings in the rest of the world . . . We were as on an island of stagnation and claustrophobia in the midst of a rapidly changing world."

Before he left for Europe, he recruited a gifted young actor named Montgomery Clift to play the lead. Clift had already made *Red River* with John Wayne but the film had not yet been released, and so *The Search* became his first appearance on the screen. Then Fred and Wechsler roamed the displaced persons' camps and bombed-out cities of postwar Germany, interviewing people and taking photographs. They returned to Zurich with dozens of case histories, which two writers turned into a story about a nine-year-old boy, separated from his parents during the war, who is picked up and cared for by a friendly GI while the boy's mother searches for him all over Germany. Fred filmed most of the interiors in Zurich but shot the exteriors in the bombed-out remains of Munich and Nuremberg. He used professional actors working alongside children recruited from the streets and the camps.

The result is a flawed but deeply satisfying drama. It begins with a poorly composed introduction—pasted on by Wechsler after Fred completed his work—delivered by a woman in a *once-upon-a-time* voice that makes it seem like we're watching a fairy tale rather than a gritty urban drama. Once that's over, however, the actors begin to play their parts and the movie becomes gripping and agonizingly sad. It features two superb performances: one by Clift as the young, easygoing GI who has no interest in playing a humanitarian hero but can't turn his back on a child in need; and the other by a nine-year-old Czech actor, Ivan Jandl, whose wary face, awkward, underfed body, and plaintive voice create a portrait of wounded vulnerability. Their scenes together are both casual and intense, and build powerfully as their relationship grows. Clift, who hadn't served during the war, prepared for the part by living with a platoon of Army engineers in the U.S.-occupied zone in Germany. After the film was released, someone asked Fred, "Where did you find a soldier who could act so well?"

It was sometimes the case that the children depicted in the film were not acting at all. For one scene, Fred put displaced children inside a Red Cross truck and told them they were to be transported to a new home. But many of them knew that the Nazis had often disguised mobile gas chambers as Red Cross ambulances, and they panicked when the doors were shut. The hysteria that Fred filmed inside the claustrophobic vehicles was real. It was a cruel but highly effective use of his young amateur cast—and a measure of how far Fred was willing to go to get what he wanted on film. In his memoirs, he describes this moment without expressing any remorse.

In a sense this was Fred's own story: a displaced war orphan seeking his way in a new and unfamiliar landscape. The film has an almost unbearable intimacy about it as the camera roams the devastation. This was the world Fred came from, one he had known so well, and now, like his murdered mother and father, it was gone.

The Search has fine acting, careful and efficient visual storytelling, and a deeply humanistic perspective that demands its audience pay attention—"a major revelation in our times," wrote Bosley Crowther of the *New York Times*, who urged every adult in the United States to see it.

The movie was nominated for four Oscars, including Clift for best actor and Fred for best director. It won for best story, and also won a special award for Ivan Jandl's powerful performance.

Fred went on to make two more compelling films about the aftermath of the war on GIs (*Act of Violence* and *Teresa*), but it was *The Search* that established him as a director who could pull off a complex, ambitious project on location and make a drama that looked like a documentary with actors who looked and sounded like real people. After it opened, he recalled, "the tiny little people" at MGM "who had been running for cover away from me a year earlier were now coming *at* me, all broad smiles, moving into close-ups and hugging me . . . This was when I became a cynic."

He got buckets of praise for the gritty social realism and quiet artistry of *The Search*, but no work at MGM for nearly a year. Then Stanley Kramer and Carl Foreman came knocking.

STANLEY MADE THE FIRST approach. After toiling for a decade in the suffocating confines of MGM, Fred was delighted with the kinetic energy and lack of pretense at Stanley and Carl's company. "Working in a small rental studio near Cahuenga Boulevard . . . ," he would recall, "there were no luxurious offices, no major-studio bureaucracy, no small internal empires to be dealt with, no waste of time or effort."

He signed a three-picture deal with the company. "I decided I had had enough of the factory system and asked to be released from MGM."

The Men, the first of the three films, was based on the draft screenplay Carl Foreman had constructed using the stories of the disabled war veterans he had met and interviewed at Birmingham Veterans Administration Hospital outside Los Angeles. Its main focus was on a fictional young Army officer named Bud who had been shot in the spine near the end of the war, and Ellen, the girl he had left behind. She now wanted to marry him despite the fact that he would most likely remain paralyzed from the waist down and sexually impotent for the rest of his life. The screenplay was a tough-minded, brutally honest portrait of what these young people were up against.

From the beginning, Fred was delighted that the artificial walls between producer, director, and screenwriter were readily breached at Screen Plays Inc. He and Carl worked together on revising the script and all three men shared the decision on who to cast in the starring role. All of them were intrigued by a newcomer named Marlon Brando, a young actor making a huge impact on Broadway in *A Streetcar Named Desire*.

"The wonderful thing about the film was that Stanley Kramer, Carl Foreman, and I were our own front office. We didn't have to bargain with anybody or persuade anybody," Fred recalled. "I remember Kramer bringing up three possibilities, and Brando was one of them. We all felt that Brando would be the most interesting. He had just finished *A Streetcar Named Desire* onstage, and it was just a question of how he would work out, not having ever worked in film."

Deeply ambitious yet equally ambivalent, Brando wanted to conquer Hollywood on his own terms. He had no interest in tying himself down to the seven-year contract the big studios were offering. Stanley's alternative universe, which consisted of a one-picture deal for far less money, was much more attractive to him, as was the quality of Carl's screenplay. Brando signed on.

The aspiring movie star arrived on the train from New York in jeans and a torn T-shirt. Stanley picked him up at Union Station and dropped him at his aunt's bungalow in Eagle Rock in northeast Los Angeles. A devout believer in Method acting, Brando immediately immersed himself in patient life at the Birmingham hospital. He confined himself to a wheelchair and drove a car specially fitted with hand controls like the vets themselves used. Brando spent four weeks living in a ward with thirty-one wary, frustrated, and often angry men. He dealt with them without a teaspoon of pity or condescension. Soon he became their leader.

In the most famous tale, Brando went drinking one night with his new friends from the ward, and when a woman at a bar started praying aloud for their recovery, Brando listened for a spell, then rose up haltingly. "I can walk! I can walk!" he cried. Then he broke into a soft shoe and danced his way to the sidewalk, his paraplegic buddies trailing after him in full mirth.

As he had done with Montgomery Clift, Fred gave Brando room to design his own performance. And as he had done with displaced children in *The Search*, Fred mixed forty-five real patients and hospital staff with professional actors to help give the film a more realistic feel.

To play Ellen, Bud's fiancée, Stanley hired Teresa Wright, a thirty-one-year-old actress who had an attractive, fresh-faced, girl-next-door demeanor yet had held her own in some of the best pictures of the 1940s against stars like Gary Cooper (*The Pride of the Yankees*), Joseph Cotten (*Shadow of a Doubt*), Dana Andrews and Fredric March (*The Best Years of Our Lives*). She'd won an Oscar for supporting actress and been nominated for two others, but Stanley got her for a mere twenty thousand dollars after Sam Goldwyn terminated her contract in a dispute over money and artistic control. She and Brando seemed to come from separate solar systems, let alone acting styles. But under Fred's careful tutelage she managed to meld her performance to that of her brilliant but unpredictable leading man.

Carl constructed many well-written scenes of Bud and his fellow paraplegics that depict their frustrations and agony as their aspirations collide with the hard reality of their injuries, and Brando and the expert supporting cast perform them brilliantly. But one of the most emotionally charged scene features Wright. Ellen confronts her parents about her decision to marry Bud, and when her father confesses his misgivings, her anger—hitherto unseen—boils to the surface.

"Love can be very fragile, El," her father tells her. "Even healthy people can't always hold onto it or take it for granted . . . How long do you think that love is going to last after you realize you've signed a contract to be his nurse for the rest of your life? It won't work. You're a young healthy girl."

". . . Oh I'm not blaming you," he adds. "I know you love him. I'd probably be ashamed of you if you felt any other way. Actually I blame Bud. Yes I do. He knows the score better than any of us. He ought to let you go. If he loved you as much as you love him he'd make you go."

Wright as Ellen strikes back with an unexpected sting that suggests a deep pool of resentment below her saccharine smile. "You're being so clever, so logical," she tells her father, her voice growing cold. "I never knew you could handle words so well . . . You weren't quite so logical a few years ago when we needed some boys to go out and get killed—or paralyzed . . ."

"Baby," he pleads, "is it so wrong for us to want a grandchild?"

Bud and Ellen are married. The doctors, nurses, and fellow paraplegics attend, but not her parents.

That night Bud spills champagne on the living room carpet of their new home, and when his right leg begins to spasm uncontrollably, he catches a flash of despair on Ellen's face and confronts her viciously. All her defenses collapse under his sustained verbal assault and she confesses her doubts about the marriage. Bud storms out in his wheelchair and returns to the hospital. Brando beautifully captures Bud's vulnerability and bitterness.

In the film's final scene, they agree to try again. Ellen smiles at him, but her expression is far from joyful. The audience can sense that every step for these two will be fraught with uncertainty and disappointment. War has robbed a handsome, virile young man—and his comrades in the ward—of his most defining characteristic: his manhood. There is no happy ending.

Bud is a compelling character because of Brando's keenly sensitive performance. But Ellen was truly Carl's creation, his first complex woman character. She is strong, idealistic, and determined to live up to her values, yet unsure she has the wherewithal to do so. She is vicious to her father because she knows deep inside that he may well be right, and she's frightened by Bud because he sees behind her façade of strength and determination. It's a finely etched, bravely realistic portrait.

"The courage, resolution, and compassion of the approach were never in question," writes British film critic Penelope Houston of *The Men*. "Zinnemann's handling of the professional and non-professional players, the balance maintained between the central story and the hospital background, the grasp of the human implications of the material, and the vitality of Carl Foreman's script, made this a film of unusual honesty."

The reviews were glowing and Carl got another Oscar nomination for best screenplay. But box-office receipts were weak. Fred was proud of his work on the picture and had enjoyed working on the film set with Carl. But doubts were beginning to eat at both men over their partnership with Stanley Kramer and George Glass, his devoted public relations wizard.

AS THE COMPANY'S PR man, Glass had one primary mission: the care and growth of Stanley's reputation. To promote the company, he argued, he had to put the spotlight solely on one man, otherwise the plotline would be too complicated for the simple-minded press to digest. A letter Glass wrote to gossip columnist Hedda Hopper in April 1950 was typical. After thanking her for her recent praise of *The Men*, he launched a plea: "Hedda, from time to time I have said to you that the best story in town is the success story of Stanley Kramer, the man who made this picture, from the conception of the idea through to its completion. His is the best of the modern Horatio Alger stories, and certainly living proof that opportunity is still around for those who have the courage and the initiative to go after it.

"I know that from this one lone guy, who started from scratch less than three years ago, this giant industry has drawn new hope during a most trying period in its history."

It was Glass who staged the publicity campaign that won for Stanley the *Look* magazine Achievement Award as Top Producer of the Year for 1950—and along with it, a full-page ad in the *Hollywood Reporter* congratulating Stanley for his "distinguished record as maker of *Champion, Home of the Brave*, [and] *The Men*."

The new picture was advertised as "Stanley Kramer's *The Men*" on movie posters and advertisements. Carl conceded that the original idea for the film had been Stanley's. But what about the contributions of Fred and Brando and himself? Carl chafed. There was tension, frustration—"the marriage had turned unhappy and sour," Carl recalled. And he blamed George Glass, Stanley's willing agent, more than Stanley himself.

Fred shared many of Carl's misgivings and added his own exquisite sense of grievance. Visiting New York, he couldn't help but notice that the newspaper and subway ads didn't mention his name nor Brando's, just Stanley's. He began to sense that Glass and Stanley were teaming up against him.

In a letter to his agent, Joseph Schoenfeld at the William Morris Agency—a letter he never sent but kept in a drawer for decades—Fred expressed his growing resentment. "George Glass's policy is to keep building the Stanley Kramer legend—about the man who goes out and does all of it, all by himself," Fred wrote. "If necessary, George is willing to pursue this policy at the expense of other people. By his own statement, he likes to see just how far he can push people before he is stopped, and as you know he is a shrewd and subtle man."

As a result of Glass's campaign, Fred complained, "Stanley absorbed a lot of credit that is not his . . . The 'team' idea which was stressed so strongly by him in our original meeting, was carried through the production phase—and yet somehow the picture now emerges as pretty much of a one-man job."

Next up for Screen Plays Inc., at Stanley's insistence, was *Cyrano de Bergerac*, based on the highly successful Broadway play starring the talented José Ferrer. It is the tale of a seventeenth-century French nobleman who is a brilliant swordsman and gifted poet with a disfiguringly large nose. Carl had deep reservations about the efficacy of such a project for the Kramer company; a period piece like *Cyrano* would be expensive to produce and did not fit their social-realism ethos and style. But Stanley was determined and Carl thought he understood why: he saw a lot of Stanley's own character in Cyrano. "Not only the nose, but rather Cyrano's panache, Cyrano's stubbornness, Cyrano's unwillingness to compromise, Cyrano's almost self-destructive honesty and integrity," said Carl.

As a low-budget movie, Carl argued, *Cyrano* was bound to fail. They couldn't afford to film it in color and give it the kind of sumptuous visual panache it needed. They got lucky with casting: Ferrer agreed to reprise his Tony award–winning performance from the Broadway production. But his salary left little money for the rest of the cast. The black-and-white movie looked thin and drab despite Rudolph Sternad's creative production design and Franz Planer's superb cinematography. It failed at the box office, although Ferrer won an Oscar for best actor—the first Latino performer to do so. Still, Stanley was now clearly in charge. He was dictating the company's agenda, no longer consulting first with Carl and the others. The creative collaboration was beginning to unravel.

"They were three men—Kramer, Foreman, and Zinnemann—each of whom was among the very best at what he did," says George Stevens Jr. "One guy gets the material, one writes the screenplay, and the other directs it. They are arguably the perfect combination for a film company." But all of them, Stevens notes, were restless with their roles: Stanley and Carl both longed to direct their own films, while Fred wanted total control of his. Each of them was tough, demanding, and blessed with a combative personality and an extra-large ego.

"It explains why these three made great films but also explains the difficulties that emerged," says Stevens.

The company had released five pictures in its first four years, four of which had been critical successes and two of which had done very well at the box office. But Stanley wanted to expand its production schedule and grow its finances. To do so, he needed a business partner with money and a solid reputation. He turned to Sam Katz, who had been a behind-the-scenes player in New York and Hollywood since the early days of the film industry. Katz had been a partner in the very successful Balaban and Katz theater chain based in Chicago, and when it was bought up by rival Paramount in 1926, he ran the combined theater empire from the thirty-five-story Paramount Theatre Building in Times Square. After helping stage a bloodless coup against Paramount's distinguished founders, Adolph Zukor, B. P. Schulberg, and Jesse Lasky, Katz moved over to MGM in the mid-1930s, where he worked for fourteen years as a production executive, part of the leadership group known as "the College of Cardinals." He had a reputation as a superficially charming but cold-blooded in-fighter. "Katz was a polished, well-groomed man with a mellifluous voice and an engaging smile" that concealed a devious way of doing business, recalled Dore Schary, who worked with him at MGM. Or as director Joseph Mankiewicz put it, "Nobody can be as happy to see anybody as Sam Katz is to see everybody." But perhaps not so happy; when he met up with Stanley

Kramer, Katz had just been pushed out at MGM as the studio attempted to cope with the rapidly changing economics of the movie business.

Katz brought Stanley more than his management experience; he also invested two million dollars in the new partnership and pledged to help raise thirteen million more. They called the new enterprise the Stanley Kramer Company, with Katz in charge of financial affairs while Stanley remained head of production. George Glass, lawyer Sam Zagon, and Carl continued as shareholders and limited partners, with George listed as vice president and Carl as treasurer.

Carl was not happy about the new deal. He didn't like the corporate name change and he didn't trust Sam Katz. But he still believed in the Stanley Kramer way of making movies, especially when contrasted with working for a large studio. He was reminded of the difference when he signed on with Warners to help write the screenplay for *Young Man with a Horn* (1950), a Kirk Douglas picture about a talented but self-destructive jazzman. It was directed by Michael Curtiz, a wily old veteran who had directed *Casablanca* and many other Warners hits but who knew as much about modern jazz as Carl did about ancient Babylon. Carl thought the finished film was a lethargic mess with none of the excitement and unpredictability of the jazz world it sought to depict. He suggested at a meeting with Curtiz, the producers, and studio head Jack Warner that the movie needed much tighter editing. "Thank you very much," Warner replied. "Next."

After that, "nobody talked to me anymore," Carl recalled.

Back at the Stanley Kramer Company, more changes were in the wind. Sam Katz reported to Stanley that the board of directors at Columbia Pictures was looking to groom someone to succeed Harry Cohn, the company's autocratic head of production. Cohn was one of Hollywood's most infamous film czars—"vulgar, domineering, semi-literate, ruthless, boorish, and some might say malevolent," as Stanley describes Cohn in his memoirs. Cohn was offering a deal in which the Kramer Company would become a major production unit for Columbia, making six pictures a year for five years—thirty films in all. The company would have unfettered discretion as to which films to make, provided each picture's budget did not exceed one million dollars. This would be an enormous undertaking, and the risks were obvious. "Anybody who had worked in Hollywood for as long as an hour and a half had heard stories about what an ornery bastard [Cohn] could be," writes Stanley. Still, the profits were potentially enormous—and looming in the near future was the prospect that Stanley would succeed Cohn as head of

Columbia, with Katz lurking in the background as kingmaker. Stanley authorized him to negotiate a deal. Even Carl, despite his reservations, had a hard time saying no.

On March 19, 1951, Cohn held a press conference to announce the agreement. He called it "the most important deal we've ever made." While the major studios were struggling, the Stanley Kramer Company seemed on its way to the top.

7.

The Falling Star

His eyes were the most fabulous shade of blue and always sparkling, and he had long eyelashes that were curled more outrageously than any girl's. His hands were long and graceful and beautiful. I think his hands are what I remember most.

PATRICIA NEAL

Gary Cooper was in the middle of his own long-term deal with Warner Bros., one that had proved to be a lucrative business arrangement but creative dead end. The first project he agreed to do was one of the most curiously flamboyant and deranged pictures of the postwar era. *The Fountainhead*, Ayn Rand's 754-page novel, was a proto-Fascist celebration of the capitalist id and a huge bestseller, written by a Russian Jewish immigrant who fled Bolshevism for America in 1926. Alice Rosenbaum had jettisoned her real name as soon as she got to Hollywood, but held tight to her self-sustaining delusions of grandeur. As Hollywood chronicler Otto Friedrich put it, "Ayn Rand was, of course, an Ayn Rand character."

She signed a deal to write the screenplay, insisting on the stipulation that the studio not change a word without her permission. And she thought Gary Cooper, the epitome of rugged American virility, was the only actor capable of playing Howard Roark, the sexy, egomaniacal architect whose fierce independence and refusal to compromise his artistic vision was at the heart of the story. Cooper agreed, even though his modest screen persona was thousands of miles from Roark's ludicrous self-regard. For once, Cooper's instinctive distaste for bombast and pretension failed him. To play Dominique Francon, his narcissistic and sex-obsessed lover, Warners signed an alluring and spirited newcomer, twenty-three-year-old Patricia Neal.

The movie is a camp classic, crammed with painful dialogue and overwrought acting, especially by Neal, who had to recite some of its most pretentious lines. "You're everything I've always wanted—that is why I can never see you again," she tells Roark in a scene that plays like a satirical parody.

Cooper, a far more experienced performer, struggled gamely with his role, but it was a losing battle. "Gary Cooper seems slightly pathetic with his candor and modesty in the midst of so much pretension," wrote *New York Times* critic Bosley Crowther, normally a fan. But one thing happened during the film shoot that shook Cooper's world: he and Pat Neal fell in love.

It had started with smoldering looks and some discreet hand-holding on the set, and was finally consummated on the night of the wrap party. Cooper was used to carrying on with his leading lady during the shooting of a picture, and with countless other women who crossed his path at the studios where he worked. Even after his marriage to Rocky, he was linked romantically to Marlene Dietrich, Carole Lombard, Madeleine Carroll, Paulette Goddard, Anna Sten, Merle Oberon, and Ingrid Bergman, among many others.

It's unclear what Rocky Cooper knew and didn't know about these affairs. But she was too intelligent and observant not to be aware of the effect her husband had on women and of his own epic weaknesses. "My mother was very pragmatic," Maria Cooper Janis recalls. "She had an amazing ability to cut to the chase and say okay, let's get on with it." And the Coopers were good companions in so many ways, their daughter says, that they had strong reasons to stay together despite frequent storms. Besides, Rocky was a devout Catholic who did not believe in divorce.

Cooper had usually played the game of flirtation, seduction, and conquest by his own easy-to-navigate rules. But Pat Neal was different. She had grown up in Knoxville, Tennessee, had studied acting at Northwestern University, and was intelligent, ambitious, and self-confident. She wasn't willing to be the Other Woman and settle for occasional sex. She had wanted Cooper from the moment they met at Jack Warner's private dining room before the film shoot began; she had wooed him with her earthy, direct style and her voluptuous young body, and once she got him she had no intention of letting him go.

Her autobiography, published nearly four decades later, tells uncomfortable truths even when it makes its author look like an unabashed predator. She writes about first meeting Rocky Cooper on *The Fountainhead* set and cruelly evaluating her rival as if she were an up-and-coming prize fighter sizing up an aging, vulnerable champion. Rocky, she wrote, "had none of Gary's down-home charm that endeared him to the common folk in the set . . . She was clearly a good companion to Gary Cooper. But I reminded myself that I was younger. Her presence that day made one thing clear to me. I had met a worthy adversary."

Once Neal and Cooper became lovers, they established a secret life at her small apartment at 2148 Fox Hills Drive in West Los Angeles. They cooked meals together, took walks on the beach, went for long car rides, and talked about their past affairs. "Gary was famous for his brief 'yups' and 'nopes,' but he never stopped talking when he was with me and I never tired of listening to him," Neal recalls.

He bought her a new Cadillac, a pearl necklace, and diamond drop earrings from Harry Winston's, one of Hollywood's finest jewelers. "He'd been taught by the women in his life how to please them," Neal purred.

She tried to please him as well. And protect him. Once after midnight they were awakened by a loud crashing sound. She ran outside to find a car wrapped around a telephone pole, with a bleeding man sitting in the street and a woman pinned inside the wreck. Onlookers asked to use Neal's phone to call the police, but she denied she had one and sent them to the corner gas station instead. She didn't want anyone to run across Cooper in her apartment. Then, to her dismay, she discovered Cooper standing in the middle of the road, wearing her dressing gown, and watching the scene unfold. When they got back inside, she was appalled that her first thought hadn't been for the accident victims. "All I really thought of was protecting Gary," she writes. "No one else mattered."

In a handful of his letters that have survived, Cooper expresses utter infatuation for his young lover. Brief, simple, and passionate, each one seems to have been dashed off just before he leaves for some other destination, but each has an almost childlike enchantment with his new companion. "Have had one hell of a rush but will write you from the east," reads one of them. ". . . I feel awfully good after talking to you yesterday! Please know I adore you and I pray for everything wonderful for you and for all you desire."

But there was a darker side to Cooper's passion. He insisted that their affair be kept secret to protect both of their careers, and sometimes she dated other men, out of loneliness and a desire to make him jealous. One night she and actor Kirk Douglas engaged in passionate kisses near an open window in her apartment. After Douglas left, Cooper stormed in and slapped her face hard enough to draw blood. "Baby, I'm sorry, let's just forget about it," he pleaded. And they did. Douglas still remembers that night and says Cooper must have struck more than one blow. "She was black and blue," he recalls.

Cooper and Neal maintained their secret for nine months until Neal joined friends on a trip to Aspen, Colorado, that somehow came to include a visit to the new house the Coopers had built there. Rocky's finely tuned antennae immediately sensed there was something between her husband and Neal and she confronted him that evening, demanding to know if he was having an affair with Neal and if he loved her. He reluctantly answered yes to both questions. Later that night, as Cooper sat brooding in the next room, Rocky told eleven-year-old Maria what had happened. "My mother said to me 'your father thinks he's in love with Patricia Neal,'" Maria Cooper Janis recalls. "And he was in the other room looking out the window and very upset. She said to me, 'It's got nothing to do with you, we both love you to pieces, and he's very upset, go in there and tell him you love him.' So I did."

Neal was dumbfounded to learn that Rocky had told Maria about her father's infidelity. Whatever Rocky's motive, her decision was enormously painful and embarrassing for Cooper, who desperately feared losing the love and respect of his cherished daughter. Rocky Cooper was a more cunning and formidable opponent than Neal had reckoned.

In October 1950 Neal informed Cooper that she was pregnant. She had hoped this was the event that would finally push him to seek a divorce from Rocky and marry her. Instead, without consulting her, Cooper arranged for an abortion. He drove her to the doctor's office, handed her an envelope stuffed with cash to pay for the procedure, and waited in the car while she went inside. Later, she was astonished to find out he had told Rocky what had happened. Soon after, he and Rocky agreed to separate, and he moved from their Brentwood home to the Hotel Bel-Air, home for many a wayward Hollywood husband. "At last," Neal told herself. "At last."

"If I had been older and wiser," she writes, "I would have realized that Gary had no reason to tell Rocky about the abortion unless he was going to stay with her.

"He was not going to pick up my option."

* * *

THROUGHOUT THE LOVE AFFAIR with Patricia Neal and the breakup with his wife, Cooper had a curious ally and confidante: Hedda Hopper, the queen of Hollywood gossip. While he was always wary of her and her archrival, Louella Parsons, Cooper found Hopper could be surprisingly solicitous and discreet. She had known and shared the details of his career, his affairs, and his health issues over an extended period, and she consistently treated him with admiration and respect. No doubt, this was in part because he was Hollywood royalty, and she knew better than to go after him. And no doubt, like a lot of women, she was charmed by the long, tall, self-deprecating Montana boy. But her notes also reveal a genuine warmth between them. "Gary Cooper has always talked very freely to me, especially if he's allowed to sit down and take the weight off his feet," she wrote.

She celebrated his roots in small-town America and accepted at face value his self-styled, country-boy humility. Talking with Hopper on the set of *Good Sam* in 1948, Cooper referred to a story she had written about wheat-field workers in the Midwest and recalled how he had harvested wheat in Montana with a pitchfork when he was young. "My hands were calloused from the first knuckle to the middle of my palm," he told her, triggering this observation in her column: "That quality of Coop's of not forgetting his hard-working days seems to creep into the characters he portrays on the screen."

Born Elda Furry, a Quaker butcher's daughter from Hollidaysburg, Pennsylvania, Hedda Hopper was an ex–chorus girl, real estate saleswoman, and the fifth of six wives of the infamous musical theater actor DeWolf Hopper, twenty-seven years her senior. He brought her to Hollywood in 1915, where she appeared in more than 120 movies over a twenty-year period as a supporting actress. A self-described "chatterbox, doomed to shoot from the hip," she knew everybody's business and was even an occasional source of intimate information for Parsons, who worked for William Randolph Hearst's powerful newspaper syndicate. Hopper got so good at ferreting out information that as she turned fifty and her movie career faltered, she decided to get into the gossip column business herself. Her big break came in 1938 when the *Los Angeles Times* picked up her column. Within five years, the column, syndicated by the *Chicago Tribune* and *New York Daily News*, was appearing in 110 newspapers with a combined circulation of 22.8 million copies. By then, she and Louella Parsons had become blood rivals.

"The studios created both of them," said Liz Smith, one of their modern heirs. "And they thought they could control both of them. But they became Frankenstein monsters escaped from the lab."

Crammed with a dozen or more punchy one-paragraph items, Hopper's column appeared five days a week, and she turned out a major Sunday feature as well. Each column boasted a photo of Hopper in a different hat; she claimed she spent five thousand dollars a year on her signature headgear. To handle the heavy and demanding journalistic load, Hopper employed two leg men, one rewrite woman, two clerks to handle fan mail, two secretaries, and a business manager. "Hi, slaves!" she'd call out each morning as she sailed into the office. "How's everybody?" She couldn't type, so she dictated complete sentences while she paced the floor, smoking incessantly. Those sentences sounded exactly like her: chatty, breezy, corny, coarse, and intimate.

"*Duel in the Sun* is sex rampant," she breathlessly informed her readers on January 3, 1947, about the new David O. Selznick production. "Its musical score matches its love-making . . . [Stars Jennifer Jones and Gregory Peck] are hotter than a gunman's pistol." And "Henry Fonda's busier than the proverbial one-armed paperhanger with hives." And "Frank Sinatra, tanned, rested, and rarin' to go, dropped by to say hello."

The headlines were often hokey: TO VICTOR BELONG THE SPOILS (Victor Mature); CLAUDE REIGNS, a portrait of the actor Claude Rains; and SILENCE IS NOT GOLDWYN about studio magnate Sam Goldwyn.

Hopper's column dished out endless marital and family advice, but mostly it gabbed about stars: their triumphs and their shortcomings. Who's getting married, who's pregnant, who's in the hospital, who's got a new job or a big starring role, who's gotten arrested or can't even get arrested anymore. She knew how to play up to them, and they knew how to play her.

Deep in the files of her papers at the Motion Picture Academy library in Beverly Hills is a telegram she received in November 1940 while on vacation in Tucson. HEDDA, YOU OLD HOP TOAD, it reads. FIRST YOU WENT TO TEXAS. NOW YOU'RE IN ARIZONA. THAT'S COW COUNTRY AND THAT MEANS COWBOYS. AND COWBOYS MEANS LOTS OF FUN FOR ALL AMERICA. SO HAVE A GOOD TIME. BUT FOR GOSH SAKES DON'T FORGET TO COME BACK TO US.

It's signed by five of the biggest Western stars of the day: John Wayne, William Boyd, Harry Carey Sr., Roy Rogers, and, of course, Gary Cooper.

The political side of Hopper was far less benign. She saw herself as the guardian of Americanism against the onslaught of Communists, New Dealers, and other interlopers who threatened the country's bedrock values. She claimed to see the struggle as a fight between those who wanted to make good entertainment—people like John Wayne, Clark Gable, Walt Disney, and Gary Cooper—and those who insisted on stuffing dangerous political messages into their pictures. But in truth, she wanted her kind of messages delivered by her kind of people. Jews, émigrés, and other non-Anglo-Saxons were outsiders, tolerated only so long as they understood their place.

She was one of the founding members of the Motion Picture Alliance, and when the House Un-American Activities Committee came to Hollywood she would play the role of Madame Defarge of *A Tale of Two Cities*, cheering from the sidelines as the committee hauled its victims to the guillotine. She welcomed the HUAC hearings in 1947, telling her readers that the main threat of Communism in Hollywood was the subtle injection of "Red propaganda" in movies. She was especially critical of mainstream pictures made by non-Communists whom she believed had been duped into following the party line by working "ceaselessly to destroy the belief of Americans in the processes which make our government function." Her hit list of subversive films included *Mr. Smith Goes to Washington* and *Meet John Doe*, both directed by Frank Capra, *The Farmer's Daughter*, and *The Best Years of Our Lives*.

"Emphasizing the negative qualities in our way of life under its present system, and neglecting the good, can be just as effective as waving the Red flag—even more so because its message is hidden," she warned in a column. "We've had many pictures pointing up our racial problems, political corruption in government, the evil of wealth, men driven to crime because of the supposed pressure of our capitalistic system. These are but a few devices which the Commies could use to get inverse propaganda in our films."

Gary Cooper's politics were less vituperative than Hopper's but no less right-wing, and surely that was one of the reasons she was so fond of him. Still, she was mainly interested in his personal life. When he fell in love with Patricia Neal and separated from Rocky, Hopper seemed to have a front-row seat. In a May 1951 phone call, Cooper told her that he and Rocky had not yet reached a divorce settlement. She warned him not to let Rocky take him to the cleaners. "Don't let her get all your money," she said. But Cooper defended Rocky. "She's not like that really," he told Hopper.

"She'll have a hard time finding another like you," said Hopper. "There aren't any men."

But Cooper replied frankly and self-deprecatingly. "It's all my own fault. Too many things during our long marriage were taken for granted. It's all my doing, but I do want to be free."

Hopper defended him. "Don't you think you deserve some happiness?"

Cooper wasn't buying it. "Listen, after twenty-five years I've had a helluva lot of happiness and many things that have been good," he replied. "Many more than most people get and many more than I deserve. Picture stars are spoiled. They get a little hoggish. They think they're the best things in the world; they're not."

"Don't think badly of Rocky," he added. "She's a good girl."

Hopper was discreet about the conversation. She used most of what Cooper told her in her next column, but did not disclose that she had spoken directly with him.

"The first night Gary Cooper got back to town, he took his daughter, Maria, to dinner," she wrote in another item. "His property settlement with Rocky is speeding along. If she won't agree on a divorce it wouldn't surprise me if Coop got one himself. He's looking for happiness."

When Cooper went to Naples, Florida, to shoot *Distant Drums* in May 1951, he sent Hopper a horse conch shell "for your mantle." And when he went into the hospital three months later for a hernia operation, Hopper hovered like a concerned aunt. "He was operated on once before, but before the job healed, he climbed a mountain with Ingrid Bergman in *For Whom the Bell Tolls*," she wrote. "And the darned thing never did heal properly."

He felt tired and run-down. He had turned fifty in May but looked ten years older. He was still a formidably handsome man, but it was hard to miss the creases embedded in his face. The two packs of cigarettes he smoked daily didn't help. His problems were coming together, all of them related, some of them self-inflicted. His career, marriage, and health were all in a downward spiral. He was frustrated and disappointed with the poor quality of the movies he was making—and with the fact that in 1950 he had fallen out of the Top Ten list of male box-office stars for the first time in fourteen years.

His old insecurities as an actor resurfaced. Jeff Corey, the talented supporting actor, was surprised when Patricia Neal brought along Cooper to some of the evening classes Corey taught in Hollywood. "He wanted to be a better actor," Corey recalled. "He was interested in acting." Corey once called on Cooper during class and asked his opinion about a scene some of the students were rehearsing. Awkward silence followed, and Corey quickly realized his mistake. "He just wanted to hide."

Cooper later confided to Corey that he had felt mortified after agreeing to consider doing the Robert Sherwood play *Abe Lincoln in Illinois*. He loved the writing, he said, but was intimidated by the role and eventually turned it down.

"I have only one or two tricks, at best," Cooper confessed. "That isn't enough, is it?"

Hollywood's brightest star was beginning to fade. In the movies, his character had always triumphed, usually on his own. "If you make me the hero it usually comes out right" wasn't working for him anymore. In real life, the hero needed a hero of his own.

8.

The Committee Returns

The concept of loyalty as conformity is a false one. It is narrow and restrictive, denies freedom of thought and of conscience, and is irremediably stained by private and selfish considerations.

HENRY STEELE COMMAGER

Although they had been fired from their jobs or frozen out of new ones and faced prosecution for contempt of Congress, most of the Hollywood Ten were still optimistic that the courts would eventually uphold their First Amendment defense. Meanwhile, they were in limbo: the firings had rendered each of them unemployable for the duration of their court cases and perhaps well beyond. Some of the writers scratched together low-paying work under various pseudonyms. Dalton Trumbo, needing money to pay for improvements to his ranch house, asked to borrow ten thousand dollars from actor Edward G. Robinson, the only millionaire friend he had. Robinson said he could only lend him five thousand dollars, then gave him five one-thousand-dollar bills and refused to accept a promissory note or an IOU. He clearly wanted no printed evidence of his generosity.

The Ten appealed to the three artists' guilds for actors, writers, and directors to support their reinstatement and help pay for their legal defense, but the response was tepid at best. In each case, the guilds were more concerned with protecting their currently employed members from future reprisals than with coming to the aid of the Ten.

None of the Ten was a member of the Screen Actors Guild, which was led by anti-Communists like Ronald Reagan and Robert Montgomery and was the least interested in aiding the accused.

Seven were screenplay writers; nonetheless, a solid majority of the Screen Writers Guild voted against a motion calling for their reinstatement and providing legal counsel for breach-of-contract lawsuits against the studios that had fired them. But the guild did vote to support amicus curiae briefs in those lawsuits and eventually in the Supreme Court case that the Ten pursued against their convictions.

After his successful and widely admired screenplays for *Champion* and *Home of the Brave*, Carl Foreman was elected to the guild's board for a two-year term in 1949 (and reelected in 1951). The only other leftist on the board was his former comrade Harold Buchman. Just like their fellow guilds for actors and directors, the screenwriters were under pressure to require all members to swear under oath that they were not members of the Communist Party nor of any organization advocating the overthrow of the government. The loyalty oath motion came up at a meeting on September 11, 1950. Carl felt the move would split the guild politically and saw it as just another means of singling out and harassing current or former Communist Party members. Leonard Spigelgass, Dore Schary's close friend and Carl's former commanding officer and guardian angel in the Army film unit, helped lead the anti-Communist purge. He pleaded with Carl not to oppose the motion. "It'll ruin you," he warned. "You're throwing your career away."

At first there was much opposition to the resolution, but as the night dragged on more and more people either went home or acquiesced. Previously the Communists had been the most adept at dragging out meetings, staying late, and outlasting their opponents, but no more. In the new age of anxiety and paranoia, the liberals on the board were determined to rid the guild of the dangerous label of being pro-Red. By midnight Carl found he was the last holdout. The others wanted a unanimous endorsement but he refused. He finally got Spigelgass to agree to a compromise: as required by the Taft-Hartley Act of 1947, all members of the board, including Carl himself, would sign the loyalty oath. But it would not be required of regular guild members. The resolution finally passed. Still, Carl's opposition marked him as a radical.

The liveliest and most public debate occurred within the Screen Directors Guild. The legendarily autocratic director Cecil B. DeMille, an archconservative and one of the earliest supporters of the Motion Picture Alliance for the Preservation of American Ideals, sought to require that all members of the guild sign a loyalty oath, and he managed to jam through an overwhelming vote in favor while the guild's liberal president, Joseph Mankiewicz, was in Europe on vacation. One of the prime reasons for DeMille's success was a requirement that each member sign his ballot—which left exposed anyone who opposed the loyalty oath. When Mankiewicz, upon returning home, objected to the measure, DeMille and his allies moved to impeach him.

Although he was a liberal, Fred Zinnemann was an Austrian émigré aiming for the top rank of Hollywood directors, and he was reluctant to become embroiled in political controversy. Nonetheless, he was so infuriated by the tactics used by the DeMille camp that he wrote an angry letter to the guild's executive board objecting to the signed ballot. "This is a coercive way of voting, adopted in all communistic and other dictatorships," Fred wrote. "In this fashion you have attempted to and succeeded in frightening a majority of the membership into voting for it. Need I point out the parallel with the 'free' elections in Russia and Nazi Germany?"

To DeMille's great surprise, Mankiewicz managed to rally a solid core of supporters. Key members of this group included William Wyler and George Stevens, two of Hollywood's most respected directors, professionally advised by Martin Gang, a liberal lawyer who was a leader of the Los Angeles Jewish community. Following a legal and political strategy devised largely by Gang, they managed to force a general meeting of the guild on October 22, 1950.

More than five hundred people crammed into the Crystal Room of the Beverly Hills Hotel on a Sunday evening for a sulfurous seven-hour debate. Mankiewicz's hour-long opening address, carefully crafted and rehearsed with the help of Gang, Wyler, and Stevens, was logical, passionate, and indignant. He wasn't opposed to the idea of a loyalty oath, he told the meeting, nor was he defending the Communists, but he wanted any measure to be adopted by an open and democratic process, not a palace coup. DeMille, using the same melodramatic style he employed when directing his overheated Biblical epics, responded with a haughty and patronizing off-the-cuff address that accused his opponents of belonging to a long list of Communist front organizations, among which he included the Committee for the First Amendment, which Wyler had helped found. "Troubled waters attract strange specimens sometimes," DeMille added darkly. There was a gasp of disbelief, and then members of the audience did what no one had ever dared do on a DeMille film set: they hissed and booed until the great man sat down.

Rouben Mamoulian, the distinguished Russian-born director, rose to say that for the first time in America the fact that he spoke with a foreign accent made him feel afraid. Wyler told the meeting that he was sick and tired of having people question his loyalty to his country: "The next time I hear somebody do it, I'm going to kick the hell out of him. I don't care how old he his or how big."

Every Hollywood narrative needs a dramatically satisfying ending, and the legendary director John Ford—a self-described rock-ribbed Republican from the state of Maine (and member of the executive board of the Motion Picture Alliance)—rose after midnight to provide one by gently mocking DeMille and then calling for a vote of confidence in Mankiewicz. After a vote of unanimous support (with four abstentions), the seven-hour session ended at two twenty A.M.

This being Hollywood there was, of course, a sequel, one that allowed Mankiewicz to quietly surrender after having declared victory. Five days after the meeting, he sent out an open letter asking all of the guild's members to voluntarily sign the loyalty oath. The liberals had won—and then capitulated. It was a harbinger of the repressive times to come.

BY THE TIME OF the Screen Directors Guild vote, the Hollywood Ten were on their way to prison. On April 10, 1950, the Supreme Court had refused to hear their appeal by a vote of six to two. John Howard Lawson and Dalton Trumbo were the first to be convicted of contempt of Congress and sentenced to the maximum penalty: a year in prison and a thousand-dollar fine. "As far as I was concerned, it was a completely just verdict," Trumbo stated with trademark disdain in a documentary film twenty-five years later. "I had contempt for that Congress and have had contempt for several since."

Within months the rest of the Ten were serving similar sentences (two of them, Herbert Biberman and Edward Dmytryk, were only sentenced to six months each) at various federal prisons throughout the country. Ring Lardner Jr. and Lester Cole found themselves in the same Danbury, Connecticut, facility where former HUAC chairman J. Parnell Thomas was doing time for misappropriating government funds for his personal profit. "Hey, Bolshie!" Thomas, who worked in the chicken pen, yelled at Cole, who was cutting grass in the prison yard with a machete. "I see you still got your sickle. Where's your hammer?"

To which Cole replied, "And I see just like in Congress, you're still picking up chicken shit."

Back in the days when he was still presiding over the committee sitting atop an elevated cushion and phone directory, Thomas had pledged that the committee's special staff was making an extensive study into "Communist propaganda in various motion pictures and the techniques employed." That had never happened. The committee seemed much more interested in making fear-inducing headlines about the Communist threat than in producing genuine evidence or testing its own assumptions. But over the years conventional wisdom has held that Communists in fact had little impact on the content of Hollywood films. This was partly because they were predominately screenwriters in a studio system that treated writers as a necessary but inconsequential cog in the movie-making machinery. Politically conservative movie producers and their sharp-eyed studio bosses claimed to have weeded out anything that smacked of leftist ideology.

It was also because party leaders generally warned their members against trying to front-load ideology into the movies they wrote. Screenwriter Richard J. Collins, one of the veteran Communists who later turned informer, testified that party chairman Earl Browder had warned against putting more than "a drop" of Communist belief in a film. It might be possible at times, Collins testified, for Communist screenwriters to work at the margins to eliminate glaring racial and ethnic stereotypes of the subservient Negro, dim-witted Italian, or red-nosed drunken Irishman. But that was all.

The one serious and methodical report of the issue supported the conventional wisdom. Researcher Dorothy B. Jones, who did a year-long study for the nonpartisan Fund for the Republic of films written or produced by members of the Hollywood Ten at four major studios, concluded that while some screenwriters made attempts to influence movie content to favor the Communist Party and the Soviet Union, they generally failed. "The very nature of the filmmaking process, which divides creative responsibility among a number of different people and which keeps ultimate control in the hands of top studio executives; the habitual caution of moviemakers . . . and the self-regulating practices of the motion-picture industry . . . prevented such propaganda from reaching the screen in all but possibly rare instances," wrote Jones.

The films of the Hollywood Ten "were, in the main, routine Hollywood fare which followed time-worn patterns of content," she concluded.

But Collins's and Jones's honest assessments, and the conventional wisdom as a whole, missed the larger point. While the movies generally did not serve as blatant propaganda vehicles, a small but significant number of films did contain a compelling left-wing critique of American society. Some of them were written or directed by Communist Party members, while others were the product of liberals and progressives who shared parts of the party's critique of American society but not its allegiance to Moscow. "There was no plot to put social content into pictures," said screenwriter and director Abraham Polonsky, one of Hollywood's most thoughtful and respected Marxists. But "social content comes from a general philosophical attitude toward society— that's what counts."

Before the war, movies like *The General Died at Dawn* (1936), written by Communist Party member Clifford Odets (and starring Gary Cooper); *Blockade* (1938), a film about the Spanish Civil War written by Hollywood party leader John Howard Lawson ("Where's the conscience of the world?" demands the hero, played by Henry Fonda); and *The Man I Married* (1940), an anti-Nazi film directed by Irving Pichel, a nonparty left-winger who was later blacklisted, all reflected the views of the people who helped create them.

But perhaps the two most radical films ever released by a mainstream studio were made mostly by liberals. *Mr. Smith Goes to Washington* (1939) was a collaboration between director Frank Capra, an anti-Communist populist, and screenwriter Sidney Buchman, a Communist Party member. Capra was known for his populist films—most notably *Mr. Deeds Goes to Town* and *Meet John Doe*, both starring Gary Cooper— but *Mr. Smith* challenged the integrity of one of America's most hallowed institutions, the U.S. Senate, depicting capitalist corruption as its animating principle. It caused howls of outrage from real-life politicians, including Joseph P. Kennedy, then ambassador to Britain. The father of future president John F. Kennedy offered to pay two million dollars to Columbia Pictures to buy up the film's negatives in order to destroy them (the offer was refused). *The Grapes of Wrath* (1940), directed for Twentieth Century-Fox by John Ford, a registered Republican albeit with socialist tendencies, from Nunnally Johnson's screenplay of the John Steinbeck novel, depicted working-class migrant workers being harassed by parasitic bankers in Oklahoma and predatory commercial farmers in California. The Okies' sole ally is a preacher-turned-Communist agitator named Jim Casy, and the only place they find refuge is a government-run migrant labor camp.

World War Two was the heyday of cooperation between left and right in the effort to defeat Fascism. Beyond the films supported by the Roosevelt administration that were clearly designed to promote cooperation with the Soviet Union (*Mission to Moscow, Song of Russia,* and *The North Star*), many others celebrated class solidarity, racial equality, and collective action, including *Woman of the Year* (1942), *Tender Comrade* (1943), and *Pride of the Marines* (1945) and dozens of others in which mainstream and Communist culture joined forces. Even MGM's musicals—one of the purest pop products of American film studio capitalism—acquired a pinkish political tinge in *Thousands Cheer* (1943), co-written by party members Paul Jarrico and Richard Collins, which climaxes with an international chorus singing *"Make way for the day called tomorrow, make way for the world that is new!"*

Similarly, after the war, there were politically meaningful movies like *The Boy with the Green Hair* (1948), directed by Joseph Losey and written by Ben Barzman and Alfred Lewis Levitt, all of them current or past Communist Party members (and produced at RKO by the anti-Communist liberal Dore Schary); *All the King's Men* (1949), written and directed by former party member Robert Rossen; and *The Best Years of Our Lives* (1946), written by Robert E. Sherwood and directed by William Wyler, both of them liberals. Abe Polonsky's *Body and Soul* (1948), directed by Rossen and written by Polonsky, and *Force of Evil* (1948), which Polonsky wrote and directed, both contained powerful critiques of capitalism (and both starred leftist icon John Garfield). Those films, along with *The Asphalt Jungle* (1950), written by party member Ben Maddow and starring ex–party member (and later informer) Sterling Hayden, were tougher and more radical than almost anything that had come before. So were Carl Foreman's *Champion, Home of the Brave,* and *The Men.* "As time went on," said Polonsky, "the films were more explicit about what they believed."

These were the kind of politically muscular films that the Motion Picture Alliance and its allies in the American Legion, the Daughters of the American Revolution, the FBI, and the House Un-American Activities Committee saw as evidence of disloyalty and subversion. They were determined to stamp them out.

The ever-vigilant, ever-dour Ayn Rand composed a long list of "Don'ts" that the alliance published in a twelve-page pamphlet entitled "Screen Guide for Americans." Rand's manifesto claims at the outset that the influence of Communists in Hollywood isn't due to their own power, but to "the unthinking carelessness" of their opponents. "Red propaganda has been put over in some films produced by innocent men, often by loyal Americans who deplore the spread of Communism throughout the world and wonder why it is spreading," she writes. The Communist purpose "is to corrupt our moral premises by corrupting non-political movies . . . by indirection and implication."

Famous for championing a narcissistic brand of libertarianism, Rand insists her guide should not be used as an industry code of conduct; "each man has to do his own thinking," she contends. But for those who find independent thinking too taxing, she offers thirteen handy rules to follow, including: "Don't Smear the Free Enterprise System," "Don't Smear Industrialists, Wealth, the Profit Motive, Success, or American Political Institutions," and "Don't Glorify Depravity."

"Don't tell people that man is a helpless, twisted, drooling, sniveling, neurotic weakling . . . Show the world an *American* kind of man, for a change." And Rand adds her own pet peeve: "Don't ever use any lines about 'the common man' or 'the little people.' It is not the American idea to be either 'common' or 'little.'"

Rand concludes with a chilling warning that presages the rise of the blacklist and the purge from the ranks of Hollywood of anyone associated with the Communist Party. Americans believe in free speech, she warns, but that doesn't mean "we owe them jobs and support to advocate our own destruction at our own expense . . . It does not require employers to be suckers."

"Freedom of speech does not imply that it is our duty to provide a knife for the murderer who wants to cut our throat."

William Wyler told Lillian Ross of the *New Yorker* that he was convinced that in the current climate he would not have been allowed to make *The Best Years of Our Live*s, which depicts bankers as cheerfully heartless people who refuse to lend money to deserving war veterans, nor would Hollywood be able to make *The Grapes of Wrath* or *Crossfire*.

"People got scared," Wyler told journalist Elizabeth Poe in an unpublished interview. "The pressure groups, the Motion Picture Alliance, scared the hell out of everybody. All our heads were going to be on a chopping block . . . It was very easy to work yourself out of this business by saying what was on your mind."

Ross quoted an unnamed studio executive who told her, "I now read scripts through the eyes of the DAR [the Daughters of the American Revolution], whereas formerly I read them through the eyes of my boss . . . I'm all loused up. I'm scared to death and nobody can tell me it isn't because I'm afraid of being investigated."

By now the studios were in a self-protective frenzy. The *New York Times* reported on September 13, 1950, that Monogram Studios had shelved a film project on the life of Hiawatha, the fifteenth-century Onandaga Indian chief who was the subject of Longfellow's classic poem. The reason: Monogram feared that Hiawatha's efforts as a peacemaker among warring Indian tribes "might cause the picture to be regarded as a message for peace and therefore helpful to present Communist designs."

That same day it reported the shelving of Hiawatha, the *Times* also reported that the Senate had passed by 70 to 7 a bill to require registration of Communist organizations and fronts, establish a Subversive Activities Control Board, and permit the summary interning of suspected subversives in case of war or insurrection. President Truman would veto the bill, calling it "the greatest danger to freedom of speech, press, and assembly since the Alien and Sedition Law of 1798," but Congress would override the veto.

Like most Western democracies facing what its leaders perceived to be an existential threat, Americans were generally in no mood to respect the civil liberties of those they perceived to be internal enemies. "The nation was ready for witch-hunts," writes author David Halberstam.

Despite the threats, the truth was that so far only ten film people had been imprisoned. But hundreds of others were feeling the heat. Everyone knew that Hollywood was vulnerable both for economic and political reasons. While some of its feistier leaders had openly defied the committee in 1947, by 1951 the Hollywood establishment was supine. "Actually, with the firing of 'The Ten,' Hollywood created for itself a monster that was to grow as gruesome as any that ever frightened the wits out of children at a horror matinee," wrote "X," a screenwriter whose insistence on anonymity was itself a sign of the anxious times, in *The Nation*. "Since that day, the film industry has been in a panicky retreat before every attack on civil liberties. It is now a hapless pushover for any witch-hunting outfit that seeks to collect blood or blackmail."

New victims were emerging. A leaked FBI report named actors Edward G. Robinson, Fredric March, John Garfield, Paul Muni, and Danny Kaye as celebrities who were furthering Communist aims. Robinson was a particularly juicy target. He had supported dozens of liberal and left-wing causes and had allowed his house to be used for a strategy meeting of the Hollywood Nineteen and their lawyers before their ill-fated trip to Washington to testify in 1947 (Robinson was not at home that night). Louis Budenz, a self-confessed Soviet spy who became an FBI informer, testified in executive session to the committee that Robinson was "an active cooperator with the Communists, under Communist discipline." Robinson met with FBI agents and made three appearances before HUAC in an attempt to refute the allegation. "My name has been besmirched and dragged through the mire by a lot of wicked, irresponsible people, by hearsay, gossip, innuendo, and unsubstantiated charges," he told the committee in an executive session in December 1950. He pleaded, "Either snap my neck or set me free. If you snap my neck I will still say I believe in America."

To co-opt the witch-hunters, Hollywood created its own mechanism for self-purification. The Motion Picture Industry Council was formed in 1948 by ten member groups that included representatives of the producers and the talent guilds. Its mandate was to promote better public relations for the industry, which meant presenting a united front on the issue of combatting alleged Red influence in Hollywood. Dore Schary, a liberal, served as the first chairman, succeeded by Cecil B. DeMille, a conservative. Another key player was Ronald Reagan, head of the Screen Actors Guild. But the driving force behind the council was the moon-faced trade union boss and Red hunter Roy M. Brewer, whose influence seemed to be expanding weekly. Under Brewer's guidance, the council's main duties were to help the industry purge itself of "subversives," condemn HUAC witnesses who refused to cooperate, and serve as a rehabilitation service for people looking to get off the blacklist.

Hollywood's anxieties echoed those of the nation at large. American hegemony was under threat. The Soviet Union tested its first atomic bomb after obtaining some of the key technology to build it from spies working inside the heart of the American defense establishment, thus validating the House Un-American Activities Committee's most paranoid vision of a government and society riddled with Communist traitors. Two of them, Julius and Ethel Rosenberg, had been arrested in the summer of 1950 on charges they had helped pass atomic secrets to Moscow. HUAC member Richard Nixon had rooted out the purported betrayals of senior State Department official Alger Hiss, who was convicted in January 1950 of perjuring himself before the committee by denying he was a secret Communist agent and sentenced to five years in federal prison. Nixon had been elected U.S. senator from California (defeating Helen Gahagan Douglas, whom he smeared as a Communist sympathizer) largely on his reputation as a Red hunter, a role that would soon win him the vice presidency. China had fallen to Mao Zedong's Communist fighters and American forces were pinned down in Korea; the political right looked for scapegoats for both these catastrophes. Joseph McCarthy announced he had obtained a list of 205 Communists working in the State Department.

Cold War paranoia was reflected in the October 27, 1951, issue of *Collier's*, which dedicated the entire magazine to reporting an imagined version of World War Three, entitled "Preview of the War We Do Not Want." The magazine followed every detail of the conflict from the first surprise attack by the Soviets to the eventual occupation of Russia by American-led forces of the United Nations.

Collier's recruited some of the nation's best-known authors and journalists—including Edward R. Murrow, Robert Sherwood, Lowell Thomas, J. B. Priestley, Margaret Chase Smith, Philip Wylie, and Walter Winchell—to spin its atomic fantasies. The issue was overseen by talented features editor Cornelius Ryan (who later gained fame for *The Longest Day*, his factual account of the D-Day invasion). To increase the sense of reality, even the magazine's cartoons—some of them drawn by famed World War Two cartoonist Bill Mauldin—and many of its advertisements were geared to reflect the imaginary war.

The war begins with Communist cells throughout the Western world launching a campaign of sabotage and open attacks, such as the detonation of a bomb in New York's Grand Central Station. The United States and its allies launch a preemptive nuclear attack on strategic targets in the Soviet Union. The Russians retaliate by dropping atomic bombs on civilian populations in London, New York, Washington, Los Angeles, Detroit, and Philadelphia. "Washington is burning to death," writes Associated Press columnist Hal Boyle. "Uncounted thousands are dead . . . For a radius of a mile from the center of the blast, the devastation is utter—a huge scorched zero as if a giant white-hot hammer had pounded the area into the earth . . . The dome of the Capitol itself is a great white shattered teacup."

Moscow is A-bombed in retaliation. The regime collapses, United Nations forces occupy the shattered Soviet Union, Stalin is assassinated, and Russia returns to Christianity and democratic rule. But not before untold millions are killed on both sides.

The *Collier's* issue both reflected and contributed to the paranoid vision of Communists as destructive, even suicidal, automatons, willing to sacrifice themselves and everyone else for their evil cause. So did the testimony of infiltrators and defectors from the party who portrayed Communists as godless, brainwashed cadres who loved no one and nothing but their heartless cause. "Where Communism is concerned, there is no one who can be trusted," warned Herbert A. Philbrick, who infiltrated the American Communist Party in the 1940s for the FBI. "Anyone can be a Communist. Anyone can suddenly appear in a meeting as a Communist party member—close friend, brother, employee or even employer, leading citizen, trusted public servant."

Communists were incapable of love or normal human emotions. "You have to forget you have a family," said Elizabeth Bentley, an American spy for the Soviet Union who defected and became an FBI informant. "We are forbidden to form close friendships and, especially, to fall in love."

Communists were disturbed and twisted individuals—misfits, neurotics, bad girls, homosexuals—who insinuated themselves into our most cherished institutions. Whereas previous generations of rightists had detected treasonous plots among foreign groups, historian Richard Hofstadter noted, the modern radical right found a more insidious conspiracy inside America's governing elite. The rise of modern media and America's global reach gave the plot against America a vast international theater for the fearful. In his landmark essay "The Paranoid Style in American Politics," Hofstadter listed three elements: a conspiracy to undermine American capitalism; a conspiracy of top government officials who had been infiltrated by Communists and were dominating and undermining American policy; and a network of Communist agents who had infected the schools, churches, and the press to subvert the country's fundamental values. "The paranoid spokesman sees the fate of conspiracy in apocalyptic terms—he traffics in the birth and death of whole worlds, whole political orders, whole systems of human values," wrote Hofstadter. "He is always manning the barricades of civilization."

The enemy, Hofstadter continued, was clearly delineated: "He is a perfect model of malice, a kind of amoral superman—sinister, ubiquitous, powerful, cruel, sensual, luxury-loving . . . he controls the press; he has unlimited funds; [and] he has a new secret for influencing the mind (brainwashing)." Hollywood, with its untamed sensuality and amorality, dominated by Jews and other outsiders, provided the perfect theater of the imagination for this paranoid vision.

The demonization of American Communists was so persuasive in part because there was an element of truth in the characterizations. As historian Ellen Schrecker points out, the most important element was the notion that the party was secretly run by Moscow. The party's connection to the worldwide Communist movement, which had been a source of strength and solidarity in the 1930s and during the war, was now a giant anvil chained to its neck. By 1951, the Hollywood party was a mere shell—down to fewer than one hundred members—battered both by its enemies and by the doubts of its own former adherents. Still, its opponents were not done.

Once again, Billy Wilkerson's *Hollywood Reporter* led the campaign to bring back HUAC to Hollywood. In January 1951 the trade paper's "Rambling Reporter" column reported "the grapevine has it that another commie infiltration of the studios has been ordered by the Soviet. Watch Out!" Later in the month, Wilkerson in his own column added that there were 568 people in the film industry "who have been mentioned as belonging to or connected in some way with front organizations; and some others who have been labeled out-and-out card-holding commies. Many of the 568 are innocent; others are guilty. All should be compelled to clear their names at the risk of losing employment until they do."

The studios were doing their best to rid themselves of Communist influence and cooperate with the Red hunters, according to Wilkerson. Still, he claimed that "a list of some 180 boys and girls, who felt it was brilliant to join all the 'causes' and march down the line with the commies, is now in all studio hands, with many of those in charge of assignments referring to the list before they make deals." For those who refused to cooperate, "we'd like to suggest that they had better find a new field for their bread and butter, because this industry will not furnish it any longer."

The committee, coming off Nixon's headlines-driven success in exposing and pursuing Alger Hiss, was at the height of its power. J. Parnell Thomas, the flamboyant chairman, had been exiled in disgrace, while the ardent anti-Semite John Rankin had been pushed out, and Nixon had departed for the Senate. The new chairman was Representative John S. Wood, a Georgia Democrat who was milder-mannered but no less of a conspiracy monger. His sidekick, Representative Francis E. Walter, a conservative Pennsylvania Democrat, was an unabashed xenophobe who loathed Reds and the foreign-born—and held them to be equivalent. Anyone who dared criticize the committee was himself guilty of subversion, as far as Wood was concerned. When the nonpartisan Fund for the Republic issued a critical report on blacklisting, Wood subpoenaed principal author John Cogley and accused him of publishing lies and half-truths. Nixon's seat had been taken over by Donald L. Jackson of California, an ex-newspaperman, who along with Harold H. Velde of Illinois, a former FBI agent, and Charles E. Potter of Michigan were long-winded, argumentative, and inclined to sanctimonious renunciations of subversives both real and imagined.

The House Un-American Activities Committee, having once tasted blood in Hollywood, was about to return for more.

LARRY PARKS, THE FIRST movie star to testify during the 1951 hearings, was called to the witness table in the Old House Office Building on March 21, the same day that Alger Hiss went to prison. Parks's starring role in *The Jolson Story* in 1946 had won him fame and an Academy Award nomination for best actor. Born in Kansas and raised in Illinois, he was the Midwest personified—soft-spoken, and thoughtful, tall and handsome, with wavy brown hair and a powerful physique—"I thought he was simply gorgeous," said his wife, actress Betty Garrett, recalling when she first met him. He was also a former Communist who had quit the party in the mid-1940s around the time his career took off. His best friend was Lloyd Bridges, another rising young star who had also been a party member. Even after leaving the party, Parks was still active in left-wing causes. He remained on the board of the Actors' Laboratory Theatre, identified as a Communist front organization by the Tenney Committee—the Joint Fact-Finding Committee on Un-American Activities in Sacramento—and had supported Progressive Party candidate Henry Wallace in the 1948 presidential campaign. But perhaps Parks's worst transgression was that he had openly campaigned against the House Un-American Activities Committee after it had exposed and pursued the Hollywood Ten. Parks himself had been one of the nineteen potentially "unfriendly" witnesses subpoenaed to appear during the 1947 hearings but had not been called to the stand once the committee decided to fold its tent early after confronting the first ten witnesses.

The Ten, operating by consensus, had refused to admit they were Communist Party members and cited their First Amendment right of free political association. Now all of them were in prison for up to a year. Parks and his lawyer decided to opt for a different approach: he would admit his former party membership, answer all of the committee's questions, and avoid the confrontational rhetoric of the Ten. After all, Parks had done nothing wrong or illegal. He had joined the party out of a sense of idealism and had left after he decided it was not living up to his principles. But he would try to avoid naming others who had been members. All of them had been good, patriotic Americans, Parks believed, and he did not want to harm any of them or cost them their jobs.

It seemed like a reasonable strategy, but it quickly backfired. Under hostile interrogation from committee counsel Frank S. Tavenner, Parks politely insisted, "I feel I have done nothing wrong ever" in joining the Communist Party. He had undergone no huge awakening nor disillusionment with the party. "I drifted away from it the same way . . . I drifted into it," he testified. But when Tavenner pressed him for the names of fellow party members, Parks bristled. "This is my honest opinion: that these are people who did nothing wrong, people like myself," he replied.

Parks, who chain-smoked his way through two hours of testimony that morning, didn't realize that he and the committee were essentially speaking two different languages. What he saw as a matter of political choices made by responsible citizens in a democracy, they saw as an epic battle between good and evil.

Representative Charles Potter pressed him. "If you had knowledge of a man who committed murder, certainly you wouldn't be hesitant to give that information to the proper authorities?" Potter demanded. So what about those "believed to be working to overthrow our government by force and violence?"

Not everyone on the committee agreed. Francis Walter sought to intervene on Parks's behalf. "How can it be material to the purpose of this inquiry to have the names of people when we already know them?" he asked Tavenner. ". . . Isn't it far more important to learn the extent of the activity, and what the purpose of the organization actually was, than to get a long list of names of bleeding hearts, and fools, suckers, hard-boiled Communist politicians?"

Tavenner wasn't buying. "This committee ought to be entitled to receive proof of information which it has in its files," he insisted. In seeking to cooperate by talking about his own participation, he said, Parks had waived his legal right to refuse to talk about others.

When Parks resumed testifying after a lunch break, he cited his Revolutionary War ancestors and talked about the legacy he wanted to leave his two young sons. Referring to the committee's demand that he name names, he asked, "Is this the kind of heritage that I must hand down to them?"

Betty Garrett later said this was the point where her husband dropped the pretense of cooperation and began speaking from the heart. He knew he would pay dearly for it. "I think my career has been ruined because of this," he told the panel.

Then he pleaded once more. "Don't present me with the choice of either being in contempt of this committee and going to jail, or forcing me to really crawl through the mud to be an informer."

The committee was unmoved. Representative Donald J. Jackson told Parks that the panel was an expression of the people's will and had the duty to probe into "the great damage [that] occurred when you became a member of an organization which has been found to advocate the overthrow of every constitutional form of government in the world."

Parks was dismissed but ordered to appear in an executive session later that afternoon. Meanwhile, the committee called Howard Da Silva and Gale Sondergaard (whose husband, Herbert J. Biberman, was one of the Ten), two actors who adopted the defiant posture of the Hollywood Ten but with one crucial difference: rather than invoking First Amendment protection of free speech and political association for not answering the committee's questions, they cited the Fifth Amendment's shield against self-incrimination. This protected them against a contempt of Congress accusation, but virtually guaranteed they would be blacklisted under the Waldorf Statement. To reiterate the point just before the 1951 hearings began, Joyce O'Hara, acting president of the Motion Picture Association of America, announced that those witnesses who did not firmly deny any association with Communist or Communist-front organizations would find it difficult to get jobs in the future.

Da Silva and Sondergaard each appeared on the stand for fewer than fifteen minutes. Neither of them worked again for years. Da Silva even found himself erased after the fact; producer Irving Allen announced that Da Silva's scenes as a U.S. Cavalry officer were being deleted from the RKO picture *Slaughter Trail* and refilmed with Brian Donlevy taking his place, at a cost to the studio of one hundred thousand dollars.

After disposing of Da Silva and Sondergaard, the committee moved into executive session. Behind closed doors, Chairman Wood made clear that if Parks refused to answer the committee's questions, he would be cited for contempt. At that point, Parks realized he had exhausted all his options. He could either name names or go to jail. He didn't mince words. "I tell you frankly that I am probably the completest ruined man that you have seen . . . I don't think that this is fair play. I don't think it is in the spirit of real Americanism."

Finally Larry Parks surrendered. He named a dozen people.

When it was over, Representative Walter sought to ease the pain of Parks's betrayal. "I think you could get some comfort out of the fact that the people whose names have been mentioned have been subpoenaed, so that if they ever do appear here it won't be as a result of anything that you have testified to."

Agonizingly honest to the end, Larry Parks replied, "It is no comfort whatsoever."

But his ordeal was far from over. The next evening, the Motion Picture Alliance held its annual meeting at the Hollywood American Legion Auditorium. The alliance was riding high and more than a thousand people attended. John Wayne, its president, expressed sympathy for Parks. "When any member of the Party breaks with them, we must welcome him back into American society," said Wayne. "We should give him friendship and help him find work again in our industry."

Guest speaker Victor Riesel, a fire-eating syndicated columnist, showed no such mercy. "The hell with Parks," he declared. "He didn't tell us anything we didn't know."

Fellow columnist Hedda Hopper stood up and excoriated Wayne. While she said she had sympathy for anyone who had seen the light, she claimed that Parks and Garrett had refused to cooperate with the FBI when an agent had visited their home four years earlier. "This man was practically thrown out of their house," she said.

Hopper claimed she was speaking for the mothers of the 55,000 American casualties who had fought Communism in Korea. "Why so much emphasis on one career?" she demanded. "I, for one, believe that the life of one soldier fighting for our freedom is worth more than all the careers in all of Hollywood . . . I'm wondering if the mothers and families of those who've died and the wounded who are still living will be happy to know their money at the box office has supported and may continue to support those who have been so late in the defense of our country."

After Hopper sat down, a chastened Wayne rose to apologize for expressing sympathy for Parks. "We do not want to associate with traitors," conceded Wayne. He suggested that he and Hopper get together and issue a joint statement about what should happen to Parks.

That same day, an unnamed source associated with the committee leaked to reporters that Parks had named "more than twelve Hollywood personages" in his executive session. "Several of those named by Parks in secret testimony Wednesday as one-time Reds are 'big names' in the entertainment world," the source claimed.

Because of his misguided attempt to be honest and honorable in a world that respected neither, Parks was now effectively a traitor to both sides: he had named names, which made him anathema to his former comrades on the left; but he had done so painfully and reluctantly, which rendered him useless to the right. Instead, he was made an object lesson. Columbia Pictures canceled his next starring role—"by mutual consent," the studio announced—effectively ending his movie career; he was largely confined to performing on the dinner theater circuit for the rest of his life. He and his wife were shunned by many of their former friends. Betty Garrett was even kicked off a committee organizing a charity luncheon for the Motion Picture Home.

"By going first Larry had shown what the rules were now, and what the price was for being honest," she recalled. Parks died of a heart attack at age sixty.

Carl Foreman, reading accounts of Parks's teary-eyed appearance, was stunned. "Carl said it was one of the worst things he ever saw," recalls Eve Williams-Jones, Carl's second wife and widow. "He said it was heartbreaking. They crucified Parks."

It was not just that Carl felt enormous sympathy for Larry Parks; he feared the day could be coming soon when he too would face the pitchforks of the committee and its supporters.

ONE OF THOSE WHO watched Larry Parks's ordeal most closely was Sterling Hayden, a rising young actor who was due to testify three weeks later. Whatever doubts Hayden had had about cooperating with the committee quickly vanished, and he realized he had only one hope if he wanted to save his promising new career: give the committee everything it demanded.

A decorated Marine Corps veteran who had done intelligence work in Yugoslavia during the war, Hayden, who had just turned thirty-five, was tall, handsome, and rangy, with rugged blond looks in a Scandinavian face with just enough lines around the eyes to make him authentically beautiful. He prided himself on his two-fisted independence and smoldering contempt for Hollywood. He was in effect Gary Cooper with the rough edges intact. Cooper was by far the better actor, but Hayden was just getting started. But unlike Cooper, Hayden had joined the Communist Party for a brief spell after returning from the war, and his left-wing views were well known around town.

Hayden knew he needed help to navigate treacherous waters. He hired Martin Gang, one of Hollywood's most morally agile lawyers, to represent him.

In July 1950 Gang wrote a letter to J. Edgar Hoover pleading for a way to clear Hayden of his political sins. "In June of 1946 this young man, in a moment of emotional disturbance, became a bona fide member of the Communist Party," wrote Gang, who knew how to speak Hoover's language. Hayden had quit just five months later, Gang claimed, after "he decided that he had made a mistake." Hoover wrote back two weeks later that while no machinery existed to create clearances for former party members, Hayden should contact R. B. Hood, chief of the FBI's L.A. office at the Federal Building.

Gang escorted his client to the FBI office. "I feel like a bear led on a chain by the lawyer," Hayden recalls in his memoirs. Like Parks, Hayden pleaded with Hood not to have to name names. The bureau chief was frank. "I would . . . suggest that if you are going to cooperate with the Bureau, you do so to the fullest extent of your ability," he replied. And Hayden proceeded to spill everything and every name he knew.

A few months later, Hayden received a subpoena from the committee. After reading Parks's testimony, Hayden said he realized "they don't want information, they want to put on a show, and I'm the star . . . I'm damned no matter what I do. Cooperate and I'm a stool pigeon. Shut my mouth and I'm a pariah." But Hayden made a quick and remorseless calculation: better to be a working stool pigeon earning a movie star's pay than an unemployed pariah.

Gang and committee investigator William Wheeler prepared Hayden for his big day with nine pages of notes on index cards. He was told to take along his wife, who was "displayed like a service flag draped in a front window." Hayden also made sure to wear his combat ribbon in the left lapel of his brown tweed suit.

Tavenner opened the questioning and Hayden replied at length. Unlike Parks, he made no attempt to justify his actions—joining the Communist Party "was the stupidest, most ignorant thing I have ever done," he told the committee.

He had joined the party in 1946 and had left in disgust six months later. "Their fight for social justice was and is a sham, a mere façade to attract people like myself who had an honest and sincere desire to do something worthwhile," intoned Hayden, in language that sounded like it flowed direct from Martin Gang's pen. "Their boundless bigotry and their intolerance of opinions which differed from their own were revolting to me."

And unlike Parks, Hayden didn't hesitate to name the names of everyone he had met, including his ex-mistress, Bea Winters, a secretary at his agent's office who he said had recruited him to join the party.

At the end of the day, the committee and Hayden traded compliments. Chairman Walter praised his "courageous and forthright testimony," while Hayden praised the committee for the "tremendous service to be rendered, not only to the country at large but to the motion-picture industry."

Hayden concluded: "I urge upon everyone who might find himself in my position to come forward and get this thing off his chest. It is a big burden, believe me."

Privately, he knew better. He thought of Larry Parks, sitting in the same chair three weeks earlier, where he had "consigned himself to oblivion . . . Well, I hadn't made that mistake. Not by a goddamned sight. I was a real daddy longlegs of a worm when it came to crawling."

Three of the people Hayden named publicly as Communists faced immediate consequences. Winters was fired from her job as a secretary at Horizon Pictures, the Sam Spiegel-John Huston production company. Twentieth Century-Fox announced that screenwriter Abe Polonsky would be completing his last assignment that week; Polonsky didn't work again in Hollywood under his own name for nearly two decades. Neither did actress Karen Morley, whose contract with Columbia was terminated.

When Hayden got back to Hollywood, reporters at the airport asked him about Winters's firing. "That's the bad part of it," he conceded, but added that he had had to make up his mind about a proper course of action and that he had done so clearly. Other people paid the price.

Hayden resumed his golden film career, as well as his alcoholism and self-loathing, all of which he chronicled in self-lacerating detail in *Wanderer*, his bestselling 1963 memoir. All he had lost was his self-respect.

THE APPEARANCES OF PARKS, Sondergaard, Da Silva, and Hayden had laid out the rules of the game for the new round of hearings. As all four had learned, defiance was no longer an act just of bravery but of martyrdom. But acquiescence alone was also not sufficient. To achieve redemption, witnesses were required to go through a three-step process: acknowledge their prior left-wing activities with deep regret, praise the committee for its important and heroic work, and demonstrate the credibility of their transformation from Red to red-blooded American by disclosing the names of other subversives. The demand for names was no longer a quest for evidence, writes Victor Navasky; "it was a test of character. The naming of names had shifted from a means to an end."

The hearings blatantly violated the Constitution's separation of powers. Congress is supposed to make laws, not judge the innocence or guilt of those accused of violating them. But from the start, the committee saw its role as that of exposing Communist Party members and subjecting them to public humiliation and ostracism without the safeguards of a trial. While those called before the committee could take along a lawyer for legal advice, the accused was not allowed to call witnesses nor cross-examine "friendly" witnesses whom the committee called to testify against them. Virtually all of the accusations went untested and uncontested. The committee was judge, jury, and prosecutor. Which is why President Truman, despite his administration's own round of Red hunting among federal employees, declared that "the committee is more un-American than the activities it is investigating."

Throughout the spring and summer of 1951, a parade of witnesses—mostly screenwriters and actors—appeared before the committee. The biggest stars faced the biggest dilemma. They did not want to name names, but at the same time they couldn't afford to defy the committee outright.

John Garfield, whose birth name was Julius Garfinkel, was the most famous among them. A working-class kid from the Bronx, Garfield was perhaps Hollywood's most recognizably Jewish actor and certainly its biggest Jewish star, and he had long been active in a wide range of left-wing causes. His strategy before the committee was to plead innocence and feign ignorance. He could not recall signing any critical letters or supporting any subversive groups, nor had he ever knowingly met a single Communist, whether in New York or Hollywood. "My life is an open book," he told the committee. "I was glad to appear before you and talk with you. I am no Red. I am no 'pink.' I am no fellow traveler. I am a Democrat by politics, a liberal by inclination, and a loyal citizen of this country by every act of my life."

Garfield denounced Communism as subversive. He told Representative Jackson that if the Communist Party had ever approached him, "I would have run like hell." But Jackson said he simply did not believe him.

Garfield "did his best to make himself appear a simpleton, marvelously naïve about politics, who had helped support a variety of Communist fronts despite his firm hatred of Communism," wrote journalist Walter Goodman.

It didn't work. The *Daily Worker* denounced him for denouncing the party, while *New York Post* columnist Archer Winsten said flatly that no one could have lived in New York in the 1930s and not have known a single Communist, and *Variety* reported that the FBI had opened a file investigating Garfield's testimony at Jackson's urging.

José Ferrer, a longtime Patriotic Front supporter who had just won an Oscar for best actor for *Cyrano de Bergerac* (which was produced by Stanley Kramer and written by Carl Foreman), "came on like a penitent fox that had just renounced its appetite for fowl," wrote cultural historian Stefan Kanfer. Before he testified, Ferrer took out a full-page ad in the *Hollywood Reporter* saying he would swear under oath "that I am not, have never been, could not be a member of the Communist Party; nor, specifically am I a sympathizer with any Communist aim, a fellow traveler, or in any way an encourager of any Communist Party concept or objective." Ferrer praised the committee for its stellar work, hastily retracting his previous opinion that it should be abolished.

"When did you change your mind on that score?" asked an incredulous Representative Bernard Kearney.

"Well, today, among other things," Ferrer replied. It was the one truthful answer he dared give.

The committee did not even pause before crashing the privacy of the marriage bed. In its executive session with Ferrer, Tavenner asked if he had at one time been married to the actress Uta Hagen. When Ferrer said yes, Tavenner asked, "Is Uta Hagen a member of the Communist Party?"

Ferrer restrained himself from denouncing the shamefulness of the inquiry. "Not that I know of," was his terse reply.

Ferrer, Garfield, and fellow actor Edward G. Robinson all played the same sorrowful tune. They were loyal Americans, good Democrats, haters of Communism, and any donations they might have given to causes favored by Communists were made out of idealism and naïveté. They had been duped by evil people and they were sorry. But since they hadn't actually belonged to the party, they couldn't name any names— they simply didn't know who was a Communist and who wasn't.

The panel treated each of them with haughty skepticism. Afterward, Ferrer and Robinson continued to work as actors, although Robinson found his opportunities sorely curtailed. Garfield, however, never worked again in Hollywood. He returned home to New York, where he was able to find roles on the stage but for very limited money. He was already suffering from a congenital heart condition and a serious drinking problem, and his health rapidly deteriorated. He soon decided he had no choice but to give the committee what it wanted: repentance and names. He consulted with Roy Brewer and columnists George Sokolsky and Victor Riesel, three of the guardians of self-purification. With the help of Arnold Forster, an old high school friend who had become director of the Anti-Defamation League of B'nai B'rith, Garfield wrote a piece for publication in *Look* magazine to be entitled "I Was a Sucker for a Left Hook." But before it could be published, a physically and emotionally exhausted Garfield fell asleep at a woman friend's apartment one evening and never woke up. He was thirty-nine. Canada Lee, his African American co-star in *Body and Soul*, who was also blacklisted, died two weeks earlier at forty-five.

HUAC WAS A MIGHTY sword in the spring and fall of 1951, slashing its way through the ranks of purported Communists and their sympathizers. It accused those who invoked their Fifth Amendment right against self-incrimination of cynically hiding behind constitutional protections. When director Michael Gordon cited the Fifth, Representative Walter demanded, "I am just wondering whether or not you aren't arbitrarily hiding behind the section of the Constitution of the United States that does not appear in the constitution of Russia or any of the iron-curtain countries."

When Hollywood dentist Michael Schoen refused to answer questions, Representative Clyde Doyle became righteously enraged: "I am a much older man than you are, Doctor, and I just want to say to you that I pray to God that you get on your knees and see if you can't clean up some of your thinking and be rid of this subversive outfit and get over to the American one."

Schoen suggested the committee would do better to expose truly un-American activities by investigating race riots and attacks on black people in the South. "I say, Doctor, that you are a very ungrateful person and a very dangerous man," Representative Potter replied.

The press played a critical role in helping the committee conduct its undue process. Partisan cheerleaders like Billy Wilkerson and Hedda Hopper had invited the committee back to town and rooted from the sidelines, but the supposedly more objective mainstream press was also a key ally. The committee arranged the venues and scripts of its hearings for maximum news coverage. Its staff steered testimony to produce bombshells or breakthroughs during the morning session in time to create a good headline for the afternoon press, then something later in the day for the next morning's papers.

The daily press tended to report these newsworthy developments uncritically. The allegations of "friendly witnesses" like Sterling Hayden were repeated without question or rebuttal. Those who were named as Communists were not contacted by reporters and given the opportunity to respond. There were virtually no articles that questioned the committee's methods. The committee provided a libel-proof forum for accusations of subversion against named individuals who were not permitted to cross-examine their accusers. "The press does not merely mirror or report the hearing; it is an indispensable part of it—like a loudspeaker on a high-fidelity sound system," wrote HUAC critic Frank J. Donner.

Alan Barth, editorial page editor of the *Washington Post*, was one of the few mainstream journalists to object to this perversion of the press's role of government watchdog. "The tradition of objectivity . . . has operated in this context to make the press an instrument of those seeking to inflict punishment by publicity," he wrote. "Allegations that would otherwise be ignored . . . as groundless and libelous are blown up on front pages and given a significance out of all relation to their intrinsic merit after they have been made before a committee of Congress."

The only way an accused person could attempt to refute the allegations was to petition to appear before the committee. Those who sought to do so—like Robinson and Ferrer—had to humble themselves. As Barth put it, "It was much as though an innocent pedestrian spattered with mud by a passing vehicle were expected to thank the driver for permitting him to wipe the mud off his face and clothes."

When the press did weigh in with a longer, non-deadline enterprise piece, it often adopted the fevered tone and reasoning of the committee. The headline for a feature by investigative reporter Seymour Korman that was distributed nationwide by the *Chicago Tribune*'s news service declared POLITICALLY INFANTILE FILM FOLK WERE EASY MARKS FOR REDS. "Why in this glittering capital of the movie industry have some of the most talented and highest paid actors, producers, directors, and writers joined or espoused a party and philosophy openly dedicated to strip them of their gold and glamor in the course of destroying America?" Korman asked. After studying the proceedings of the committee and interviewing some of those involved, Korman came up with four reasons: that the Communist Party had sent some of its "biggest guns" to Hollywood to recruit newcomers; that the town was filled with "misguided idealists and self-styled liberals" who were easy targets; that the "movie colony dupes of the Reds were incredibly stupid or gullible"; and that the studio heads had been negligent in failing to clean house "despite oft-repeated warnings." Korman cited unsourced "estimates" that Communists and fellow travelers "have poured more than 12 million dollars into the Red coffers."

The few journalists who wrote critically of the Red Scare eventually faced their own day of reckoning. Elizabeth Poe Kerby, who wrote an exposé of the blacklist for *Frontier*, a small, liberal, California-based magazine, and later became a researcher for the Fund for the Republic's detailed study, was accused by "friendly" HUAC witnesses of being a Communist sympathizer. Mississippi senator James Eastland's internal security subcommittee held closed-door hearings on "Communist Party Influence in the Press," sending thirty of its thirty-eight subpoenas to current or former staff members at the *New York Times*, whose editorials criticized both the blacklist and racist Jim Crow practices in the South. The *Times* issued a ringing editorial defending its right to challenge government policies, but it also pledged to rid itself of anyone who was found to be a Communist Party member, and three employees who took the Fifth Amendment before Eastland's subcommittee were fired or forced to resign.

Bert Andrews of the *New York Herald Tribune*, the city's other great daily, won the Pulitzer Prize for National Affairs Reporting in 1948 for his stories about ten State Department employees who were fired after false allegations of disloyalty. But Andrews later became an unofficial advisor to Representative Richard M. Nixon during his pursuit of Alger Hiss, and the *Tribune*, fed by Nixon, led the pack in breaking stories about his investigation into Hiss's alleged Soviet sympathies. The *Tribune* went on to publish "The Red Underground," a regular weekly column of unsourced allegations of Communist sabotage and subversion, many of them supplied by the FBI.

DESPITE THE COMMITTEE'S BULLYING tactics, most of the witnesses refused to cave. In the first set of hearings from March to May 1951, twenty out of thirty who were called to appear refused to name names. Some were ongoing Communist Party members who were following party discipline, although their numbers in Hollywood had likely declined to fewer than one hundred people due to the crackdown and to disillusionment with Moscow. Others simply felt they could not violate their own consciences for the sake of a paycheck.

"People's names have been mentioned in this committee," testified Hollywood agent George Willner. "I have noticed the following day they have lost their jobs. They have been guilty until proven innocent."

"Is that due to the fact that the names have been mentioned here or the company they keep?" asked Representative Kearney.

"I think it is probably due to the atmosphere in this hearing and the smell that comes from this hearing," replied Willner, who had already been fired from his job.

But those who did name names had enormous impact. Richard J. Collins, thirty-six, was one of the best-liked and most highly respected screenwriters in Hollywood, and co-writer of *Song of Russia* along with Paul Jarrico, a close friend and fellow Communist Party member. Collins was one of the original Nineteen whom the committee had subpoenaed in 1947, but he hadn't been called to the stand. Still, he had found no work in Hollywood afterward. Broke and disheartened, by 1950 he told the FBI he was ready to cooperate. When Collins appeared before the committee on April 12, 1951, he named twenty-three people, among them Robert Rossen, who had written and directed *All the King's Men,* which had won three Academy Awards in 1950, including best picture, and Budd Schulberg, author of *What Makes Sammy Run.* Collins also fingered a somewhat obscure screenwriter named Martin Berkeley. All three men had left the party years earlier, and Collins later said he had assumed wrongly that naming them would not damage their careers (all three eventually testified and named names themselves). Even worse in terms of personal betrayal, Collins named screenwriter Waldo Salt, at whose wedding Collins had been best man. Worse still: he named his ex-wife, actress Dorothy Comingore, whom Collins had recruited to join the party. Later, after she invoked the Fifth Amendment when called to testify, Collins successfully sued her for sole custody of their two children, claiming among other things that her radical politics rendered her an unfit mother.

Parks's and Hayden's testimonies were no great surprise to their former comrades—neither was a key figure in the party. But Collins's testimony was a shock. He had been an active party member since the late 1930s and had, by his own estimate, attended five thousand hours of meetings. "I could not conceive at all that Dick Collins had gone to the FBI and done that," Carl Foreman would recall. "He seemed to me to be a person of such great integrity."

Director Edward Dmytryk's turnabout was equally shocking because he had been a faithful member of the Hollywood Ten and had served four and a half months in prison without public complaint, even though he had quit the party several years earlier. But inwardly he was seething. He felt that he and the others among the Ten had served as sacrificial lambs, tricked by their Communist lawyers into using a legal strategy that was designed to get them declared in contempt of Congress. He was broke and had no way to support his wife, actress Jean Porter, who also was effectively blacklisted because of her husband, and their new baby.

Dmytryk's letters to Jean from prison indicate that although he was the one behind bars, her torment was worse than his. "Hey Baby!" he writes her in July 1950. "You're feeling kind of low, aren't you? Yeah, you've really had a time! I knew it would be tougher for you than for me, but I hoped you'd be able to stick it out somehow. I guess it's even tougher than I thought it would be." She and the baby were constantly ill with colds, but her main concern was about how she and Eddie would survive financially. He tries to reassure her, even suggests she try to borrow money from movie star Dick Powell, an old friend. "Darling, I don't know why you've gotten so panicky about my working when I get out," he tells her. "We'll get along fine."

But Dmytryk privately was just as worried as his wife. "I was the only director in the group," he recalled. "I couldn't sell my talent under the table . . . I had no place to hide."

Dmytryk and his non-Communist lawyer, Bartley Crum, searched for some means to expunge his name from the blacklist, but there was only one: "I had to purge myself. HUAC and the Hollywood right each had to have its pound of flesh, and neither would accept a compromise. They had an eye-for-an-eye attitude, and they weren't letting anyone off the hook."

When he testified on April 24, he gave them what they wanted. He told the committee he had changed his mind about cooperating because circumstances had changed since 1947: the Cold War was now raging and the Soviet Union was the enemy; U.S. troops were fighting Communist forces in the Korean War, which eventually claimed 37,000

"Easy does it, old boy," matinee idol Ronald Colman advised young Gary Cooper for his first feature film role in *The Winning of Barbara Worth* (1926).

The Good Life: Gary Cooper
and his elegant wife, Veronica,
boarding a yacht in 1936.
PHOTOFEST

An insouciant Hedda Hopper,
Hollywood's gossip column queen,
in one of her trademark hats.
"Gary Cooper has always talked very
freely with me," she told her readers,
which was mostly true. PHOTOFEST

The horn-rimmed glasses, the quizzical expression, the omnipresent cigarette—Carl Foreman in 1961.
COLUMBIA PICTURES/PHOTOFEST

"Audiences still want to see courageous motion pictures," said studio head Dore Schary, a fighting liberal and Carl's first champion. The photo appears on the book jacket for *Heyday*, Schary's 1979 autobiography.
PETER LEDERER/LITTLE BROWN

The Red hunters of HUAC in 1947—from left to right, Rep. Richard B. Vail, Chairman J. Parnell Thomas, Rep. John McDowell, chief investigator Robert E. Stripling, and a young and dedicated Rep. Richard M. Nixon.
ACME/LIBRARY OF CONGRESS PRINTS AND PHOTOGRAPHS DIVISION

Stripling and Thomas search a strip of Hollywood celluloid for signs of Communist influence.
ASSOCIATED PRESS/LIBRARY OF CONGRESS

"Oh boy, a spotlight!" exclaims matinee idol Robert Taylor as he rushes to testify before HUAC in 1947. *Washington Post* cartoonist Herblock was one of the committee's most stinging critics.
HERBLOCK FOUNDATION/LIBRARY OF CONGRESS

"Lights, Camera, Action": Gary Cooper (seated to the left) charms the press and the committee at HUAC's October 23, 1947, hearing.
ACME/LIBRARY OF CONGRESS

Cooper strikes three poses—bored, quizzical, and confident—as he deftly fouls off HUAC's softball questions in what was his most nuanced performance of 1947. PHOTOFEST

The star-studded Committee for the First Amendment gathers outside the Capitol to protest the HUAC inquisition. Front row, from the left: actors Marsha Hunt, Richard Conte, June Havoc, Humphrey Bogart, Lauren Bacall, Evelyn Keyes, Danny Kaye, and Jane Wyatt, with director John Huston in the back between Havoc and Bogart. PHOTOFEST

Seven of the Hollywood Ten in 1950 on their way to the federal courthouse in Washington, D.C., to face trial for contempt of Congress. From the left: Sam Ornitz, Ring Lardner Jr., Albert Maltz, Alvah Bessie, Lester Cole, Herbert Biberman, and Edward Dmytryk. All of the Ten would be convicted and serve prison time. ASSOCIATED PRESS/LIBRARY OF CONGRESS

Actor Larry Parks, "the completest ruined man that you have seen," testifies before HUAC, March 21, 1951. PHOTOFEST

Actor Sterling Hayden—"a real daddy longlegs of a worm," he later wrote—names names in April 1951. PHOTOFEST

Director Edward Dmytryk, who defied HUAC in 1947 and went to prison, cooperated four years later and escaped the blacklist.
ASSOCIATED PRESS/LIBRARY OF CONGRESS

Screenwriter Martin Berkeley in his young and handsome days, displaying his serious writer's uniform of t-shirt, pipe, wispy mustache, and thoughtful expression.
COURTESY OF BILL BERKELEY

WESTERN UNION

W. P. MARSHALL, PRESIDENT

The filing time shown in the date line on telegrams and day letters is STANDARD TIME at point of origin. Time of receipt is STANDARD TIME at point of destination

LA995:   13 AM 12 08

L.LLU329 PD=FY LOSANGELES CALIF 12 732P=

HON MR TAVENNER =

        COUNCIL HOUSE UNAMERICAN ACTIVITIES COMMITTEE
        CONGRESS OF US WASHDC=

I MARTIN BERKELY WHO WAS NAMED TODAY BY RICHARD COLLINS
BEFORE THE HOUSE UNAMERICAN ACTIVITIES COMMITTEE IN
WASHINGTON AS A QUOTE MEMBER OF THE COMMUNIST PARTY UNQUOTE
MAKE THE FOLLOWING STATEMENT QUOTE I HAVE READ TODAYS
DESPATCHES FROM WASHINGTON THAT A WITNESS APPEARING BEFORE
YOUR COMMITTEE RICHARD COLLINS HAS ACCUSED ME OF BEING A
COMMUNIST. I AM NOT NOW NOR HAVE I EVER BEEN A MEMBER OF
THE COMMUNIST PARTY NOT WILL I BECOME ONE, AND COLLINS IS
GUILTY OF PERJURY. I RESPECTFULLY URGE YOU TO ALLOW ME TO
COME TO WASHINGTON TO APPEAR BEFORE YOU TO LAY MY
ANTI=COMMUNIST POSITION BEFORE YOU IT IS WELL DOCUMENTED I
HAVE FOUGHT COMMUNISM CONSISTENTLY INSIDE MY GUILD AND OUT=
        MARTIN BERKELEY...

Martin Berkeley denies everything in a telegram to HUAC, April 12, 1951. Later he would deny his denial.
NATIONAL ARCHIVES

American lives; and American Communists had betrayed their country by stealing atomic secrets. "The Communist Party is conspiratorial, subversive, and even in certain cases treasonable," he testified.

He named twenty-six people.

It was simple, said Eddie Dmytryk: "I didn't want to be a martyr for a cause I didn't believe in."

9.

The Screenplay

Of course, the whole story behind the filming of High Noon *is a comedy of errors and omissions—and a frantic scamper for credit by everyone since the film achieved some success.*

STANLEY KRAMER

The Men failed at the box office; despite an incandescent performance, Marlon Brando would have to wait a little longer to become a big-time movie star. But Carl Foreman received his second Oscar nomination for screenwriting. He lost again—this time to Charles Brackett, Billy Wilder, and D. M. Marshman Jr. for *Sunset Boulevard*. Still, his string of personal successes led him to try to revive a project he'd first pushed two years earlier and still felt passionate about.

A United Nations representative had approached Screen Plays Inc. in 1948 seeking to interest Stanley and Carl in making a movie about the organization. Carl believed in the UN and wanted to help, but rather than turn out a propaganda film he started playing with the idea of setting it in the Old West in a town under threat from outside forces. At first he saw it as a hopeful parable about the new world order. But as the climate of fear began to take hold in Hollywood his vision began to darken. The HUAC hearings, the plight of the Hollywood Ten, the abject surrender by the big studios—all struck him as signs of moral and political collapse in a community he had once respected. "It was these events that made me think of a story about Hollywood under the political gun, as it were, and its reaction," he recalled. "The certain lines of defense were shortening, and people were falling away and the authorities—*our* authorities, the studio heads and the Eric Johnstons, who had been so brave at the beginning—were all changing their tune and people were more and more scared all the time."

At the same time, Carl had become intrigued with the concept of a story that would run in real time, like the recent Hitchcock thriller *Rope*—the clock ticking and the suspense building for ninety minutes as the plot unwound toward a final showdown between the lawman and the bad guys. He dashed off a short outline and called it *High Noon*, an appropriate title for a picture in which the clock would be a major factor.

To supplement his income, Carl occasionally did writing gigs for other production companies besides his own, and he was currently working on *The Clay Pigeon* (1949), a modest noir-style melodrama for RKO, which had recently been acquired by Howard Hughes. Richard Fleischer, Carl's buddy and close neighbor, was directing—it was Fleischer who had directed *So This Is New York*, the Kramer company's first picture—and they carpooled to the studio together every morning from their homes in the San Fernando Valley and back again in the evening. There was plenty of time to kill crossing the Hollywood Hills and the two men would discuss *High Noon*, working out some of the potential characters and plotlines. Fleischer liked the idea a lot and wanted to direct it but was too busy with other things.

Carl next discussed the idea with Stanley Kramer, who also expressed interest. But the two men got sidetracked on other films. They had finished *Champion*, their boxing movie starring Kirk Douglas, then launched immediately on the combat melodrama *Home of the Brave*. Stanley wanted to keep that movie's racial story matter secret, so he used the *High Noon* title as a cover on the screenplay and press announcements to disguise what they were doing. Still, Carl kept working on the real *High Noon* on the side.

A draft treatment, dated January 11, 1950, and crafted by Carl with Dick Fleischer's input, is entitled *High Noon: An Original Story by Carl Foreman*. It is set in the fictional frontier town of Hatfield. Marshal Will Tyler is turning in his badge two days after marrying his bride, Elizabeth, when the stationmaster arrives to inform him that Clyde Doyle, a convicted killer, has been released from prison and is arriving in an hour on the noon train. Doyle's two brothers are waiting for him at the station. When he gets there, they plan to kill Tyler.

During the next hour, Tyler discovers he will have to face the Doyles alone. The judge who sentenced Doyle to prison abruptly leaves town, one of Tyler's deputies resigns and the other is away on business, Elizabeth walks out on him after he refuses her plea to flee, and no one in the community answers his call for volunteers. As the minutes tick by, he makes out his will and sets off down a silent street to meet his fate—"the loneliest man in the world," as the draft puts it. The silence is broken by gunshots. Ten minutes later, the three Doyles lie dead while a wounded Tyler drops his badge and holster in the dirt, embraces Elizabeth, and rides with her out of town.

The draft, which runs slightly more than three pages, is just a rudimentary sketch of what *High Noon* would become. Yet it contains many of the themes and concepts of the final film: the head bad guy arriving on the noon train to meet his gang, the conflict between the marshal and his new bride, the abandonment of the lawman by the people he had counted on for support, the lonely walk down an empty street to a showdown against overwhelming odds, the references to time passing quickly. "There are no dissolves, fades, or other time lapses," Carl writes. "Everything that happens takes place as the actual minutes tick by."

But when Carl showed the treatment to friends and colleagues around the company, he discovered to his surprise and embarrassment that his *High Noon* story was not original. Art director Rudolph Sternad recalled reading a short story with a similar plot in *Collier's* or the *Saturday Evening Post*.

Indeed, "The Tin Star" by John W. Cunningham Jr. had run in *Collier's* in December 1947. As the story opens, Sheriff Doane, an aging widower with painful arthritis, is preparing for a showdown with four gunmen who are coming to town to kill him. One of his deputies quits out of cowardice, while the other, named Toby, promises to stand by him but plans to quit afterward. The job of sheriff is just too tough and unappreciated. Doane agrees. "You risk your life catching somebody," he says, "and the damned juries let them go so they can come back and shoot at you . . . It's a job for a dog, son."

Mayor Percy Mettrick shows up, seeking to pressure Doane into resigning rather than face the younger gunmen. "Who the hell do you think you are, Doane?" demands Mettrick, washing his hands of the matter. ". . . Whatever happens, don't be blaming me."

Doane rides off to the cemetery to pay his weekly visit to his wife's gravesite. "No, Cissie, I could have gone," he tells her. "But you know— it's my town."

Hearing shots, Doane races back to town to find one gunman dead and Toby wounded in the leg. Doane manages to shoot another gunman, but he can't hold the pistol after squeezing the trigger because of the pain.

Jordan and Colby, the two remaining killers, grab Toby and use him as a human shield. Doane manages to kill Colby by switching his gun to his left hand but takes a bullet in the neck from Jordan. The two men exchange shots; Doane is hit in the stomach and the knee while Jordan is shot in the chest. As a dying Jordan lifts his gun to shoot Toby, Doane throws himself across Toby's body and absorbs the final bullet.

As the story ends, Toby takes the dead sheriff's gun and his tin star, "holding the two things tightly, one in each hand, like a child with a broken toy."

"Get the doc," he tells Mettrick. "I've got a busted leg. And I've got a lot to do."

"The Tin Star" is a story about the demands of duty on men of honor, and about courage—when the moment of truth arrives, some men have it and some don't. It's also about the passing of the torch from one generation to the next. The plot details are a bit convoluted, but the characters are sharply drawn. And while many of the themes and plot details differ, its basic narrative thrust is uncomfortably similar to Carl's concept for *High Noon*. The reference to the clock and the train, the cowardly actions of the mayor and one of the deputies, the mechanics of the final shootout—all have echoes in the story Carl was starting to create. But with one important difference: "The Tin Star" concludes with an affirmation of the values of society, whereas *High Noon* ends with a ringing rejection.

Carl was chagrined to discover the overlaps between his story and Cunningham's. Perhaps he had read the story in 1947 and then forgotten all about it? He suggested to Stanley that they buy the film rights to the story just to be safe. But Stanley was immersed in planning for *Cyrano de Bergerac* and had lost interest in *High Noon*. Although Westerns usually did well at the box office, they were expensive to shoot and needed a big-time star, lots of action scenes, and Technicolor to guarantee success, all of which didn't appeal to some of the more pragmatic moneymen who counted on Stanley and his team to work quickly and cheaply. But Carl was determined to go ahead; he paid Cunningham eight hundred dollars out of his own pocket for the rights. He harbored the hope that he might be allowed to produce and direct *High Noon* himself under the Kramer company trademark. It was, after all, his baby. After completing the screenplays for *The Men* and *Cyrano*, he started to work on it.

*   *   *

BY THE TIME CARL finished a more detailed, fifteen-page treatment in January 1951, circumstances had changed dramatically for him and the Kramer company. Stanley had formed his new enterprise and was about to sign the deal with Columbia Pictures. It would require the company to deliver six pictures per year over a five-year period—an enormous undertaking for a company that had only made five pictures in its four-year existence. Stanley, George Glass, and Sam Katz immediately turned their attention to acquiring properties, hiring talent, and hammering out a production schedule for the first year. Stanley told Carl he would have to forgo directing *High Noon* or any other picture for the foreseeable future. The company needed him working full-time cranking out scripts and helping produce the movies that resulted.

There was, however, one unfinished piece of business that Stanley needed Carl's help with. The company owed United Artists one more film under its original distribution contract and *High Noon* was the obvious candidate. Carl could finish writing it and he could produce it as well. The film would be branded a Stanley Kramer production, but Carl would be credited as associate producer and he would have a larger role than in the past in overseeing the making of the movie.

At around the same time, Fred Zinnemann returned to Hollywood after filming *Teresa*, the story of an Italian war bride and her GI husband, in Italy and New York. He was thrilled when he read the detailed *High Noon* outline and listened to Carl talk about the project. "I thought it was nothing short of a masterpiece—brilliant, exciting, and novel in its approach," Fred would recall. "I could hardly wait to come to grips with it." Carl's heart sank; he realized he would have to shelve his hope of directing the picture himself and turn it over to his more experienced colleague. Still, Carl liked and trusted Fred, had enjoyed their partnership on *The Men*, and was more than willing to collaborate with him again. *High Noon* moved forward.

Neither man seemed fazed by the fact that they had never made a Western before. "I had grown up with the Western," Carl would recall. "It turned out there was very little research to be done." He was wary of the obvious limitations and "encrusted clichés" of the Western, and he was not interested in cattle drives or stunning vistas or multiple gunfights. "I was simply tired of endless cattle stampedes and I wanted to present human rather than purely pictorial values," Carl recalled.

Still, he had a genuine appreciation for the classic values of the old-fashioned Western, especially those of his silent-movie idol William S.

Hart, whose Western characters always kept their word. It's clear that Carl was thinking of Hart as he started to sketch out his own heroic lawman for *High Noon*. "His films were remarkably authentic, and psychologically accurate," Carl later wrote. "More, in their lean simplicity, their unadorned concern with basic motives and passions, and their direct thrust to an inevitable conclusion, they bore a strong relationship to the Greek classics, and more often than not, like them they ended in tragedy."

Both he and Fred also had huge respect for John Ford, the American cinema's most honored director and a visual poet of the American West. Carl's new script in many ways followed the path first blazed by Ford's classic Western *Stagecoach* (1939). At its heart, *Stagecoach* was a social drama, almost a comedy of manners, about class, loyalty, community, and civilized values. Ford filled his stagecoach with a variety of outcasts, hypocrites, and thwarted idealists. The hero is an escaped convict seeking justice for the murder of his brother. His companions and soulmates are an alcoholic physician and a kindhearted prostitute. Each rises to various challenges with courage and grit. In the end, the hero triumphs over Apache raiders and goes on to confront his brother's killers in a showdown that his lover begs him to avoid. He guns down the villains, then rides off with her to his ranch across the border, with the blessing of a sheriff who looks the other way as they escape. Decency triumphs. The film is Ford's optimistic vision of the West as a place of new beginnings. *High Noon* borrowed many of the same themes; its hero triumphs through personal courage and gun violence. But its vision became something far darker.

Fred Zinnemann's reputation was that of an art-house filmmaker who knew how to work with talented young actors but had never directed a hit movie. Some observers thought it was ludicrous to give him a Western, that most quintessential and lowbrow of American cinematic forms. But Fred had grown up in Vienna reading the novels and short stories of Karl May, Germany's literary equivalent of Zane Grey. The Wild West of May's melodramatic books bore little or no resemblance to the real one, but that didn't matter; they were faithful to the mythic American West in his mind—and in the minds of tens of thousands of readers. One of the books Fred treasured from childhood and brought with him from Europe was the 1891 novel *Der Schatz im Silbersee* (*The Treasure of the Silver Lake*), in which two of May's classic heroes, Apache chief Winnetou and mountain man Old Shatterhand, track down a gang of killers searching for the legendary treasure. "My father was into the West and that's what got him wanting to come to America in the first place," says Tim Zinnemann.

But Fred didn't care primarily about the Western setting. What appealed to him most about making *High Noon* was the same thing he looked for in almost all his pictures: the struggle of a lone person confronting a terrible decision. *High Noon* would have intense scenes of people facing danger who were forced to reveal their true selves in front of the story's hero. "It's a picture of conscience as against compromise," he said. "Just that, nothing else."

HIGH NOON WAS CARL'S eleventh screenplay in just over a decade and the writing went quickly. He would send pages to Stanley and Fred as he wrote, and they would meet periodically for discussions. Fred's major contribution to the screenplay was to emphasize the railroad tracks at various moments in the story and have them disappear into the far horizon to underscore the isolation of the town and the looming threat. Fred even had Rudy Sternad do a sketch of the tracks to show the image he was looking for. Stanley suggested they hold the final shootout in a cemetery, but Carl rejected the idea. Otherwise things went smoothly, with Carl fleshing out scenes and dialogue.

The setting for his story is now called Hadleyville, a name that sounds a bit more like Hollywood and also echoes Mark Twain's novella about a small town's hypocrisy, *The Man That Corrupted Hadleyburg*. Not so long ago, Carl writes, the town was at the mercy of local rancher Gil Jordan, a ruthless feudal baron, and his gang of thugs. But five years ago, Marshal Will Doane and a handful of hard-riding deputies had defeated the gang and arrested Jordan for murder. He was sentenced to hang, but influential friends in the territorial capital applied pressure to have the sentence commuted to life imprisonment. These days Doane only needs two deputies to help him enforce the law. But now word has come by telegram on a Sunday morning that Jordan has been pardoned and is on his way home on the noon train to join with the remnants of his gang and seek revenge on Doane.

Alongside the plot, the prime focus of Carl's first draft was on character development. He had learned over the years that, as he put it, "if I understand my characters, it's a much easier story to write. Time and again I fall into traps. I get terribly interested in the plot and get so involved in that I get too lazy to stop and say, 'Wait a minute, really, who are these people? What do they want? What are they about?'"

The main character is Doane, a second-generation Westerner in his mid-thirties. Doane, who is not a native of the town, has an unromantic view of his job as marshal but "has enjoyed the prestige it has given him, and the knowledge that he is respected and liked by the townspeople." Now he is getting married and is leaving his post with regret. He is doing so at the behest of his new bride, a young woman who has convinced him to move to another town and open a general store. "He is, certainly, not an average man," writes Carl, "but a very human one."

Amy Fowler, whom Doane has married this morning, became a Quaker after her father and brother were killed while taking part in a vigilante action. "Young, attractive, intelligent, strong-willed, Amy is determined not to be a sheltered toy-wife but a full partner in her marriage, and it is she who has planned their future," Carl writes. "More, Amy's Quaker heritage had given her strong intellectual and emotional convictions against any form of violence, and marriage to Doane would have been unthinkable had he remained a peace officer."

Carl has also created another strong woman character, Helen Ramirez, a local businesswoman. She is half white and half Mexican and thus "a victim of the era and environment with rigid social standards." She is "neither acceptable to the 'pure' American women of the region nor eligible for a 'good' marriage. Consequently, in addition to being intelligent, shrewd, and strong-willed, she is also hard and resentful. Physically she is handsome, full-breasted, passionate. More, she has style, personality." The widow of a local saloon owner, Helen had become Gil Jordan's mistress during his reign over the town. But after his arrest and imprisonment, she selected Doane as his successor, and she still cannot forgive Doane for ending their affair—"a privilege she reserves for herself." Helen insists on controlling her own life, including her body.

What's striking is that both these women characters are exceptionally modern, independent, and intelligent, not just for the 1880s time period the screenplay is set in but for 1951 when Carl created them. Not many women with their stature and autonomy appeared in Western novels or films. And both sprung directly from Carl's own imagination. He had never before written female characters of such flair and strength; the women in *Champion* are largely cardboard cutouts, representing virtue, sin, and sensuality. Ellen, the lead character in *The Men*, is stronger and more complex, a mix of naïve idealism and fierce determination, but she is still incompletely drawn. Amy and Helen, by contrast, are something new, and their strength and the contrast between them are among the things that make *High Noon* exceptional. Carl's widow, Eve Williams-Jones, says he based these characters in part on his own mother and grandmother, both of them strong, talented women. His mother could sew, make hats, and play the piano beautifully. His grandmother wrote poetry. Both were gifted storytellers.

"I was trying to write some women's parts within the framework of a male story, and also within the framework of a male industry," Carl would recall. He especially wanted Helen Ramirez to be a character of "stature, individuality, a person in her own right, a strong character."

Carl has added one other main character to the mix. Harvey Pell is Doane's friend and chief deputy and recently he has become Helen's younger lover. Beneath his friendship with Doane lurks "a nagging sense of inferiority" and envy. Although Pell has taken Doane's place in Helen's bed, he feels he has not really replaced the older man in her heart. Pell is immature, ambitious, and anxious to prove his manhood and importance. He had hoped to be named Doane's successor as marshal, and resents Doane for the fact it hasn't happened. He comes to see the unfolding crisis as his opportunity to get what he wants.

As Carl worked on developing the main characters, Stanley launched the process of casting the picture. The big question was who should play the lead role. Stanley, Carl, and Fred discussed names such as Gregory Peck, Henry Fonda, Kirk Douglas, Burt Lancaster, Marlon Brando, William Holden, and Charlton Heston, but each of them either was unavailable or unwilling to work for the kind of salary that the Kramer company was willing to pay—fifty thousand dollars or so. But to Stanley's surprise, one big star was willing to negotiate. Gary Cooper, who was in the middle of the seven-year deal with Warner Bros. that at this stage guaranteed him $295,000 annually for one picture a year, was so hungry for a decent part that he was ready to take a major pay cut.

At first Stanley and Carl were reluctant to consider him: at age fifty he looked at least ten years too old to play the marshal. And Cooper was exactly the kind of big studio celebrity actor that both men tended to deprecate. "The name of Gary Cooper was already, at that time . . . a fun name for Hollywood: *yep* and so forth and so on," Carl would recall. "He was a kind of relic; old, old times." Stanley was equally wary. "[Cooper] wasn't at the peak of his career either," he recalled. "Everybody felt he was old and tired."

But Bruce Church, the Salinas lettuce grower who had helped finance *The Men* and *Cyrano* and who was willing to invest two hundred thousand dollars in this new picture, was a big Cooper fan. He urged Stanley and Carl to make a pitch to Cooper's lawyer, I. H. Prinzmetal. Tired of the second-rate screenplays he was getting from Warners, Cooper said he loved Carl's story and was genuinely excited by the chance to play the marshal. He claimed the role reminded him of the Montana lawmen his father used to tell him about. "My concept of a sheriff was that of a man who represented the people," said Cooper. "Alone he could never do his job—he had to have help." To everyone's surprise, Cooper was prepared to accept one hundred thousand dollars—less than half his usual salary—plus a percentage of the profits. Stanley, for one, assumed there would be none. It was a great deal for the Kramer company.

Carl recalled that Cooper came onboard before he had finished the screenplay. The contrasts between them surely made for an interesting first encounter. Cooper was pure Hollywood aristocracy, lavishly paid and well connected. He'd been a major star for two decades, and even though the luminosity of his stardom was fading, he was still at the heart of the filmmaking establishment. There's a photo from a New Year's Eve party at Romanoff's in the 1950s of Cooper in evening wear with a long-stemmed glass of champagne in his hand, looking relaxed and well groomed, standing and joking with Clark Gable, Van Heflin, and James Stewart, his good friends and noble peers. Or Cooper at the Parthenon with Rocky and Maria, or Cooper strolling along the Seine or meeting Pope Pius XII at the Vatican, or bowing to Queen Elizabeth in London, or sitting at a table with the dashing young John F. Kennedy in a naval officer's uniform. Cooper was always well dressed and handsome and comfortable with royalty of all kinds, a man so elegant that a men's magazine had gone to his house to photograph his clothes closet.

Like Cooper, Carl Foreman now lived in Brentwood, an haut-bourgeois neighborhood just west of Beverly Hills. But Carl's idea of social life was poker night with John Weaver, Herb Baker, and Dick Fleischer, or a barbecue at Stanley Kramer's little beach cabana, or bowling at La Cienega Lanes on Saturday night followed by coffee at Dominick's. But what Cooper and Carl had in common was respect for the work and an abiding hunger to succeed. Cooper needed a good screenplay and Carl knew that *High Noon* was the best one he'd ever written. On this they totally agreed.

Even though Cooper was a relative bargain, his hundred-thousand-dollar fee blew a huge hole in Stanley's budget and left a mere $35,000 for the rest of the cast. He and Carl had to work carefully and skillfully to put together a talented set of supporting actors.

They hired the Academy Award–winning character actor Thomas J. Mitchell for the part of Jonas Henderson, the jocular but hypocritical town selectman who claims to be the marshal's best friend but publicly disowns him at the crucial moment when Doane pleads for the community's support. Mitchell had won an Oscar for best supporting actor for *Stagecoach* in 1940, and had performed brilliantly in classics like *Mr. Smith Goes to Washington* and *It's a Wonderful Life*. Stanley signed him for $6,000 for one week's work. Kramer struck similar time-sensitive deals, although for far less money, with Lon Chaney Jr. ($1,750), Otto Kruger ($1,500), and Henry Morgan ($1,000), all of them veteran character actors. Each signed on for just one week's work, which meant Carl and Fred had to design a shooting schedule to use all of them during the first week of filming. Stanley got Lloyd Bridges, a potential future star, for five weeks at $800 per week.

Bridges was a handsome, blond-haired Northern California boy who had worked in the theater in New York in the early thirties before returning home in 1936 to get into the movies. He was briefly under contract at Columbia, but got stuck with bit parts and no real training or career development. Seeking to improve, he joined the Actors' Laboratory, where he was exposed to acting techniques and radical politics in equal measure and became a devoted student of fellow actor Roman Bohnen, chairman of the Actors' Lab executive board. Like his good friend Larry Parks, Bridges became a member of the board, and then around 1943 Bohnen asked him if he'd ever given any thought to joining the Communist Party. There was, as Bridges later recalled, "no law against it and they were fighting the Nazis and the Fascists." So he joined up. He remained in the party for a year or more, then drifted away. But he remained on the board of the Actors' Lab and involved in radical causes, including the campaign to abolish HUAC.

Bridges had been best man at Parks's wedding to Betty Garrett in 1944, and he watched with horror the public humiliation heaped upon his friend by HUAC. A few weeks after Parks's disastrous appearance before the committee, Bridges paid a visit to the FBI with his new lawyer, Martin Gang, to tell everything he knew about the party, including the names of Bohnen (who had died in 1949) and other former comrades. All of which he kept secret from his fellow *High Noon* cast members, including the fact that he was due in October to give testimony in executive session to Bill Wheeler at HUAC.

Stanley and Carl next contracted for the three "gunnies"—the members of Gil Jordan's gang, including his younger brother, Milt, who spend most of the movie drinking, smoking, and bickering while waiting for their boss's train to arrive. Stanley signed Sheb Wooley, Robert Wilke, and, in his first movie role, Lee Van Cleef, who was a client of Earl Kramer, Stanley's talent-agent uncle. All three went on to become superbly familiar faces in a decade or more of Westerns, and Van Cleef became an iconic Western star (although in *High Noon* he didn't have a single line of dialogue; his hawklike face said it all). Jack Elam, another fixture in Westerns, had a bit part as the town drunk. Earl Kramer also brought in a client named Katy Jurado, a dark and sultry Latina actress who was a proven star in Mexico, where she had made seventeen films in Spanish, but had only appeared in one previous American movie.

As in *The Men*, Carl was closely involved in many of these decisions and Fred had veto power. But Stanley alone got the credit for the most intriguing yet problematic casting choice.

GRACE KELLY WAS A twenty-two-year-old fledgling actress with a couple of Broadway performances, television shows, modeling gigs, commercials, and one small movie role on her résumé when her agent, Jay Kanter of MCA, suggested her for the part of Amy Fowler, the marshal's virginal but strong-minded new bride. Kanter was the same agent who had worked with Stanley to line up Marlon Brando for *The Men*. Kelly was strikingly beautiful—a natural blonde with perfect skin, piercing blue eyes, and a beguiling smile—and incredibly unsure of herself. But perhaps her most noteworthy trait, in Stanley's eyes, was her willingness to work for $750 a week.

Grace had the plummy accent and icy demeanor of a native-born aristocrat from Philadelphia's affluent Main Line. But she wasn't exactly what she seemed. Her parents were Irish Catholics and she was raised in East Falls, an affluent Philly neighborhood but nowhere near the Main Line. Her father, Jack, whom she adored, was a gold-medal Olympic oarsman, owner of a bricklaying business, charismatic but failed mayoral candidate, and world-class philanderer. Her mother was a beauty queen and model who taught physical education at the University of Pennsylvania. Her older sister, Peggy, was Jack Kelly's favorite, while Grace was a flat-chested, chubby, and myopic teenager, subject to bouts of extreme melancholia. "The idea of my life as a fairy tale is itself a fairy tale," she told Donald Spoto, one of her biographers.

Jack's brother, George, was an actor and a playwright, and he saw something promising in his shy, frustrated young niece and helped steer her toward the stage. At age seventeen, she moved to the Barbizon Hotel for Women at Lexington Avenue and East Sixty-Third Street in Manhattan, where Jacqueline and Lee Bouvier, Sylvia Plath, Lauren Bacall, Gene Tierney, and Liza Minnelli all lived at one time or another, and she studied acting at the American Academy of Dramatic Arts, whose alumni included Spencer Tracy, Katharine Hepburn, Edward G. Robinson, Rosalind Russell, and Kirk Douglas. Her first serious boyfriend was one of her teachers, a divorced actor and a Jew. After graduating she did lots of small-town theater work and TV commercials, then won a supporting role in a Broadway revival of August Strindberg's *The Father*, starring Raymond Massey, in 1949, four days after her twentieth birthday. She was doing summer stock in Denver when she got the part in *High Noon*.

When they met to discuss the role, Fred Zinnemann found her "beautiful in a prim sort of way," but tense and awkward. She wore white gloves to the meeting—"a thing unheard in our low-class surroundings," Fred recalled—and neither of them could manage any small talk. Their conversation was awkwardly brief and Fred was relieved to dispatch her down the hall to meet with Carl Foreman.

All of them were uncertain about her. She seemed young, stiff, and uncertain. Stanley, who had hired her before Cooper came aboard, became even more worried once he did. Grace was twenty-eight years younger than Cooper; would they really fit as husband and wife? "She was too young, too inexperienced, too nervous," Stanley would recall. Still, she was in.

NEXT CAME THE SEARCH for locations for the film shoot, which Stanley oversaw with Fred's and Carl's input. The interiors would largely be shot in the low-rent Motion Picture Center Studios at 846 Cahuenga Boulevard, where Carl kept his main office even after most of the Kramer Company moved several blocks north to the more lavish confines of Columbia's studios at 1438 North Gower. As for the exteriors, Fred wanted to find a small Western town in the middle of nowhere, "with miles of empty space at the end of each street and a railroad track pointing straight into infinity." He and the film's art director, Ben Hayne, scoured New Mexico and Arizona looking for someplace with an evocative, old-fashioned main street and railway station. They found an authentic setting outside Gallup, but Stanley vetoed it because of the expense of hauling the cast and crew so far from home. Instead, he found something closer around the colorful town of Sonora in Tuolumne County, the old gold-rush territory in the foothills of the Sierra Nevada mountains some 330 miles northeast of Los Angeles. There was a main street in the nearby town of Columbia that included a firehouse, livery stable, and old church that seemed to perfectly suit their needs. And the town of Warnerville had a railroad station, water tower, and old narrow-gauge train tracks.

With most of the casting and locations accomplished, Stanley backed away, devoting his time and energy to dealing with the massive commitment he had made to Columbia Pictures. He began feverishly buying the rights to stories and rounding up more directors and writers. Following the examples of *Home of the Brave* and *Cyrano de Bergerac*, he bought the rights to several plays, including *The Member of the Wedding*, *Death of a Salesman*, and *The Four Poster*, which he figured he could turn quickly into screenplays. He gave Carl a $790,000 budget cap for *High Noon* and left him and Fred to flesh out the cast and crew.

Both men understood that with such a limited budget, they would have to take a rigorously disciplined approach to making the film. The shooting schedule, for example, had to be brisk—Carl budgeted for thirty-two days, including Sundays off—and it had to be organized around the fact that some of the key supporting players were only signed for a week or two yet had to film their scenes together. Fred knew he needed a director of photography who could do set-ups and lighting quickly and efficiently and shoot scenes correctly the first time. He turned to an old friend and colleague.

Floyd Crosby was a rail-thin veteran cameraman whose early professional experience, like Fred's, was in documentary filmmaking. Born in New York City in 1899, Crosby studied at the New York Institute of Photography, then became an apprentice photographer on an ethnographic expedition to Haiti. Like Fred Zinnemann, he crossed paths early in his career with documentary film legend Robert Flaherty, working for Flaherty and famed German filmmaker F. W. Murnau on *Tabu* (1931), which is still considered one of the most beautiful outdoor pictures ever made (it won an Academy Award for cinematography). Over the next two decades Crosby specialized in documentaries in exotic locales like Tahiti, Honduras, Brazil, and India. He also made short documentaries for the Air Force during World War Two, rising to the rank of major. Crosby, whose son David later became a founding member of two groundbreaking rock bands, the Byrds and Crosby, Stills, and Nash, was known for his uncompromising standards, like his mentor Flaherty, and he did very little shooting for mainstream Hollywood features until 1950 when he worked on Robert Rossen's *The Brave Bulls*. Fred was confident that Crosby could help him create the stark, documentary-style visual effect he was looking for.

Carl was also looking for an ally he could trust, and he turned to Elmo Williams, who was developing a reputation as one of Hollywood's finest film editors. Williams was a good-looking Oklahoma farm boy who came to Hollywood in the early 1930s to escape the Dust Bowl. While working as a carhop at the Hi-Ho Drive-In at the corner of Westwood and Wilshire Boulevards, he met an up-and-coming film editor named Merrill White, who hired him as an assistant and taught him the craft of film cutting. Williams worked for several studios, then enlisted in the Army during the war and joined the Capra film unit alongside Carl and other budding young writers and filmmakers. After the war he worked for RKO and met up with Dick Fleischer, who told him about the fun he had had working with Stanley and Carl and discussed the *High Noon* project. After Williams expressed interest, he got a call from Carl, who regularly played volleyball with him and called him by the nickname Mole.

"Mole, I need you over here," Carl told him. ". . . I need somebody that's on my side." Williams added, "Apparently he was already having some difficulties with the Kramer Company."

And so gradually, over the course of a few weeks, Stanley, Carl, and Fred signed up a small but very talented band of professionals—from the famous star to the able supporting cast to the master craftsmen and technicians behind the camera. Backing them up, at least in theory, were some gifted artists and craftsmen in the Kramer Company, including composer Dimitri Tiomkin and art designer Rudolph Sternad. They were up against a miserly budget and a tight shooting schedule. And they faced the sense that, rightly or wrongly, *High Noon* was not a priority for the new company and its hyperactive but distracted leader. "Almost from the start, it was apparent that *High Noon* was going to be an orphan, a ransom paid to UA [United Artists], completely overshadowed by the really important Columbia product—in short, a B picture on the overall slate," Carl would recall.

Stanley Kramer would later dispute Carl's claim and insist that he personally had overseen the making of *High Noon* and had never short-changed the production. It's the first of several conflicts and contradictory accounts that have raged ever since the movie first appeared. But for Carl, as he worked on the first full draft of the screenplay, these issues would turn out to be the least of his problems. The House Un-American Activities Committee was planning a return visit to Hollywood in September, and Carl's name was on its list.

10.

The Informer

The so-called "liberals" were stunned by my revelations . . . It shocked them to their superficial little souls. "What does this man Berkeley mean," they shrilled in their emasculated voices, "turning our secure little world into a battleground?"

MARTIN BERKELEY

Of the twenty-three people whom former Communist Richard J. Collins named as party members in his testimony on April 12, 1951, one of the most obscure was a fellow screenwriter named Martin Berkeley. Collins said he had been a member of a group that met regularly at Berkeley's ranch house on White Oaks Avenue in Encino in the late 1930s or early '40s, although he believed Berkeley had subsequently fallen out with the party. Within hours of Collins's testimony, a telegram arrived for committee attorney Frank Tavenner from Berkeley angrily accusing Collins of lying. I AM NOT NOW NOR HAVE I EVER BEEN A MEMBER OF THE COMMUNIST PARTY, the telegram declared, and he urged Tavenner to invite him to Washington TO LAY MY ANTI-COMMUNIST POSITION BEFORE YOU. IT IS WELL DOCUMENTED I HAVE FOUGHT COMMUNISM CONSISTENTLY INSIDE MY GUILD AND OUT. Berkeley also sent a telegram to his son, Bill, then a freshman at Yale, warning him not to believe what he would read on the front page of the next day's *New York Times*.

The wire to HUAC was partially true: Berkeley had indeed become an active Red hunter in recent years, supporting the anti-Communist purge inside the Screen Writers Guild. But the first sentence was a blatant lie. Not only had Berkeley been a full-fledged member of the

American Communist Party, but the first meeting of the Hollywood branch of the party had been held at his house in June 1937. He'd been among the most loyal of members when Hitler and Stalin signed their nonaggression pact in August 1939. Berkeley was one of those comrades who turned on a dime from a staunch enemy of Fascism to an ardent advocate for "peace." He wrote an article passionately making the case why America should stay neutral in the war between Britain and Nazi Germany, condemning "the reckless bigwigs" who were "determined to alter the course of neutrality, where all our hard won gains will be lost."

Soon he would be displaying that same depth of passion in going after his former comrades.

Born in Brooklyn in 1904, Martin Alton Berkeley—the family name was originally Berkowitz—had been a theater actor and a playwright for a decade before moving to Hollywood in 1937. He worked for five years for MGM, then five more at Twentieth Century-Fox. His output was reliably steady and steeped in melodramatic clichés.

The Sparks Fly Upward, his play about Abraham Lincoln's childhood, features a climactic death scene in which Abe's mother, Nancy, tells her young son, "Be kind to your sister and your Pappy . . . Live always like I taught you to live . . . Stand firm for what you believe like your Pappy does—stand firm for the truth—and keep your head high."

In Berkeley's play *Obsession: A Love Story* Joyce tells Gordon, her star-crossed lover: "It's been so empty without you . . . Trying to keep the old chin up . . . It was a living hell."

Gordon replies, "I thought I could forget you."

Berkeley's screenplay, *Will James' Sand*, a B Western released in 1949, is set in "Desert Country, fit for neither man nor beast." The great horse Jubilee escapes a train fire by "racing like the wind." Berkeley was often assigned to work on animal pictures, including polishing work on *My Friend Flicka* (1943), which led Ring Lardner Jr. of the Hollywood Ten to the observation that Berkeley was unable to write dialogue for humans.

There's a strong tone of vituperation mixed with condescension when Berkeley's former comrades recall everything from his appearance to his writing to his politics. Much of this is colored by post-facto anger over his betrayal of them. But Berkeley clearly felt alienated and isolated from his fellow screenwriters: they were Hollywood's cool kids and he was the class clown. Fellow playwright Allen Boretz, who had a big Broadway hit with the comedy farce *Room Service* (later made into a Marx Brothers' movie), first met Berkeley in his agent's office in New

York. Boretz was struck that a Brooklyn Jew had such bland German-like features: "rather weakly handsome, I would say—tall, blond, blue eyes, with a kind of Teutonic face," he recalled.

Berkeley became Boretz's eager understudy. "He became my toady. He followed me around wherever I went. He talked to me constantly, wanting to understand who I was, and what I was, and how I had come to write like that."

In Hollywood, where clichéd writing was no impediment to employment, Berkeley found steady work for a decade. But Boretz said Berkeley came to him one day in a panic because MGM had assigned him to a Laurel and Hardy picture and he was afraid he would be fired because he knew nothing about writing comedy. Boretz took pity and whipped out the screenplay for him. When Berkeley turned it in his producer suspected it'd been written by someone else, but still used it.

Boretz said Berkeley had gradually lost faith in himself because he lacked the skills of a top screenwriter like Dalton Trumbo. "He had some talent but no great talent. He was no Trumbo, let us say. He was not even a . . . me."

Still, Berkeley was proud of his success. He bragged to his son Bill, "I've never written a great movie, but I've never written a movie that lost money."

Berkeley's irate telegram to HUAC prompted Richard Collins to offer many more telling details about his former comrade. The branch meetings at Berkeley's Encino home had been held in a playroom separated from the main house by a driveway, Collins recalled. Berkeley often wore blue denim trousers and a jacket to the meetings, and smoked a pipe stuffed with Revelation tobacco. He and his second wife, former actress Kathleen Kincaid, had eventually moved to Tarzana around 1941 to a larger house on a hilltop with horse stables behind it. Collins recalled a meeting he attended there after Germany invaded the Soviet Union. By 1942 or 1943, Collins said, Berkeley's obnoxious behavior had alienated many of his comrades and some feared he had turned into an FBI informer. In short, Collins seemed to know all about Martin Berkeley.

To make things worse, the committee had obtained the details of Berkeley's party membership cards for 1943 and 1944. The committee also learned from Jason Joy, director of public relations at Twentieth Century-Fox, that the studio had dropped Berkeley from working on the script for *Behind the Iron Curtain*, an anti-Communist picture, after the FBI "put the finger on him" for his alleged Communist ties.

A month after Collins's testimony and Berkeley's telegram, the two men met for lunch. "Berkeley had asked Collins if the committee really had in its possession authentic Communist Party cards, or if they were phonies," read a HUAC memo afterward. "Collins stated that he told Berkeley the cards were authentic."

Based on that piece of intelligence, Martin Berkeley decided it was time to come clean. He confessed to Bill Wheeler, the committee's chief Hollywood investigator, that he had indeed been a party member from 1936 to 1943 and confirmed that he had hosted several party meetings at his house. "The Committee has some pretty strong evidence against Berkeley and he knows it," Tavenner told the lawmakers.

Bill Berkeley, Martin's son from his first marriage, recalls arriving at his father's home in Pacoima in the San Fernando Valley in the summer of 1951 to find Wheeler had been staying there for several days while interviewing his father. During these sessions, Berkeley gushed names like a newly drilled oil well. Not a dozen names, like Larry Parks, nor two dozen, like Richard Collins, but 150 names, including seventy-five names of people who had not previously been identified as party members. "It is my opinion that he is the most important witness to date," Wheeler wrote to Tavenner. "The hearing in Hollywood is shaping up very well if Berkeley testifies here."

Wheeler went on to list the names of a dozen or so new targets for whom "dossiers, exhibits, and questions should be prepared."

One of them was Carl Foreman.

BY JUNE 1951 CARL was deeply immersed drafting the *High Noon* screenplay, with occasional input from Fred Zinnemann and Stanley Kramer. Carl's script became sharper as the climate of fear and loathing worsened around him. Old friends were no longer talking and people were crossing the street to avoid each other. FBI agents were paying visits to people's homes. Party members like screenwriter Abe Polonsky knew their phones were wiretapped. Meanwhile, many were whispering about poor Larry Parks, whose agonizing performance on the witness stand in March had crystallized everyone's deepest anxieties. An air of panic had set in. A *Life* magazine reporter wired her editor that people were anticipating the next set of committee hearings like "a group of marooned sailors on a flat desert island watching the approach of a tidal wave." This gathering sense of dread became the emotional core of Carl's story.

Because Carl was writing about the death of Hollywood, he decided to begin the screenplay with a flashback and a dissolve: scenes of an empty, desolate Hadleyville, looking like a ghost town while the opening credits rolled, followed by a dissolve to the town as it had been before its destruction, on the day that Gil Jordan and his men came back to town. At the conclusion of the movie, after Doane and Amy depart, Carl intended to dissolve back to the ghost town.

It was a misfire: too gimmicky, too obvious, and lacking the immediacy that was the central driving force of the screenplay. It undermined the whole concept of a story unfolding in real time. "I honestly don't remember why I dropped it," Carl would recall. "Maybe Stanley or Fred didn't like it."

If so, their objections indicate what a collaborative project *High Noon* truly was. Even a writer as sure-handed and experienced as Carl needed smart, critical readers. Most of all, he needed to embrace his own concept. Using constant shots of clocks to show real time passing would give the film a sense of urgency. What would make *High Noon* thrilling and frightening was its internal momentum driving the story inexorably toward a final confrontation not just between good guys and bad guys but between courage and fear.

Suddenly the beginning became obvious to him: he would start with the gunmen, the precipitators of the crisis to come, gathering on a rocky copse of trees while the film's credits unroll.

ON A SUNDAY MORNING already seared by heat, a man waits on the outskirts of a small Western town. A lone rider appears, waves briefly, and approaches him. Then a third rider gallops toward them. A church bell tolls in the distance. Although it's only mid-morning, the three men look sweaty and grimy from their ride. The third man takes out his pocket watch, checks the time, and snaps it shut. He nods to the others and they begin a slow, deliberate canter into town. The men ride with brazen ease, their rifles and handguns in plain view. They pass a church where congregants are filing in for the morning service and turn down the main street past a firehouse, grain store, and barbershop, passing townsfolk who watch them with growing concern. As they approach the marshal's office, one of the men rears his horse.

"You in a hurry?" the leader of the group asks angrily.

"I sure am," the younger man replies.

"You're a fool!" the older man exclaims.

As they ride off, the camera cuts to the interior of the courtroom next to the marshal's office where a judge is presiding over the wedding of Will Doane and Amy Fowler amid a small group of the town's most upstanding citizens. Then the camera cuts back to the three men riding past a saloon. "Did you see what I saw?" a man loafing outside says to his companions. "Open 'er up, Joe! We're going to have a big day today."

The riders end their procession at the train station, where they dismount and demand of the stationmaster whether the noon train is on time.

So begins Carl Foreman's screenplay of *High Noon*. In a series of small, deft strokes, he introduces major elements of his frontier drama: the gunmen who constitute an ominous menace, the community in various states of unease, the ticking clock moving slowly toward the moment of reckoning.

Next, the camera takes us back to the marshal's office and a brief ceremony: Will Doane removes his badge and pins it to his holster, which he leaves hung on the wall. But as he and his new bride prepare to leave, the stationmaster bursts in with a telegram announcing that the authorities have pardoned Guy Jordan (the chief villain has a new first name), and he adds that three of Jordan's men are waiting for their boss to arrive on the noon train. The marshal glances at the clock on the wall: it's ten forty A.M. Noon is just eighty minutes away. His friends quickly usher Doane and Amy out the door and onto an old buckboard. A hesitant Doane climbs aboard and heads out of town with his new bride.

But when they reach the parched prairie, Doane suddenly pulls up. He sits silently for a moment, frowning with thought as Amy stares at him.

"It's no good, I've got to go back," he tells her. "They're making me run. I've never run from anybody before."

Amy doesn't understand what he's thinking nor why, but he says he doesn't have time to explain it to her. Despite her plea to keep going, he turns the buckboard around and heads back to town.

When they get back to the marshal's office, Will explains to her that Jordan is coming back to town to kill him. Running away won't help: Jordan and his three henchmen can easily overtake their wagon on the open prairie. Better to stay in town, he tells her, gather his deputies and his friends, and confront Jordan and his men here. Still, Amy pleads for them to leave immediately. "You don't have to be a hero—not for me!" she tells him.

"I'm not trying to be a hero," he replies angrily. "If you think I like this, you're crazy!"

But Amy resists. As she sees it, Will is reneging on his promise to start a new life with her. "You're asking me to wait an hour to find out if I'm going to be a wife or a widow," she tells him. ". . . If you won't go with me now—I'll be on that train when it leaves here."

"I've got to stay, Amy," he replies. She walks out the door.

As Carl must have known, the scene is particularly resonant because Cooper is repeating the same sentiments his character expressed more than two decades earlier in *The Virginian*, his first major starring role. Back then, the young and virile hero spoke with the confidence of youth. But now the protagonist is older and far less self-assured. Like his younger self, he knows he has no choice but to confront his enemy, but he is more aware of the mortal danger he faces and less certain of the outcome.

The heart of *High Noon* follows: a series of scenes in which Will Doane seeks in vain to enlist help from his friends and neighbors, all of whom find reasons to turn him away. It begins with Percy Mettrick, the judge who has just presided over the wedding, who makes clear he has no intention of standing alongside the marshal in his hour of need. As he hurriedly packs his law books, papers, and gavel, Mettrick gives Will a cynical civics lesson, relating how the citizens of Athens in the fifth century B.C. deposed and banished a tyrant. When the tyrant returned with an army of mercenaries the residents welcomed him back and stood by while he slaughtered members of the legal government. Mettrick says he himself had escaped a similar fate in a small town eight years earlier. "Will, why must you be such a fool?" asks Mettrick, as he folds and packs up his American flag. "Have you forgotten what he is? Have you forgotten what he's done to people?"

Mettrick, whose soul is calibrated only for survival, cannot understand Will's stand. "Look, this is just a dirty little village in the middle of nowhere. Nothing that happens here is really important . . . Get out!"

As Mettrick pulls out, Harvey Pell arrives. Doane is visibly relieved to see his principal deputy, until Pell makes clear that he has one nonnegotiable condition for helping take on Jordan and his gang: Doane's support for Pell to become the next marshal. But Doane won't submit to Harvey's blackmail. When Pell asks why not, Doane replies, "If you don't know, there's no use me telling you."

Pell is too narcissistic and immature to begin to understand. He believes Doane is angry with him because he's been sleeping with Helen Ramirez, Doane's ex-lover. Pell storms out. Doane loses not just a deputy but also someone he considered a friend. The clock on the wall reads two minutes after eleven.

Next up is Herb Baker, one of Will's former deputies. Baker (named after one of Carl Foreman's closest friends, as are Weaver and Grogan in subsequent scenes; Carl put their names in every one of his screenplays) tells Will that he can count on him for support and firepower. "Why, you cleaned this town up—you made it fit for women and children to live in . . ."

"I was hoping people'd feel that way," says Doane.

"What other way is there?"

Baker sounds slightly perturbed when Doane says he has no other men lined up yet, but pledges to return in ten minutes "loaded for bear."

Doane's next visit is to the hotel suite of Helen Ramirez. She is surprised and angry to see her former lover and she assumes he has come to plead for her to intervene with Jordan to spare his life. When he explains that he has merely come to warn her of Jordan's return, she calms down. "I'm not afraid of him," she says.

"I know you're not," says Doane, "but you know how he is."

"I know how he is . . ."

These vague references to Jordan's brutal past behavior are far more effective than a graphic account of his crimes would be. Those acts are left instead to our imagination. Similarly, we must accept Will's inability to articulate the personal code that requires him to stay and take on the Jordan gang. Carl Foreman is challenging us to draw our own conclusions about the morals and motives of the characters.

Helen tells Will she's decided to leave town, adding, "If you're smart, you'll get out yourself."

"I can't," he replies.

"I know," she says. Although they are estranged, these two characters understand and sympathize with each other more deeply than anyone else in *High Noon*. As Doane heads down the hotel stairs, the clock on the landing reads 11:11.

The marshal heads next to the saloon, where we discover that there are people in town who are happy Jordan is coming back. "You must be crazy, coming in here to raise a posse," Gillis the bartender tells Doane. "Guy's got friends in this room—you ought to know that!" Doane leaves the bar empty-handed.

Still, the most painful rejection is yet to come. Mart Howe, the retired town sheriff, is Doane's mentor and friend, and the lawman has always believed in Howe as a leader and role model. "You've been my friend all my life," Will tells him. "You got me this job. You made them send for me . . . From the time I was a kid I wanted to be like you."

But Howe is locked inside his own sense of grievance and resentment. He believes his life as a lawman has been wasted. "You risk your skin catching killers and the juries let them go so they can come back and shoot at you again. If you're honest, you're poor your whole life and in the end you wind up dying all alone in a dirty street. For what? For nothing. A tin star . . ."

As for the people of Hadleyville whom Will is defending, Howe speaks a bitter truth: "They really don't care."

The room goes quiet as the two men look at each other. Displaying a vulnerability he would never show to others, Will begs Howe for guidance. "What should I do, Mart?"

But Howe has an answer that Will cannot accept. "They're coming to kill you," he tells Doane. "Get out, Will! Get out!"

Will makes one more plea. "Will you come down to that station with me?"

Howe says no. He says he is too arthritic and would be of no help to Will. In fact, Will might well get himself killed trying to protect him. "You know how I feel about you, but I won't go with you."

Howe's excuses are hollow, but Doane doesn't waste his breath refuting them. He heads next to the home Sam Fuller, a town selectman, who hides in the bedroom but orders his wife to lie and tell Doane that he's gone off to church. Will doesn't even bother to act surprised.

Meanwhile, the interaction between Harvey and Helen grows hot-tempered. She seems to take pleasure in telling Harvey the truth about his shortcomings, especially when compared to Doane. "You're a nice looking boy, you have big wide shoulders. But . . . it takes more than big wide shoulders to make a man, Harvey. And you've got a long way to go."

"You know something?" she adds cruelly. "I don't think you'll ever make it."

When Pell reaches for her, she slaps him hard.

Doane's next stop is the church, where he disrupts the morning service to plead for volunteers. The minister at first dismisses Doane's appearance, noting that the lawman seldom attended services and had chosen to get married that morning not in church but in a civil ceremony. The preacher softens his tone when Doane explains why he has come, but can offer no practical guidance to his flock as to their moral obligation to the marshal. "The Commandments say: Thou shalt not kill . . . but we hire men to do it for us," he tells the congregation. ". . . The right and the wrong seem pretty clear here, but if you're asking me to tell my people to go out and kill and maybe get themselves killed— I'm sorry—I don't know what to say."

So much for the ability of organized religion to guide and shape the public conscience.

Several congregants are ready to support Doane, but others resist. Then Jonas Henderson, the marshal's old friend and ally, rises to stand beside him. "What this town owes Will Doane here, you could never pay him with money, and don't ever forget it," he begins. Doane listens gratefully. But as Henderson continues, his oration turns from support to betrayal. "Now, there's people up north who've been thinking about this town, and thinking mighty hard. They've been thinking about sending money down here—to put up stores, build factories." But a violent shootout on the streets would lead them to change their minds, "and everything we worked for is going to be wiped out in one day."

Henderson concludes by telling Doane to get out of town immediately. "It's better for you—and better for us." Both religion and commerce— the twin pillars of American capitalism—have rejected the lawman and abandoned him to his fate. A stunned Doane leaves the church empty-handed.

He makes his way down the empty streets to the livery stable and eyes a fast horse. Just then Harvey Pell enters. He's been drinking heavily at the saloon, and he tries clumsily to force Doane to saddle up and leave town. The two men end up in a brutal fist fight that the marshal eventually wins. He stumbles to the local barbershop, where he gets a clean towel to wipe the blood and dirt from his face. The barber also happens to be the local undertaker, and Doane can hear a carpenter in the next room hurriedly hammering together coffins for the showdown to come. The barber glances at the clock on the wall: 11:53.

Meanwhile, Amy Fowler, waiting for the noon train, has gone upstairs at the hotel to meet Helen Ramirez. She pleads with Helen to relinquish her hold on Doane, but Helen explains that Doane's refusal to leave town has nothing to do with her. When a surprised Amy asks why Will won't leave, Helen replies, echoing Doane's own words. "If you don't know, I can't explain it to you."

Helen lashes out at Amy. "What kind of woman are you? How can you leave him like this?" Amy explains that her father and brother had both been killed in a gun battle and that's when she became a Quaker. "I don't care who's right or wrong! There's got to be some better way for people to live!"

Doane returns to the marshal's office, where Herb Baker is waiting. But when he learns that Doane has not been able to recruit other deputies, he backs out and abandons the marshal to his fate.

After Herb leaves, Doane sits at his desk, overwhelmed by his anger and helplessness and almost in tears. The clock reads two minutes to twelve. He stares at his gun, as if weighing suicide. But he pulls himself together. Then he hears the train whistle: noon has arrived. He writes a brief last will and testament and heads out the door. The street is deserted. A buckboard passes him with Amy and Helen heading toward the station. They ride past silently.

Will Doane knows now he is totally alone. He slowly moves forward to meet his fate.

EVEN BEFORE MARTIN BERKELEY fingered him, Carl Foreman was on at least one list of subversives. He'd been named as a Communist sympathizer by the Tenney Committee in Sacramento. But Carl's 1950 stand against the loyalty oath as a member of the board of the Screen Writers Guild had singled him out as well to the FBI and HUAC. Adele Buffington, a right-wing screenwriter, was feeding reports to both the bureau and the committee in her campaign to rid the guild of leftists.

The subpoena arrived on June 13, just as Carl was in the process of finishing the *High Noon* script. Bill Wheeler delivered it by hand. He was a pleasant young man in a gray suit, with pomaded black curly hair, rosy cheeks, and the stocky build of a former high school football player beginning to go to seed. He told Carl he was truly sorry to be the bearer of such bad news, but if he could help in any way he'd be happy to meet. He handed Carl his card and invited him to call any time.

Carl broke off work and went straight home. Four-year-old Kate was delighted her daddy had come home so early and she jumped into his arms. But Estelle was stunned to learn the reason why. She and Carl agreed to keep it quiet for the time being. He needed time to ponder what to do and how exactly to do it. Someone involved with the party must have squealed. "Who do you suppose the son of a bitch was who did this to us?" he asked angrily.

Carl knew his options were limited. He couldn't take refuge in the First Amendment; the courts in the case of the Hollywood Ten had already ruled against that strategy. It was a sure path to a prison sentence and public ostracism. But to invoke the Fifth Amendment and refuse to testify was to suggest one had something to hide. It was the act of a guilty person, and the only thing Carl was guilty of was being a former Communist.

The only sure way out was to name names. After all, he was no longer a party member. He owed his former comrades nothing; none of them were good friends, although some of them had been in the past. Why should he stick his neck out for a cause he no longer believed in? Still, he couldn't stomach becoming an informer. It was a violation of the code he had grown up with in Chicago. No one in his old neighborhood had ever cooperated with the cops or stooled on his friends. "No hero me, and no saint, believe me, but way too much to pay," he later recalled.

One thing he knew for certain: he had to tell Stanley right away that he'd been subpoenaed. Stanley was out of town, so Carl phoned him. He took the news well. They'd been through a lot of difficulties in the past and licked them, he assured Carl, and there was no reason why they shouldn't do the same this time. They would work it out.

When Stanley got back to L.A., they met in his office, just he and Carl. If things get bad, Stanley told him, then Carl could work from home for a while, still on salary but with a lower profile. Surely it would all blow over after a year or so. Carl felt relieved. Despite their growing estrangement over the company, when it came to the crunch Stanley was on his side. They were brothers.

The warm feelings didn't last long. When Stanley told George Glass and Sam Katz about Carl's subpoena, they both expressed alarm. The Columbia deal was just getting started. The studio and its mercurial boss, Harry Cohn, had been signatories to the Waldorf Statement, agreeing that they would fire anyone named as a Communist, and Cohn would be furious to learn he was going into business with a former Communist facing a HUAC subpoena. Then Glass revealed that he, too, had been subpoenaed by HUAC. At first Glass insisted he would not cooperate. But then he agreed to meet with Martin Gang, Sterling Hayden's old lawyer, who set up a session between Glass and Bill Wheeler. Glass's conciliatory attitude impressed Stanley. If George was willing to cooperate for the sake of the company, why couldn't Carl? So far as Stanley was concerned, this was not a political or moral issue but rather a question of personal loyalty to Stanley and the company. He was beginning to have doubts about Carl's.

During all of this time, Carl was putting the finishing touches on the dialogue in the *High Noon* script. He found himself inserting words that he was hearing from his so-called friends, especially in the church meeting scene. There was a heavy whiff of betrayal in the air.

"It was now happening to me rather than to friends of mine and it was all falling into line," he would recall. ". . . A lot of the dialogue was almost the dialogue that I was hearing from people and even in the company . . . You could walk down the street and see friends of yours recognize you, turn, and walk the other way."

Carl was careful not to tell anyone that the script was taking on an anti-blacklist shading. No one was feeling brave enough to take on HUAC and he knew that divulging to Stanley and the others what he was up to would only heighten their anxieties and cause them to either kill the project or pull him off it. While he trusted Fred Zinnemann, he felt Fred didn't need to have this particular knowledge added to the burden of preparing for the film shoot. Still, Carl felt it was time to tell Fred and Gary Cooper about the subpoena. He was being called to testify right around the time when the film shoot was scheduled to begin. Later, his appearance date was postponed until September 24—almost exactly in the middle of the shoot. Both men deserved the opportunity to walk away from the picture if they felt Carl was too radioactive to work with.

Fred was marvelous about it. Don't worry about me, he told Carl, just do whatever you have to.

Carl was anticipating more resistance from Cooper. After all, he was a member of the executive board of the Motion Picture Alliance for the Preservation of American Ideals—the group that had invited HUAC to investigate Hollywood in the first place—and he had been a friendly witness during the committee's first round of Hollywood hearings in 1947. They met in Cooper's most discreet rendezvous spot—his silver Jaguar convertible—near Cooper's Brentwood home, and Carl told him the whole story.

Cooper asked questions: How does Kramer feel about this? What about Zinnemann? Carl answered him, and then offered Cooper his out. "If you want to leave the picture, now's the time to do it," Carl told him. "No hard feelings."

Cooper refused. It's going to be a good picture, he told Carl. He said he had always figured that both Stanley and Carl were left-wingers, but he liked the script. You know how I feel about Communism, he added, but you're not a Communist now and anyway I like you, I think you're an honest man, and I think you should do what you think is right. "I'm not leaving the picture," said Cooper, "so that's it."

Carl was deeply moved. The conversation seemed to cement their partnership. From then on, Carl felt, he and Cooper were not just colleagues on a film project but allies. Cooper said he would explain the situation to Bruce Church, who, like Cooper, was a conservative Republican. Later on, he even volunteered to speak to the committee and tell them what a patriotic American Carl was—a suggestion that was vetoed by Cooper's lawyer, I. H. Prinzmetal, and by Carl himself.

But things were hardening with Stanley and the other partners. Sam Katz called Carl for a meeting and Carl went to his office at Columbia. Katz said he understood and respected Carl's position, but perhaps there were options Carl hadn't considered. Do you have a lawyer? When Carl said no, Katz said he knew a man who could help.

AFTER HIS SUCCESSFUL DEFENSE of Sterling Hayden at the HUAC hearings in April, Martin Gang quickly established a reputation as the go-to lawyer for those seeking to forge some kind of compromise with the committee in order to continue working. He represented screenwriter Richard Collins and script reader Meta Reis Rosenberg during their testimony in April when each of them expressed their deep remorse for having joined the Communist Party and named the names of former comrades.

Gang wound up representing more informers than any other Hollywood lawyer—by his own estimate, some twenty movie people and thirty more in other professions. His justification was simple: he was helping worthy but misguided people stay out of prison and keep their jobs. He would not represent anyone who took the Fifth Amendment, arguing that if they were *former* Communists, as all of his clients claimed to be, they had not broken any law and therefore did not need the amendment's protection. He claimed that his clients never initiated naming anyone, but simply confirmed names that the committee already had obtained. His own duty, he solemnly declared, was to his clients.

Gang's parents were Eastern European Jews who came to the United States in the 1890s, and he himself was born in Passaic, New Jersey, in 1901. After graduating from Harvard, he spent part of the 1920s in Weimar Germany, where he eventually earned a doctorate in economics from the University of Heidelberg. He watched the systematic destruction of the German middle class by runaway inflation and open street warfare between Fascists and Communists. It made him suspicious of extremists of both political stripes and determined to pursue compromises to appease the powers that be. When he returned to America, he wound up earning a law degree from the University of California at Berkeley and made connections that brought him to Los Angeles at a time when the big studios were making the transition from family-owned businesses to modern companies. He joined Loeb, Walker, Loeb, a Jewish-owned firm that exercised a virtual monopoly on entertainment law. "Even when the big studios were run by Jews," he recalled, "they didn't care what you were or who you were if you had talent."

Gang eventually launched his own entertainment law firm, and his long list of celebrity clients included Bob Hope, George Burns, Frank Sinatra, Rita Hayworth, Burt Lancaster, Lucille Ball, and Myrna Loy. He put up with their tantrums and their quirks. "Movie people are like everybody else, only more so," he liked to say.

He represented Olivia de Havilland in her landmark lawsuit against Warner Bros. in the early 1940s establishing the right of a performer to terminate his or her contract at the end of seven years, rather than have it extended at the sole discretion of the studio. He also handled financial matters for right-wing columnist Hedda Hopper and left-wing screenwriter Dalton Trumbo, who called Gang "the industry expert in frying producers."

Starting with the Hayden case, Gang got to know committee staff members like Frank Tavenner and Bill Wheeler and boasted of his ability to work with them. "Like most of these people, they're human beings and you can appeal to their decency," he told Victor Navasky. "And Wheeler and Tavenner were very helpful where people were not members of the Communist Party—they wouldn't be helpful if they thought they were still members of the Communist Party."

"I think I helped educate the committee that they'd do better with honey rather than vinegar," he added. "Over the years they learned."

Wheeler, said Gang, was "a nice man. I got to be very fond of him, I think I educated him kind of because I used to take him to dinner with people who were on his list. A lot of people he was personally convinced were okay he never pursued it. He met with them and talked to them and made up his own mind." Wheeler "was doing a job and what I tried to do was to help my clients by presenting the facts to him in such a way that my clients would not be unnecessarily hurt. And if that's a crime, you can convict me."

There was another component to Gang's role as well. Gang was a pillar of the Jewish community in Los Angeles, and he served as a bridge between the gentiles of HUAC and the Jews of Hollywood, both the studio moguls and those on the left. He himself didn't believe the committee was anti-Semitic, but there were plenty of irresponsible people on the right compiling lists and making allegations. He wanted to protect genuine liberals—but not Communists—from being blacklisted. "I didn't like the committee but I worked with it, because I had a responsibility to my clients and their lives," he recalled.

Members of the Communist Party and those who had left the party but retained a sense of loyalty to their former comrades felt contempt for Gang—a feeling Carl shared. Rumor had it that Gang and his law firm made large fees off their political clients. (In fact, Gang plausibly claimed that his partners were not happy with his taking on these controversial cases, saying they made more enemies than friends and cost the firm between fifty thousand and one hundred thousand dollars in lost legal fees.)

Gang met Carl at Columbia executive B. B. Kahane's office. He told Carl he believed he could help him, provided Carl was willing to cooperate. All Carl had to do was repeat a handful of names that the committee already knew.

But Carl was adamant he wouldn't name names, not even of those like the Hollywood Ten who had already been identified as Communists by multiple witnesses. "It was such a cowardly thing to do," Carl said, and besides it was not a practical means of escape "because once you started naming somebody, they wouldn't let you go until you named some live ones."

Gang then lost patience. I'm a liberal, just like you, he told Carl, and I want you to come out of this okay. But these are terrible times, he went on. Carl should be aware that the government was preparing to reopen the concentration camp at Tule Lake, California, that had been built to detain Japanese Americans during World War Two. Only this time, Gang warned, the detainees would be leftists like Carl. "He had set out to frighten me, and he did," Carl recalled. Still, Carl refused to budge.

Gang reported back to Sam Katz that Carl Foreman was being intransigent.

WHILE CARL WAS SECRETLY agonizing over what to do, fellow screenwriter (and director) Robert Rossen was also suffering. Rossen's career should have been in high gear: in 1950 *All the King's Men* had won three Academy Awards, including best picture. But Rossen was well known to be a former Communist Party member. He was one of the original nineteen men who had been subpoenaed by HUAC in 1947 and he often expressed disappointment that he hadn't been called to testify. He seemed to have a taste for martyrdom.

Ever since that session the committee was on Rossen's tail. Investigators had found 1943 party membership cards and numbers for him and his wife, Susan, and had developed a four-page typewritten single-spaced dossier on his Communist front connections and activities. An April 1951 memo named him as "one of the twelve most important Communists in the motion picture industry."

Raised on the Lower East Side of New York, Rossen was known as a combative and difficult but highly talented writer. His screenplays for Warner Bros. in the 1930s and early forties helped set the studio's trademark style of hard-bitten, fast-paced urban melodramas with gangsters, cops, and gunplay. He had gone on to become a leading director. His second film as a director was *Body and Soul*, the powerful 1947 boxing picture written by Abe Polonsky and starring John Garfield, both of whom were also prime HUAC targets.

Carl had first met Rossen in the late 1930s at the League of American Writers, where Rossen taught screenplay writing. Carl was not a big fan: he felt Rossen was more interested in telling stories of his many battles and principled stands against the studio bosses than in helping newcomers learn the trade. But he respected Rossen's talent, and now he felt sorry for him as well.

By the summer of 1951, Rossen was drinking heavily. He would stop by the Foreman house almost every afternoon between four and five, ask Estelle for a drink, and wait for Carl to get home from the studio. Rossen was in agony: he felt squeezed by the HUAC investigators on the one hand and by his former comrades on the other. Carl, who was wrestling with the same dilemma, didn't know what to say. "Now I had inherited Bob," he would recall, with more than a touch of condescension. "Somehow, he was mine."

Rossen did Carl one big favor: he introduced him to Sidney Cohn, a labor lawyer from New York. Besides Rossen, Cohn had several Hollywood clients who had been called by the committee, including screenwriters Leonardo Bercovici, Marguerite Roberts, and her husband, John Sanford. Cohn went to Sunday brunch at the Rossens', and Bob and Sue invited Carl to stop by as well. Cohn agreed to meet with Carl afterward at his hotel, the Beverly Crest. Cohn listened quietly as Carl poured out his story. Afterward, Cohn asked two questions. Was Carl still a party member? And was he willing to become an informer and name names in order to salvage his career? Once Cohn was persuaded that the answer to both questions was a solid no, he agreed to represent Carl before the committee.

Carl told Cohn he was willing to go to jail for a year to defend the principle of not naming names. He said he believed that Stanley Kramer would hold his job for him and take care of Estelle and Kate while Carl was in jail. But Cohn said Carl would be crazy to accept any kind of prison sentence. You're a screenwriter, not a labor leader, he told Carl. You have no leadership responsibilities, but you *are* responsible for your wife and daughter and any other members of your family who you help support. Why should you go to jail? The committee is morally corrupt and not worthy of your sacrifice. "You will beat them by *not* going to jail," he told Carl.

Cohn said he favored a strategy that would keep Carl out of prison while preserving his honor. Cohn called it the "diminished Fifth." A witness would assert he was not now a member of the Communist Party and had not been one at the time the subpoena was served. But when asked if he'd *ever* been a member, the witness would invoke the Fifth Amendment's right against self-incrimination. There were two problems with this strategy. Legally, it was dubious: most lawyers argued that once a witness denied current membership, he waived his right to invoke the Fifth Amendment—it was all or nothing. And morally it was questionable: many of Carl's friends on the left believed that answering any of the committee's questions was a form of collaboration. But Carl was looking for an honorable position that he could live with, and Cohn's idea suited him. Whether it would keep him off the blacklist was another matter. Carl was pretty sure it wouldn't. "It's the kind of situation in which you can't win," he later recalled, "but you feel you have to act in a certain way."

Cohn was adamant that the committee was a collection of gangsters who deserved no respect. "Always bear in mind," he told Carl, "that these people on the committee, they want to kill you. They would love you only if you turned whore for them . . . No matter what you say they are going to try and destroy you."

11.

Citizen Kane

Morality, we are told, is a voice of conscience from within in harmony with a voice of authority from without. We have seen what happens when the citizen delegates his conscience to the state.

VICTOR NAVASKY

Carl Foreman handed in the finished screenplay on July 30, 1951. Then he and Fred Zinnemann went to work, going over the script line by line and shot by shot, paring it down to the bone for the sake of both the drama and the budget. "We worked together beautifully, even when we snarled and screamed at each other," Carl recalled, "because we were friends and we loved the story."

Under Fred's critical eye, Carl made five sets of revisions by September 4. Several speeches were cut down or deleted altogether. Overt sexual references between Doane and Amy were deleted, while the sexual tension between Harvey Pell and Helen Ramirez was increased and made more explicit.

While collaborating with Fred was demanding but productive, Carl found that working with his partners at the Stanley Kramer Company was increasingly difficult. "It soon became obvious that it wasn't going to be an easy picture to make," Carl wrote later. "As its producer, I found myself short of just about everything—money, interest, manpower, facilities . . . The production department, now headquartered at Columbia and disdainful of the little Western, was slovenly and careless. Mistakes were made in the name of economy which later added costs to the picture . . . It was like being back at a major studio again."

The biggest problem was the result of an ill-considered attempt at cost cutting. Back in February Stanley's location team had chosen the evocative little town of Columbia near Sonora in the foothills of the Sierra Nevada mountains as the location site for many of the exterior street scenes. But when Fred went up there in early July, he discovered that the trees on the main street, barren in winter, were now so leafy they blocked much of the view. While various sites around Sonora would still work for the train station, the old church building, and the livery stable, Stanley and Carl decided to rent the Western storefronts at the Columbia studio's ranch in Burbank just over the Hollywood Hills to serve as Hadleyville's main street. "Dressed" interiors of the marshal's office, the saloon, the judge's office, the hotel lobby, and the barn could also be filmed at the Columbia Ranch.

Harry Cohn had purchased the Burbank property, originally either a horse stable or dairy farm, in 1934. It was just forty acres—a postage stamp compared to the sprawling 2,776 acres of the Warners' movie ranch or other spreads belonging to Fox, RKO, and Paramount. But Columbia's rental charges were so low that the ranch had become the site for many pictures, including the setting for Shangri-La in Frank Capra's *Lost Horizon* (1937), and reached its heyday later in the 1950s when Screen Gems, Columbia's television division, shot more than a dozen TV sitcoms there. Two years after *High Noon*, Fred would return to shoot Hawaiian street scenes for *From Here to Eternity* for Columbia. While much of the street was destroyed in a January 1970 fire, its last big-screen appearance, ironically, was for *Guilty by Suspicion* (1991), a movie about the blacklist in which the director, played by Robert De Niro, shoots a *High Noon*–inspired picture on the set.

Street noise from cars, construction sites, and planes flying into the nearby Lockheed Air Terminal (now called Bob Hope Airport) constantly interfered. Still, inauthentic as it seemed, the Burbank location had one big advantage from Fred's point of view: the smog that inevitably settled into the San Fernando Valley every morning by the time shooting began. It made the sky appear pale and featureless, with no billowing clouds to interfere with the washed-out look he and Floyd Crosby were aiming for.

Early on, Fred and Crosby agreed on a realistic, unfiltered appearance for the actors and the sets that would give *High Noon* the visual feel of an old newsreel.

They studied the Mathew Brady Studio's photographs of the Civil War and went for the same grainy textures and flat light. There would be no handsome young chiseled hero set against dramatic backgrounds.

Instead, it was Cooper's aging, gaunt, and slightly stooped, black-clad marshal walking stiffly against an empty sky, emphasizing his outcast status within his own community. Fred and Floyd—spiritual sons of the great film documentarian Robert Flaherty—were striving for the anti-Western: gritty, grimy, and real.

"We agreed that we would do nothing to make the photography pretty," Crosby would recall. "We wanted the feeling of a hot, stark, small western town. To achieve this, I did not filter the skies, as we felt that white skies would add to the feeling of heat. We also had the print made a few points lighter than normal to add to the effect of heat."

Fred in his handwritten screenplay notes mentions *Sweat on Doane's shirt. Sweat on girls.*

"The makeup men were busy all day applying glycerin [for sweat] to everyone's faces," recalled actor Larry Blake, who played the bartender.

To underscore the gritty effect, Cooper agreed to be shot with no filter to conceal the deeply etched lines on his face. He looked every day of his fifty years and, in truth, considerably older. It was a vanity-free appearance.

Fred in his thoughtful and meticulous manner carefully laid out three visual elements that he intended to emphasize throughout the picture. The first was the marshal's lonely journey on foot through the mostly deserted town in a vain search for comfort and support. The second was the motionless, ominous railroad tracks, which represented the looming threat that would soon arrive. Finally, he planned to underscore the urgency of the marshal's plight by an obsessive focus on clocks in every interior scene. The clocks would get larger as the story unwound and time raced by, their pendulums moving more and more slowly until, according to Fred, time would finally stand still, "gradually creating an unreal, dreamlike almost hypnotic effect of animated suspension."

Throughout August, as Fred went over the script with Carl, he made notations in red ink or pencil on virtually each page in his small, tidy handwriting, telling himself (and Carl) how he wanted things to look and feel. His original script, on file at the Motion Picture Academy library in Beverly Hills, is an extraordinary guide to the thought process of a cinematic artist in the act of creation.

Some of Fred's notes are designed to emphasize the visual appearance of a scene. *Dust and beards on riders!* he notes on the first page. And sometimes he is describing the motives and feelings of the characters.

On the second page, after Helen first spots the three riders from her hotel window and turns back to talk to Harvey Pell, Fred captures with precision her mixed feelings for her young lover:

1. *Occasional tenderness*
2. *Occasional maternal feeling*
3. *But she never tells him*
4. *He feels it & it rankles quite seriously*

Fred is also aware of Helen's enduring longing for Doane, her former lover. When the marshal comes to warn her that Guy Jordan is coming back to town, Fred writes in pencil:

Don't go—still in love with him—that's what the scene is about

Fred continually focuses on Helen's feelings. And he tries to find ways to visually express her inner struggle:

Gets up, walks up & down
Great inner conflict. She hates to see Doane die. Wants to go & help him.
But she decides she can't do it. He is not her man.

Fred lists the detail elements he plans to include. After page 85 of the script, he inserts a typewritten page listing twenty-one separate shots of clocks registering the march of time—almost double the number in Carl's first draft. Fred's list starts with the first scene in the marshal's office, where the clock registers 10:40, and continues to a final look at the clock at noon when Fred wants to pan to a clock face with no hands on it. He writes: *Pendulum—slow motion—pan up to clock—no face.*

On another page, Fred writes out in ink the various walks—nine in all—that the marshal takes through town seeking help:

Doane plods:
#1 Office to Hotel (to warn Helen)
#2 Hotel to Office (to see if selectmen arrived)
#3 Office to Saloon (to raise posse)
#4 Saloon to Howe (to ask Howe) Drunk LONG WALK!!
#5 Howe to Fuller (to ask Fuller)
#6 Fuller to Church (to ask community)

#7   *Church to livery stable past saloon why?* (in pencil he adds: *to run away, inner panic*)

#8   *Stable to Barber Shop 264–5 (to wash)*

#9   *Barber to Office*

And he writes occasional notes to Carl, sometimes to criticize the screenplay and other times to ask for Carl's help in understanding what's going on:

Carl: explain to me in detail what Helen is thinking about in (scene) 76 (p. 25), also sc. 31-39-35.

He criticizes the screenplay when the stationmaster tells Amy: "We'll get three whistles if the train's going to stop."

Phony suspense point! Everybody knows that Jordan is on that train

When Carl's screenplay notes that "Helen is aware of what Amy is thinking," Fred complains: *Can't photograph thoughts.*

Because time and money were both at a premium, the story had to be shot out of continuity. Fred knew he had to work quickly, and he memorized every shot in advance and in its exact order to facilitate the building of sets, rental of props and horses, and countless other details. "Working fast is very helpful because it maintains the energy of the performance," Fred said. "But you have to have the actors prepared to a point where they know exactly when, what, where, et cetera."

To help them prepare, Fred relied on Stanley's unusual tradition of formal rehearsals. The *High Noon* rehearsals started at the end of August, a week before the film shoot was to begin. No one bothered to tell Cooper—they had assumed that because he was such a big star and rehearsals were not stipulated in his very detailed contract he would not be interested. But after a day or so Cooper, who was still recuperating from the hernia operation he had undergone a few weeks earlier, called Carl to ask why he had not been invited. "After that he was there every day," Carl recalled. Cooper even brought along Slim Talbot, the Montana rodeo star who had served as his stand-in and occasional stuntman at film shoots for more than two decades.

It was during those first days of rehearsal that Carl and Fred discovered Katy Jurado's English was poorer than they had thought. Among other things, she couldn't pronounce *Doane*, the marshal's last name. That's when they decided to change it to Kane, which lent an appropriate Old Testament flavor to a story about vengeance, justice, and a community's moral failure. They also changed the names of the two bad-guy brothers from Guy and Milt Jordan to Frank and Ben Miller.

Lloyd Bridges had loved the rehearsals for *Home of the Brave*, and he felt more and more comfortable with Cooper and Katy Jurado as they rehearsed their scenes together. But he felt hemmed in psychologically by Fred. The director sat there, not saying much until Bridges tried out a loping Western walk as he felt his way into his character, a preening young man of ego and ambition. "You're not going to do that, are you?" Fred asked him.

"I was searching, you know, rehearsing," replied Bridges, who was beginning to absorb some of his character's sense of resentment.

While the actors were getting comfortable with their roles and with each other, Carl and Fred were still discussing how the climactic gunfight should play out. One gaunt, physically awkward, and rapidly aging lawman would be going up against four younger, meaner killers. How could Will Kane plausibly survive?

"It seemed that the odds against . . . our marshal were just too much, too great, and to be really realistic about it he should be killed (and) go down bravely but dead," Carl recalled.

But there were two problems with killing off Will Kane. First of all, once he became a star Gary Cooper seldom died in his movies—the only exceptions being *The Plainsman* (where Wild Bill Hickok lingers for one too many poker games), *For Whom the Bell Tolls* (there was no way to avoid the fact that Robert Jordan dies in Hemingway's novel), and *The Pride of the Yankees* (even Hollywood couldn't escape the fact that Lou Gehrig had died of the muscle-wasting disease that now bears his name). Just like John Wayne was not supposed to die in a movie, neither was Gary Cooper. No one wanted to upset audiences who routinely expected to see their celluloid heroes triumph.

But Carl also rejected a pessimistic ending because of its meaning. "Freddy, if we let him go, if he dies, what we'll be saying is you can't win, you just can't win, so just give in," Carl told Fred. "And I don't think we should do that, because maybe he has a chance to survive." Fred, in the end, readily agreed.

ONCE THE PRODUCTION MOVED to the film set, *High Noon* became Fred Zinnemann's show. Floyd Crosby, the film's director of photography, had never worked with Fred before, and he was amazed at his friend's rigorous sense of discipline and the power of his personality. "Everything was first take, first time," he recalled. "Zinnemann is a very efficient director. He knew that script, the whole script, by heart. I don't mean all the dialogue, but he knew every scene in it. He'd memorized it, and he knew what he wanted; and he was very easy to work with."

Fred quickly established a routine. "Zinnemann gets the actors in, everybody else leaves," said Crosby. "He rehearses with them sitting down, then calls the cameraman back, the gaffer, and various people. Then he blocks out the scene, what the moves will be. Now they rehearse with all the marks, then the cameraman. Now the stand-ins, who have been watching what the actors do, come in and take their place. Now it's your set, you do the lighting. When finished, you turn it back to the assistant director, then the director comes back, maybe one more rehearsal, then you shoot."

The only catch with Fred, Crosby recalled, is that he expected you to be ready when he was. "When you say you're ready, and he starts rehearsing . . . he doesn't want to stop and have you change the lighting. Some directors don't mind if you do that." Not Fred. "You'd better have it right when you turn it over to him."

Floyd also felt confident because he loved the screenplay. "It was the only script I ever read where I was convinced it was going to make them a great picture," he recalled.

They began the film shoot on Wednesday, September 5, at Motion Picture Center Studios with two days devoted to the sequence where Kane disrupts the church service to plead for help. *Fear. Everybody is scared and nervous*, Fred wrote in the margins of the script. At the conclusion, when the slippery Jonas Henderson advises Kane to leave town, Fred notes, *Sends man to certain death.*

Immediately there was a problem. Fred felt that Floyd wasn't properly lighting the room: there was too much light on the walls and not enough on the people. Stanley viewed the rushes that evening and he agreed they looked too dark; he ordered that the film be developed two points lighter than Crosby had stipulated. Nobody was very happy, but they moved on the next day. There was no time for reshooting.

That Friday they shot the interiors of the homes of Mart Howe and Sam Fuller. They also shot the exterior scene of Will and Amy mounting the buckboard and heading out of town.

The next day, they moved to the Columbia Ranch to film interiors of the courtroom and the marshal's office. This allowed them to finish with Thomas J. Mitchell's scenes and to introduce Grace Kelly. In the wedding scene, Kane lifts Amy, his new bride, onto a ledge and demands a kiss. Cooper's back was hurting and it pained him to pick her up, but he did it for several retakes. This scene also wrapped up Mitchell's work on the movie, which meant they didn't have to go into overtime for the second-most-expensive actor in the film.

Later in the day they filmed the scene in which Kane tries to explain to Amy who Frank Miller is and why Kane feels compelled to return to town. *Doesn't want to tell her how bad Miller is*, notes Fred.

The film company worked six days a week, nine to ten hours each day, with an hour's break for lunch. At times the heat was intense— Burbank peaked at ninety-nine degrees on Wednesday, September 19—especially for Grace Kelly and Katy Jurado in their tight and elaborate costumes. Cooper ate on the set with the cast and crew, but there were times when he lay down on the ground and rested his sore back or grabbed a nap under a tree near where he parked his silver Jaguar. The filming of *High Noon* was moving along at a brisk pace averaging four pages per day of the 111-page screenplay.

Fred tried to leave room for creative innovation. Sometime during that first week, he learned that his friend George Stevens was using a huge Chapman crane in shooting *Shane* for Paramount. Fred managed to borrow it for a day. The crane, which had only been invented a few years earlier, had a special boom that allowed it to lift a camera and operator as high as forty feet. "It's a pull-back-and-up at the same time," said Crosby. ". . . That was his idea. That was what he wanted."

Using the crane, Fred and Crosby created a shot that started off focusing tightly on Kane walking down the empty main street on his way to confront Frank Miller's gang and then rose up into a boom shot that encompassed the entire town, the deserted street, and the tiny lone figure of the marshal who looks around, turns, and begins the long walk to meet his enemies and his fate. As the shot rises sharp-eyed viewers can briefly spot modern telephone poles and lines and the Warner Bros. studio in the distance.

John Ford had once told Fred, "You could be a pretty good director if you could stop moving the goddamn camera all the time. There has got to be a *reason* for moving it. Use the camera like an information booth." Fred felt he honored Ford's instruction in designing the boom shot. The camera did not move much in *High Noon*, but when it did it served as an exclamation point expressing something important—in this case the supreme loneliness of a man facing death. It is one of the most memorable shots in the film, a fitting visual summation of all that has come before—and the perfect setup for what comes next.

CARL FOREMAN WAS ON the film set every day, working alongside Fred Zinnemann and observing. But Stanley Kramer was seldom around. In an unpublished interview in 1973, Stanley acknowledged, "I spent less time on that set than on any picture which we'd made . . . because we had already moved to Columbia and started preparation on *Death of a Salesman.*" Stanley felt compelled to "hedgehop" between the various *High Noon* sets and his new Columbia office. "It was at my insistence that he [Carl Foreman] be there and I literally set it up that whatever time I was away Foreman represented me. So that he was really like an associate producer on the film." The associate producer's role was more formal than Stanley stated: a September 14, 1951, letter from him to Carl specifically lists Carl's services on *High Noon* as "Writer and Associate Producer."

Still, Stanley insisted that he view the dailies each evening, and he didn't much care for what he was seeing. He told Carl and Fred he felt the photography was too washed out and bland. "Soon screams of anguish about the lousy quality of the photography were heard," Fred would recall. "Floyd stood his ground and never wavered . . . It took a lot of courage on his part; after all, he had to remember that it was not I who was paying his salary."

Stanley remembered it differently. He insisted that he actually pressed Crosby to make the images even grittier. "It was supposed to be shot in the heat of the summer and it was," he recalled. "But we never got the perspiration and since it was being done in black and white, Floyd Crosby, who was the photographer, I don't think was too happy with me—but in the lab even as we were shooting the dailies I was having them process the dailies printed sometimes four or five points lighter than he had indicated on his camera report in order to wash it out more."

Stanley also wasn't happy with some of the acting he was seeing in the rushes. He clearly did not care for Gary Cooper's laconic, minimalist technique. "As the scenes were shot, I was fascinated by Cooper's performance," Stanley says in his memoirs. "He seemed not to be acting but simply being himself. I don't know whether this was true. Perhaps he carefully considered each scene and decided how to best proceed but I don't think so . . . The character Cooper played was meant to be a simple man, not a superhero, strong but not unafraid, a human being. I think Cooper could have played him in his sleep—*there were times I thought that was just what he was doing* [author's italics]."

Later on Stanley was even more blunt. "Actors, I have to tell you, are not my favorite form of human life," he told an interviewer in 1975. Stanley said he loved Spencer Tracy for Tracy's honesty and his ability to subtly portray emotions, and he thought Marlon Brando was a huge talent. But as for Cooper, "he was not my favorite actor," although he admitted that Cooper belonged in *High Noon*. "That part was made for him, the pebble-kicking, non-reacting, all underneath kind of man who is tight-jawed and restrained. Cooper was interesting to me, but I don't think that what he did was necessarily acting." You can hear the disdain eating like acid through Stanley's efforts to sound diplomatic.

Even Lloyd Bridges, who had high regard for Cooper, wasn't sure at first what to make of his low-key, low-energy performance. "He made it so easy," Bridges told Leonard Maltin. "Matter of fact, most of the time I was working with him, I didn't feel I was on camera. That first scene I thought, 'My God, is this it? Will this be a print?'"

"He was such a down to earth, simple, no airs of any kind," Bridges added. "He was what you saw on that screen."

Stanley was equally unhappy with Grace Kelly. "She was miscast," he told author Donald Spoto. "She was just too young for Cooper. She didn't believe she did well in the role, and I didn't think so either."

The criticism rained down the heaviest on Carl, who considered it part of his job to shield Fred Zinnemann and the others from Stanley's scorn. "From the very first day, nobody at our Columbia front office was happy about it," Carl recalled. "The photography was questioned. There were remarks about slowness, dullness, too much under-playing. Somehow, although everyone had read the script, nobody seemed to remember that the small pieces of mosaic they saw in the dailies were part of a carefully designed pattern, that suspense is often increased by retarding pace, that strong emotions need not to be shrieked through a megaphone to be understood and felt."

Surely Stanley must have been feeling that *High Noon* was cursed. Carl's political problems were a lurking headache: the film could be easily condemned as the product of a backlisted left-wing writer. And now it looked like the picture itself wasn't any good. Carl was also certain that Stanley and George Glass were beginning to hear echoes of their own words and betrayals in the mouths of the cowardly townspeople.

As the date of Carl's HUAC appearance grew near, things only seemed to grow worse between him and Stanley. "We seemed to buck each other on practically everything," Carl recalled. "I was in no mood to compromise anymore, and I fought for everything I thought necessary all the way. Finally, he washed his hands of the whole picture, his attitude inferring that he was giving me enough rope."

UNBEKNOWN TO ANYONE WORKING on *High Noon*, on September 5—the first day of the film shoot—George Glass, accompanied by lawyer Martin Gang, gave sworn testimony to Bill Wheeler in an executive session at the Taft Building in Los Angeles, where Gang's law firm was located. Glass described how he and his wife, Harriet, had attended a Communist Party recruitment buffet dinner at screenwriter Ring Lardner Jr.'s house in late 1944 or early 1945. He said he later had attended various events at the houses of four other party members accompanied by his close friend, publicist Charles Daggett. But Glass denied he had ever joined the party. He conceded that he had given a lecture on public relations to a class at the People's Educational Center, which the committee considered a Communist front organization, and that he and Harriet had taken a three-month Spanish language course there. He even supplied a copy of his lecture, "How to Plan a Campaign," to enter into the record.

When Wheeler asked him what he thought of Communism, Glass replied, "I think it stinks . . . It is not only alien to my thinking but it is dangerous and certainly anti-democratic in the extreme." Still, Glass defended his admiration for trade unionism and said he saw no contradiction between supporting labor unions and supporting capitalism. It was a quick—perhaps thirty minutes—and relatively painless session, except for the fact that George Glass named twelve people, some of them his closest friends. He would repeat nine of those names the following January during a public appearance before the committee.

Glass's cooperation increased the pressure on Carl to do the same. The atmosphere got colder a few days later when Carl took time off from the film shoot to meet again with Stanley, only this time the two men were accompanied by their lawyers. Stanley was abrupt, according to Carl's account, and he seemed upset that Carl had brought along Sidney Cohn. He said he was not willing to let some New York lawyer dictate what would happen to his company; he'd rather shut it down. As for Carl, Stanley called him "Mr. Foreman" throughout the meeting.

Then as they moved into the second week of filming, things came to a head. While Cohn was back in New York, Carl was summoned to another meeting at Columbia with Stanley and all the other partners—Sam Katz, George Glass, and Samuel Zagon. He arrived to find them all sitting around the table and Stanley announced their verdict: Carl was to stop working on *High Noon*, hand in his resignation, and turn over his stock holdings. All of this was designed to insulate the company from Carl before his testimony. At a later date an appropriate settlement would be made.

Carl resisted. He said he did not want to appear before the committee as a man who had already been tried and convicted by his own partners. Nor did he want to abandon the picture at this crucial moment of production.

Stanley said he himself would take over the picture. Carl objected, pointing out that Stanley had had little direct involvement up until then and in any case had many other new tasks at Columbia. But Stanley warned Carl that if he didn't stay away from the set voluntarily, he would be barred physically.

Two days later, George Glass went to the Columbia Ranch with an envelope containing two letters dated September 12, 1951, and signed by Stanley. The letters suspended Carl from the company and from any role on *High Noon*, effective immediately. "You are hereby further instructed and directed not to come upon the premises of Motion Picture Center Studios nor upon any location where said motion picture is being produced."

"This was not my idea," George told him.

Carl called Sidney Cohn, who was adamant that these actions were illegal. You're the treasurer of the company, Cohn told him, and they can't fire you from *High Noon*, nor can they suspend you without going through a legal process. They can't even hold meetings without your being present. "Tomorrow," Cohn said, "I want you to report to your office at the Columbia studio and call for the company's books and inform them you're doing an audit."

Carl was certain the security guards wouldn't let him in the building, but when he showed up the following day he was allowed inside. When he got out of the elevator, he saw Zagon and Katz. They looked surprised to see him. He entered his office, and a few minutes later one of Zagon's law partners, Raymond Sandler, came by and asked what he was doing there. When Carl said he was planning to audit the books, Sandler left in a hurry.

Later that day, Stanley went to Fred and said he felt he had to remove Carl from the picture. He told Cooper the same thing. Stanley assured them both that he would be taking over Carl's role as producer. But both men echoed Carl's concern that Stanley would not have the time to oversee *High Noon* when he was so busy at Columbia on other projects. In any event, Cooper said, he liked working with Carl and wanted him to remain on the set. Fred said the same thing. So did Bruce Church, the Salinas financier, who had come to Hollywood with his family for their annual visit; his wife and two daughters had just had tea with Katy Jurado on the set.

Stanley was surprised by this polite but firm rebellion by the picture's essential people, and his discomfort was compounded by the fact that Carl had not yet signed the standard agreement deferring part of his salary during the film shoot. This was normally a routine procedure, but it had been overlooked in the rush to get *High Noon* rolling. Without the deferral, Stanley feared, Bank of America would refuse to issue the loan the company needed to complete the film. Stanley and the other partners were stuck. The following day Carl received a new letter. This one restored his role as writer and associate producer of *High Noon* until the film was completed. It also stipulated that "neither we nor you will release any publicity in connection with your relations as an employee officer, or director of this corporation without first consulting with each other and obtaining each other's consent thereto." Stanley phoned Carl that same day and asked for another meeting, just the two of them.

Carl arrived at the Columbia office on Tuesday afternoon, September 18. According to Carl's account, Stanley sounded bitter and resentful. "Well, you've won," he said. Not really, Carl replied. He had never wanted to hurt Stanley, and even now Carl said he hated to see him humiliated or feel defeated. Carl said he didn't want to leave the company. But if Stanley insisted, he would do so. Just give me a decent settlement, Carl told him.

Then Stanley started talking about Carl's plan to invoke the Fifth Amendment on the witness stand. The minute you do that they'll think you're a Communist and they'll suspect me as well. Stanley, pleaded Carl, I know we haven't been getting along lately, but we were once good friends and when this thing is over I hope we'll be friends again. If they ask me about you, I'll say you're a fervent anti-Communist, and I won't do anything to hurt you or the company. Everyone else had caved too quickly to HUAC's pressure. If he and Stanley held firm, Carl said, they could beat this. "Let's fight as long as we can," he pleaded.

The two men agreed to wait sixty days before making a final decision on Carl's fate. If, at the end of that time, the pressure was still too great, then Carl would agree to quit the company. If that became necessary, he was confident that Stanley would protect his interests. There would be no need to bring in the lawyers.

The meeting had lasted two hours. Carl felt closer to Stanley than he had for more than a year. They shook hands and embraced.

Over the years Carl Foreman gave many accounts of his meetings and interactions with Stanley Kramer and his other business partners and what he deemed to be their duplicity in their dealings with him. Stanley, by contrast, almost never spoke publicly about his disagreement with Carl and often praised him for his skills as a writer. There was one notable exception: an interview he gave to author Victor Navasky in the 1970s for *Naming Names*, Navasky's seminal book on the blacklist, in which Stanley contends that Carl was not honest about his past Communist connections and what he planned to say on the witness stand. In fact, Stanley claimed, Carl had made veiled threats against him. Stanley had reason to be anxious. He too had taught a workshop in screenwriting in spring 1947 on Thursday evenings at the People's Educational Center, the L.A. night school that the attorney general had later designated as a Communist front. During the same term, Carl had taught a similar course on Mondays. In June 1951 a supposedly reliable informant told FBI agents that Stanley "had the reputation of being sympathetic to Communism."

When Martin Berkeley made a voluntary appearance at the FBI's L.A. office early in September to answer questions, he said he knew nothing derogatory about Stanley personally but insisted that "the Kramer outfit is Red from the top to the bottom."

"In my negotiations with Foreman there was this veil of unspoken ideas about how my past connections could militate against me," Stanley told Navasky, adding, "If he had leveled with me, if I had known all the facts, that would have been one thing. But he really didn't . . . We had a couple of meetings in which I locked the door and looked him right in the eye, and I just felt he didn't look me back in the right way, and we parted. That's it."

Stanley went on. "I never heard the phrase 'qualified Fifth.' All I got from Foreman was the threat, 'I could name other names besides these.'"

In his autobiography, written a decade later, Stanley is more sympathetic to Carl. He never claims that Carl lied to him about being a Communist or threatened him with exposure. "He told me he was no longer in the party, and I believed him," he writes. Stanley says Carl explained that if he admitted to the committee that he had been a party member, he would have been legally required to provide the names of fellow members.

"My only problem with his stand was that it endangered our company. I realized his testimony would put all of us under a shadow, and I had a responsibility I couldn't ignore. We argued this out at some length, but he had no solution to his problem and I had no solution to mine."

They were two proud, prickly, creative, and self-made men, each one grown wary of the other and worried that the world he had built was about to come undone. The reservoir of affection and admiration each had genuinely held for the other was drained nearly dry.

Their two-hour private meeting was the last time they ever spoke.

"He and I had a sad parting," Stanley Kramer writes, "about which I feel bad to this day."

12.

"Bombshells"

I am not going to hang anybody that doesn't deserve it.

MARTIN BERKELEY

The walls were closing in on Carl Foreman, or so it must have felt. He was in the middle of the *High Noon* film shoot, while starting preliminary work on *The Happy Time* and *The Member of the Wedding*, the two pictures he would be dealing with once *High Noon* was completed. And of course he had to prepare for his own special performance before the House Un-American Activities Committee.

The morning after his meeting with Stanley Kramer, Carl decided to stay home from the film set to get some sleep because he knew he wouldn't be needed. At around ten, Carl flipped on the television to KTTV, the local station owned by the *Los Angeles Times*, to catch the opening of the hearings, which the station was broadcasting live. There was a fellow screenwriter, a slightly familiar-looking man in glasses, marching forward to the witness table.

From the moment he swept into crammed and claustrophobic Room 518 of the Federal Building in Los Angeles with his wife, Kathleen, and his legendary Washington lawyer, Edward Bennett Williams, by his side, Martin Berkeley took command of the committee's hearings like a professional actor storming into an amateur production of *Witness for the Prosecution*.

First came a touch of melodrama. Williams, who was also counsel for the Red-hunting senator Joseph McCarthy, announced that his client had received three phone calls over the previous week threatening his life and that of his wife if he testified. The latest had come two days earlier from a man who had warned, "If you name any names that have not already been named you will be sorry."

Nonetheless, here he was, Martin Berkeley, defying death to bring the truth to the committee and the American people.

Then, a touch of contrition. After being sworn in, Berkeley told the committee that his previous telegram denying he had ever been a Communist had been "very silly."

"I did it in a moment of panic," he explained, "and was a damn fool."

And now the true story supposedly could begin. Berkeley said he had first gone to Communist Party meetings in New York in 1936 and had joined the party later that year. When he got to Hollywood the following year, one of his friends sent him to meet screenwriter Guy Endore, who introduced him to fellow screenwriter Frank Tuttle, and he went to Frank and Sonia Tuttle's home, where he heard V. J. Jerome give a lecture on the evils of Trotskyism. Jerome had been briefly assigned as West Coast commissar, dispatched by national party headquarters in New York to put together the infrastructure and raise money to launch the new Hollywood branch. "His job was so good that we are all here today because of it," said Berkeley, venturing a teaspoonful of irony.

Then a solemn caveat. "I will not mention a name unless I am dead certain that this person was a member . . . " Berkeley insisted, "because I am not going to hang anybody that doesn't deserve it." But apparently dozens and dozens of people did deserve it. Berkeley spent the next hour serving up name after name, mopping the sweat off his shiny brow with a large white handkerchief as he proceeded. By the time he finished, he had named more than 150 people—close to half the total number of film-industry Communists—a never-to-be-broken HUAC Hollywood record.

"My dad was not cruel or difficult, so for him to do what he did seemed a fair amount out of character," says his son Bill, a teenager at the time. "To me, it was the act of somebody who was just desperately trying to survive. But because of him, a lot of people lost their livelihood."

According to Martin Berkeley, Jerome and his comrades had several objectives, including organizing the Screen Writers Guild, forming the Directors Guild, expanding the Hollywood Anti-Nazi League, and forging the Motion Picture Democratic Committee to support FDR's reelection campaign. The first local party meeting had been held at Berkeley's house in June 1937 because he had a large living room and ample space for parking. He rattled off the list of distinguished attendees, including Donald Ogden Stewart, Dorothy Parker, Dashiell Hammett, and "that very excellent playwright, Lillian Hellman."

Jerome worked closely with John Howard Lawson, a founder and first president of the Screen Writers Guild, whom Berkeley labeled "the grand Poo-Bah of the Communist movement from that day, I promise, until this. He speaks with the voice of Stalin and the bells of the Kremlin." The two commissars had assigned Berkeley to infiltrate the International Alliance of Theatrical Stage Employees trade union coalition and help get rid of its corrupt leadership.

Then he sprinkled some more names into his tale, including actress Virginia Farmer and screenwriters Waldo Salt and Arnold Manoff.

And then Carl Foreman: "That is spelled F-O-R-E-M-A-N. I believe he wrote the screenplay of *Cyrano de Bergerac* and *Champion* and other very fine pictures."

Committee attorney Frank Tavenner asked whether Carl held a position at the Screen Writers Guild. "I am glad you asked me that, sir, because that is very important," Berkeley replied. "There is on the Guild today only one man I know who was ever a Communist. This man has never, to my knowledge, disavowed his Communism. His name is Carl Foreman."

He added, "I hope he appears here, sir, and clears himself, because it will help me clear the guild and that is a job I want to do."

Watching at home, Carl was stunned. He'd only met the guy once or twice, so far as he could recall, and never at a Communist Party event.

Berkeley denied that party members wielded much influence over the content of the films they worked on. He described how actor Lionel Stander had once boasted that he had managed to whistle four bars of the "Internationale," the Communist workers' anthem, in the 1938 film *No Time to Marry* in a scene where he was waiting for an elevator. "But that was about the extent of what the Communists were able to do," Berkeley said. "A picture goes through too many hands. It is controlled by too many minds for any single writer or producer or actor to affect its content."

The main goals of the Communist Party in Hollywood, he added, were prestige and money. He recalled how members had launched various groups to collect funds for Democratic candidates. "That money never got where it was going, I'm sorry to say. It went, organizationally, I am convinced, to the Communist Party."

As for his own break with the party, Berkeley said he had first gotten into trouble when he was assigned at MGM to write a screenplay with a prominent right-wing writer. His comrades pressured him to quit the assignment, but he refused. He also had been shaken by the 1939

Ribbentrop-Molotov pact. He had become convinced that the party was stealing money donated to the anti-Fascist cause: "My belief was that these men were essentially thieves." He had also been upset when loyal comrades Paul Jarrico and Richard Collins had tried to load *Song of Russia* with pro-Soviet propaganda.

He had left the party in 1943 in a burst of antagonism, aligned himself with the anti-Communist faction of the Screen Writers Guild, and helped form a committee "whose sole purpose was to get control of the guild board away from the Reds and return it to the membership." It had worked, he claimed, with his usual lack of modesty. "We got rid of the rats . . . and Hollywood is a better place in which to live, let me tell you.

"Since then, I have devoted every moment that I could to fight the party.

"I am not a reactionary, I am not a Fascist . . . I am a liberal, middle-of-the-roader who says that the liberal movement in this country was destroyed by the Communists."

Of course there was a terrible price to pay for his high-minded idealism. Berkeley said he had been largely unemployed since he had walked away from the party. His former comrades were conspiring against him. His own agent, George Willner, had deliberately sabotaged his career by turning down potential screenwriting assignments. "A writer employed for ten straight years, writing commercial success after commercial success, suddenly for nineteen months finds he can't get a job," complained Berkeley, who didn't allow the fact he was under oath to constrain his admiration for his own work.

Representative Potter asked him if he believed that party members were dedicated to defending the Soviet Union "over and above their citizenship responsibility to defending the United States of America."

Berkeley's reply: "Mr. Potter, I believe that anyone who was then a member of the party or joined the party since 1945 and who retains his membership today is a traitor." This became a definition that the committee readily embraced and adopted for its own.

The congressmen thanked him profusely, not just in the name of the committee but, as Chairman Wood put it, on behalf of "every liberty-loving American citizen."

Then they swept him into an executive session where he named a dozen more names, after which the tributes continued to flow. "What you have done is probably as valuable as calling up the National Guard for the whole state," gushed Representative Walter.

Berkeley returned the compliment. "I think this committee has done a great deal to break the backbone of the party," he replied. He then suggested that Congress double HUAC's appropriation, and threw in some praise for Bill Wheeler as well. "I have never seen a man work as hard as that boy over there does."

Even as he testified that afternoon, the *Los Angeles Herald & Examiner* hit the streets with the front-page headline: DEFIES DEATH THREAT TO ACCUSE 'BIG SHOTS' and a photo of an anxious-looking Berkeley mopping his brow. "Death threats today failed to stop former Broadway Playwright Martin Berkeley, now a Hollywood film writer, from creating the biggest sensations to date in the Los Angeles hearings of the House Committee on Un-American Activities." Berkeley, the *Herald* reported, "dropped one bombshell after another" and "electrified the committee."

The next morning's *Los Angeles Times* featured a banner headline over the nameplate: COMMUNIST QUIZ GOES ON DESPITE THREATS. The lead paragraph was Berkeley's claim that "uncounted millions of dollars have been siphoned from Hollywood into the coffers of the Kremlin." An inside story listed all 152 names; but not one of them had been contacted for a response, although the paper did report that an actress named Patricia Segar Miller had contacted the *Times* to make clear she was not the Patricia Miller cited on Berkeley's list. The *Times* was a feudal kingdom of conservative purity but its rules on coverage were not all that unusual: none of the major newspapers bothered to contact the people named as Communists in the hearings. Legally, it was not required; all testimony given to a congressional hearing, no matter how libelous or unsupported by evidence, could be reported without fear of legal consequence, and therefore no newspaper seemed to bother with it.

The same front page further reflected the circumstances fueling the anti-Communist fever. The lead headline proclaimed REDS ASK NEW TRUCE TALKS, while an accompanying piece reported that Allied and North Korean troops were "locked in a swaying death grapple" in the mountains of eastern Korea. Yet another article reported the latest Defense Department figures that 83,257 American soldiers had been killed or wounded or were missing in the fifteen-month-long conflict. The numbers were mounting, and so was the sense that America was again under siege.

SHAKEN AND SICKENED BY what he'd seen and heard on TV, Carl decided he had to go to the Columbia Ranch that afternoon to let the cast and crew know what had happened before they read it in the evening papers. He told them when he got there about Berkeley's testimony and the fact that he himself would soon have to testify. He said he might be away from the set for several days, but he didn't want any of these matters to affect the film, and he expected everyone to continue their hard work for Fred.

Like many Hollywood film sets in those troubled times, the cast and crew of *High Noon* were deeply divided and on edge over politics, with suspicions high and some people avoiding each other. But they had worked together closely and professionally on the set. People seemed shocked by what Carl told them, but they generally smiled and offered their support. As Carl walked back to the parking lot, he heard Cooper call after him. "Uncle, that's the best speech I ever heard," said Cooper. He choked up and put his arm around Carl.

"Do what you have to do," Gary Cooper told him. "But kid, don't let them put you in jail."

13.

The Witness

I have already told you that I am not a Communist.

CARL FOREMAN

In the days before he was due to testify, Carl Foreman had a persistent daydream: that he would enter the witness stand as Abraham Lincoln, with a shawl around his shoulders and a wart on his cheek, and deliver a glorious burst of folksy eloquence that would shame the committee and trigger a standing ovation, putting an end to the madness of the Hollywood inquisition.

Reality was far less noble. Carl and Sidney Cohn spent the weekend prepping for his testimony, while the cast and crew of *High Noon* finished their work week on Saturday and prepared to fly up to the town of Sonora, 320 miles to the north, for a week of location shooting. With the project he had worked on so intensely removed from his sight, and the hearings bearing down on him, Carl suddenly felt alone and afraid. The career he had worked so hard to build was unraveling and there was nothing he could do to stop it. It was as if *High Noon* were truly happening to him.

The only person he could turn to for comfort was his wife, Estelle. They made love Sunday night and it was better than it had been in years. "We were together," he would recall. "We were joined."

Early Monday morning, Carl dressed in a dark blue suit and what he called "a very sincere tie." He picked up Cohn at the hotel and the two men drove to the Federal Building on East Temple Street in downtown Los Angeles, an imposingly gray and impersonal rectangle of concrete and glass with stripes of dark windows running up the sides that from a distance looked not unlike prison bars. They took the elevator up to the fifth floor; in Room 518 five microphones bristled from a polished tabletop near the front facing the committee members. Carl sat down and took a quick sip of water.

Frank Tavenner started with the basics: where and when was Carl born, where had he gone to school, when did he move to Los Angeles and what were his various jobs and screen credits there, and what was he working on now? Carl gave a quick plug to *High Noon*—and a backward swipe at the committee—describing the film as "the story of a town that died because it lacked the moral fiber to withstand aggression."

"It is a suspense story," he told Tavenner, "and I hope it will be a good one."

Then Tavenner cited Martin Berkeley's recent testimony that Carl was a member of the Communist Party. Was it true? Carl consulted with Sid Cohn, then declined to answer, invoking both the First and Fifth Amendments. "However, I should like to say this—"

Tavenner first cut him off—"I asked you no further question"—then changed gears: "I think I should give you the opportunity to answer." It was a far cry from the aggressive handling of earlier witnesses. The committee clearly was learning the benefits of appearing to be courteous in public.

Carl explained that on September 11, 1950, he had voluntarily signed an oath as a member of the executive board of the Screen Writers Guild pledging that he was not a member of the Communist Party, nor of any organization dedicated to the violent overthrow of the U.S. government. "That statement was true at that time, sir, and is true today."

It was a convoluted way of saying he hadn't been a party member for at least a year; Tavenner immediately sought clarification. What about between 1945 and 1950? he asked.

Carl declined to answer on the same grounds as before.

Did you surrender your party membership while you were in the Armed Forces?

"I have already told you that I am not a Communist . . ."

Did you rejoin the party after you left the Army?

"I decline to answer that . . ."

Were you a member of the Communist Party while you taught screenwriting at the People's Educational Center?

"I decline to answer . . ."

Had Carl at any time renounced his party membership?

"I have never admitted that I was a member of the Communist Party."

Do you deny it now?

"I decline to answer . . ."

Carl was fencing with Tavenner and it was a dangerous game. He could be charged with contempt of Congress for his partial answers and selective use of the Fifth Amendment. And of course, his failure to fully cooperate would almost certainly land him on the blacklist.

Bill Wheeler was sitting next to Tavenner and whispering in his ear. The next question: Had there been conflict within the Screen Writers Guild between Communists and anti-Communists?

Carl said he really didn't know because in the days before the war, "I was a very unimportant guy in Hollywood and in the guild as well."

Tavenner asked Carl to speak louder. Carl again reached for a glass of water.

Didn't you violently oppose the Screen Writers Guild loyalty oath?

Carl said yes, but so had many other guild members. "When the resolution was finally written to my satisfaction, I voted in favor."

Tavenner pressed on. How many members of the guild were also members of the Communist Party?

Carl declined to answer.

Representative Clyde Doyle took over. Doyle, who fashioned himself a man of sweet reason, reminded Carl that the committee's stated mission was to investigate subversive activities. He understood why Carl did not want to snitch on others, Doyle said, "but how about yourself, can't you help us from your experience to make this study?"

Carl said it was a fair question, and he added, "I hope you will believe this: if I knew anyone who now or ever had treasonous intentions toward the United States of America and its form of government or its Constitution, I would consider it not only my duty but my privilege to report it to the nearest authorities."

Doyle said his son had been killed in the war and he honored every person who had served in the military, as Carl had. But he said he had learned too much about the perfidy of Communists to honor any of them. "Foreman, we know of your great ability and your splendid service to the Armed Forces . . . leave names out if you will, as far as my questions are concerned . . . [but] what do you know about the functions of the Communist Party, if anything, that would help us get at the problem? Is that a fair question?"

But Carl wouldn't bite. He fell back on pleading patriotism. "I am an American, I was born here and I love this country. I love it as much as any man on this committee."

Doyle ran out of time. The soft sell hadn't worked. Now Donald L. Jackson, a former Marine and former journalist, took over with a more aggressive approach. "How many known or self-admitted Communists are members of the Screen Writers Guild?"

"I wouldn't have any idea, sir."

Jackson, who had replaced Richard M. Nixon on the committee after Nixon's election to the Senate, asked why Carl had opposed a loyalty oath for guild members.

He had, said Carl, because he believed the United States was engaged in a war of ideas with the Soviet Union and for America to win that struggle, people must be free to express themselves. "I have a feeling that the imposition of oaths somehow smacks of police state methods and I kind of don't like it."

Jackson then went for the patriotic jugular. Wasn't Foreman aware that every one of the eighty thousand Americans killed or wounded in Korea had taken such an oath?

Carl pointed out again that he himself had ultimately taken the oath. He had no problem with oaths, so long as they were voluntary.

The two men were talking past each other. Jackson dismissed Carl as untrustworthy. "I personally will place no credence in the testimony of any witness who is not prepared to come before this committee and fully cooperate," he declared.

Jackson read an editorial from Saturday's *Herald Express*, a Hearst paper, praising the committee's "splendid job" and honoring the late screenwriter James McGuinness—he had died in December 1950—and fellow members of the Motion Picture Alliance who had fought against Communism. Representative Francis Walter chimed in, saying it was "very, very disturbing" to hear that some of the committee's most passionate supporters were now being blacklisted by Communist sympathizers for their pro-American views.

Carl didn't hesitate to challenge this. "Mr. Walter, please don't be disturbed," he replied, "because that information is absolutely incorrect." He pointed out that he was soon to produce a picture that starred Adolphe Menjou and was directed by Edward Dmytryk and that Gary Cooper was starring in his current picture, *High Noon*—all of them associated with the Alliance. "Really, sir, you have been misinformed," he told Walter.

Jackson jumped back in. "Do you think that Mr. Dmytryk was doing the American thing, the right thing, in coming before this committee and giving us the benefit of his knowledge regarding Communism and Communist activities?"

Carl dodged and weaved. "I don't think it is very important as to what I think, Mr. Jackson. I think it is important to Mr. Dmytryk what he thinks."

Charles Potter came next, expressing his disappointment that Carl was withholding information. Once again, Carl fell back on his record of personal loyalty and patriotism, citing the honorary membership he had been given by the Paralyzed War Veterans of America for *The Men*.

"I am afraid, Mr. Foreman, that they are disappointed in your testimony today," Potter replied.

By now the hearing had drifted into a near-comatose slump. It was a dispiriting ritual. The committee had tried to entice Carl to be a good American and come clean, and when he refused, they had tried to shame him. Carl had been polite and deferential, and he had spiritedly defended his own patriotism, but he had ducked all the key questions. He had not uttered one word of criticism of Communism. All he would concede for the record was that he wasn't a Communist now, and hadn't been one in 1950 when he signed the Screen Writers Guild loyalty oath. There would be no Larry Parks moment of truth.

"The witness is excused," concluded Chairman Wood. It had only taken an hour. Carl headed home to Brentwood.

The house was flooded with telegrams, flowers, and phone calls of support. Someone even sent over a box of glassware addressed to *The Home of the Brave*. Carl felt exhausted, but there was no sense of relief either for him or for Estelle. They both knew the crisis wasn't over. Estelle was exhausted as well, so in the evening she stayed home while Carl's buddy John Weaver drove him to Union Station, where he boarded the night train to Sonora. He spent Tuesday on the set. The morning headlines were relatively mild. The *Los Angeles Examiner* led with Walter's allegation that former Communists who had informed on the party were being blacklisted by movie producers and employment agencies. It quoted Carl as denying the allegation, which made him look like he was speaking on behalf of opponents of the committee, a role he had no desire to be cast in.

Back in Hollywood, the Kramer people met with Harry Cohn's crew of executives at Columbia to assess the damage that Carl's invocation of the Fifth Amendment had caused. This wasn't the first time they had been embarrassed politically. Two months earlier, Sam Katz had learned that Joseph Losey, a talented young director who had just been offered a three-picture deal to help the Kramer Company with the growing load of films, was to receive a HUAC subpoena. Katz had told Losey he would have to sign a loyalty oath before the deal could go through. Losey had fled to Europe instead.

The understanding that Stanley and Carl had reached before he testified now went out the window. After the meeting, Columbia issued a statement in Stanley's name. "There is a total disagreement between Carl Foreman and myself," it read. "Interests and obligations involved are far greater than his or those of this company," Stanley added, somewhat cryptically. Therefore, the shareholders and directors would meet as soon as possible, and "necessary action will be taken at that time."

PARTNER TURNS ON RELUCTANT FILM QUIZ WITNESS read the headline in the *Washington Post*, an accurate if brutal summation.

When reporters reached him in Sonora, Carl refused to comment. He called the office in Los Angeles, but he was told that Stanley, George Glass, and Sam Katz were all out of town and unavailable to talk to him.

In his letter of September 14, twelve days earlier, Stanley had pledged that neither side would issue public statements about Carl's status with the company without first informing and obtaining the consent of the other.

"They didn't wait the sixty days," Carl would recall. "They quit right then and there and threw me to the wolves."

In one sense, Carl was lucky: the committee had quietly decided not to seek to prosecute witnesses who had selectively invoked the Fifth Amendment. But there was the blacklist to contend with. Two days later, after the committee adjourned its Hollywood session for the fall, the Motion Picture Industry Council announced that twenty-eight "unfriendly" witnesses would face industry sanctions in keeping with its policy of "repudiating those who did not cooperate with the committee." The council had been set up by Dore Schary and fellow studio executives three years earlier to protect the industry's public image by helping enforce the Waldorf Statement's ban against employing subversives. It didn't list the names of the newly targeted twenty-eight, but Carl's was one of them. His old friend and mentor was now one of his persecutors.

When Sidney Cohn finally reached Sam Zagon, Stanley Kramer's lawyer, he accused the Kramer Company of breaking their word to Carl. Zagon replied, "Well, it's obvious that he's got to go."

WHILE CARL WAS TESTIFYING that Monday, Fred Zinnemann and the *High Noon* cast and crew flew to Sonora on a chartered DC-3. Everyone seemed to relax once they landed in the cool foothills of the Sierra

Nevadas, far removed from the smog-drenched heat and toxic politics of Los Angeles. "The northern California countryside was ravishingly beautiful," Fred would recall. "It was great to be in the open from dawn to dusk."

But the first morning on location, disaster nearly struck. Floyd Crosby and Fred set out to shoot one of the key moments in the *High Noon* narrative—the arrival at noon of the train carrying the newly released Frank Miller. The empty train tracks symbolizing the threat to come were one of Fred's three cherished visual elements, and he wanted to film the train's appearance in the most powerful possible way. He and Crosby decided to position the camera between the two rails to capture the approaching train head-on, starting as a distant dot on the horizon and culminating with the engine coming to a screeching halt within inches of the camera. Both Floyd and Fred were on their stomachs behind the camera tracking the locomotive as it grew larger and larger in the viewfinder. "It looked beautiful," Fred recalled, "moving rapidly with white smoke billowing. Then it let out black smoke, which looked even better. What we didn't know was that this was a signal that the engine's brakes were failing."

With the engine bearing down on them, Crosby and his assistant tried to snatch the camera out of the way but the tripod's hooks got caught on one of the rails. Both he and the assistant—and Fred, who was standing just behind them—jumped to safety at the last possible moment. The camera was crushed by the oncoming locomotive, but the film magazine remained miraculously intact. The exposed film was saved, and the shot appeared in the movie. But it cost eight thousand dollars to replace the camera.

Carl's arrival gave him and Fred a chance to again review one of the more difficult decisions they faced during the film shoot. Carl's script contained a subplot involving a second deputy named Toby. In "The Tin Star," John Cunningham's short story, Toby is the sheriff's loyal main deputy. Carl used the same character in his screenplay, but his version puts Toby out of town bringing in a prisoner while the main story is taking place. Toby is in a hurry to get back to Hadleyville to attend Kane's wedding, but he is unaware that Frank Miller is returning on the noon train and so he has a limited sense of urgency.

Carl wrote three short scenes, scattered through the screenplay. In the first, Toby cuts the rawhide thong around the prisoner's hands to enable him to smoke. In the second scene, the prisoner hits Toby on the head with a rock and tries to escape but is overcome by Toby and knocked unconscious. In the third scene, Toby and the recaptured prisoner arrive at a stagecoach station, where Toby ties him to a hitching post, goes inside, and reacquaints himself with a sultry young Mexican woman he has met before. He decides to linger there for beer and seduction under the assumption that he has already missed the wedding and doesn't need to hurry back to town.

Carl and Fred have both maintained that they added the subplot scenes for "protection" because they feared the film might otherwise feel too claustrophobic and intense. "People go to a Western expecting to see a lot of vistas and things like that," Carl recalled. "We wanted a safety valve. Suppose we were wrong? One must have conviction, agreed, but I think there are valid cases for protection takes."

"Stanley liked it, Fred liked it, everybody liked it."

The three scenes were scheduled to be filmed outside Sonora near the end of the location shoot, but Fred claimed they were never completed because the weather turned bad while the fight scene was being shot on the day before they were due to return to Hollywood. Fred insisted that he had hated the subplot because it "destroyed the unity of time and place which was so enormously important," and stalled the relentless action of the film. Both Fred and Carl said the scenes were never intended to be used, and Fred insisted they had abandoned the scenes after two or three attempts. But film editor Elmo Williams claims they shot the entire sequence of three scenes and that he included it in the director's master cut at Fred's request.

In fact, says Roberta Haynes, the actress who played the young Mexican woman and who is likely the last surviving member of the cast, all three scenes were completed. The shooting schedule backs her up; it shows that two and a half days were devoted to the three scenes—September 28 and 29 and October 1. And Carl supports Williams's claim that Fred included them in the director's cut made immediately after the film shoot was completed. Later on, as we'll see, the fate of the three scenes took on great importance when *High Noon* was edited.

The last day on location was devoted to filming the fight scene between Will Kane and Harvey Pell in the livery stable. Lloyd Bridges says Gary Cooper was reluctant to do the scene because his back was hurting and he had other physical ailments as well. But in the end he decided to perform it without a stunt double.

Before the filming began, Bridges smuggled his wife, Dorothy, and seven-year-old son, Beau, who were visiting the set, up to a hayloft to watch. Lloyd explained to Beau that it would be a pretend fistfight and no one would get hurt. But when at the end Cooper threw a bucket of water on Beau's supposedly unconscious dad, the boy burst out laughing. "My father did not tell me he was going to get knocked out," recalled Beau, himself now a highly respected actor, more than sixty years later. "Then Cooper goes over and throws a bucket of water on him, and I wasn't ready for that. And I just lost it and started cackling and laughing and I destroyed the shot."

The two men had to film the entire fight scene again. Cooper never uttered a word of complaint.

Beau said his father bawled him out all the way back to the hotel, but when Cooper got on the elevator with them he invited Lloyd and his family to join him for dinner. "He was a sweet man," Lloyd Bridges would recall.

Cooper in general was relaxed and friendly on the set. Roberta Haynes noticed how easygoing and informal he was, and she got to know him better the following year when she worked with him on *Return to Paradise*, which was filmed in Samoa. "He was wonderful to work with and very cooperative," she recalls. "He was very private but he never played the big star. I loved working scenes with him." As for his reputation as a lady-killer, Haynes said he never was anything other than a gentleman to her. "In fact, he said to me I shouldn't feel bad if he didn't make a pass at me because he was on [medication] for his ulcers."

Grace Kelly, who arrived from Denver a few days before rehearsals began, never seemed to fit in with the rest of the cast and crew. She looked uncomfortable and seemed unfriendly. Fred Zinnemann recalled that she seemed "tense and remote," but he wasn't displeased, because her stiffness served her in the role of the troubled new bride who felt betrayed by her husband's insistence on confronting the Miller gang.

Gary Cooper was more kind. "I knew this: she was very serious about her work and had her eyes and ears open," he would tell Hedda Hopper after the film shoot was completed. "She was trying to learn, you could see that. You can tell if a person really wants to be an actress. She was one of those people you could get that feeling about and she was very pretty. It didn't surprise me when she was a big success."

"I also feel like she fills a much needed gap in motion pictures," Cooper added, offering his professional opinion as a longtime connoisseur of beautiful women and their capacity for passion. "It's been quite a few years since we had a girl in pictures that looked like she was born on the right side of Park Avenue. Looks like she could be a cold dish with a man until you got her pants down and then she'd explode."

For her part, Kelly expressed warm feelings about Cooper as well. "He's the one who taught me to relax during a scene and let the camera do some of the work," she would recall. "On the stage you have to emote not only for the front rows, but for the balcony too, and I'm afraid I overdid it. He taught me the camera is always in the front row, and how to take it easy."

The warm feelings articulated by Kelly and Cooper led many people on the set to conclude they were having an affair. Cooper, after all, was famous for sleeping with his female costars as if it were a contractual obligation, and Kelly would soon acquire a reputation for the same kind of sexual conduct. For several years after *High Noon*, she was reputed to have slept with various of her leading men, including Clark Gable, William Holden, Ray Milland, and Bing Crosby. "Grace almost always laid the leading man," novelist Gore Vidal once claimed. "She was famous for that in this town."

When Patricia Neal visited Cooper on the Sonora location, she noticed that Kelly studiously ignored her. "I was used to being snubbed in public, but this I couldn't figure," Neal writes. "Unless she felt I was competition."

She finally asked Cooper, "Is Grace interested in you?"

"Nope, I think she's set her cap for Freddie," Cooper replied. But Neal adds, "He wasn't totally convincing." She didn't ask him again.

Grace's parents, who must have had an inkling about the dangers their beautiful, love-starved daughter faced in Hollywood, dispatched her eighteen-year-old sister, Lizanne, to live with her at the Chateau Marmont during the film shoot and act as a junior chaperone and all-around wet blanket. When Cooper took Grace for a drive in his silver Jaguar in search of a good meal, Lizanne reportedly would squeeze herself into the back of the two-seater and tag along.

The problem with the tales of Grace Kelly's promiscuity is not only that there's no reliable way to verify them, but that they all fit a certain template. Sex in Hollywood, as anthropologist Hortense Powdermaker noted in her 1950 study *The Dream Factory*, was often a joyless, hollow, and transactional exercise, with older, powerful men exploiting younger, attractive women. "It's good to be skeptical," says film historian Jeanine Basinger. "When you spend time in Hollywood here's what you hear: number one, all the men were gay, and number two, all the women were nymphomaniacs. It was how men talked about women and nobody thought much about it."

Roberta Haynes, who was an attractive brunette with aspirations of stardom, recalls being chased around the office by producer Jerry Wald, who was almost twice her age. But when it comes to Grace Kelly, Haynes believes Cooper was telling the truth. She recalls seeing Grace sitting on Fred Zinnemann's lap on the film set several times during their week in Sonora and concluding they were having an affair.

If so, they weren't the only ones. Roberta also contends that Carl Foreman and Katy Jurado were sleeping together during the location shoot, although Jurado stayed away when Estelle Foreman arrived in Sonora for a visit. Carl himself made a teasing reference to helping Jurado with her English during the film shoot. "I used to work with her a lot," he recalled. "That was very pleasant."

Despite her lack of English language skills, Jurado's performance captivated Zinnemann, Foreman, and Kramer. She fit their fantasies of the smoldering, dark-skinned, Latina sexpot, and her sneer and her arrogance, mixed with a certain vulnerability enhanced by her hesitant pronunciation, made her perfect for the role of the proud but humbled businesswoman. "I wanted a Mexican gal and she had a fire and a thing for it and I think she was wonderful," Stanley would recall.

Although *High Noon* was only her second American film, twenty-four-year-old María Cristina Estella Marcela Jurado García was already a full-fledged movie star in Mexico. The film that made her famous was *Nosotros los Pobres* ("We, the Poor"), one of the greatest of Mexican epic melodramas about the urban poor, released in 1948. After *High Noon*, she would go on to dozens more Hollywood pictures, usually playing a Native American or "half-breed." She was nominated for an Academy Award for playing the Comanche wife of Spencer Tracy's character in *Broken Lance* (1954). In *Stay Away Joe* (1968) she played Elvis Presley's half-Apache mother. "I love to act any character at all," she once told Louella Parsons. "But just once I would like to be my Mexican self in an American motion picture."

After the film shoot was over, Grace Kelly complained about her own performance. Ever the perfectionist, she compared herself with withering disapproval to one of Hollywood's most accomplished stars. "You look into Gary Cooper's face and you see everything he's thinking," she said. "I looked into my own face and I saw nothing."

Grace felt that Fred Zinnemann had not been helpful professionally, despite his infatuation with her. "I couldn't get the kind of direction from him that I needed as a neophyte, and I wasn't equipped enough for moviemaking at that time to do it for myself," she recalled. "After I saw the finished picture, I was horrified! I remember thinking, 'Well, this poor girl may never make it unless she does something very quickly.'

I rushed back to New York and started taking classes again with Sandy Meisner," her highly regarded acting teacher.

Fred confessed that he had difficulty working with people he didn't think were talented. Not being an actor himself, he believed his role was to help free performers to do their most creative work. "All I do is use my instinct for casting and let the actors feel that I trust them and have respect for them, and encourage them," he said. But "if by some chance I get a mediocre actor, I get very frustrated."

Grace Kelly, apparently, was a mediocre actor by Fred Zinnemann's demanding standards.

THE CAST AND CREW returned to Hollywood on October 3 with just a week of shooting left and began filming the scenes in Helen's hotel room at Motion Picture Center Studios the following day. Two days later they returned to the Columbia Ranch in Burbank to put the finishing touches on the climactic showdown, including the final shoot-out between Will Kane and Frank Miller.

Much of the gunfight had been staged at the ranch before the film company had gone to Sonora. Fred's highly detailed notes make clear that the creation of the sequence was an elaborate collaborative effort, involving not just Fred and Carl but also Stanley Kramer, production designer Rudolph Sternad, and composer Dimitri Tiomkin. Then Fred and Sternad roughed out a series of sketches showing every shot Fred would need and the relation of each camera cut to the ones that came directly before and after. "Thanks to this exact pre-planning, the actual production time was reduced very considerably," Fred writes. The *High Noon* creative machine was humming.

The shoot-out had to be plausible and exciting, and it had to end with one live marshal and four dead gunmen.

The solution that they came up with was a perfect fit. In the opening segment Will Kane is able to shoot and kill Ben Miller, Frank's impulsive younger brother played by Sheb Wooley, after Ben inadvertently alerts Kane by breaking a shop window and taking a woman's bonnet. This reckless act allows the marshal to get the drop on him. It's a highly appropriate fate for Ben, an arrogant man-child whose undisciplined act of petty thievery gets him killed.

In the second segment, Kane manages to kill Jack Colby, played by Lee Van Cleef, after the gunman blunders into the livery stable where Kane has taken cover, leaving himself exposed and an easy target. We know almost nothing about Colby, who has no speaking lines in the film, except that he plays the harmonica and seems bored and impatient as he waits for his vengeful boss's train to arrive. His impatience proves fatal. Two bad guys down, two to go.

Amy, Kane's estranged new bride, is sitting with Helen Ramirez on the soon-to-depart train when she hears the gunfire. Fearing the worst, she leaps from her seat and rushes wildly up the main street. She comes across a dead body that she fears is her husband's until she gets close enough to see it's one of the gunmen (Ben Miller). She then makes her way to the nearby marshal's office, where she reads Kane's last will and testament. Meanwhile, Kane is pinned down in the livery stable by the two remaining gunmen, Frank Miller and Jim Pierce. They hurl burning lanterns into the barn to smoke him out. He turns loose the horses inside and climbs on one as they stampede from the burning barn. Miller and Pierce give chase and trap Kane inside the saloon, where he faces another cross fire. Pierce has his back to the marshal's office; Amy grabs the gun that an angry Harvey Pell had left hanging on a hook and shoots Pierce in the back through the window. Seeing what has happened, Miller seizes Amy and marches her out into the street with a gun to her head, forcing Kane to come out as well. Amy wildly reaches up and claws at Miller's face, and as he throws her to the ground Kane opens fire, killing him. These last two killings not only are plausibly staged, but they restore the partnership and the trust between Kane and his new wife. The two have confronted terrible danger and survived, and they share a quality no one else in Hadleyville possesses: courage.

It took three days to finish shooting the gunfight at the Columbia Ranch, leaving three more days for filming back at Motion Picture Center Studios. The last day was October 11.

The proof of Fred Zinnemann's relentless efficiency came in dollar signs: he completed *High Noon* in the allotted thirty-two days at the budgeted amount of $790,000. Meanwhile, at a nearby film set, his good friend George Stevens was making his own classic Western: *Shane*, admittedly a far more visually sumptuous film, shot in Technicolor largely on location in picturesque Jackson Hole, Wyoming. It took seventy-five days to shoot—twenty-seven above what had originally been scheduled—at a cost of $2.9 million.

Afterward, Carl held a modest wrap party for the cast and crew. It felt a little like a wake. Stanley Kramer, Sam Katz, and George Glass all stayed away. "One or two secretaries and a few of the production staff at the Columbia offices dropped in, but no one else," Carl recalled.

14.

The Exile

I was convinced of Foreman's loyalty, Americanism, and ability as a picture maker.

GARY COOPER

It took nearly a month for Sidney Cohn to work out a severance package for Carl Foreman. Their opening demand was for four years' pay, based on the company's projected profits and the value of Carl's shares. Stanley's lawyers first offered $18,000 but quickly raised it to $55,000. Carl's forfeiture of credit as associate producer of *High Noon* was part of the bargaining from the beginning. The film's opening credits began with "Stanley Kramer Presents," but no producer was listed.

The final agreement, dated October 22, 1951, cited "differences of opinion" between the production company and Carl "with respect to the rights and obligations of the parties in connection with the completion of the product of said motion picture photoplay, and with respect to other matters." He was relieved of his duties and would be paid his entire compensation for *High Noon* as previously agreed to. In return Carl waived his credit as producer or associate producer but retained the screenplay credit. No dollar amount was stipulated, but Carl and Cohn later put the final figure at roughly $150,000—the equivalent of $1.4 million in 2016 dollars, and far more than any other blacklisted screenwriter had received for an early termination of a contract (most got nothing). Once it leaked out, the reported amount of the final settlement engendered jealousy and astonishment among Carl's colleagues and former comrades and was no doubt one of the reasons some of them later accused him of secretly selling out to the committee.

When the day came for the signing, all of the documents were laid out on a large table in Sam Zagon's law office at the corner of Hollywood and Vine. At three P.M., Carl passed by Stanley, George Glass, and Sam Katz in the hallway without speaking. Sidney Cohn led him into the conference room, where Carl signed all of the papers, and Cohn suggested he go somewhere nearby while Sidney stayed behind to witness the signing by the others. The door was slamming shut on one of the most creative partnerships in Hollywood.

Carl walked to the Brown Derby just a block down Vine Street and ordered a drink at the bar. Peering into the darkness he noticed two men sitting at a nearby table. It was Bill Wheeler, HUAC's Hollywood investigator, and Lloyd Bridges. Wheeler, always affable, gave Carl a grin, while Lloyd waved weakly. Carl walked over. He told Wheeler what a coincidence this was because he had just come from signing a settlement agreement ending his relationship with the Stanley Kramer Company—a process that had been set in motion when Wheeler had handed him a subpoena five months earlier. "And what are you doing here, Bud?" Carl asked Bridges, using Lloyd's nickname.

Bridges looked embarrassed. He launched into a tangled explanation of his brief involvement with the Communist Party: he hadn't known what he was joining, and he had been in it only for a few weeks and had left without knowing what it was all about, and now Wheeler was helping him get out of the mess he found himself in. Wheeler nodded and explained to Carl that Lloyd would be testifying in a closed session and everything would be all right.

Carl nodded but didn't say anything; he just got up and left.

AS IT TURNED OUT, Lloyd Bridges didn't get off the hook so lightly. Unlike Carl, he hired Martin Gang and gave testimony in executive session to Wheeler in which he confessed his past membership in the party and named a half dozen other members. Still, he hadn't passed the test. For a year after *High Noon* came out, he had problems finding work. Film producer Frank King told Gang that Bridges's name was on studio lists as politically unacceptable. Gang wrote letters on his client's behalf, only to learn that Roy Brewer, now serving as chairman of the board of the Motion Picture Alliance, had tagged Bridges as an unrepentant Red.

There's no indication that Gang's letters did any good; Bridges still had trouble getting parts. Looking back forty years later, Bridges was careful to deny he had ever been involved with the Communist Party. "I felt after I did *High Noon* that my future would be pretty rosy, but anyone who was sort of liberal in those days or wanting to do anything about improving humanity kind of suffered," he recalled. "And I was part of an organization called the Actors' Lab and there apparently were quite a few Communists in that organization, so I suppose that was one of the reasons I was put on the list. Didn't work for several years." Bridges eventually got the starring role in *Sea Hunt*, a television program that revived his career. But it was a syndicated show, not a national network program, presumably because the networks were more cautious about hiring people whose names were on someone's list.

In fact, Bridges was one of a half dozen or so people involved with *High Noon* who were either outright blacklisted or deemed politically tainted. Carl had hired two of them—supporting actors Howland Chamberlin and Virginia Farmer—knowing full well that they were about to be called to testify and would soon be blacklisted. "I did this because, as far as I was concerned, this would be their last job and they would certainly need the money," Carl later recalled. He did not care that his "former friends at the company would say that son of a bitch, right down to the last he was taking care of his Communist friends." Chamberlin got $750 for one week of work.

Both Chamberlin and Farmer had been named by Rena Vale, a former Communist Party member turned star witness for the California legislature's Red-hunting Tenney Committee in the early 1940s— testimony that was readily available to HUAC's investigators. Vale described several meetings of party members working in the arts that had been held at Farmer's house in Santa Monica; Chamberlin, who was a member and organizer of the party's cultural unit, had been an occasional participant, Vale said, as had Chamberlin's wife, actress Leona McGenty.

Chamberlin, with his slicked-back hair, pencil mustache, and eternally cynical expression, played many an unprincipled stool pigeon in his career as an actor. In *High Noon* he played the sneeringly sardonic hotel clerk who takes pleasure in explaining to newly married Amy Kane the reasons for his deep personal dislike of her husband. But on the witness stand before HUAC, Chamberlin was a defiant man of principle. "My present occupation is an actor, and I find it deeply repugnant and profoundly un-American to be smeared, blacklisted, and strangled economically by my presence before this committee," he declared.

Chairman Wood immediately objected: "Just a moment, just a moment will you, please . . . Will you please cease just a moment when I interrupt you? . . . Will you please spare us your opinion as to the standing, intelligence, veracity, moral character of members of this committee and its staff, and answer the questions that are directed to you, because we are not concerned at all about your opinions of us."

Chamberlin had spent most of his acting career on the stage. His first motion picture was *The Best Years of Our Lives* in 1946, and he'd had nearly a dozen small movie roles since then. Citing director William Wyler's claim that he couldn't have made the picture five years later because of the atmosphere of fear, Chamberlin added, "I charge that this committee is responsible in helping create this kind of an atmosphere which features censorship." The committee couldn't wait to dismiss him from the witness table.

Farmer's appearance was even briefer. She tried to read a statement invoking the principles of her Pilgrim ancestors in explaining her opposition to the committee, but Wood cut her off. Farmer's statement concluded, "Never have I felt . . . so deservedly the daughter of my fathers and mothers as I do in taking the stand that I take today, upon the First and Fifth Amendments of the Constitution before this committee."

Actor Jeff Corey also took the fifth when called. Corey had played the psychiatrist in *Home of the Brave* and was one of Stanley Kramer's favorite character actors. He told the committee he had been graylisted in April 1951 after fellow actor Marc Lawrence named him as a former party member. "Hitherto I had been quite busy as an actor, but my professional fortunes have waned considerably, coincident with the mentioning of my name."

Chairman Wood cut Corey off when he sought to explain why he was invoking the Fifth Amendment, saying he wanted no further speeches. "I seem to have worn you gentlemen out successfully," Corey replied—and soon left the witness table.

Corey became a speech therapist, coached drama students, and did construction work. He didn't get another professional acting job until 1961.

"All I had to do was drop the two required names in the basket, and I would have been permitted to work," he said. "I didn't choose to. I thought it degrading, and a man has to live with himself."

High Noon cameraman Floyd Crosby never got his day in front of the committee. Crosby didn't find out he was blacklisted until the following year when Fred Zinnemann tried to hire him to work as a second-unit cameraman on *From Here to Eternity* at Columbia Pictures. Fred met with resistance, and when he pushed for a reason, someone at the studio explained, "Well, he's on the list." Crosby said he had belonged to a group that wanted to make left-wing films. "I don't know if it was a blacklist, but a graylist, anyway," he said. He wound up signing a statement saying he had never been a Communist and sent one copy to the cameraman's union and the other to Columbia. He got the job on *Eternity*, but other mainstream studios were reluctant to employ him, even though he was considered one of the best in the business. He finally got hired by independent filmmaker Roger Corman. Crosby helped Corman churn out discount B-style pictures such as *Attack of the Crab Monsters*, *Machine Gun Kelly*, and *Teenage Caveman*, followed by a series of Edgar Allan Poe films that became cult classics, including *The Pit and the Pendulum*, *House of Usher*, and *The Raven*. Connoisseurs of great camera work discerned and admired his distinctive touch in these films, but Crosby seldom got to practice it in high-profile mainstream movies.

"Floyd Crosby was certainly not a Communist, but during the fifties, some studios did not like him," Corman recalled. "However, that meant nothing to me. I used him simply because he was a good cameraman."

TWO DAYS AFTER THE separation agreement to leave the Kramer Company was signed, Carl Foreman announced that he was forming his own production company, with the financial support of Gary Cooper and others, including Robert L. Lippert, a wealthy California investor looking to launch a new film production company and a distribution network. Henry Rogers, a friend of Carl's who was a leading figure in Hollywood in entertainment publicity, agreed to do PR for the new company. The announcement topped the next day's *Daily Variety*.

Cooper said he, his wife, Rocky, and his father-in-law all wanted to be stockholders in the new company. "Use my name," Cooper told Carl. "I mean it." Then the actor went off to Idaho for a hunting and fishing trip with his pal Ernest Hemingway.

Carl was skeptical; he told I. H. Prinzmetal, Cooper's lawyer, that a business relationship with Cooper was surely doomed because of politics. But Cooper refused to see any difficulty: Carl had testified truthfully, Cooper reckoned, and should now be allowed to go on with his life and career. Prinzmetal's usual role was to protect his star client from bad decision-making. But Prinzmetal said Cooper in this case was capable of making his own decision. "It's not a gesture," Prinzmetal assured Carl. "He really feels that you're going to be a very profitable operation."

In standing up for Carl, Cooper was delivering an unsubtle blow to his friends and allies on the hard right and demonstrating moral courage and a newly refined sense of political right and wrong. Pat Neal encouraged him to do so. She felt Cooper, who had a deep aversion to personal conflict, had let her down by not pressing Warners for her to get the juicier female role in *Bright Leaf* (1950), the second film they did together (the part went to Lauren Bacall instead). Now she urged him to stand up for Carl. "You mustn't let him down," she told Cooper.

Within days, the unofficial guardians of Americanism in Hollywood mobilized to sabotage Carl's plans. Gossip columnist Louella Parsons attacked Carl on her radio program, and I. E. Chadwick, head of Independent Motion Picture Producers Association, registered a protest with Lippert, who was one of his newest members. In addition, Steve Trilling, production executive at Warners, warned Prinzmetal that Cooper's partnership with Carl could jeopardize the studio's investment in future Cooper films. Even more troubling, Prinzmetal told Carl that Jack Warner had called him and threatened to invoke the morals clause to break Cooper's contract.

Behind the scenes, John Wayne was also putting the heat on Cooper. "Was Wayne pressuring him? Oh yeah," Maria Cooper Janis recalls. "I don't know if he met with him personally, but I know very clearly from hearing the family talk, and my father at one point said Wayne's bit was if you do this [with Foreman] you'll never work in this town again. He was very ugly about it."

The most virulent public opposition was conducted by Hedda Hopper, who didn't hesitate to name and shame one of her favorite movie stars in her column. "I'm amazed to hear that Gary Cooper would become a stockholder in Carl Foreman Productions," she wrote on October 30, six days after Carl's announcement. "Foreman not only would not answer the $64 question but was an unfriendly witness before the House Un-American Activities Committee."

When he read Hopper's column, Carl fired off a telegram, noting that he had told the committee he had voluntarily signed an oath in September 1950 stating that he was not a member of the Communist Party. "My only desire, Miss Hopper, is to go on making the kind of pictures that I have been associated with in the past and in that manner to make a positive contribution to the American way," he wrote.

But Hopper was not remotely appeased. Two days later, she published Foreman's telegram in her column and noted he had only answered part of her question. "No, Mr. Foreman, my reference was to the full $64 question—*Are you now or have you ever been a member of the Communist party?*

"Okay, Mr. Foreman, that is $32 worth of the $64 question, and I believe, knowing Mr. Gary Cooper's Americanism and his contemplated association with you, he would be as interested as I am in the remainder of the answer."

Cooper folded that same day. While his PR agent issued a statement in Hollywood, Cooper personally called Hopper from Idaho. "I was convinced of Foreman's loyalty, Americanism, and ability as a picture maker," he told Hopper, whose news story was published on the front page of the next morning's *L.A. Times.* "My opinion of Foreman has not changed." However, Hopper reported, "since the announcement Gary said he had received notice of considerable reaction and thinks it better for all concerned that he does not purchase any stock."

"Gary said he will be back sometime next week, and meanwhile he plans to roam the hinterlands of Idaho in search of fish and game with several male companions."

It had taken just a week from Carl's announcement of Cooper's support for one of Hollywood's biggest stars to change his mind. Even Gary Cooper couldn't stand up to the blacklist.

Foreman graciously said he had pleaded with Cooper to withdraw from the agreement because the pressure might harm Cooper's career. If he felt let down by Cooper, Carl never said so.

"Gary Cooper is the finest kind of an American and one of the most decent men I have ever met," said Carl in his written response to Cooper's withdrawal. "I regret to lose him as a business associate and I hope to keep him always as a friend."

Others were getting cold feet as well. José Ferrer's agent shot down the prospect of Ferrer signing to do a film for Carl's company. "I don't care what Joe Ferrer says," the agent, Kurt Frings, told Carl. "I will never allow him to work with you. He would only get in trouble." Frings told Carl he had fled Europe when the Nazis came into power and feared something similar could be happening in the United States. He urged Carl to make his peace with HUAC or face the prospect of being sent to an internment camp once the backlash began. Carl also met with Bette Davis and her new husband, actor Gary Merrill. Davis urged him to buy a script she owned and cast her in the movie. Here too nothing happened.

The pressure continued to build. Henry Rogers, the PR man, was told by his business partner, Warren Cowan, that talent agents were threatening to pull their prestige clients like James Stewart, Fred MacMurray, and Rosalind Russell from the firm. Rogers told Carl that most of the pressure was coming from John Wayne. So Carl told Rogers to set up a meeting. He and Wayne met the following Saturday morning at a wood-paneled office in Beverly Hills. The two men were so tense that they agreed to go for coffee to settle their nerves. Then they returned to the office and got down to business.

John Wayne was Hollywood aristocracy, whereas Carl Foreman, for all his Oscar nominations, was just a writer. Still, the two men went toe to toe. Carl told Wayne that Henry Rogers was innocent of any Communist tarnish. Wayne said he believed him and that all Rogers had to do was terminate his contract with Carl's company and Wayne and his pals would leave him alone. But Wayne's real purpose was to convince Carl to go back to the committee and cooperate. Wayne said he was still angry with Gary Cooper for betraying the principles of the Motion Picture Alliance by backing Carl—after all, Cooper was an Alliance board member—and that Carl would be hurting Cooper further if he didn't recant. As for Carl, Wayne warned, he would never work in film until he testified again.

Carl said he might just go to Europe and work there for a while until things settled down. What makes you think you'll be able to leave? Wayne asked him. Carl took that as a threat. The meeting ended with Wayne still frustrated and Carl feeling scared. He resolved to obtain a passport straightaway.

Carl felt bullied by Wayne, who had dodged military service during World War Two and seemed to be trying to assuage his guilt by waging political and economic war against those deemed to be Communists. But even on this battlefront, Wayne arrived on the scene after the war already had been won and Hollywood's small band of Communists were in full retreat. "His role," in the acidic words of cultural historian Gary Wills, "was to emerge after the battle and shoot the wounded."

Carl had one other bizarre meeting that winter, with Martin Berkeley, his chief accuser, arranged by Prinzmetal, Cooper's lawyer. To Carl, Berkeley seemed strangely deflated—not at all the ebullient witness for the prosecution who had blown the whistle on his former comrades with such passionate enthusiasm. Things hadn't quite worked out for

Berkeley. His old friends on the left despised him for being a stool pigeon, while those on the right distrusted him for much the same reason, and both sides were repelled by his undisguised pleasure in the spotlight. Carl accused Berkeley of having lied about seeing Carl at Communist Party meetings. To be perfectly honest, Berkeley replied, he couldn't recall exactly where or when he had seen Carl, but he was quite sure he had. Carl then recited for Berkeley chapter and verse of their two meetings over the years, neither of which had taken place at party events. Berkeley squirmed but insisted that he had testified correctly. In the end, Carl desperately wanted to sue Berkeley for perjury but Sidney Cohn convinced him it would be an utter waste of time. Any successful lawsuit would require Carl to testify fully about his party membership and name other members as well—something Carl would never do.

BOB ROSSEN URGED CARL and Estelle to get passports in case Carl had to leave the country to find work. At first Carl resisted, but after his chilling meeting with John Wayne, he decided to follow Rossen's advice. He and Estelle took the train to New York and applied for their passports far from the high-volume hysteria of Los Angeles, while they checked out the Broadway scene to see if there might be a place for him there as a writer. They saw twelve plays in fourteen days, but Carl was unimpressed with much of the work and came to the conclusion he desperately wanted to stay in films. After they picked up their new passports, Carl and Estelle boarded a train and returned to L.A.

Carl was a committed movie guy. He passionately believed in them as the most successful and popular art form ever invented. The golden age of movies might be over—Carl wasn't exactly sure it had ever truly existed—but he was certain that the best, most creative work in popular culture was still being done in Hollywood. He had never really wanted to work anywhere else, and he still hoped he wouldn't have to. He remained convinced that somehow, after the dust settled, he would be allowed to keep working.

But any hopes Carl still held for his new production company were soon shattered. By January 1952 he was hearing from friends that Roy Brewer had put out the word that anyone who worked on a movie with Carl would find himself blacklisted. Bob Lippert, the producer who had agreed to help finance Carl's first three films, met with Carl to say that Brewer had threatened him directly. "Maybe you ought to go to England," Lippert told Carl.

In the end, Carl had no choice but to agree. His dream of forming his own independent company had died, killed in the cradle by forces he could barely see, let alone fight against.

In retrospect, Carl had been either extraordinarily optimistic or extraordinarily naïve—perhaps both—to think that he could survive the blacklist with the help of loyal friends. Whatever their initial intentions, there was no way Stanley Kramer or Gary Cooper or anyone else could or would stand up against the repression.

"My partners, you know, saw their own futures and careers trembling in the balance, because of their guilt by association with me, and they behaved as a great many other people did," said Carl.

Walter Bernstein, a Communist Party member who wrote screenplays and television dramas under various pseudonyms for a decade after he was blacklisted (and also wrote *Inside Out*, a compelling memoir of the era), is a stern critic of informers and all of the justifications for betrayal that people offered for naming names. But he agrees that liberals like Stanley Kramer stood no chance of protecting their colleagues on the left. "If they'd taken a stand they would have been canned," says Bernstein. "Sure, it would have been great if [Kramer] had stood up and quit or been fired and gone on to something else. But it was the Cold War. No one was willing to do that."

George Stevens Jr., whose father was one of Hollywood's most celebrated directors, agrees. "There's no underestimating the sense of fear and vulnerability and ruthlessness of the studios," he says. "People were worried about being put out of business. What could Stanley Kramer have done? Nothing."

IN LATE APRIL, CARL booked a one-way passage on the French ocean liner *Liberté*, hopped a train at Union Station in Los Angeles, and returned to New York. Bob Rossen, now seeking work on Broadway, was there to greet him. Rossen went out with Carl almost every night. While he had been right to urge Carl to get a passport, it turned out that he had failed to secure a new one for himself. Rossen was trapped in the United States: he couldn't leave the country but he couldn't get work in the only field he knew and cared about. But there was nothing Carl could do to help him. "He was a very ambitious man and a talented man, and he couldn't work," Carl recalled. On May 6, 1952, the day the ship set off across the Atlantic, Rossen joined Sid Cohn in waving good-bye to Carl from the pier.

Carl was in cabin class and was certain he would be shunned by any Hollywood folks on board. Right away he ran into one of the biggest stars, Clark Gable, who was traveling with producer Cy Howard, an acquaintance of Carl's. Both men were booked in first class, of course. Carl didn't want to embarrass them or himself, but Howard insisted he join them for dinner. Carl wore his dinner jacket, which men of stature tended to pack wherever they went. Like Gary Cooper, Gable was a supporter of the Motion Picture Alliance and a staunch anti-Communist, but Howard said Carl would like him—"he's really a nice guy." At dinner that evening Gable told Carl he vehemently opposed Communism but respected Carl's decision not to rat on his friends.

When the *Liberté* pulled into Southampton port six days later, Carl felt a sense of liberation that could not be deflated even after the British immigration officer granted him only a thirty-day stay. It was a beautiful day, and Carl took the train to London and checked into the swank Savoy Hotel. Then he walked the streets of Westminster, past Westminster Palace, Ten Downing Street, and St. James's Park, comforted somehow to see these monuments to British civilization and parliamentary democracy at a time when he felt betrayed by his own country. He was surprised to learn that people knew and respected his work and were puzzled and indignant over the blacklist and the Red scare. "It seems as if I can write my own ticket here if I want to," he wrote to Fred Zinnemann in a cheerful "Hi Freddie" letter a few weeks after he arrived.

Early on he went to see James Carreras, a business associate of Bob Lippert, the film distributor Carl had hoped to work with back in Los Angeles. Carreras was charming and friendly but told Carl frankly, "Lippert should never have sent you over to me. I make terrible pictures . . . I just make pictures to make money . . . but this is not what you want to do." The funding fell through almost immediately on a picture Carl had hoped to make with Marlene Dietrich. He traveled to Paris, Rome, and Berlin, and he met fellow exiled screenwriters like Ben and Norma Barzman. Everyone was cordial and supportive, and various film studios offered him assignments under the table at very low rates of pay. But Carl had his settlement money from the Kramer Company and his pride; he resolved to himself not to take anything just for the sake of working.

Almost immediately he discovered he was suffering from the worst writer's block of his life. He couldn't even write a short letter to Estelle. He tried working on a screenplay, but "every page was agony, and every page was lifeless and dull."

Martin Berkeley's "bombshell" testimony gets the over-the-banner headline and photo of him and wife Kathleen on the *Los Angeles Times* front page of September 20, 1951. But the paper's lead stories concern fighting in Korea as the U.S. casualty rate reaches 83,257. Meanwhile, the temperature in Burbank, where *High Noon* is being shot, hits 99 degrees. LIBRARY OF CONGRESS

Room 518 of the Federal Building in downtown Los Angeles is crammed with congressmen, reporters, and spectators as Berkeley (see arrow, top left) blows the whistle on more than 150 of his former comrades. L.A. HERALD EXPRESS/L.A. PUBLIC LIBRARY

Carl Foreman, dressed in blue suit and "a very sincere tie," faces the microphones on the witness table at HUAC's September 24, 1951, public hearing. COURTESY OF EVE WILLIAMS-JONES/ WRITERS GUILD FOUNDATION

Reps. Francis E. Walter, John S. Wood (chairman), and Donald Jackson with microphones in position as HUAC meets on September 20, 1951. PHOTO BY HOWARD BALLEW, L.A. HERALD EXPRESS/L.A. PUBLIC LIBRARY

Marlon Brando and Stanley Kramer dine at Armando's in Brooklyn in 1950, the year they made *The Men*, Brando's first feature film.
PHOTOFEST

Patricia Neal and Gary Cooper attend a Hollywood party in 1952 at the height of their affair.
PHOTOFEST

Gary Cooper, Fred Zinnemann, and Grace Kelly consult on the set of *High Noon*. PHOTOFEST

The *High Noon* cast in costume and Carl Foreman take a television break. Were they watching the HUAC hearings in downtown Los Angeles? PHOTOFEST/UNITED ARTISTS/PARAMOUNT

Gary Cooper rests his aching back between scenes at the *High Noon* film shoot alongside his cherished silver Jaguar convertible.

Cooper and his fourteen-year-old daughter, Maria, on the set of *High Noon* at the Columbia Ranch in Burbank, September 1951.

The indomitable Helen Ramirez (Katy Jurado) listens warily as her narcissistic young lover, Harvey Pell (Lloyd Bridges), schemes to replace his mentor and friend, Will Kane, as marshal of Hadleyville. UNITED ARTISTS/MARGARET HERRICK LIBRARY

Will Kane and his new bride, Amy, just after their wedding ceremony, face four dear friends, played by (left to right) Lon Chaney Jr., Thomas J. Mitchell, Harry Morgan, and Otto Kruger, all of whom will soon betray him. PHOTOFEST

"Is melody, Ned . . . please don't hate me,"
composer Dimitri Tiomkin told lyricist
Ned Washington about the complex folk tune
he had written for *High Noon*.
PHOTOFEST

Tex Ritter, cowboy crooner and king of the
B-Westerns, 1941. His mournful rendition of
"Do Not Forsake Me, Oh My Darlin'" was the
most authentic. PHOTOFEST

Elmo Williams, who claimed he "saved"
High Noon with his deft editing, shows off
his 1953 Oscar for film editing.
MARGARET HERRICK LIBRARY

Two of art director Rudolph Sternad's storyboards from *High Noon:* the three waiting "gunnies," and the lonely marshal on an empty street as the train whistle blows. UCLA ARCHIVES

"At that time I had it very bad," he would recall. "When I sat down to the typewriter, instead of writing 'Fade in' or 'Scene One,' I would find myself writing, in effect, a letter to the editor, any editor! *Dear sir. Do you know what they're doing to me?*' You see, I was full of rage and self-pity."

Most of those letters ended up in the trash. But Carl sent the longest and angriest—an eleven-page dissection—to his friend Bosley Crowther, the *New York Times* critic whose rave review of *High Noon* would help propel it to success. He started off by declaring how "tremendously pleased and proud" he was of the film. But then he launched into a "completely and unequivocally off the record" account of the genesis of and making of the film and his bitter falling out with Stanley Kramer: the Columbia deal, the purchase of the rights to "The Tin Star," how Stanley had stepped away and left him and Fred to work on *High Noon* on their own, how he had written it as an allegory for the blacklist, how Stanley, Sam Katz, and George Glass had sought to bully him into cooperating with the committee and tried to fire him from the picture when he refused, how Cooper and Zinnemann and Church had forced Stanley to back down, and how Carl had decided to go to London for a while because "I finally got tired of watching the darkness settle in on Hollywood, tired of watching people being hammered and pressured until they crumbled, tired of being offered black market deals and all the rest."

He mentioned the prospect of a writer-producer contract with the prestigious Rank Organisation, Britain's leading entertainment company. "On the whole, I think I'd like to work here," he told Crowther. "Certainly it's nice to be wanted." The problem, "between you and me," he added, "is that all I know or really care about is America and the American scene. I don't know if I could do an honest job on an English picture, or a French or Italian one—at least until I'd lived in those places for quite a while." Time would tell, Carl concluded.

Estelle finally reached him on the phone. "I thought you were only going for three weeks," she told him. "What's happening? You haven't written. Are you coming home?" The answer was no. A few weeks later, Estelle and Kate left for London.

They arrived to a husband and father who seemed lost in many ways, untethered from the place he loved and the work he felt he had been born to do. "The whole fabric of one's existence was torn in many respects forever," he would later write, and "it created in almost all the writers I know a feeling of vast unease and depression and loss of confidence."

Carl Foreman's exile had truly begun.

15.

The Music Men

Do not forsake me, oh my darlin', on this our wedding day . . .

After the film shoot was finished, Fred Zinnemann and film editor Elmo Williams spent ten days assembling a director's rough cut, mostly using Fred's master shots. It was nearly two hours long, according to Williams. And it included the three scenes involving the subplot with Toby the deputy. But under the rules of the game, the final cut belonged not to the director, but to the man whose name topped the company masthead.

Stanley Kramer was deeply dismayed by what he saw. Stanley had never liked the dailies but had been too busy to interfere with what was, to his mind, a minor film for which he had few expectations. But now all of his unhappiness poured out. The rough cut was too long and lacking in tension and excitement, and he intensely disliked it. "I was terribly disappointed when I saw the first cut," Stanley confirms. "This was not the fault of Williams. Whatever blame there was belongs to me. In that first cut, the picture I had in mind was not what I saw. Maybe it wasn't too bad, but it wasn't too good either. Something was missing."

After this, Williams's and Stanley's accounts begin to diverge. According to Williams, a frustrated Kramer didn't know what to do next. One of Stanley's earliest jobs in Hollywood had been cutting film, and he took great pride in his editing skills, which he had used on several of the company's previous films—most especially on *Champion*, its first and biggest hit. So Stanley was inclined to try to edit *High Noon* himself, but he had no idea where to begin, or so Williams would later claim. "He intimated to me he was going to take over the picture,"

Williams recalled. "He was going to Palm Springs for a week and think about it . . . And he implied to me maybe they'd change editors too."

Williams says he pleaded with Stanley to give him a crack at reediting the picture while Stanley was away. "And he kind of reluctantly said, 'Well, what the hell, go ahead.'"

Williams says he used lots of trims and scraps from the cutting-room floor, shots of the railroad tracks, the ticking clocks, and an empty chair to try to build dramatic tension. "They were pieces of film at the beginning or the ends of takes," he recalled. He eliminated the three scenes involving Toby, and ruthlessly pared scenes between Grace Kelly and Katy Jurado or between Jurado and Lloyd Bridges. "Every time you left Cooper and his problem the picture lost its tension," Williams recalled. "And I decided early that that's where the flaw was in the script."

Over the years Elmo Williams's version of his edit became more and more elaborate, even as his memory for details began to recede. In a November 2000 interview when he was eighty-seven, he claimed for the first time that he had filmed new shots of clocks and of the empty chair in the corner of Judge Mettrick's courtroom. "I went out and shot the inserts myself. I didn't do the camera work, but I took a cameraman and shot the clocks," he said.

Stanley returned from Palm Springs but was sidetracked on other matters for several days, giving Williams more time to polish and refine his version. He worked on it until the very last minute, then recruited Harry Gerstad, the company's supervising editor and Williams's boss now that Carl Foreman was officially out of the picture, to help him by splicing together pieces of film. They took the finished product to Stanley's house that evening and showed it to Stanley, his wife, Ann, and George Glass. As the showing began, Williams recalled, "Stanley's talking to George all the way through it. I thought, Oh Christ . . . I knew I didn't have his attention. But by the time the prologue was finished he was quiet . . . didn't say another word." When it ended, "he walked over and shook my hand."

Everything was fine, said Williams, except he had cut so much that the film was down to sixty-eight minutes, at least twelve minutes short of the required length for a first-run feature film. So Williams went back and restored scenes of Kelly, Jurado, and Bridges.

Over the years Elmo Williams took credit for saving *High Noon* and regaled journalists and authors with tales of how he had single-handedly turned it into a classic. In his various retellings, he suggested that Fred Zinnemann had been so smitten by Grace Kelly that he had given her far too many scenes, that Gary Cooper's various aches and pains had rendered his performance wooden and tedious, that Carl Foreman had written and Fred Zinnemann had filmed several peripheral out-of-town subplots, not just one, and that it had been Williams's idea—not Carl's or Fred's—to insert many of the clocks to give the film narrative tension.

"I hate to defend myself, but it was my editing of the film that made it what it was in the end," Williams said in 2000.

Stanley Kramer mocked Williams's claim that he had saved *High Noon*. "Now Elmo was a very good editor, [but] Elmo is not now nor was then the creative brain of our century," said Stanley in an unpublished 1973 interview. "I think that Elmo's contribution was that he said why don't I use the clock and see if I can't jazz up the thing in juxtaposition to the railroad track. I said absolutely . . . we should do that."

But Stanley's own version of the edit is equally dismissive of Fred and Carl's work. In essence, Stanley claims it wasn't Elmo Williams's editing that saved *High Noon* but his own. When he saw Fred Zinnemann's director's cut, says Stanley, "the idea of the man in the town trying to seek support . . . was not jarring your teeth as we thought it should."

"I was certainly aghast," said Stanley. "There were problems, but I knew what to do with it. I was the one who did the final cut of this film—I alone, and I stand by whatever flaws or virtues the film has to this day."

Stanley claims it was he, not Williams, who put the emphasis on the ticking clocks. He claims that the director's cut "had shot a few clock scenes . . . but not enough of those clock views, I now decided. We put more clocks on tables, walls, mantels, and so on, and shot short takes of them, which we inserted one by one into the film."

Elmo Williams insists that Stanley Kramer did not edit one frame of the film. "Kramer did not cut a version of the picture," said Elmo in a 1978 interview with author Lawrence Suid. "I cut the next version, and the next and the next . . . It was essentially my version of the picture."

Both Williams's and Kramer's conflicting versions of the rescuing of *High Noon* from creative oblivion deeply outraged Fred Zinnemann and Carl Foreman. Both men insisted that the clocks had always been part of the original script—which adhered faithfully to Carl's real-time concept driving forward the narrative. Indeed, there are fourteen specific references to clocks and time in Carl's script, plus four other times when characters look at their pocket watches. Fred added even more shots of clocks, as reflected in his handwritten notes on the film set. What Williams did create was four more quick shots of clocks and pendulums in the dramatic montage of people and scenes at the moment when the whistle blows announcing the arrival of the noon train.

Carl, who left the film entirely by the end of October after signing the severance contract with Stanley's company, had his own version of what happened. He maintained that Stanley had cut the film ruthlessly, in part perhaps because he was deeply angered by the way Carl had modeled the betrayals of Jonas Henderson and the other cowardly townsfolk after Stanley's own behavior toward Carl.

"Stanley didn't like it, and took over," Carl wrote in 1952. "He cut it brutally, almost, it seemed, with venom. Everyone agreed the version was bad. He gave in, finally, and Elmo Williams took over and returned the cut to Fred's original version."

In those early days just after the film was released, Carl praised Williams for preserving the film and preventing Stanley from destroying it. "Elmo Williams is, I think, the best, most creative editor in Hollywood. One of the best, anyway."

Later on, however, Carl was less complimentary. In a 1982 letter to Williams, Carl said he was grateful to him "for not allowing Kramer and Gerstad to destroy the film. I have always thought that you liked the film and tried to preserve it, and that you did what you did in order to pacify Kramer . . . [who] knew very well that he was the basis for the characters of Henderson and Fuller in the script." But Carl added, "It really isn't fair for you to take all the credit for its success, as you have done over the years."

When the respected film critic Arthur Knight wrote a piece praising Williams's editing, Carl fired off a blistering letter upbraiding Knight for portraying Elmo as "the demon editor . . . who saved *High Noon* by cutting in all those clocks." Carl lamented that Knight had fallen for Williams's "perpetuation of this nonsensical myth."

Fred Zinnemann predictably seethed for years as the various editing legends were retailed in books and magazine articles. He finally exploded in 1988 after his good friend and fellow director Bertrand Tavernier asked him if it was true "that *High Noon* had been made in the cutting room."

"I hoped that the record would be set straight some day, but wanting to avoid unpleasant public disputes which might have hurt the picture I kept silent for many years while that insidious campaign grew into a myth," Fred wrote to Maria Cooper Janis.

"While there is no question that the final editing was brilliant, there was not much elbow room for cuts or for major structural changes, as most scenes were frozen in their places by the progression of time clearly shown on various clocks. Thus, despite all assertions to the contrary, the picture could make sense only in the form originally intended by Foreman and myself."

Where does the truth lie? Carl's claim that Stanley Kramer set out purposely to butcher *High Noon* in the editing room because of his anger with Carl is hard to swallow. After all, a mutilated fiasco of a film would have reflected as badly on Stanley, whose company would have been held ultimately responsible, as on Carl and Fred, and it would have cost Stanley his investment. It's far easier to accept the idea that Stanley truly believed the film was a disaster and saw himself as the only person who could save it. It's readily conceivable that Stanley tried to edit the film, cut it deeply and perhaps angrily, was frustrated with the result, and turned it over to Elmo Williams when he volunteered to give it a try. Williams's cut brought the film part of the way back to Fred's original version, but with a tighter and tenser narrative that stayed more focused on the marshal and the clocks.

This explanation takes into account all four men's versions while treating each of them with some skepticism. In the end, it's the only one that makes sense.

THE MEN WHO MIGHT truly lay claim to saving *High Noon* had nothing to do with its filming or editing, but everything to do with the song that helped make it famous.

The leader of these music men, Dimitri Tiomkin, was born in the Ukraine in 1894 to a wealthy Jewish physician and his wife. At age seven he began training as a musician at the St. Petersburg Conservatory, with its battalions of pianists, fiddlers, and composers. "Music has always produced vivid personalities and notable eccentrics, and so did old Russia," Tiomkin boasts in his lively and quirky autobiography, *Please Don't Hate Me*, and he himself certainly qualified as one.

While the conservatory bored him, Tiomkin played piano at movie houses in St. Petersburg to earn money and spent late evenings at the Homeless Dog, a bohemian basement café whose owners vanished soon after the 1917 revolution. He himself fled Russia and the Bolsheviks in the early 1920s. He wound up in Paris in a two-man classical piano act with a fellow Russian, then sailed to New York, where they performed on the vaudeville circuit back in the days when mainstream audiences actually paid attention to classical music.

His major nemesis in America, as he cheerfully confesses, was the

English language, which he butchered in speech all of his adult life and never quite mastered—"like loving a beautiful woman who slaps you in the face," he writes. He couldn't pronounce the words, couldn't string together a grammatical sentence, couldn't figure out which words went where. "We go theater with party. What show is?" was typical.

While making a speech to the exclusive Lambs Club in New York, he tried to tell a funny story about a fat Russian admiral. The audience laughed all the way through, but in the wrong places. "You might as well tell them in Italian," suggested the toastmaster, George M. Cohan. "They'll understand it better."

It wasn't just the language. "Dimi" couldn't master the long strides Americans used for walking; his were short steps like a ballet dancer. "Walk like a man," his Viennese-born wife, Albertina, commanded him in vain. And he couldn't break the habit of kissing a married woman's hand upon introduction. All too often, the woman in question would reach for his hand expecting a handshake and inadvertently smack his face as he bent over.

Still, he was a great success musically. He mastered jazz piano and composition, collaborated with George Gershwin, and gave piano recitals throughout the country, arriving in Hollywood in the early 1930s just as demand was soaring for music to fill the soundtracks of the new talking pictures. He hooked up with famed director Frank Capra and wound up composing the music for *Lost Horizon* (1937), *You Can't Take It with You* (1938), *Mr. Smith Goes to Washington* (1939), *Meet John Doe* (1941), and *It's a Wonderful Life* (1946). His movie scores were lush and melodramatic, with classical echoes—just the kind of aural pastiche that Hollywood loved. When Tiomkin won an Oscar in 1955 for the musical score for *The High and the Mighty*, he thanked Brahms, Strauss, Wagner, Beethoven, and Rimsky-Korsakov. Some in the audience thought he was being pretentious, but others understood that he was actually paying tribute to all the great composers he had stolen from. Altogether, he was nominated for nearly two dozen Oscars and won four.

He first met Stanley Kramer and Carl Foreman in the Army Signal Corps. Tiomkin was too old and unfit to be drafted, but he volunteered at Frank Capra's behest and he loved the work. By his own estimate, he churned out scores for hundreds of pictures, from short training films to full-length documentaries. He could command an orchestra of any size and all the recording equipment he desired, day or night. "Having always been harassed by studio economies I found myself in the lap of musical luxury," he recalled fondly.

When Stanley and Carl formed their independent film company after the war, they turned to Tiomkin for music scores. They couldn't pay him anywhere near what the major studios offered, but he liked working with talented young people. Tiomkin composed the scores for *So This Is New York, Champion, Home of the Brave, The Men*, and *Cyrano de Bergerac*. Sometimes Stanley and Carl found Tiomkin's music too lushly dramatic. Fred Zinnemann in particular felt Tiomkin had overstuffed *The Men* with musical clichés, and he upbraided Tiomkin after a sneak preview in San Francisco. "I remember that he wept—real tears—but it was too late for changes," said Fred.

Curiously enough for a Jewish boy from the Ukraine, Tiomkin's most enduring claim to fame as a composer lies with his music for Westerns: *Red River, Duel in the Sun, Giant, Gunfight at the O.K. Corral*, and of course, *High Noon*. Perhaps he was able to musically connect cowboys with Cossacks, or perhaps, like a lot of newcomers to America, he was swept up by the romantic myth of the Old West. His biographer, Christopher Palmer, compares Tiomkin's scores to the epic paintings and sculptures of Frederic Remington and Charles M. Russell. "They, like him, viewed the West from an expansively romantic, essentially nineteenth-century viewpoint," writes Palmer, "and their pictures decisively influenced the ideology and iconography of the Hollywood Western."

Himself a bubbly eccentric, Tiomkin managed to cope with the extreme fantasies of Hollywood's aristocracy. While working on *Duel in the Sun*, he faced a demand from the passionately imperious producer David O. Selznick to come up with orgiastic music for a rape scene featuring Gregory Peck and Jennifer Jones, Selznick's mistress and wife-to-be. Tiomkin made several attempts that Selznick found too sedate. "It isn't orgasm music," he said of Tiomkin's final effort. "It's not *shtup*. It's not the way I fuck."

"Mr. Selznick, you fuck your way, I fuck my way," an exasperated Tiomkin replied. "To *me*, that is fucking music!" Selznick eventually surrendered.

Stanley Kramer and Carl Foreman may not have always loved Tiomkin's scores, but they knew they were getting a bargain, and Stanley gave him free range when it came to the orchestral score for *High Noon*. The result was one of the most innovative and evocative scores in motion picture history—and a song that set off yet another creative whodunit.

* * *

JUST AS HE DID with the editing of the picture, Elmo Williams sought to take complete credit for choosing and inspiring the music. He said the story told in *High Noon* felt to him like a folktale, the kind an old man might tell his grandson, or something from a Carl Sandburg poem, and he wanted music that would feel the same way—a folk tune like "Ghost Riders in the Sky" as sung by Burl Ives, one of the most popular singers of the era. Williams discussed this idea with Tiomkin, but the composer couldn't grasp what he wanted and in any case was too busy working on music for two of the new films the Kramer Company was making at Columbia. That's when Williams turned to the Burl Ives recording. He knew it wouldn't be used in the final film, but it had the kind of thumping folk-style beat he was looking for.

Williams's method was to cut his films to music. He had worked at the Capitol Records studio in Hollywood on early television shows and had experimented with combining film and music to fill airtime, and he worshipped the power of rhythm. When editing film, he used a process called "temp tracking"; it's standard procedure in many modern films, but Williams could rightfully claim to be one of the first to regularly use it. "I find in cutting that every show has its own rhythm and if you screw around with it you screw the show up," he recalls in an unpublished interview with film historian Rudy Behlmer. ". . . I used to put a click track in my synchronizer when I was cutting and usually take the rhythm from the leading character in the show—the speed he walks, the speed he talks, whatever it is. I'd take it and I'd find a kind of medium rhythm with the main character, and when I cut a picture and get through with it and think I've got a good shape, I stick the click track in my synchronizer and I wind it through. You'd be amazed; when the cuts are right they fall right on the beat, just as though you had added the music from the beginning . . . It really works and you know when you've got a show right."

Elmo Williams says he used "Ghost Riders in the Sky" as the temp track for the rough cut he showed Stanley Kramer, and that Stanley was quickly sold on the idea of using a similar-style ballad for *High Noon*. Stanley turned to Tiomkin, who at first resisted, according to Williams, complaining, "I am not cowboy! I cannot write horse opera! Cossacks I can write, but not cowboy!" It's a nice story, but Tiomkin had already written highly successful scores for two classic Westerns, *Duel in the Sun* (1946) and *Red River* (1948), and it's difficult to imagine he had any reservations about composing music for *High Noon*.

In any event, Williams claims that Tiomkin eventually relented and wrote a Western theme song—some said he stole the melody from a

Ukrainian folk song. Then Tiomkin hired lyricist Ned Washington to write the words. A slim, dapper, pencil-mustached man of fifty who was born and raised on the poor side of Scranton, Pennsylvania, Washington was a journeyman lyricist with a superb track record in Hollywood and Manhattan. Among his biggest hits were lyrics for "When You Wish Upon a Star" (1940), an Academy Award winner (he also shared an Oscar for his lyrics for *Pinocchio*'s overall score), as well as "Stella by Starlight" (1944) and "My Foolish Heart" (1950). After *High Noon*, he would go on to write lyrics for several more Tiomkin melodies, including the "Theme from *Rawhide*" (1958) and "Town Without Pity" (1961). All in all, he was nominated for eleven Oscars as a co-songwriter and won three.

Ned Washington, according to Elmo Williams, was baffled by Tiomkin's description of what he was looking for. Here too, just as he did as film editor, Williams says he stepped to the fore and saved the day: he described to Washington his folksong concept and an inspired Ned went to work.

Dimitri Tiomkin's version of what happened, presented in his memoir, is very different. For one thing, it doesn't even mention Elmo Williams. Instead, Tiomkin says he was brought in after the film was shot and Fred Zinnemann's rough cut was put together, after which the consensus among Stanley Kramer, George Glass, and the rest of the Kramer Company was that the picture "looked like the ugliest duckling of all." Tiomkin was not so pessimistic. He believed the right song could help save it—everybody, it seems, felt a personal duty to save *High Noon*—and he convinced Kramer to try out a theme song that could be sung, whistled, and played by the orchestra all the way through the film, an innovative approach that had rarely been used in movies before.

Contrary to Williams's claim, Tiomkin says he was well-versed in the melodies of the Texas range and Mexican border as well as traditional frontier tunes and was not at all put off by the assignment. His wife, Albertina—always the sharp-eared, sharp-eyed critic—vetoed his first songwriting attempt, but during the course of a long day at the piano he modified it, expanded it, and made it more complex to the point where she approved. Then he needed a lyric, something supple enough to stretch with the twists and turns of the unconventional melody he'd composed. And he wanted words that would tell the story of the picture with style, sentimentality, and pathos.

Enter Ned Washington, who when he first heard the twisting melody did indeed seem puzzled. "What are you doing, Dimi, playing variations?"

"Is melody, Ned," Tiomkin replied. "Is melody for you writing words. Please don't hate me."

Washington, a professional's professional, came back with "Do Not Forsake Me Oh My Darlin'."

Ned's simple poem not only fit the notes and the sentiment, but also revealed and reflected the central ideas of the film. The song's narrator is Will Kane himself, addressing Amy, his new bride, expressing the fears and longings in music that Kane can't find the words to articulate in the actual film:

> *Do not forsake me, oh my darlin'*
> *On this our wedding day.*
> *Do not forsake me, oh my darlin'*
> *Wait, wait along.*
> *The noonday train will bring Frank Miller*
> *If I'm a man I must be brave*
> *And I must face that deadly killer*
> *Or lie a coward, a craven coward*
> *Or lie a coward in my grave.*
>
> *Oh to be torn 'twixt love and duty*
> *S'posin' I lose my fair-eyed beauty*
> *Look at that big hand move along*
> *Nearin' high noon.*
> *He made a vow while in state's prison*
> *That it would be my life or his'n*
> *I'm not afraid of death, but oh*
> *What will I do if you leave me?*
>
> *Do not forsake me, oh my darlin'*
> *You made that promise when we wed*
> *Do not forsake me, oh my darlin',*
> *Although you're grievin', I can't be leavin'*
> *Until I shoot Frank Miller dead.*
>
> *Wait along, wait along, wait along, wait along . . .*

"It's a masterpiece in its way," declares Tiomkin, and he was right. Ned had created a true folk tale, unconventional yet powerful, poignant, and dramatic. The lyric deftly summarized the plot of the film: the initiating event ("*The noonday train will bring Frank Miller*"), the backstory ("*He made a vow while in state's prison*"), the psychological tension ("*Look at that big hand move along nearin' high noon*"), and the hero's desperate dilemma ("*Oh to be torn 'twixt love and duty*"). The song not only narrates the plot, it lays out the implications of the coming showdown and explains the marshal's inner conflict in a way that he himself cannot articulate. "The song, at first glance, seems very simple in both structure and message," writes music scholar Deborah Allison. "A slightly closer look exposes a work of considerable complexity."

Next, Tiomkin needed the right performer to capture the poetry and the pathos of the song. It's likely that in this instance he took the advice of Elmo Williams, who had worked at Capitol Records and knew about the company's top country music star, Tex Ritter, a former B-movie cowboy hero and balladeer from the remote northeast corner of Texas, with a low, husky voice and smooth singing style.

Woodard Maurice Ritter was born in 1905 on a ranch forty miles from Shreveport, Louisiana, in one of the poorest counties in Texas. He went to a one-room schoolhouse that held two classes after they nailed a flimsy wooden partition down the middle one day. He was one of six children and he and his two brothers sang in church every Sunday. But Tex Ritter was no country yokel. He went to the University of Texas at Austin, graduated pre-law, went on to law school at Northwestern University in Chicago, and found his way into Western music shows to help pay his tuition. Singing at first was just a hobby—Ritter still thought he'd become a lawyer—but a visit to the theaters and dance halls of New York City in 1928 changed his mind. He abandoned his suit and silk tie for cowboy boots, a bolo tie, and a ten-gallon hat. He wound up singing cowboy tunes on the radio, then toured the country in a series of Western plays and musicals, including *Green Grow the Lilacs*, the forerunner of Rodgers and Hammerstein's *Oklahoma!*

In his late twenties Ritter landed in Hollywood, where he met Hoot Gibson, Roy Rogers, Gene Autry, Ken Maynard, and Buck Jones and followed their lead into the singing cowboy movies. His first starring role was in *Song of the Gringo* for Grand National Pictures in 1936; it was the start of a decade of formulaic but stirring B Westerns. "Movie fans knew what to expect . . . a staunch hero, a damsel in distress, galloping horses, fistfights, gunplay, and villains for the hero to vanquish," writes Bill O'Neal, Ritter's biographer.

When Grand National went bankrupt in 1938, Ritter went on tour to make money, and he basically never stopped. He sang product-endorsement jingles for Frostilla shaving cream, milk cartons, playing cards, bandannas, and paper dolls. For seven years he was on the *Motion Picture Herald*'s list of Top Ten Money-Making Western Stars. By the time he made his last movie in 1945, he had appeared in sixty Westerns, mostly for "Poverty Row" outfits like Grand National, Monogram, and PRC. Still, he was at the apex of his recording career; in January of that same year he held down the top three places on *Billboard* magazine's country music chart. He recorded for Capitol Records for thirty-two years.

Ritter and two guitarists—one of them the legendary finger-picker Merle Travis—arrived at Tiomkin's house on a Sunday in full cowboy regalia. They looked at a few photo stills from the movie while Tiomkin explained the plot. Then the maestro sat down at the piano and played—and sang—the song, his Russian accent contorted into a tortured Texas Panhandle drawl, which vastly amused his small audience. "Tex and his cowboys nearly fell off their chairs laughing, and Ned Washington doubled up with mirth at hearing such a parody of his song," Tiomkin recalled.

Nonetheless, they got the idea. Ritter and his boys recorded the song, with Tex singing in a soft, plaintive style that was both intimate and haunting, while the two guitars played gently behind him.

"It wasn't supposed to be Gary Cooper's voice necessarily; it could have been his thoughts," Ritter recalled. "But it was used instead of [instrumental] music to create the mood."

It was a unique use of a theme song. Movies like *Laura* (1944) and *The Third Man* (1949) had used haunting themes throughout their stories, but the music in each was solely instrumental: the songs set a mood but did not tell a literal story. An anonymous writer at *Billboard* captured *High Noon*'s innovation exactly: "The song does not merely advance the story line. It *is* the story line."

"What is remarkable in this coupling of music and film," the writer adds, "is the 'economic' use to which the song is put. It would be difficult to get any more out of the song. It pays all possible dividends; it sets moods, tells the story, chord sequences are used as a leitmotif, etc."

Tiomkin, who loved selling his music almost as much as he loved composing it, suggested that Ritter record the song for Capitol, but the company was not interested because Western movie themes were not considered big sellers. So Tiomkin took the song to Mitch Miller, a producer at Columbia Records who had a well-tuned ear for commercially popular music. Miller recorded a more synthetic and melodramatic version of the song with Frankie Laine, a pop singer who was younger and sexier than Ritter. Laine belted it out as if he were singing "Bolero" during a cattle stampede, with a female chorus behind him. When Capitol's executives realized that Columbia was about to outflank them with Laine's 45, they summoned Ritter for a recording session on May 14, 1952.

Capitol released Ritter's austere version on June 21, and Columbia released Laine's more lathered rendition a week after, and soon there were four more recorded versions of the song as well. Laine's leaped to the top of the charts, while Ritter's trailed behind. When *High Noon* was finally released in late July, the runaway popularity of the theme song helped pave its success, which in turn triggered a new wave of record sales. Laine's record sold more one million copies, while Ritter's sold eight hundred thousand. Still, "for many of us who were captivated by *High Noon* the only version of the title song that ever rang true was by Tex Ritter," writes Bill O'Neal.

Neither Tiomkin nor Williams mentions Stanley Kramer in their accounts of how the music was created, but Stanley of course has his own version. He says it was his idea from the beginning to use a ballad for *High Noon* and that he decided he wanted something along the lines of a Burl Ives song. Stanley says Tiomkin and Washington brought him a folk song that he vetoed because it wasn't powerful enough. He then dug out the Ives recording of "Ghost Riders in the Sky" and played it for Tiomkin and Washington. "Tiomkin was very irritated with me, but they went back and they did it again," Stanley recalls. "Now the next time they came back on the stage and played it, it was 'Do Not Forsake Me, Oh My Darlin'.'"

ONE THING EVERYONE AGREES on: Stanley Kramer loved the song and believed it could be the key to rescuing the film. He loved it so much he inserted it a dozen different times in the edited version of the picture. Then he held two movie previews, the first in Pomona, the second in Long Beach. Stanley went to the first and couldn't help but notice the audience growing restless each time the song was reprised. By the fifth iteration there was laughter and jeering. It was way too much of a good thing.

Tim Zinnemann recalls attending the preview at Long Beach with his father when he was ten years old and hearing members of the audience laugh and boo. Afterward, he and Fred stood alone in the lobby while various studio officials talked in hushed and somber tones that confirmed they had just witnessed a disaster. Tim went to the men's room and overheard two of the studio guys talking. "Oh hell, what does a European Jew know about making Westerns anyway?" one asked the other. The upshot, recalls Tim: "The movie sucks . . . and everybody was pointing at Fred Zinnemann and saying it's all his fault and I told you so."

Stanley's response was to pare down the "Do Not Forsake Me" segments. The melody still appears a dozen times during the picture, but most of them are shorter in duration and several are lower in volume. Tiomkin's orchestral score offers several variations of the melody; at one point even Lee Van Cleef's character, one of the bad guys waiting for Frank Miller's train, plays the tune on his harmonica. The melody remains omnipresent without being overwhelming, and it becomes an even more haunting accompaniment to the story. Still, no one involved was anticipating a critical or box-office success.

Another bad omen came when Harry Cohn, the famously despotic head of Columbia Pictures and architect of the Kramer Company's new multi-movie contract, asked to see the film. He suggested to Stanley that perhaps Columbia could distribute the film as their first joint offering. Stanley replied that the picture was already promised to United Artists, and in any event it wasn't ready to be shown yet. But Cohn couldn't wait. When Kramer arrived at Motion Picture Center Studios the following Sunday morning, Tiomkin told him Cohn had been there earlier and taken home a print of the rough cut for viewing.

Stanley was furious. He was already having his doubts about the deal with Columbia, and Cohn's arrogant behavior set him off. The next morning he stormed into Cohn's plush all-white office—said to have been modeled after Benito Mussolini's totalitarian-deluxe office suite in Rome—and started screaming at him.

"I said I wouldn't let him see it if he was the last man on earth," Stanley recalled. "I called him every name under the sun, and [told him] I want to break the contract."

Cohn looked at Stanley as if he were insane. "What are you upset about?" Hollywood's *Il Duce* demanded of his new junior partner. "The picture is a piece of crap."

16.

The Process

I can tell in five minutes if a person is a Communist. I'm never wrong.

ROY M. BREWER

While Carl Foreman was driven from the Promised Land of Hollywood, his celebrated accuser was embraced. Martin Berkeley was quickly recruited to become an important cog in the intricate machinery of the blacklist.

It was a multilayered process. The Motion Picture Industry Council presided over the official version, sending its members—the studios, unions, and talent guilds—lists of names of those like Carl who had been called to appear before HUAC and had refused to cooperate, as well as those named as Communists by so-called "friendly" witnesses. These suspected subversives were purged from the employment rolls. Until they repented and cooperated with the committee, they were banned from working in Hollywood.

But the studios had pledged to go even farther. The 1947 Waldorf Statement committed them to firing anyone who was in the Communist Party whether they had been called to testify or not. In practice this extended well beyond party members to anyone who had ever supported an organization identified as a Communist front by HUAC, the Tenney Committee, the FBI, or citizens' groups like the American Legion, as well as *Alert*, *Counterattack*, and *Red Channels*, the Red-baiting publications that listed such fronts and their members.

This was a vast undertaking. Rather than simply working off lists of names compiled from these various sources, the process quickly evolved into something far more elaborate: the "graylisting" of anyone who failed to sign a loyalty statement. Each major studio assigned a top-ranking official to be responsible for vetting employees and "keeping Communists and suspected Communists off the payroll," as studio executive Y. Frank Freeman of Paramount put it. Freeman, a regular informant for the FBI, told the bureau that at Paramount, "no talent whatever is hired without being as thoroughly screened as it is possible for the studio to do . . . The same situation exists at such studios as Universal-International, Warner Brothers Pictures, and Columbia Pictures."

The graylist sounded less sinister than the blacklist, but as former Hollywood Ten member Edward Dmytryk pointed out, it was in many ways worse. "I was blacklisted, I knew why I was blacklisted, and when I so desired, I knew how to get off the blacklist," he recalled. "The graylisted, on the other hand, although generally left-wingers, were almost never Communists and usually had no knowledge of their transgressions or even that they had transgressed. They knew they weren't working, but they didn't know why."

It was a diffuse, often haphazard system, subject to the whims and failings of those who ran it and the so-called experts—ex-Communists, former FBI investigators, amateur right-wing ideologues—who fed it. Roy Brewer, the union leader who became chairman of the Motion Picture Alliance, was its de facto ruler. The American Legion played an important role. In March 1952 its leaders met in Washington, D.C., with Eric Johnston, president of the Motion Picture Association, and representatives of the eight major Hollywood studios. The Legion expressed sympathy with the efforts of the studios to purge themselves of all Communists and sympathizers. At the same time, they warned that if they weren't satisfied with the studios' efforts, local Legion posts around the country would be free to organize boycotts of particular movies and the studios that made them. The Legion followed up the meeting with a letter to the eight studios, naming some three hundred people it considered suspect. All of them were required to sign loyalty oaths and denounce past transgressions if they wanted to continue to work in movies.

The system was financially corrupt: those seeking clearance had to hire well-connected lawyers or else employ former FBI or HUAC agents who formed the "smear-and-clear" organizations that published lists of alleged subversives and then helped people clear their names for a fee. But its moral corruption was equally striking. When actress Gale Sondergaard pleaded with the Screen Actors Guild to support her legal effort to oppose the blacklist, the guild board, led by Ronald Reagan, declared it would fight any blacklist, but added: "On the other hand, if any actor by his own actions outside of union activities has so offended American public opinion that he has made himself unsaleable at the box office, the Guild cannot and would not want to force any employer to hire him." Using this twisted reasoning, Reagan, Brewer, John Wayne, Hedda Hopper, and other enforcers of the blacklist could deny it existed.

The Motion Picture Alliance played a key role in the clearance process. In its October 1951 newsletter, the Alliance issued an invitation to those who felt they had been wrongly accused or who were ready to recant their previous involvement with Communism. "If there be any such," read the invitation, "the Motion Picture Alliance hereby offers its cooperation to help them clear their names or their consciences."

But a bitter divide opened up within the Alliance over the question of just how to deal with reformed Communists. The hard-line faction, led by Hopper, argued that ex-Communists should receive no help in returning to work. Just as she had scorned Larry Parks's tearful anti-Communist testimony in March 1951, she now questioned the sincerity of Eddie Dmytryk's repentance because he apparently hadn't demonstrated a suitable level of remorse for his past radicalism. In a column, Hopper endorsed the view of Albert Maltz, a Hollywood Ten member who had once been one of Dmytryk's closest friends. "I think Maltz hit the nail on the head," wrote Hopper, "when he wrote: 'Dmytryk has not now made a peace with his conscience. He has made it with his pocketbook and his career.'"

The opposing faction, led by Brewer, argued that redemption should be possible and helped Dmytryk find work. Brewer and actor Ward Bond, one of John Wayne's best friends, formed an informal committee to coordinate and rule on the acceptability of letters submitted to the studios by employees seeking clearance. They recruited right-wing newspaper columnist George Sokolsky and American Legion national commander James F. O'Neil to the group. But since none of these men nor anyone else in the Alliance had first-hand knowledge of so-called Communist activity, they called upon Martin Berkeley, their favorite ex-Communist, for advice. Happy to be in the middle of the action, Berkeley met regularly with Brewer and Bond to go over the letters and "determine whether the letter writer is telling the truth, is hedging or is deliberately falsifying his or her explanation."

Brewer also got together frequently with Ronald Reagan to clear performers. "Reagan and I spent countless hours helping to rehabilitate those who wanted to make a clean break from the party and get their lives back," Brewer recalled. Reagan, who was beginning to make his personal transition from liberal Democrat to conservative Republican, met his future wife, actress Nancy Davis, at a lunch where she complained that she was being confused for an actress with a similar name who was on the American Legion's blacklist. Reagan helped her clear her name, and then married her.

All told, according to historian Larry Ceplair, more than five hundred people from the entertainment industry were blacklisted or graylisted. Sokolsky testified to HUAC that he personally had helped "rehabilitate" three hundred people and allowed them to get back to work.

In August 1952—six weeks after Carl Foreman landed in England—Berkeley reported he was working again as a screenwriter, speaking regularly before groups like the American Legion, and writing newspaper columns and magazine pieces that managed to blend ultra-Americanism with naked self-promotion. "Our work will never finish," he vowed in one column. "The forces of democracy need us and we need them. You can count on us."

Berkeley kept in regular contact with Hopper, paying homage to her power and patriotism while casting her as his savior and benefactor. Sometimes Hopper played along, as when she promised to intercede with her friends at the big studios to get him more screenplay work. "I am back on Freedom Road again and people like yourself made it possible," he writes to her, in one of a steady stream of letters and notes. His tone is submissive and pandering. In another letter he reports he'll be speaking before the national convention of Roy Brewer's IATSE trade union. "Believe me I'll tell them how people like you and Roy and Ward [Bond] and Bob Arthur and all the rest came to my side while the white-livered 'liberals' sulked in their tents."

If Hopper responded to any of these letters, there's no record of it in her papers at the Motion Picture Academy archives.

Berkeley was working both ends of the process, feeding new names into the system while at the same time clearing repentant ex-Communists to return to work. In November 1951 he met again with HUAC's Bill Wheeler and gave him a list of twenty-one more names of alleged party members that he and fellow informant Richard Collins had come up with. Berkeley also told Wheeler that the party leadership had issued a directive back in 1938 identifying a select group of elite members who were to be set aside and placed in a special category so that they could swear under oath that they weren't members. Berkeley said Sam Ornitz, a screenwriter and party member, had told Berkeley's wife, Kate, that Dore Schary was one of those receiving this special status.

It was the perfect kind of smear—someone told someone else who then told Berkeley who then told Wheeler—unprovable yet also irrefutable. It never would have held up in a court of law, but it was perfect for the court of public opinion that was HUAC's preferred forum.

In a marathon closed session in January 1952, Berkeley gave HUAC another twenty names of current or former Reds. He began with a rundown of his latest speeches, four of them before American Legion groups. He had received a standing ovation at each one, he boasted. "And it would do your hearts good to have seen the way they have reacted to my testimony . . . [and] to know how highly these individuals on this present committee are regarded by the Legion and by the public in general."

But he quickly shifted into complaint mode. Other than four weeks of writing on a "charity job" arranged by Robert Arthur, a Motion Picture Alliance leader who worked as a producer at Universal Pictures, "I cannot get a job and none of the rest of us can get jobs, and none of us are going to get jobs unless something is done. I worked for ten straight years without a day's layoff with an average of forty thousand to fifty-five thousand dollars a year . . . I have as fine commercial credits as any writer in the business, and suddenly there isn't any work. I know there is a blacklist."

Berkeley insisted that his Communist enemies were out to get him and every other cooperative witness. "Ask yourself how many non-Communists or anti-Communists were employed by Sidney Buchman and Carl Foreman . . . and Adrian Scott and Robert Rossen," he said in a speech at the Masonic Temple in North Hollywood. "All these men were producers—all have been identified—every last one of them used the comrades almost exclusively."

The notion that Carl had hired Communists "almost exclusively" for *High Noon* was ludicrous, as Gary Cooper could personally attest. But at this point no one was prepared to step forward publicly to contradict Martin Berkeley. Still, even Bill Wheeler, his main ally, understood that Berkeley was making these allegations of a blacklist of anti-Communists because he himself needed a job. "Berkeley is disgusted with the motion picture industry principally because he has not yet become employed," Wheeler wrote to his boss, HUAC chief investigator Louis J. Russell.

Berkeley pleaded for the committee to issue a statement demanding that the studios hire the friendly witnesses. "I think that the committee has handled the producers with kid gloves long enough," he wrote to Wheeler. A statement "would help build a fire under the companies and, unless something is done soon, we might as well be dead . . . Can you help us?"

"PS," he added: "Have more information for you!"

Berkeley returned to HUAC when his son Bill was denied admission to the Navy's officer training program after graduating from Yale. Berkeley asked Wheeler to find out if Bill was being singled out because of his father's self-confessed former Communism. "If the Navy is eliminating this boy because of his father's prior conduct I personally feel this course of action is uncalled for," Wheeler told staff attorney Frank Tavenner. Bill says he was the only member of his class to be rejected and that the Navy cited phony medical reasons. Thus the son of one of the country's most high-profile anti-Communists was effectively blacklisted as a result of his own father's testimony.

Berkeley is generally credited as HUAC's champion namer of names, at least when it comes to Hollywood, but his total numbers are usually underestimated. Beyond the 150 or so names he gave publicly in September 1951, he added six more in executive session that same day, plus twenty on January 29, 1952, and thirteen others in April 1953, for a grand total of at least 189.

When he wasn't testifying, Berkeley kept up the Red-baiting drumbeat in print. He wrote articles for the *American Mercury* accusing four past or present congressmen of being Communists and claiming that the party was trying to seize control of radio and television. "The backbone of the Communist movement is crushed in Hollywood," he declared. "But the Reds are fighting back." Having lost control of the movie business, the Communists were now seeking to seize the airwaves— "right in your own living room!"

WHILE THE RED-HUNTERS and self-styled Americanists were riding high, Hollywood's liberals were in full retreat, led by the former leaders of the Committee for the First Amendment—which was now listed by HUAC as a Communist front organization. While William Wyler seethed, fellow director John Huston wrote an abject letter to his lawyer explaining how he'd been tricked into supporting the Hollywood Ten and how once he had learned their true motives for refusing to reveal their Communist affiliation, "I was shocked beyond words."

Screenwriter Philip Dunne, another former CFA leader, began collaborating with Roy Brewer, who offered to help clear anyone whose innocence Dunne could prove. "I then was faced with a moral dilemma," Dunne recalled. "If I accepted his offer, would I be shaking hands with the devil by tacitly endorsing his right to sit in judgment on his fellow citizens?" Dunne decided to do so, but with one condition: the letters these folks wrote would be addressed to him and not to Brewer. Dunne estimated that he and Brewer helped clear fifteen people and get them back to work.

Dore Schary, Carl Foreman's old mentor, had been one of the most defiant HUAC opponents in 1947, and the frequent object of Hedda Hopper's withering scorn. When he returned to MGM as head of production in 1948, Hopper had declared that MGM should be renamed "Metro Goldwyn Moscow"—a remark that her syndicate had been forced to retract after Schary threatened a five-million-dollar libel suit.

But in a meeting with the special agent in charge of the FBI's Los Angeles office in December 1950, Schary said he was prepared to cooperate, according to a memo to J. Edgar Hoover that the agent wrote afterward. Schary said MGM was "very concerned that they do not hire any members of the Communist Party or Communist sympathizers in connection with any film production." He went on to describe how he had convinced actress Betsy Blair to sign a loyalty oath before hiring her for an MGM production, and to defend Danny Kaye, who Schary said "is no more political than the draperies hanging on the wall." Before he left, Schary said he had recently submitted a script to assistant FBI Director Lou Nichols concerning a possible FBI movie.

Hoover remained skeptical. "I would view with some reservations Schary's profession of anti-communism now," he wrote at the bottom of the memo. "It is of course not popular nor profitable to be known as fellow travelers now but these 'Johnnies come lately' raise in me a question about their basic sincerity."

By 1952 Schary no longer felt strong enough to stand up against Hedda Hopper as well. "What about Communists?" Hopper demanded of him in an interview. "You once said that you would not fire a Red until it had been proved he was dedicated to the overthrow of our government by force and violence."

"I've changed that viewpoint," a contrite Schary replied, "simply because I'm now convinced they mean to overthrow the government by force and violence. I wouldn't hire a Communist, and I would fire anybody I discovered to be one."

To help make clear where he now stood, Schary and MGM produced a thirty-five-minute documentary called *The Hoaxters*. It branded Communism as "a bitter and cynical hope that appealed to bitter and cynical men," and called Karl Marx the "fourth pitchman of the Apocalypse," alongside Hitler, Mussolini, and the imperial militarists of Japan. Despite the fact he had died nearly seventy years earlier, Marx "still rides," according to the narrator, "bringing with him the same old snake oil which has brought men to their knees and to their graves. The only difference is that his bottle has a different label, a red one."

Schary's film did carry a warning against repression. "In continuing to make Communism ineffective we must not betray our own values, for there are angry voices in the land, homegrown tyrants who play the reckless game of slander in order to achieve their ends." Remember, it warns, "Hitler was an anti-Communist." And beware of "the hoaxter trying to destroy America in the name of America."

Schary defends *The Hoaxters* in his memoirs, saying its main intent was to equate Fascism and Communism and attack both the radical right and the radical left. Still, his last word on the blacklist was one of regret: "A heavy cost in courage was paid by the industry and a dreadful price was paid by those we could not protect."

THE HOAXTERS WAS ONE of more than two dozen Hollywood films designed to meet HUAC's demand that the studios atone for their past ideological sins. John Wayne led the way in helping create a subgenre of anti-Communist pictures in the early 1950s, most of which were not very good and none of which made money. Wayne's personal contribution was *Big Jim McLain*, his paean to HUAC and its investigators. The Warner Bros. film, which came out in August 1952, one month after *High Noon*, begins in the hearing room with the real members of the committee grilling an uncooperative witness (played by an actor), who turns out to be a professor of economics at a local university. When asked by Chairman Wood which side he would support in a war between the United States and Soviet Union, the mealy-mouthed academic invokes the Fifth Amendment. "Anyone who continues to be a Communist after 1945 is guilty of high treason," intones the narrator, echoing the standard articulated by Martin Berkeley in his landmark testimony.

But the real narrative of *Big Jim McLean* is the story of Operation Pineapple, the committee's investigation of Communist influence in

Hawaii. Wayne plays Big Jim, a committee investigator reportedly modeled on Bill Wheeler, and a strapping young James Arness (later to be *Gunsmoke*'s Marshal Matt Dillon) plays fellow investigator Mel Baxter. Both men are square-jawed, two-fisted patriots who can't stand Commies and devote their lives to exposing their nefarious schemes. Still, when he arrives in Honolulu, Big Jim at first seems more focused on romancing an attractive and compliant young doctor's receptionist, played by Nancy Olson, who eventually helps him build a case against her boss, one of the island's top Commies. The Reds themselves are sinister, dishonest, racist, and homicidal—sort of like the standard Warner Bros. bad guys but even more repugnant. They manage to capture and kill poor Mel, but Big Jim hunts them down and busts them. Still, the big fish get away on a legal technicality. "Sometimes I wonder why I stay in this job," Jim complains, sounding more than a little like Will Kane.

Big Jim McLean is predictably silly nonsense, "a vaporous and reckless romance" wrote Bosley Crowther. "The over-all mixing of cheap fiction with a contemporary crisis in American life is irresponsible and unforgivable. No one deserves credit for this film."

The other big anti-Communist film of 1952 was far more intriguing in its assumptions and obsessions. *My Son John*, directed by Leo McCarey (another charter member of the Motion Picture Alliance) and starring Robert Walker, Helen Hayes, Dean Jagger, and Van Heflin, was a domestic comedy turned nightmare with a hysterical mother, a half-crazed father, and a sinister son with something to hide. John Jefferson has neglected to come home from Washington in time to see his two younger brothers ship out to fight in the Korean War. When he does make it home, he mocks his father's obsessive, simple-minded Americanism—Dad is a local American Legion commander—and religiosity. John swears on the Bible to his doting but doubtful mom that he's not a Communist, but an FBI investigator who comes visiting raises her suspicions. And when she discovers that John has a key to the Washington apartment of a young woman who has been charged with espionage, her deepest fears are confirmed. Walker and Hayes are gifted actors who bring a sense of Oedipal dread to the relationship between John and his profoundly troubled mother. Poor remorseful John comes to realize the error of his ways, but before he can make amends he is gunned down outside the Lincoln Memorial by his former comrades. But his taped confession, in which he admits his perfidy and denounces Communism, is played as a posthumous commencement address at his alma mater. "I am a living lie, I am a traitor," he tells the graduating seniors. "I am a native American Communist spy. And may God have mercy on my soul."

My Son John, wrote a dismayed Bosley Crowther, "is a picture so strongly dedicated to the purpose of the American anti-Communist purge that it seethes with the sort of emotionalism and illogic that is characteristic of so much thinking these days."

Crowther listed the elements in *My Son John* "that may cause a thoughtful person to feel a shudder of apprehension at the militancy and dogmatism it reveals—its snide attitude toward intellectuals, its obvious pitch for religious conformity, and its eventual whole-hearted endorsement of its Legionnaire's stubborn bigotry. And to make this concern more considerable, there is the fact that the picture is played with remarkable skill at illusion by almost everyone."

Senator Karl Mundt of South Dakota—a HUAC alumnus now risen, like Richard Nixon, to the ranks of the U.S. Senate—applauded *My Son John* as "undoubtedly the greatest and most stirring pro-American motion picture of the past decade . . . It should be seen by the people of every American home." But audiences shied away. *My Son John* drew less than one million dollars in ticket sales and failed to make *Variety*'s Top Ninety pictures for 1952.

Despite these efforts at cinematic contrition, Hollywood was still suspect. In the December 1951 issue of the *American Legion Magazine*, journalist J. B. Matthews, a former HUAC investigator, asked "Did the Movies Really Clean House?" His conclusion: "The answer is no . . . Although times have changed for the better, the complete house-cleaning job in Hollywood remains to be done." Matthews wrote that the three hundred or so members of the Communist Party, added to the hundreds more fellow travelers and liberals who had been involved in purported Communist front organizations, meant "we have a story of Communist penetration of the film industry which is truly shocking."

Matthews singled out *High Noon* as one of the pictures in which Communists and "Communist-collaborators" were still involved. He named not just Carl Foreman but bit-part actors Howland Chamberlin and Virginia Farmer, Stanley Kramer—presumably because of the course he had taught at the People's Education Center in 1947—and even Fred Zinnemann, who had signed the amicus curiae brief for the Hollywood Ten's appeal to the Supreme Court. All of them, apparently, deserved to be purged.

Hedda Hopper agreed. She called Matthews's article "sickeningly accurate."

AT THE STANLEY KRAMER Company, Sam Katz and George Glass were the people in charge of ensuring that no Communists or Communist sympathizers were on the payroll, as Marsha Hunt found out in 1952. A talented and attractive actress, Hunt was signed for a major role in the Kramer production of *The Happy Time*, a cheerful comedy about a teenaged boy's coming of age in the 1920s. Hunt had signed a notarized statement the previous year denying she had ever been a Communist after her name appeared in *Red Channels*, a blacklist newsletter, citing her participation in purported Communist front groups like the Committee for the First Amendment. Her agent sent a copy of the statement to Katz, who called her soon after and pleaded with her to sign a new one, which he composed and sent over to her. "You'll never work in films again if you don't sign it," Katz warned. "It will kill you in the industry."

Hunt refused to sign because she didn't care for a paragraph that said she had been guilty of bad judgment and was sorry. She crossed it out and wrote instead, "If any of these activities furthered the cause of Communism, I regret having done them."

This proved insufficient. The executives at Columbia, the Kramer Company's new overseers, feared that *The Happy Time* would be picketed, George Glass told Hunt. He pleaded with her to take out an ad saying she was not a Communist and regretted having belonged to Communist front groups. Hunt says she refused; Glass kept calling.

Finally, after the film shoot ended, she went to see him. "They want it now," Glass told her. "This is a time for expediency, not integrity." Afterward she met twice with Roy Brewer and had a three-hour meeting with Katz. "If you don't [sign], you will be hurting the only company that has employed you," Katz told her. "You are making it so no company will hire any of you liberals." She told him that the company could itself take out the ad, but she wouldn't. As a result of her principled intransigence, she was graylisted for more than a decade. Hunt had made some fifty pictures in her previous seventeen years in the business; she made only eight more in the twenty years that followed.

17.

The Movie

I'm going to go back and find my business manager and agent, producer, and three-name writers and find out why I didn't get High Noon *instead of Cooper.*

JOHN WAYNE

After the two disastrous sneak previews in Pomona and Long Beach, and with Fred Zinnemann off on a new project and Carl Foreman gone altogether, just about everyone at the Stanley Kramer Company thought *High Noon* was a loser. But one film-studio veteran strongly disagreed.

George J. Schaefer, who was sixty-three, had started in the movie industry in 1914 as a secretary to film pioneer Lewis J. Selznick. Schaefer had navigated his way through the executive ranks at Paramount in the early 1930s, and had eventually risen to become president and chief executive officer of RKO Radio Pictures, where he championed the early work of Orson Welles, including *Citizen Kane*. After leaving RKO in 1942, he independently produced and distributed films, and he helped Stanley cut successful distribution deals with United Artists for *Champion* and *Home of the Brave*. After viewing *High Noon*, he believed Stanley had another potential winner.

Schaefer helped organize special trade screenings in April 1952 that yielded positive reviews. "A basic Western formula has been combined with good characterization in *High Noon*, making it more of a Western drama than the usual outdoor action feature," wrote *Variety*'s William Brogdon. "With the name of Gary Cooper to help it along, and on the basis of the adult-appealing dramatic content, the business outlook is favorable."

Schaefer and George Glass, Kramer's astute and loyal PR man, worked with Max Youngstein, head of production and marketing at United Artists, to create a marketing campaign that emphasized the movie's suspense, its mature approach to relations between men and women, and the idea that it was unusual and nonformulaic—not your standard Hollywood Western. Spewing exclamation points, the movie trailer labeled it "Stanley Kramer's masterpiece of suspense!" featuring Gary Cooper as "A man who was too proud to run!" It boasted that "Never have so few moments had such excitement!" United Artists had recently been reorganized and its leaders were desperate for a hit; they got behind the picture enthusiastically.

High Noon opened on July 14, 1952, at one of New York's most majestic old movie houses, the Loew's Mayfair at Seventh Avenue and Forty-Seventh Street, where it ran for two months. It also opened in Philadelphia, Boston, Pittsburgh, Minneapolis, and Portland, Maine. It was an immediate box-office hit, boosted by the astonishing popularity of "Do Not Forsake Me, Oh My Darlin'" and the excellent reviews the film received.

The *New York Times* led the way. "Every five years or so," Bosley Crowther began, "somebody—somebody of talent and taste, with a full appreciation of legend and a strong trace of poetry in their soul—scoops up a handful of clichés from the vast lore of Western films and turns them into a thrilling and inspiring work of art in this genre. Such a rare and exciting achievement is Stanley Kramer's production, *High Noon*, which was placed on exhibition at the Mayfair yesterday."

Anticipating the long conflict over credit, Crowther said it was impossible to know who was responsible for the film's quality, but he named Kramer, Foreman, Zinnemann, and Cooper as all likely candidates.

"What is important is that someone—or all of them together, we would say—has turned out a Western drama that is the best of its kind in several years. Familiar but far from conventional in the fabric of story and theme and marked by a sure illumination of human character, this tale of a brave and stubborn sheriff in a town full of do-nothings and cowards has the rhythm and roll of a ballad spun in pictorial terms. And, over all, it has a stunning comprehension of that thing we call courage in a man and the thorniness of being courageous in a world of bullies and poltroons."

Crowther came back a few days later with a second paean to the film. He lavished praise particularly on Carl for his taut, realistic screenplay.

"Mr. Foreman has no dangled puppets, he has truly and artfully conceived real characters whose motives and dispositions are clear and credible," Crowther wrote. "The marshal, played by Gary Cooper, is not the usual, square-jawed, stalwart sort; he is a tired and unglamorous sheriff who would gladly crawl off in a hole if he thought that would mean an avoidance of a showdown—but he knows it won't. He is a man with the sense to meet a challenge, not duck in the hope it will go away."

Stanley, who still thought of *High Noon* as a forlorn mutt of a film, was stunned by Crowther's raves. "We went to New York and Bosley Crowther said 'Do you know how good this is?'" he recalled. "Bosley Crowther really created *High Noon*." After the extraordinary *New York Times* review, Stanley said, the other critics "seemed to fall in line."

Otis L. Guernsey Jr. of the *New York Herald Tribune* joined the choir. He called *High Noon* "an American movie achievement which can stand beside the tallest from anywhere and look most of them in the eye."

So did *Time* magazine. "Zinnemann's direction wrings the last ounce from the scenario with a sure sense of timing and sharp, clean cutting," wrote *Time*, which called *High Noon* "a taut, sense-making horse-opera that deserves to rank with *Stagecoach* and *The Gunfighter*."

The summer of 1952 was a scorcher and the new technology of electric-powered air-conditioning no doubt helped drive people to the theaters. *High Noon* was the only new film to make *Motion Picture Herald's* "Box Office Champions" for August, and it finished the month as the national leader, according to *Variety*. It quickly became United Artists' biggest earner since *The African Queen* the year before. The film brought in $2.5 million in eighteen weeks and was the main reason for UA's return to modest profitability in 1952. It became the eighth biggest grossing picture of the year with $3.4 million (*Big Jim McLain* was twenty-seventh, with $2.6 million). Gary Cooper, who had taken less than half his usual salary for the picture in return for a percentage of the net profits, eventually earned a reported six hundred thousand dollars.

It was an astonishing success for such an austere and unusual piece of entertainment. What audiences saw was a modest, terse, almost dour eighty-four-minute black-and-white Western with no grand vistas, no cattle drives, and no Indian attacks, in fact no gunplay whatsoever until its final showdown. Yet its taut, powerful storytelling, gritty visual beauty, suspenseful use of time, evocative music, and understated ensemble acting made it enormously compelling.

"It's a great movie," says film critic Leonard Maltin. "Its compactness is one reason. For all its purposefulness, it doesn't beat you over the head. It's telling a story. And it's very well cast: all of those character actors are just perfect. The blend of location and back lot is seamless. And that music is inspired."

THE FILM BEGINS QUIETLY, with a man hunched on a rock in a thin grove of trees, waiting for two companions, while Tex Ritter's haunting version of "Do Not Forsake Me" plays and the credits unwind. From that calm, subdued opening moment, *High Noon*'s story marches forward relentlessly and purposefully toward its violent climax and doleful conclusion.

The clocks and the theme song are the two threads that are braided throughout the movie, although they serve very different purposes. The clocks constantly remind us that time is running out for our hero. They help build and underscore the tension and anxiety of his fruitless search for support. There are no dissolves in *High Noon*—none of the usual fade-ins and fade-outs connoting the unseen passage of time—because time passes directly in front of us. Every minute counts—and is counted. The song, whose melody is played at least twelve times during the picture, reminds us of Will Kane's dilemma and what's at stake for him. His life and his happiness are on the line, yet he cannot walk away from his duty. After the debacle of the film's two sneak previews, Stanley Kramer had artfully reduced the amount of song time but still used snippets of the melody as an evocative, subliminal reminder that a fatal confrontation is coming.

As he walks the deserted streets of Hadleyville seeking volunteers, Will Kane is engaged in a journey into the unfaithful heart of his community. His travels become a series of bitter disappointments: the judge, the deputy, the former volunteer, the saloon customers, the selectmen, the church members, the retired marshal, even his lovely new bride—they all turn away from him in his hour of need.

The lawman's search is for the meaning of his life. Kane has lived by certain bedrock assumptions: that good men will stand together and confront evil when it arises, that wives and friends will provide moral support, and that the pillars of civil society—church and state, and the ministers, judges, and elected officials who represent these institutions—will rally to support law and order and human decency. All of those assumptions are challenged and upended as *High Noon* unfolds.

Kane's individual meetings with the characters who betray him are the moral core of the movie and the moments when Cooper and the supporting cast are at their finest. Thomas Mitchell, Grace Kelly, Lloyd Bridges, Katy Jurado, Otto Kruger, and James Millican (uncredited as Herb Baker, the unfaithful volunteer) all hold their own in their scenes with Cooper. They do most of the talking (and self-justifying) while Cooper responds with quiet stoicism and deepening despair to each disappointment. And film editor Elmo Williams astutely re-shuffles the order of Kane's search to put his former mentor Mart Howe toward the end. It's an appropriate shift because in many ways Howe's rejection is the most disheartening. The two actors play the scene beautifully. Lon Chaney Jr. as Howe seems to make almost perfect sense as he runs down his list of reasons why he can't accompany Kane to the showdown. But his excuses are all hollow and self-serving, and Chaney's doleful delivery betrays him. He knows he is abandoning his friend. Kane knows it, too. He doesn't continue to plead; he simply gets up and leaves. The scene is one of Cooper's best moments. His line readings express his deep respect and affection for the older man (actually Chaney was five years younger than Cooper). He never raises his voice or shows anger. But he makes clear by his physical movements and the blank expression on his face that this rejection by his friend and mentor is the ultimate betrayal.

WILL KANE IS NOW fully alone, his isolation underscored in *High Noon*'s most memorable visual moment—the reverse high-crane shot in which the camera pulls up and away from the lone figure of the marshal, standing in the middle of Hadleyville's deserted main street. Then he turns and walks slowly toward the train station to meet his fate.

"Look, no one is there," says director Wolfgang Petersen, who first saw and fell in love with the film as a teenager in post–World War Two Germany. "Where are the people? They are just gone. Not even a dog can be seen. He is completely alone."

Like his acting, Gary Cooper's movements throughout *High Noon* are minimalist. He is dressed in black vest, hat, and pants in contrast with the blank white sky. He walks gingerly, reflecting his character's existential burden (and the actor's ailing back and sore hip), and his line readings are slow and careful, like a man bearing a crushing burden. He may be in a tight spot and desperate for help, but he won't beg or compromise. His utter relief when Harvey Pell, his chief deputy and friend, shows up for work quickly dissolves when Pell makes clear he won't back Kane unless the marshal agrees to do an unacceptable favor in return. Kane doesn't hesitate; he immediately says no, then resumes his search for allies. He literally has no time to waste on scoundrels. He knows his life is ebbing away with the ticks of all those clocks, but he doesn't cut any moral corners.

None of the people who made *High Noon*, including Stanley Kramer, was enthusiastic about hiring Cooper. Yet in the end they owe him so much. His carefully controlled performance, his ability to portray simultaneously strength and vulnerability, is an enormous asset. It gives his character, and the entire picture, plausibility, intimacy, and human scale. Will Kane is no superhuman action hero, just an aging, tired man seeking to escape his predicament with his life and his new marriage intact, yet knowing he cannot. There's none of Cooper's usual light touch or self-confident insouciance. He tries and fails once or twice to be charming or ingratiating—when he lifts up Amy, his new bride, and demands a kiss, or when he tries to kid Harvey about the deputy's impetuousness. But mostly he is bone-tired and achingly sincere. Cooper falls back on directness and determination.

It is a brave performance, and it is hard to imagine any other actor pulling it off with the same skill and grace. Certainly none of the gifted young bucks whom Kramer, Foreman, and Zinnemann considered and might well have preferred—Brando, Holden, Heston, Peck, Douglas— could have done it with such convincing authenticity, despite all their talent. In *High Noon*, Gary Cooper is indeed the truth.

The suspense builds with each rejection, until finally at one minute before noon, Elmo Williams takes out his film editor's scissors and glue-pot and cuts and pastes a montage of faces, settings, and clocks that manages to review the entire narrative so far in ruthlessly swift strokes, as Dimitri Tiomkin's score builds in tempo and volume. Then suddenly, the inevitable whistle of the noon train slashes open the montage to announce that evil has finally arrived.

When it comes, it wears a very human face. Frank Miller, played by veteran character actor Ian MacDonald, isn't tall or muscular or physically intimidating in any way. He wears a nondescript Western businessman's outfit and a no-nonsense manner. There are no handshakes for his younger brother or his hired gunmen, and no acknowledgment of Helen Ramirez, his former lover, whom he espies boarding the train a few yards down the platform. Miller just loosens his tie and checks his revolver. "Let's get started," he demands.

Kane is just as terse and determined. As Tom Hanks points out,

Cooper speaks just seven words of scripted dialogue in the last fourteen minutes of the film. There are no brave or angry speeches, no high-volume exposition, no heart-stirring declarations. "Gary Cooper is not just Sheriff Will Kane in *High Noon*—he is also a mysterious and cryptic teacher of the art of acting on the screen," says Hanks.

Other legendary performers have also praised the pure craft of *High Noon*. In Fred Zinnemann's files is a handwritten note from Katharine Hepburn on behalf of herself and Spencer Tracy:

> *Dear Freddy, Spence and I were completely bowled over by your picture— It is a memorable job—Thrilling and inspiring and full of such integrity . . . I cannot remember being so completely absorbed—it seemed three minutes long—Cooper and the dark woman were so touching, in fact all the cast were so good—the music extraordinary—the writing, photography. It is so all of a piece that it delivers the most powerful punch I have received in a long long time. Your own qualities of simplicity & strength are certainly right there all the time—Never a cliché and never a clever touch—just wonderful & simple & overpowering—You gave us a tremendous life & again reminded us of what a lovely business this is—affectionately, Kate Hep*

HIGH NOON HAS ALL the trappings of Western movie patriarchy. Its hero is a man of standard masculine characteristics—inarticulate, stubborn, adept at and reliant on gun violence. But it also has two strong female characters who struggle to come to terms with the sudden crisis at hand and must choose whether to embrace or reject the man they both love and yet are deeply in conflict with. As feminist film critic Gwendolyn Foster says, the movie mounts "a subtle attack on gender expectations throughout both narratives."

Neither woman fits the conventional models that Western films usually impose on their female characters. Amy Fowler Kane, the marshal's young bride, is a Quaker from Missouri—pale-skinned, blonde, attired in a prim white wedding dress—but is not a typically submissive spouse. She confronts her new husband about his decision to return to Hadleyville and abandons him when he refuses to accede to her pleas. "I don't understand any of this," she complains at first, but gradually she comes to see the full implications of his decision and of her own. While Grace Kelly believed her performance was wooden and failed to mesh with the other actors, it actually seems appropriate for the role of an uninitiated outsider who doesn't know the history of the town nor the sensibility of her new husband.

By contrast, Helen Ramirez, Kane's former lover, a brothel owner and half-Mexican—brown-skinned, dark-haired, black-bodiced, and voluptuous—understands his predicament and longs to help him. But because he has previously rejected her, and perhaps because she knows his cause is hopeless, she chooses to walk away and protect herself instead.

Helen had been Frank Miller's lover when he ruled Hadleyville through terror and violence, then had jumped readily into the arms of Kane after he defeated Miller and sent him to prison. After Kane ended their affair, she turned to Harvey Pell, his strong, handsome, but utterly immature deputy. She makes no apologies for using her sexuality to control the men around her. "There are very few men who cannot be managed, one way or another," she tells Amy.

Helen, better than any other character, understands intuitively that what's at stake is not just Kane's life but the fate of the entire community. Kane "will be a dead man in half an hour, and nobody is going to do anything about it," she tells Pell in what is perhaps the most perceptive comment by any of the film's characters. "Don't ask me how I know. I know. And when he dies, this town dies, too. It smells dead to me already."

Fred Zinnemann was clearly fascinated by Katy Jurado's performance and his camera lingers on her face in almost all of her scenes. "The close-up is how you indicate who's in charge, who's the strong person," notes film scholar Charles Ramirez Berg. By giving more of these to Jurado, "Zinnemann and Foreman were turning the stereotype upside down."

The long-standing Hollywood tradition in Westerns that the dark-skinned bad girl winds up taking a bullet for the man she loves is also subverted in *High Noon*. Rather than dying, Helen Ramirez leaves her former lover to his fate, cashes in her assets, and boards a train for a new start in another town. "What surprises us in retrospect is how much the film questions the values that make up the supposed fabric of American society, a fabric that can be ripped asunder with unsettling ease," writes Foster.

In the end, Amy finally surrenders her own Quaker principles and submits to her husband's values in order to save his life. She picks up a revolver and kills one gunman and helps Kane kill another. When it's over, Kane lifts her crumpled body from the street, embraces her, and leads her to the buckboard that will deliver them far from Hadleyville. But first he drops his badge on the ground. The gesture is a condemnation of the corrupt community they are leaving. But it's also a renewal of his promise to Amy: no more gunfights, no more law enforcement.

High Noon's sensitive focus on Helen and Amy—remarkable for its era and genre—is one of the elements that make it an extraordinary movie. "It is the women who control the point of view of this film," says film historian Joanna E. Rapf.

DESPITE *HIGH NOON*'S SUCCESS, the movie has stirred wariness and rejection from many critics of stature. Robert Warshow, whose 1954 essay "Movie Chronicle: The Westerner" is a classic, admires the film's documentary-style visuals and understands that the movie is one of many that seek to transform the genre "from the boisterous adolescent beauty of the 1930s and '40s to a sense of seriousness and realism, both physical and psychological."

"As lines of age have come into Gary Cooper's face since *The Virginian*, so the outlines of the Western movie in general have become less smooth, its background more drab," writes Warshow. "The sun still beats upon the town, but the camera is likely now to take advantage of this illumination to seek out more closely the shabbiness of buildings and furniture, the loose, worn hang of clothing, the wrinkles and dirt of the faces." The true theme of the Western is no longer "the freedom and expansiveness of frontier life, but its limitations, its material bareness, the pressures of obligation."

But Warshow ultimately dismisses *High Noon* as a "'social drama' of a very low order . . . altogether unconvincing and displaying a vulgar anti-populism." He says the film shouldn't have to explain why the marshal must face his enemies alone—"a question that does not exist in the proper frame of the Western movie, where the hero is 'naturally' alone." As a result, complains Warshow, while "the hero of *High Noon* proves himself a better man than all around him, the actual effect of this contrast is to lessen his stature: he becomes only a rejected man of virtue." Cooper riding away at the end with his bride "is a pathetic rather than a tragic figure."

Two of the most revered icons of the Western movie tradition, director Howard Hawks and actor John Wayne, also argued that Will Kane's pleas for help from ordinary townsfolk somehow sully his professionalism and make him appear weak and helpless. When the residents turn him down contemptuously, the movie portrays them as cowardly and unworthy of the marshal's sacrifice. In the end, he confronts the Miller gang alone not to protect a corrupt and selfish community that doesn't deserve to be defended, but because his own honor demands it. Wayne was especially dismayed that the movie portrayed churchgoers and public officials as cowards and hypocrites. He interpreted this as an attack on American values, which in many ways it is.

Hawks and Wayne eventually went beyond their visceral dislike for *High Noon*. They made an enduring cinematic rebuttal, *Rio Bravo* (1959), considered by many critics to be one of their best movies. "I didn't think a good sheriff was going to go running around town like a chicken with his head cut off asking for help, and finally his Quaker wife had to save him," Hawks told author Joseph McBride. Hawks said he decided to "do just the opposite, and take a real professional viewpoint . . . We did everything that way, the exact opposite of what annoyed me in *High Noon,* and it worked and people liked it."

Fred Zinnemann also came in for much criticism. Film critic Andrew Sarris, who helped import the French auteur theory of filmmaking to the American critical scene, never felt Fred was a true creative cinematic artist of the stature of John Ford, Howard Hawks, Alfred Hitchcock, or Orson Welles. Sarris decried *High Noon* as his "runner-up" for the title of "most overrated Western . . . with its mannered, fussy performance by Gary Cooper and the pallid presence of Grace Kelly. Also, this is the favorite Western for people who hate Westerns." Robin Wood, the great British film critic, blasted Fred's direction as "external and shallow . . . His handling of the actors is almost uniformly abominable."

Sarris, like Warshow, put his finger on what many Western lovers believe: that *High Noon* is just a barely disguised social drama using a Western setting and costumes. Even Fred's own remarks lent support to this view. He saw the story told in *High Noon* as a classic clash between an outsider and a corrupt community, one of his favorite themes and a conflict that happens all through history. "*High Noon* is not a Western, as far as I'm concerned," he wrote. "It just happens to be set in the Old West."

Westerns, which were arguably America's first and foremost indigenous movie genre (starting with Edwin S. Porter's *Great Train Robbery* in 1903, considered the first narrative film), were indeed in the process of changing direction by the time *High Noon* came along. For decades they had presented myths about the taming of the frontier: in telling tales of heroic sheriffs and cavalrymen defeating criminals and hostile Indians they portrayed the civilizing of the West as a courageous and moral enterprise. But films like *High Noon* presented a different, more complex message:

that a community established through violence and avarice could be cowardly and corrupt, with no place for brave men and women.

Charles Silver, director of the Film Study Center at the Museum of Modern Art, lumps *High Noon* with a string of anti-Romantic, anti-populist Westerns, along with William Wellman's *Ox-Bow Incident* (1943) and Henry King's *Gunfighter* (1950). "There was little regard for either the nobility of the Western myth or the cinematic potential of the imagery of the American West," Silver writes. A longtime champion of John Ford's Westerns, Silver contends *High Noon* explicitly contradicts Ford's evocative and visually poetic work.

But it's also possible to view *High Noon* as a worthy link between two of Ford's most important Westerns: *Stagecoach* (1939) and *The Man Who Shot Liberty Valance* (1962). In the former, a fresh-faced outlaw and a reformed prostitute, played by John Wayne and Claire Trevor, survive Indians, bad guys, and society's disapproval, then leave town on a buckboard. In escaping the suffocating strictures of a corrupt society, their liberation is a celebration of their independence and their innocence. Carl and Fred both greatly admired *Stagecoach*, and they clearly borrowed heavily from its plotline and visual appearance.

By contrast, *Liberty Valance* is an elegiac ode to a mythic West that never was. The hero, played again by John Wayne, guns down an evil malefactor but allows another man to take the credit, and he loses the love of his life and his self-respect in the process. A sadder, more self-critical film, made by a director who as he aged embraced emotional complexity and contradiction, *Valance* takes the measure of the sacrifice of love and honor of those who helped tame the West. *High Noon* is the bridge between these two superb films—the passageway between innocence and experience and between triumph and resignation.

In the end, the question of whether *High Noon* is a genuine Western seems a bit silly. It is filmed like a Western, is set in a Western town, uses a Western musical theme, and operates within the classic story framework of one man facing a showdown with the bad guys. And of course, it stars one of the genre's most recognizable and reliable performers.

Ultimately, argues film historian Michael Selig, "*High Noon* is an expression of the genre attempting to find itself. Will Kane stalks the streets, from saloon to church, searching for the community of altruistic individuals that used to exist in Hadleyville. As he is rejected again and again, his face registers fear, an emotion new to Western heroes." *High Noon*, says Selig, manages "to deepen and change the narrative line of the Western without fundamentally altering the role of the individual heroic action."

Audiences have always loved *High Noon*, even if the higher-brow critics have not. There's something about Gary Cooper marching slowly down a deserted Western street, a six-shooter holstered on his hip, that has stirred and reassured three generations of viewers. It is a symbol of moral bravery for an uncertain age.

The film was enormously influential. Its success—and the subsequent success of *Shane* (1953), which was filmed at the same time but not released until the following year—inspired an entire sub-genre of one-man-versus-evil Westerns. In *Bad Day at Black Rock* (1955), a one-armed World War Two veteran played by Spencer Tracy solves the murder of the father of a Nisei war hero, defeats the killer and his accomplices, and rallies the decent folks of a demoralized Western town. Sergio Leone's *Once Upon a Time in the West* (1968) begins with a *High Noon*–ish scene of three bad men waiting at the depot for a train to arrive (but it is Charles Bronson who gets off the train and kills all three). *High Plains Drifter* (1973), the first Western directed by Clint Eastwood, is a fantasy sequel to *High Noon*: a mysterious man shows up in a small town after its sheriff has been murdered and takes revenge on the three killers and on the townsfolk who had stood idly by while the sheriff was killed.

But film historian David Thomson believes Will Kane's most faithful cinematic heir is Harry Callahan, the modern-day San Francisco police lieutenant who goes one-on-one with murderous criminals in *Dirty Harry* (1971) and its various, more tawdry sequels, his righteous actions always portrayed in stark contrast to the cowardly equivocations of his morally corrupt superiors. At the end of *Dirty Harry*, after gunning down the villain, Eastwood flings his inspector's badge into a pool of dirty water, echoing Cooper's same action twenty years earlier at the conclusion of *High Noon*. But whereas Cooper's gesture is one of sadness and resignation, Eastwood's is one of contempt.

CLEARLY *HIGH NOON* IS a Western, but is it also, as Carl Foreman insisted, a blacklist allegory? Almost no one thought so at the time, including Fred Zinnemann. When he first read Carl's first draft, he said many years later, "I felt the situation as described by Kramer and Foreman very fascinating and I saw no parallel with any political upheavals. I don't believe that there are any. I think that this is a mystique that's been created and there's nothing to it."

Bosley Crowther, after receiving Carl's eleven-page letter, hinted at the politics in a column he published in August 1952. He called *High Noon* "a drama of one man's bravery in the midst of a town full of cowards. It is a story that bears a clear relation to things that are happening in the world today, where people are being terrorized by bullies and surrendering their freedom out of senselessness and fear."

Will Kane, Crowther added, "is a man with the sense to meet a challenge, not duck in the hope it will go away. The marshal can give a fine lesson to the people in Hollywood today."

An anonymous editorial writer for *The Nation*, a progressive magazine, also got the message. "There must be times these days," the editorial declared, "when Mr. Foreman feels that he too has been deserted by those who should have helped him stand off the bullies and tough guys whose aggressions have so largely destroyed the moral fiber of the Western town that goes by the name of Hollywood."

The official mouthpiece of the Kremlin, for what it's worth, saw nothing left-wing about *High Noon*. The movie, *Pravda* complained, was a celebration of the American capitalist myth that one man was what truly mattered. In *High Noon*, the guardians of Communist orthodoxy sniffed, "the idea of the insignificance of the people and masses and the grandeur of the individual found its complete incarnation."

Dave Kehr, film curator at the Museum of Modern Art, is also no fan of *High Noon*. He has written that Gary Cooper plays an "inflated archetype in his most overrated film," which Kehr calls a "didactic political fable." Still, Kehr respects its political acuity.

"What convinces in *High Noon*," writes Kehr, "is the film's sense of social malaise, of a community drained of coherence and conviction in the face of overwhelming fear—certainly a plausible portrait of a country in which, according to a Gallup poll in September 1951, about half the respondents believed that the Korean conflict represented the beginning of an atomically charged World War III."

Still, seen on the screen at a distance of more than sixty years, *High Noon*'s politics are almost illegible. Rather than appearing to be a brave opponent of the blacklist, some critics have suggested that Will Kane could just as readily be seen as Senator Joseph McCarthy bravely taking on the evil forces of Communism while exposing the cowardice and hypocrisy of the Washington establishment.

It's an intriguing exercise to compare and contrast *High Noon* with *On the Waterfront* (1954), another classic film to emerge from the blacklist era and one whose politics were supposedly the exact opposite.

On the Waterfront was written by Budd Schulberg and directed by Elia Kazan, both of whom were former Communists who—unlike Carl Foreman—denounced the party and named names before HUAC. The film's hero, Terry Malloy, a New Jersey dockworker played by Marlon Brando, turns state's witness and testifies against a corrupt union boss (played by Lee J. Cobb, who was also a cooperative HUAC witness) who rules by bribery and terror. Terry's conversion from a loyal stooge in the union to a whistleblower is an act of personal courage.

Yet despite the intentions of their creators, the two films seem like compatible companion pieces when viewed from a modern perspective. Both are about brave men who, when abandoned by friends and allies, choose to stand alone against evil forces and triumph.

Wolfgang Petersen, who watched *High Noon* for an article in the *New York Times* in 2001, captured well the film's celebration of personal courage and its impact on him as a German teenager in the early 1950s. "People were not really talking about the past or about responsibility," he recalled. "And then I saw this movie, and it was so clear to me: There is good. There is bad. It was about heroism, you know, about courage . . . It was very powerful."

WHEN THE AWARDS SEASON began in early 1953, *High Noon* started out strong. It won the best film and best director prizes from the New York Film Critics, as well as top honors from the *Film Daily* newspaper, the Associated Press, *Photoplay*, and *Look* magazine, and was nominated for a Golden Globe. Carl won best screenplay from the Screen Writer's Guild. Finally, the film was nominated for seven Academy Awards. *HIGH NOON* LOOKS TO SWEEP OSCARS was the headline on *Variety*'s annual straw poll article. The newspaper predicted the movie would win best picture, best actor, and best screenplay. Foreman's "victory looks virtually certain," it noted.

But Hollywood's conservative lobby was determined to deny Carl an Oscar. Predictably, the counterattack began with a column by Billy Wilkerson in the *Hollywood Reporter* that disparaged Carl's award from the Screen Writers Guild, one of Wilkerson's favorite political punching bags.

"Some of the guild crowd are giving out with the argument that a man's literary talent and his writing accomplishments have nothing to do with his politics, or vice versa," he wrote. "In the present circumstances—national and international—this is a rather stupid argument, because when any man uses his talents and industry to grab

American dollars which directly or indirectly help out a cause that is dedicated to the overthrow of our form of government, the least any loyal American can do is NOT VOTE AN AWARD to such a man.

"The honoring of Foreman and the nominating of Michael Wilson in the same Screen Writers Guild sweepstakes not only are an affront to the upholders of our democracy, but indicate plainly that within the Screen Writers Guild there is still too much sympathy for the commie line."

Hedda Hopper joined in with a series of columns between December 1952 and March 1953 pushing for rival films in the various categories *High Noon* was nominated for—with the notable exception of best actor, where her old friend Gary Cooper was a nominee.

The American Legion also attacked the film on political grounds. "We feel that the continued employment of Communists and Communist sympathizers in the production of motion pictures is totally indefensible," wrote Robert A. Bunch, Washington, D.C., district commander for the Legion, in a letter to United Artists when *High Noon* opened. "The situation is assuming the proportions of a national scandal, particularly in view of the fact that America's young men are dying on the battlefields of Korea at the hands of the ideological brothers of the Hollywood Communists."

UA's response ignored the substance of Bunch's allegations, merely noting that it had not produced *High Noon* but as its distributor had a legal obligation to market it.

Luigi Luraschi, head of foreign and domestic censorship at Paramount Studios, regularly submitted written reports to "Owen," his CIA handler. In a letter dated March 9, 1953, he reported that as a member of the board of the Motion Picture Academy he had been lobbying to undermine *High Noon*'s chances for the best picture award despite "a lot of activity from the . . . left flank." Carl Foreman's screenplay, he claimed, spinning his own fantasy, was "full of messages . . . I don't know whether things got hot or not, but Foreman was taken off, the propaganda presumably taken out, and the picture made as it is being released today. For the average fan it will seem O.K. For the Communist and for his propaganda purposes abroad, where he may see fit to press the issue, it is still full of subtleties which are a part of the construction and which can't be taken out."

"Can't understand how Cooper got sucked in," Luraschi added. "He's a savvy guy, but I guess the Western cloak fooled him."

The Oscars ceremony took place ten days later. It was the first time the event was televised (by NBC) and the first to be held simultaneously in Hollywood and New York. The result was an audience of forty-five million viewers, then the largest in television history.

If the *Hollywood Reporter* is to be believed, no one was rooting for Carl to win best screenplay, including members of *High Noon*'s own production company. "We were told that none of the Kramer boys wanted to accept the screenplay award if Carl Foreman won it for *High Noon*," wrote the *Reporter*. "They drew for the 'honor' yesterday afternoon, we were told, and Rudolph Sternad was stuck with the short straw!"

They were spared the supposed embarrassment of picking up an award for a man who had been hounded out of Hollywood because of his political views. The Oscar was won by Charles Schnee for *The Bad and the Beautiful*, a much inferior screenplay. Fred Zinnemann lost out as best director to John Ford for *The Quiet Man*, Ford's fourth Oscar.

The best picture award went to *The Greatest Show on Earth*, Cecil B. DeMille's lumbering circus epic. There was a strong element of political submission in DeMille's victory; he was, after all, still crusading to expel from Hollywood anyone with a leftist tinge, and more people probably feared than respected him. Bosley Crowther called DeMille's film "spectacular but old-fashioned" compared to the "intelligence, dynamism, and moral fiber" of *High Noon*.

Stanley Kramer, in retrospect, said he was convinced it was politics that defeated *High Noon*. "I still believe *High Noon* was the best picture of 1952," he wrote more than forty years later. "But the political climate of the nation and the right-wing campaigns against *High Noon* had enough effect to relegate it to an also-ran status. Popular as it was, it could not overcome the climate in which it was released."

At Dimitri Tiomkin's urging, Tex Ritter attended the ceremony, sat next to Gary Cooper's mother, and sang "Do Not Forsake Me Oh My Darlin'" live on national television. The music won two Oscars: one for Tiomkin and Ned Washington for the song and another for Tiomkin's innovative musical score, which used the "Do Not Forsake Me" melody as its core motif. Elmo Williams and Harry Gerstad also won the Oscar for best film editing. It was no small irony that Williams, who had leaped to take all the credit for "rescuing" *High Noon*, had to share the editing Oscar with a man who, at least according to Williams, had done nothing but splice together a few reels of film under Williams's direction in time for the fateful showing in Stanley Kramer's living room.

Gary Cooper was up against Marlon Brando (*Viva Zapata!*), Kirk Douglas (*The Bad and the Beautiful*), José Ferrer (*Moulin Rouge*), and Alec Guinness (*The Lavender Hill Mob*). Four of the five nominees had starred in films made by the Stanley Kramer Company, a tribute to Stanley's talent for choosing and attracting the very best performers. Despite *High Noon*'s alleged Communist connection, Cooper was the one bona fide member of the Hollywood establishment among the five nominees and few people were surprised when he won his second Oscar for best actor. What was surprising was the man who went to the podium to collect it for him. Cooper had run into John Wayne on location in Mexico, and had asked Wayne to represent him. It was typical of Cooper's sense of modesty and professionalism that he would not take time away from his current project, the profoundly mediocre melodrama *Blowing Wild*, to attend the Oscars. Wayne may have hated *High Noon*, but he couldn't refuse a fellow member of Hollywood's aristocracy no matter what the politics. Looking svelte and dashing in his evening wear, he gave a gracious but rueful acceptance speech:

> *I'm glad to see that they're giving this to a man who is not only most deserving, but has conducted himself throughout his years in our business in a manner that we can all be proud of him. Coop and I have been friends, hunting and fishing for more years than I like to remember. He is one of the nicest fellows I know. I don't know anybody nicer, and our kinship goes further than that friendship because we both fell off of horses into pictures together.*
>
> *Now that I'm through being such a good sport, I'm going to go back and find my business manager and agent, producer, and three-name writers and find out why I didn't get* High Noon *instead of Cooper. 'Course I can't fire any of these very expensive fellows, but I can at least run my 1930 Chevrolet into one of their big, black new Cadillacs.*

Carl Foreman's response upon hearing these remarks was to offer Wayne his services as a screenwriter: "I'm over here in London, Duke, you can get me any time."

18.

Writer's Block

Why does a man love his home country? Because the bread tastes better, the sky is higher, the air is spicier, voices ring out more clearly, the ground is softer to walk on.

BERTOLT BRECHT, *THE CAUCASIAN CHALK CIRCLE*

A few months after Estelle and Kate Foreman joined Carl in London, the city was enveloped by one of the worst environmental disasters in its history. The Great Smog of December 1952 was caused by a thick layer of the soot from coal-fired furnaces and stoves that always blanketed the city during winter combined with a windless cold front that locked down the black cloud like an impenetrable dome. For five days, people could barely see out their windows and the smog penetrated flats and houses through doors and window frames, like the worst days of the American Dust Bowl twenty years earlier. The smog killed at least four thousand people—estimates put the final toll as high as twelve thousand—and sickened one hundred thousand more.

"Carl couldn't get home from the office because the smog was so thick you couldn't see a foot in front of your face," Estelle recalled. "I don't know how he got home but he finally did . . . And I remember when I got undressed that night, I was wearing a white slip and threw it on a chair. And when I woke up the next morning, there were black streaks on it from all the oily smog that came through the window."

"There wasn't any central heating in this so-called flat," she added, "and I came down with a godawful something or other."

While the smog lifted after a few days, the mood of anxiety and despair that Estelle felt did not. She was in a strange city with a five-year-old daughter and an angry, depressed husband suffering from writer's block.

"Carl was kind of a different man when I got there. He was not the husband who had left. He was angry now, all the time. He tried to sit at a typewriter and write (but) he was too angry."

Oscar night was a terrible ordeal. Not only did Carl not win best screenplay, his name was not even mentioned by the other *High Noon* winners. Gary Cooper wasn't at the ceremony, and the others—Elmo Williams, Harry Gerstad, Dimitri Tiomkin, and Ned Washington—neglected to thank the writer who was the true father of the film. "They tried not to mention him at all," says Jonathan Foreman, Carl's son. "It was like this weird Stalinism—he didn't exist, there wasn't a writer. It must have been agony for him. It's a cowardly business, Hollywood. Full of desperate and selfish cowards."

At least he had enough money, thanks to the severance deal with the Kramer Company. Carl rented a place for himself, Estelle, and Kate just off Kensington High Street, then a more comfortable flat at nearby Duchess of Bedford's Walk. It was important to maintain a high and visible profile so that visiting Americans and members of the British film industry would not forget he was there. He played cards with William Wyler, Sam Spiegel, and other Hollywood notables when they passed through London. And he indulged in high-stakes gambling, one of his biggest weaknesses. He recalled one night of gin rummy at film director Anatole Litvak's hotel room at Claridge's. At one point, Carl calculates, he was three thousand pounds ahead—a huge sum in those days. By the end of the night he had lost it all back.

"I felt it was important to project the image of a normal, red-blooded American who liked to play cards and who could stand the smell of cigar smoke," Carl recalled.

He was drinking too much as well and occasionally sleeping with other women. "Carl changed completely," Estelle recalled. ". . . Perhaps it isn't true, but I think he felt at that time that nothing was any use any more, including loyalty to one's spouse. So he began leading a completely different life. We had a very happy marriage until then; it was quite the reverse afterwards."

He befriended several influential Brits, including film director Terence Young and producer Anthony Havelock-Allan, who worked for the Rank Organisation, an entertainment conglomerate that not only made pictures but owned movie theaters and studio complexes.

Havelock-Allan helped Carl land a ten-thousand-pound-per-year deal there as a writer-producer.

It didn't last long. Earl St. John, a Rank executive, told Carl that he had met with Arthur Krim and Robert Benjamin, the joint heads of United Artists, Rank's American business partners, at a board of directors' meeting. St. John informed them proudly that he had in hand two excellent scripts that had been worked on by their old friend Carl Foreman, whose *High Noon* had helped rescue UA from insolvency. To his surprise, the two men strenuously objected. Even if Carl used a pseudonym, they warned, they could not touch his work because it would be impossible to keep its provenance a secret. An FBI memo from around this time also mentioned Carl's new role at Rank. Someone knowledgeable was telling the bureau everything.

Carl's deal was canceled. "It was obvious that I had no future at the Rank Organisation," he recalled.

He was also depressed to discover that after his departure from Hollywood, four of his old screenwriting buddies, Melvin Levy, Stanley Roberts, Sol Shor, and David Lang, had named him in testimony before HUAC. Even worse was when he read that Bob Rossen had reversed course and named fifty-seven people to the committee.

"I felt terribly guilty about it, because I remember seeing him on the dock [at New York harbor] as I left, [a] very forlorn figure," Carl recalled. Rossen was drinking too much. He had to work. He needed money. He felt he had to testify. Carl was certain that Rossen's spirit had been damaged. His work suffered, although he went on to make one more great picture, *The Hustler* (1961), which he directed, produced, and co-wrote. Rossen died in 1966 at age fifty-seven, and Carl was certain the blacklist was responsible. "He couldn't live with the fact that he had destroyed his own image of himself as an uncompromising fighter whom nobody could push around."

TONY HAVELOCK-ALLAN HAD a heart-to-heart with Carl, raising the toughest and most sensitive questions. How will you ever find fulfillment if you can't work in Hollywood? Why not go home, name a few names, and get back to work? "He was a very lucid and articulate man," Carl would recall, "and certainly he put his finger on all the latest and latent fears that I had, and I went through a night of absolute despair and fear and desolation. There seemed to be no hope of any kind."

Kirk Douglas recalls seeing Carl in London around this time. His friend was like a caged animal, anxious and depressed and feeling like a pariah. "I was a big star then and I'm talking to Carl," says Douglas. "Suddenly he says to me, 'Well, Kirk, if you don't want to have lunch with me I'll understand.' I said 'Carl, I'm your friend,' and we had lunch, but that remark showed me just how sensitive he was. I thought, *Jesus, this is what happens to a guy who thinks all his friends have turned on him.*"

London, a longtime haven for political dissidents ranging from Karl Marx and Friedrich Engels to Charles de Gaulle, Haile Selassie, and nine governments-in-exile during World War Two, was a clearinghouse and rendezvous point for many of Hollywood's political outcasts. Some of them gathered on weekends at the north London home of blacklisted screenwriter Donald Ogden Stewart and his radical journalist wife, Ella Winter, widow of the muckraking author Lincoln Steffens. The champagne was warm and flat and the food famously bad, but the art was fabulous—the walls were lined with drawings by Picasso, Chagall, Mondrian, and Klee—and so were some of the visitors from abroad, including Charlie Chaplin, Ingrid Bergman, Katharine Hepburn, and James Thurber. And the conversation was often relentlessly political.

Nora Sayre, a young American writer living in London who spent weekends at the house, said it was hard for locals to grasp the sense of loss that these American expats felt. "The English assumed that the exiles were overjoyed to have left the repulsive country which had abused them," writes Sayre. "But few of the English acquaintances understood that these Americans missed their own culture—or that they sometimes felt like amputated limbs."

Carl tended to avoid the Stewart-Winter house. He wanted to be supportive of his blacklisted friends, but he did not want to wallow in their victimhood or his own. He especially did not want to fall into the trap of becoming a predictable critic of the United States feeding the cherished predispositions of the anti-American faction of the British left. "I didn't want to be part of the political émigré group," he said, "because I felt that was incestuous and bad and we'd always be talking about *it*. And I wanted to work."

He worked hard to meet and mix with a wide range of British society. Members of Parliament from both the left and right, writers, journalists, performers, and visiting royalty from Hollywood were all part of his social circle. "He handled himself magnificently in England," said Sidney Cohn, his lawyer and friend. Even after *High Noon* became a stunning success, Cohn recalled, "never once did he publicly or privately take any pot shots at the United States . . . Whenever he spoke about the American film industry . . . he didn't glorify it but objectively praised the good things about it . . . Never once did he sell out or do the expedient thing."

Things eventually began to look up. Alexander Korda, the London-based owner of an independent film production company, hired Carl to help him deal with the various scripts that came his way. Korda had no patience or attention span to read such things, and he relied on Carl to vet them and doctor the ones Korda decided to buy.

When his friend Joseph Losey showed up in London in January 1953, Carl met him at the airport. Losey was a talented but prickly filmmaker who had fled the United States and a three-picture deal with the Stanley Kramer Company in 1951 to avoid a HUAC subpoena. Carl "was extraordinarily warm and generous," Losey would recall, "and he made the arrival in England possible because I was without family, without work, and I was pretty bleakly alone. I remember it was a Sunday, and we walked at length in Hyde Park and talked about the situation."

Carl helped Losey get some small jobs for cash with British television shows, and then helped him line up his first British director's gig. Carl and an American businessman named Robert Goldstein bought the rights to a novel called *The Sleeping Tiger* (1954) and arranged for Alexander Knox, Alexis Smith, and Dirk Bogarde to play the lead roles. Carl and fellow blacklisted writer Harold Buchman wrote the script under the pseudonym "Derek Frye," and hired Losey to direct it under the name "Victor Hanbury." Sidney Cohn helped finance the project. The film, a twisted and intriguing crime thriller, was a mild success critically and financially. It enabled Losey to obtain a British work permit, residency, and union membership, and he was grateful for Carl's help. "That kept me alive," Losey recalled, "so I owe him a great deal for that."

But working in England was always fraught in those first years. When Alexis Smith arrived in England from Hollywood to do *Tiger*, she was unaware that her director was on the blacklist. She and Losey were having dinner that first night at a local hotel when Lela Rogers, mother of Ginger Rogers and one of the more hysterical members of the Motion Picture Alliance for the Preservation of American Ideals, walked through the door. Losey and Smith fled through the kitchen to avoid being seen together. During the film shoot, Dirk Bogarde smuggled Losey from the studio in the trunk of his car to avoid running into

Ginger. Losey also recalled meeting up with John Barrymore Jr., an actor whom he had worked with in Hollywood, only to discover later that Barrymore had been pressured to report to the FBI during his trip to London.

Losey quickly grew to understand the cynical game that he was being compelled to play: "The English market wanted to employ me because first, they knew that I knew my job; second, they got me very cheaply; third, they thought I would make pictures for the American market; fourth, they thought I would attract American stars; and fifth, in some strange way they thought they could keep it all secret."

Carl went on to secretly work on screenplays for the David Lean comedy *Hobson's Choice* (1954), *The Man Who Loved Redheads* (1955), and *Heaven Knows, Mr. Allison* (1957), according to Sid Cohn. *The Man Who Loved Redheads*, a comedy based on a Terence Rattigan play, later turned out to be one of the favorite films of Francis Walter, who became chairman of the House Un-American Activities Committee in 1955. Walter, of course, had no idea that an unrepentant former Communist had worked on it.

THE WORST WAS YET to come. On the Fourth of July 1953—an ironic date, as he couldn't help but note—Carl and Estelle received a special-delivery letter from the U.S. Embassy ordering him to report the next day and take along their passports. Carl went in as ordered, but he left the passports at home. The officer on duty told him the documents were no longer valid. If Carl and Estelle tried to use them to travel anywhere except back to the United States, they would be breaking the law.

Carl and Estelle were among thousands of alleged radicals who were either denied passports or had their travel documents confiscated during the Red Scare era. Announcing the policy in May 1952, then Secretary of State Dean Acheson stated that the department had decided to deny a passport to anyone whom there was "reason to believe" was in the Communist Party, or anyone whose "conduct abroad is likely to be contrary to the best interest of the United States," or anyone who would be "going abroad to engage in activities which will advance the Communist movement." It was a sweeping laundry list of "anyone who's" that included teachers, trade unionists, lawyers, journalists, writers, and performers, ranging from historian W. E. B. Du Bois to singer Paul Robeson to novelist Howard Fast to members of the Hollywood Ten. A Board of Passport Appeals was established to hear cases but only if the applicant first signed an affidavit denying past or present membership in the Communist Party. The panel relied on confidential information from the FBI and other sources that it routinely refused to disclose to the applicant.

In Carl and Estelle's case, the department formally ruled against them in September 1954 and the appeals board upheld the decision four months later. "Other than their uncorroborated statements, there is no evidence of their having severed their connection with the Party," read the State Department's ruling. Even if their membership had been terminated, "the evidence of record does not indicate that it was terminated under such circumstances as to warrant the conclusion that they ceased to act in furtherance of the interests and under the discipline of the Communist Party." In other words, the claim was that Carl and Estelle had not really resigned from the party or, if they had, that they were still acting under party discipline, or that they could not prove otherwise. Needless to add, the State Department presented no evidence or witnesses to support this Orwellian allegation.

Now the Foremans were truly stuck in London; they couldn't even return to the United States to visit relatives because their travel documents would be seized once they arrived home. The ruling forced Carl to turn down an offer to adapt *War and Peace* for Italian producer Dino De Laurentiis because he couldn't travel to Rome where the film would be shot. Carl was cut off not only from work but from the benefits of U.S. citizenship. These were no longer the actions of an out-of-control congressional committee or a cowardly bunch of studio heads. It was the United States government—*his* government—effectively rendering him a man without a country. "That was when I really began to feel very sorry for myself and was full of both self-pity and rage," Carl recalled.

As a resident alien in the United Kingdom, Carl was required to report regularly to his local police station to have his registration card validated. Now he went to the Home Office to inform them he no longer had a valid U.S. travel document. A civil servant listened carefully and without expression, then asked Carl to go home, write down everything in a letter, and submit it to the department. Although Britain was under the rule of a Conservative government with close ties to Washington, Carl and Estelle's residency papers were renewed that year and each subsequent year that they lived in London. Whatever else might frighten it, Britain's government was not afraid of American dissidents.

More help was on its way. By the time Sidney Cohn filed suit for Carl and Estelle in federal district court in Washington, American courts were beginning to question the State Department's actions on constitutional grounds. In two pivotal cases in 1955, judges ruled that the department had to give applicants a hearing in which they could examine and challenge the evidence against them (although it took another nine years for the Supreme Court to rule definitively that the right to travel abroad was a fundamental one). Faced with the requirement that the government actually make a legally valid case for denial, the department backed down. A judge ruled in January 1956 that based on the recent court rulings the secretary of state did not have sufficient grounds to deny passports to Carl and Estelle. The department withdrew its opposition without explanation and cabled the London embassy to reissue passports to both of them.

But the passports weren't all that Carl was after. Leo Jaffe, vice president of Columbia Pictures, met with Carl in London and told him that Columbia recognized the fine work he had done for the Stanley Kramer Company and was keen to hire him back. But the blacklist was still an issue. Jaffe proposed that Carl take the standard informant's route—hire a well-connected lawyer, name a few already-known names to the committee, and get himself cleared. Carl insisted he wouldn't consider it; but he added that he was ready to be more critical publicly of the Communist Party and its methods. He asked Sidney Cohn to approach the committee again.

"I think Sidney and I both took the position that Paris was worth a mass," Carl later recalled. "That you could deal with the devil with a long pole and if you were lucky you could stay away from him and make him serve your purposes rather than the other way around."

Cohn first reached out to Edward Bennett Williams, the Washington lawyer who had been instrumental in clearing several Hollywood clients, including Martin Berkeley. According to Cohn, Williams said he would charge fifty thousand dollars plus 10 percent of Carl's fee for the first picture he did after being cleared. Cohn didn't find the price outrageous—he figured Columbia would pay Williams anything he asked in order to get Carl back on the payroll—but he decided he himself could go to the committee.

Through the Motion Picture Association, Cohn set up a meeting with Francis Walter, the Pennsylvania Democrat who had recently become HUAC's chairman. Cohn told Walter that the committee was inadvertently harming America's image abroad with its support of the blacklist, that it was shameful that small-timers like Roy Brewer, Ward Bond, and George Sokolsky could dictate to the motion picture industry who could be hired and who could not. "These guys couldn't get themselves elected dog catchers," Cohn said.

The chairman had his own complaints. He told Cohn his daughter was attending Sarah Lawrence College, where she was unpopular because of his position on the committee while the daughters of Bob Rossen and Sidney Buchman were basking in sympathy because their fathers had been targeted. "In effect, why should his daughter have to be punished among her peers for [him] performing his duties at the House committee?" Cohn recalled Walter saying.

Cohn told Walter that Carl would be happy to testify and tell college students like those at Sarah Lawrence exactly what was wrong with the American Communist Party and why he had left it. "He'll tell you all about it, but don't ask him to name any names because he won't do it."

Walter had been on record five years earlier as doubting the need for witnesses like Larry Parks to name names. After all, the committee already had the names. It was more important, he had said then—and still believed—for witnesses to denounce Communism. On that basis, he now invited Carl to appear again.

19.

The Return

We don't like political blacklists in England.

WINSTON CHURCHILL

On August 8, 1956, at three P.M. Carl Foreman entered Room 226 of the House Office Building on Capitol Hill accompanied by Sidney Cohn, his lawyer. In the transcript—the details of which have never been published before—the session is described as an official meeting of the committee, but the only HUAC members present were Chairman Francis Walter and staff director Richard Arens.

Carl went over his testimony from 1951, claiming he had testified as freely as possible at the time, but adding, "I had and have strong convictions regarding the naming of anyone that I might have known during the time when I was a member of the Communist Party." It remained "a matter of personal conviction for me."

But this time, unlike in 1951, he openly admitted he had been a party member and he tried to explain why. During the years of the Great Depression the party had led the fight for the unemployed, for civil liberties, and against Nazism. But the party's submissive attitude toward the German-Soviet pact of 1939 had deeply disturbed him. His time away from the party after he joined the Army had allowed him to think things over, and he had decided to make a break.

Still, Carl remained a reluctant and diffident witness. He couldn't recall when he had first come into contact with the party, nor who had recruited him to join, nor any of the particular activities he had undertaken while a member. "I was a very unimportant little fellow who came to meetings and listened and was very much impressed sometimes," he testified.

He described his membership in passive terms of "drifting in" and "drifting out" of the party. After the war all his time had been soaked up by the new film production company he had joined. He had been working up to sixteen hours a day. "The company became the only important thing in my life," he said.

His language as he testified was stilted and tenuous. "I entered the party with the best of motives and I left when I came to the inescapable conclusion that the party was not the place for those motives to become effective."

Arens asked if Carl would be willing to name people "if the chairman gives you his solemn promise that this record will be protected as an executive record and will not be made public." According to the official transcript, Carl gave a one-word answer: "No."

Walter intervened. "I do not think that is important, because the thing that is important here now is the opportunity that Mr. Foreman has sought to try to let the world know what a phony, if that is the word, Communism is and the deception that was practiced . . . [in] the hope as he expressed to me that he may make a contribution toward keeping people out of this movement."

Carl grasped the opening. "I would like to place myself on record, as I would like to have done years ago, as being against this institution which has trapped a lot of people into betraying themselves and in the worst possible way, and accepting evils which are absolutely unspeakable . . . It was wrong and harmful."

So there it was, at last: Carl Foreman's denunciation of the Communist Party. It was given placidly and with no great enthusiasm, and he didn't explain why he couldn't have done so "years ago." But it was now on the record.

Carl went on to bemoan America's image overseas, saying it had suffered because of the Red Scare and McCarthyism. "There have been times in the last four years in Europe . . . when it has just been embarrassing to be an American and defend our basis of civil liberties . . . I find myself in the position of apologizing for and explaining America overseas."

He cited the official hounding of Paul Robeson and the denial of his passport as a public relations disaster for the United States. Arens interrupted to allege that Robeson was "a hard-core member of the Communist conspiracy." Carl came back sharply: "That is beside the point, if I may say so. In the Far East they consider themselves colored people. As far as they are concerned, Robeson is just another colored man and he is being discriminated against."

"As Americans, we should be tickled to death that he goes to the Soviet Union or he goes to England and gives a concert . . . What is America afraid of?" Carl's defense of Robeson sounded more passionate than his renunciation of Communism.

Arens picked up on this. He asked Carl if his break with Communism was complete. "I have no sympathy, admiration, regard, or anything like that for the Communist Party in any way," Carl replied.

"They have a lot of people hoodwinked in terms of confusing the Communist Party with liberalism. It is not liberalism . . . It is an absolute menace to everything liberal here in this country." The party "has nothing to offer the American people, it has no place in American life . . . It has revealed itself as being hopelessly tied to another party in another country."

Carl conceded he had never publicly denounced Communism. And his praise for HUAC was muted. When Walter asked if the work of the committee had hindered the party, Carl replied, "Yes it has. I thought it was self-evident."

More than two hours had passed. Carl had stuck to his principles. He had acceded to Walter's demand that he denounce the Communist Party, but he had given no names, and had even lectured the committee on America's image in the world. Walter, saying he spoke for "the entire committee"—although no other congressmen were there—pronounced himself satisfied. "I am sure you have made a contribution toward the objective that we have all been striving for, namely to make the unmistaken and unwary mindful of the fact that they can be used without too much difficulty."

BUT THE COMMITTEE WASN'T quite finished with Carl. A week after his appearance, Sidney Cohn got a phone call from Arens saying that the testimony wasn't good enough. The chairman was being pressured— Arens didn't say by whom—and Carl would have to go back in and name a few names. "That's impossible," Cohn told Arens.

Columbia Pictures needed some public acknowledgment from the committee that Carl had appeared as a cooperative witness before it felt comfortable signing him to a contract. Several months went by but no such statement was forthcoming. But eventually Cohn received a transcript of the hearing and sent it to Columbia, which took Walter's "thank you" at the end of the session as sufficient.

In March 1957 Columbia issued a press release announcing that it had signed Carl to produce four pictures for the studio over the next three years. The artfully worded statement said while he had invoked the Fifth Amendment in his original 1951 testimony, he had been "granted an opportunity to appear again before the Committee in executive session and had testified without recourse to the Fifth Amendment." Columbia marked the announcement by throwing Carl a glittering party at Claridge's, with special guests such as actors Alec Guinness and Diana Dors and director Carol Reed.

Back home, the anti-Communist lobby went on high alert. *Hollywood Reporter* columnist Mike Connelly reported that HUAC was planning to hold another executive session "to probe a report that one of its members received money to clear a show-business personality of suspicions of being a Red." It's clear from the timing that Connelly was referring to Francis Walter, but there's no record that an investigation was ever conducted.

The Veterans of Foreign Wars on April 1, 1957, in *Guardpost for Freedom*, its semimonthly publication, said it had queried Walter, who told them—falsely—that there had been no formal hearing, just a "staff consultation," and that it was "unfortunate" that Columbia claimed Carl had been cleared. The VFW declared: "It is clear from the chairman's reply that as far as the Committee is concerned, Foreman stands today just where he stood in 1951 when, as an uncooperative witness, he invoked the Fifth Amendment."

The VFW went on to accuse Columbia of breaking the 1947 Waldorf Statement by signing Carl. "By doing so, it has encouraged those who may be called as witnesses in the future not to cooperate. If Foreman can get away with it, these people will reason, then they, too, may be able to protect Communists and still continue to make big money in the industry."

Two weeks later, the Red-baiting newsletter *Aware* jumped in, chiding the committee for "setting a lower standard for Foreman than for the hundreds of others in like positions who have appeared before you."

Soon the executive committee of the American Legion passed a resolution demanding that Columbia honor the Waldorf Statement by canceling its deal with Foreman "until he testifies freely and completely."

The pressure on Walter grew to the point where he issued his own statement on June 12 saying that Carl had appeared under oath for what he characterized as a "staff inquiry . . . not a formal hearing." He added that the committee had never characterized Carl as a "cooperative witness" nor did it ever grant "clearances."

Walter also insisted he had not given Carl special treatment. "I wasn't interested in getting names from Foreman of people who had already been identified as Communists," he told reporters. "I wanted someone who could get up and tell what a sucker he'd been. I thought Foreman was the kind of important man we needed for this, and I think he did a service to the country in his testimony."

Columbia Pictures refused to back down. As far as they were concerned, Carl Foreman was now cleared.

The studio received surprising support from Hearst Newspapers columnist Louella Parsons, who declared, "Nobody in the world so thoroughly dislikes leftists more than I, but right is right, and when the United States Government clears a man, that's good enough for me."

Many of Carl's former comrades were not so trusting. Some suspected either that he had secretly named names or that Columbia had paid off Francis Walter, or perhaps both. "Foreman's success was [an] indication to some people that maybe there had been a little hanky-panky," wrote blacklisted screenwriter Walter Bernstein. "His movies had been highly profitable for Columbia Pictures and it wanted to keep him working. Possibly money had changed hands. There was no proof of this, only supposition."

Joe Losey, who says he read a transcript of Carl's executive testimony, confirmed that Carl had not named names. Nonetheless, "he made statements that would have stuck in my throat," said Losey. "I never understood how he could do that. I'm reasonably sure he didn't believe what he said, and I charged him with this privately. But he said, 'Well, you don't appear before people like that if you aren't prepared to give them something. What did you want me to do?'"

When Carl visited Los Angeles, he agreed to meet with two dozen blacklisted screenwriters at Michael Wilson's house to answer questions. At a late-night session, Carl insisted he had made no deal with the committee, that his lawyer had only made a deal with Columbia. Dalton Trumbo, one of those who attended, decided to believe Carl, if for no other reason than his clearance had revealed a chink in the blacklist that others might exploit. "Obviously there was corruption somewhere," Trumbo later told Victor Navasky, "but as long as a man didn't inform, if he had been fucked by a corrupt system and could take advantage of that corruption without harming anyone else, possibly without harming himself . . . I see no harm in it. It seems a mild sin, a venial one. And with a few exceptions forgiveness can be granted. I don't admire it, but then I'm not called upon to admire it."

The truth was that many of the comrades simply did not trust Carl. They had not liked his embrace of Sidney Cohn's original strategy of pleading the "diminished" Fifth Amendment, nor did they see Carl as a genuine comrade. He seemed too committed to his own career and too ready to jettison others. Some perhaps were jealous of the fact that he had received a large payout from the Kramer Company when he lost his job, that he had lived well in London, and that he always seemed to come out ahead financially. His old friend Hy Kraft, another blacklisted screenwriter, lumped him with Elia Kazan and Abe Burrows—both of whom had named names before the committee—as someone who'd had a convenient change of heart.

Others were even less forgiving. Nearly sixty years later, Norma Barzman, who spent nearly three decades in Europe in exile with her husband, fellow screenwriter Ben Barzman, and wrote a lively and evocative memoir about it, still refuses to discuss Carl. Asked why, she replies, "Because he stooled."

ONE OF CARL'S LARGEST paydays in London was also one of his most frustrating experiences. In 1954 he discovered in a catalog of new books notice of a World War Two novel by French author Pierre Boulle about British prisoners of war in Thailand forced to build a strategic railroad bridge by their brutal Japanese overseers. Carl had felt hamstrung as a writer in the United Kingdom because he felt uncomfortable writing critically about his British hosts. But *The Bridge Over the River Kwai*, which focused on the Japanese colonel in charge of the POW camp and the British colonel commanding the prisoners, suited him well. "It was a Frenchman's cold, detached, sardonic view of the English and the Japanese," said Carl. ". . . They were both island races and both were much preoccupied with race . . . and the two colonels . . . were both obsessed, both somewhat ridiculous, and both potentially dangerous in their obsessions." Within days he bought a six-month option for three hundred British pounds.

Sidney Cohn introduced Carl to independent producer Sam Spiegel, one of Hollywood's great improvisational operators, who had made *The African Queen* (1951) and *On the Waterfront* (1954), and Spiegel bought the film rights and commissioned Carl to write the screenplay for noted British director David Lean. It was a brief and brutal partnership. Carl and Lean fought intensely, especially over the ending. In the novel, British saboteurs try and fail to blow up the completed bridge, which suffers only minor damage. But in the film, the British colonel who has dedicated himself and his men to completing the project suddenly recognizes his folly and falls on the detonator, causing a spectacular explosion and the bridge's total destruction. "To me, the ending is confusing; I hate the awkward last-second realization, and the dialogue doesn't fit," Carl complained. He and Lean parted ways in June 1956. When Spiegel went to Carl for advice about hiring a new writer, he suggested fellow blacklist exile Michael Wilson.

Wilson, a thoughtful and unrepentant Marxist, had won an Academy Award for best screenplay for *A Place in the Sun* (1951). He had been subpoenaed by HUAC in June 1951 and fired by Twentieth Century-Fox three days later. He had been a defiant and uncooperative witness when he testified in September, four days before Carl. "The consequence of these hearings," Wilson declared in a prepared statement he wasn't allowed to read to the committee, "will be appalling pictures, more pictures glorifying racism, war, and brutality, perversion and violence. I do not think any honest pictures will be written by frightened writers and I know they will not be written by informers."

Along with fellow blacklisted filmmakers, Wilson became involved in making *Salt of the Earth* (1954), the story of a strike by Mexican-American mine workers in New Mexico. The independent production was harassed by anti-Communist forces and the film boycotted and suppressed, although it has received critical recognition over the decades and has been preserved by the Library of Congress on the National Film Registry. Afterward, Wilson moved his family aboard—they lived in France for eight years—and he continued to work and write under a pseudonym.

David Lean claimed he simply trashed Carl's script and rewrote the screenplay himself, with some polish and tightening from Wilson. "It was really Mike's and my script," Lean told Kevin Brownlow, his biographer.

But neither Foreman nor Wilson nor Lean got the screen credit, which went to novelist Boulle, who spoke little English and had not written a word of the screenplay. When the movie premiered in London in October 1957 and went on to become an international box-office hit, Spiegel gave sole credit to Boulle and denied that Carl had been involved at all. The novelist did not attend the Academy Awards ceremony in March 1958 where *Kwai* won seven Oscars, including best screenplay for Boulle. After the ceremony, when reporters asked Lean who had really written the screenplay, he replied, to Spiegel's embarrassment, "Now that's the sixty-four-thousand-dollar question, and as you have not got sixty-four thousand dollars I'm not prepared to tell you." The next day Carl announced to the United Press in London that it was he who had written the script along with "some contributions by David Lean." He said his authorship could be authenticated by the fact that three characters in the film were named Weaver, Grogan, and Baker—friends of Carl's whose names appeared in all of his screenplays. Somehow Carl neglected to mention Michael Wilson.

Wilson had already embarrassed the Motion Picture Academy in 1956, the year that *Friendly Persuasion*, starring Gary Cooper, was made from a script Wilson had written before he was blacklisted. When the film was released, there was no listed credit for screenwriting, although everyone in Hollywood knew Wilson had written it. A week before the Oscar nominations were announced, the Motion Picture Academy's Board of Governors passed a resolution declaring that any nominee who was blacklisted was ineligible for a prize. Still, *Friendly Persuasion* was nominated for best adapted screenplay and Wilson was duly eliminated from the list of those eligible. Ironically, the winner that year for best original screenplay was "Robert Rich," the pseudonym of another blacklisted writer, Dalton Trumbo, for *The Brave One*. On Oscar night no one came forward to accept the award, and Trumbo spent the next two years gleefully refusing to confirm or deny he had written the script.

The subsequent Oscar victory in 1958 of Pierre Boulle proved, in the words of blacklisted screenwriter Ring Lardner Jr., that the Motion Picture Academy "had added a new trick to its repertoire: It could close its eyes firmly when its leg was pulled." Soon after, the academy repealed its ban on blacklisted writers and performers.

Wilson went on to spend fifteen months working on a *Lawrence of Arabia* screenplay for David Lean before the two men had an epic falling out that mirrored Lean's bitter break with Carl. Lean and a new screenwriter, British playwright Robert Bolt, denied that Wilson had played any role in writing *Lawrence*, which became another international hit in 1962. (In 1963 the Writers' Guild of Great Britain recognized Wilson's role in writing it, adding his name to Bolt's, but in the United States the writing credits were not revised until 1995.) Topping off a stellar career, Wilson later co-wrote the screenplay for *Planet of the Apes* (1968) with Rod Serling. He died in 1978.

A few years earlier, after both Foreman and Wilson had returned to Hollywood, Carl presented Wilson with the Writers Guild Laurel Award for lifetime achievement. In introducing Wilson, Carl joked that "our bloody Oscar has been sitting in Pierre Boulle's living room, and I suppose that by now he's given up wondering how the hell it ever got there." Maybe they could work out "a custody arrangement," he joked. It seemed funny at the time, but the anger and frustration that both Foreman and Wilson had felt in 1957 had been deep and intense.

While he was denied proper credit for *Kwai*, Carl at least had the solace of a major paycheck. According to Brownlow, Sid Cohn had arranged for Carl to receive a 22-percent profit participation deal that paid him $250,000 in the first four years of *Kwai*'s release. By contrast, Michael Wilson's payment for his work on *Kwai* was ten thousand dollars.

ROBERT GOLDSTEIN, THE BUSINESSMAN who had helped Carl with *The Sleeping Tiger*, also arranged one of the more bizarre meetings of Carl's time in London: a one-on-one session with Hedda Hopper at her suite in the Dorchester Hotel. It started off stiffly, as had Carl's meeting with John Wayne in Hollywood several years earlier. Then Hopper brought out a bottle of Jack Daniel's she'd smuggled in from the States and ordered a bucket of ice. Carl started talking about what had happened to him with *High Noon* and found, to his surprise, that Hopper shared his intense dislike for Stanley Kramer.

It took them three hours to polish off the bottle. Hopper was sixty years old, but in the dimming late afternoon light, aided by a serious quantity of Tennessee whiskey, she began to look thirty years younger. Suddenly Carl felt the urge to have sex with her, and he could see that she felt the same. Nothing happened, and Carl staggered home drunk. After that an unspoken truce took effect between them; there were warm, affectionate, newsy letters from him to her, and supportive mentions of him in her columns. Bygones were bygones. It was another bizarre step on Carl's road back to respectability.

John Wayne was a different matter. He had been less strident than Hopper in condemning former Communists to eternal damnation in the blacklist days, but as he grew older Wayne's views became more dogmatic and self-righteous and his memory more selective. In a wide-ranging *Playboy* magazine interview in May 1971 in which he attacked liberals, blacks, civil rights and anti-war demonstrators, and Native Americans, Wayne singled out for special abuse Carl Foreman and the late Robert Rossen. The makers of *High Noon* and *All the King's Men* had created films "that were detrimental to our way of life," Wayne insisted. *High Noon*, he went on, was "the most un-American thing I've ever seen in my whole life," and he would never regret "having helped run Foreman out of the country."

In response, Carl fired off an angry letter to a British film magazine saying it would be pointless to try to refute "Wayne's silly and somewhat senile maunderings." But he added, "It was disgusting of Wayne . . . as well as cowardly, to attack a dead man—Robert Rossen, a very talented writer and director who was in fact killed by the American blacklist and so cannot defend himself against the dashing hero of so many Westerns."

When Wayne went to London in the summer of 1974 to film one of his last movies, *Brannigan*, a third-rate detective story (co-written by Christopher Trumbo, Dalton's son), he appeared on Michael Parkinson's celebrity interview TV program to discuss his career and politics. He again branded *High Noon* as un-American, although his memory of its pivotal scenes was as faulty as his reasoning. "Here's this church," said Wayne, "supposed to be an American church, and all the women are sitting on one side of the aisle, and all the men on the other. What kind of an American church is that? And all the women are telling the men to get out there and fight those killers, and all the men are afraid, what kind of a Western town is that? And then at the end, there's this sheriff, he takes off his badge and he steps on it and grinds it into the ground . . . I think those things are just a little bit un-American."

Wayne also claimed that the only blacklist in Hollywood had been one enforced by Communists and fellow travelers against Americanists like screenwriter Morrie Ryskind. When Parkinson brought up the ordeal of Larry Parks, Wayne said that Parks hadn't worked much before he was called by HUAC to testify, and that he had gotten plenty of work once he had denounced Communism.

Both statements were blatantly false.

Carl had tried to keep a low public profile in London when it came to the blacklist, but Wayne's remarks enraged him. He wrote a scathing rejoinder that appeared in *Punch* magazine. "A week or so ago," it began, "I was in the counting house, fondling the paltry residue of all that good old Moscow gold we used to get so regularly from Comrade Beria, back in those marvelous subversive Hollywood days (it would come in bullion, wrapped in back issues of the *Daily Worker* . . . when the children rushed in screaming hysterically, 'Daddy, Daddy, come quick! John Wayne is on the telly and he's saying ever such nice things about you!'"

Carl wrote that "old Duke suffers from the Foreman–*High Noon* syndrome, a nervous disease causing anger, truculence and visible discomfort." He pointed out that Wayne's description of the church scene in the film was wildly distorted, as was his claim that Will Kane had stepped on his marshal's badge and ground it into the dirt at the film's conclusion (in fact, Kane takes off his badge and drops it to the ground, but no stepping on or grinding occurs). He also accused Wayne of more "selective lapses of memory." For example, "Ask him if there was ever a political blacklist in Hollywood, and he will look you in the eye and say, oh, dear me, no, never—Ask him if he was a leading member of that scurvy gang of character assassins calling themselves the Motion Picture Alliance for the Preservation of American Ideals, which together with the House Un-American Activities Committee and a gaggle of frightened studio bosses persecuted and hounded hundreds of innocent people out of the American film industry, and he will tell you that to the best of his memory, it was a fine group of patriotic Americans devoted to celebrating national holidays."

Carl went on to say it was "indecent, if not to say vicious" for Wayne to lie about what had happened to Larry Parks. Finally, as his outrage peaked, Carl listed the "suicides and broken homes and heart attacks and people dying long before their time, like John Garfield and Joe Bromberg and Robert Rossen and others."

It was a telling moment. For all his success in London—the pictures and the money and the contract with Columbia—Carl Foreman's blacklist wounds remained deep and unhealed.

ONE OF THE CASUALTIES was his marriage to Estelle, which never recovered from the damage caused by the move to London. After a decade of struggle and heartbreak they separated, and Estelle took Kate and moved back to Los Angeles. She hoped, but didn't really believe, that it would be a temporary split. "He decided we should move back to L.A. and he would join us in a few months. And it didn't sound right," she recalled. "So anyhow we went and . . . that was really the end of the marriage. It was 1963."

By this time, Carl was deeply involved with a twenty-four-year-old film production secretary named Eve Smith. She found him difficult, yet fascinating. "He was very acerbic and short-tempered," Eve recalls. "And he was very angry—it was like someone had cut his arms off." Why did she stick with him? "He was somebody very strong. I'd lost my father and I think I found another very strong person. But he was also quite needy, and I was good with needy people."

They were married in 1965, soon after he and Estelle were divorced. They had two children: Jonathan in 1965 and Amanda in 1968. "I am indeed very happy," Carl wrote to a friend, "perhaps for the first time."

Suddenly life was good. Carl became president of the Writers' Guild of Great Britain, a governor of the British Film Institute, and a member of an official commission to establish a national film school—honors that no American had ever received before. He bought a thirty-foot cabin cruiser he christened *Lady Eve*. On weekends, they haunted London's art museums and theaters and the National Film Theatre, or roamed Hyde Park with the kids, hanging out often at Speakers' Corner near Marble Arch in the northeast corner of the park. He loved the Poets' Corner in Westminster Abbey where Shakespeare, Chaucer, Milton, Johnson, Keats, Shelley, Wordsworth, Dickens, Kipling, Hardy, and Tennyson are buried or memorialized. "That's London," he said. "It's a writer's town devoted to small neurotic lonely sensitive insecure idiots like me. It's mama saying, 'All right, sonny, so go ahead and be a writer, don't be afraid.'"

When he had arrived in London, Carl recalled, "I was in a highly emotional state of great anger and some self-pity . . . It took me a long, long time to get over it, and I am very grateful to this country. England has been an inspiration."

Still, there was a feeling of loss that Carl never quite overcame. "He recovered but the damage had been done and it is so catastrophic because it happened at what should have been the height of his career," says his son, Jonathan. "All those false starts and he'd finally made it, and they'd taken it away. He called it economic capital punishment."

Lionel Chetwynd, a young Canadian intrigued by filmmaking, met Carl in 1968 when Chetwynd got an assistant managing director's job at the London office of Columbia Pictures. He was drawn to Carl's intelligence and honesty, but he also saw the sadness. "He was a mordant man, there was a glumness about him, even when he smiled," Chetwynd recalls. "Victor Hugo spoke about melancholy as the happiness of being sad. Carl understood things in terms of honor and dishonor. It was the code he lived by. The people I most admire stood up for something and got beaten up for it. And that was Carl."

BY NOW HE WAS openly back at work, this time with his own production company, which he called Highroad. The first picture he wrote and produced under his own name was *The Key* (1958), starring William Holden and Sophia Loren. It was the story of a rescue boat captain during World War Two who inherits an apartment and the beautiful woman who lives there from a fellow seaman who is killed on a mission. The captain falls in love with the woman but fears he will not survive his next mission, and he arranges for her to be passed on to yet another seaman. He manages to survive, but she feels he has betrayed her and she flees to London leaving him behind. "To me it was the opposite side of *High Noon*," said Carl. "In *High Noon*, the main character conquered his fear and lived. *The Key* was about a man who gave into despair, a kind of fear, and lost everything."

The Key came and went with little notice, but Highroad's next production, *The Mouse That Roared* (1959), was a pleasant surprise, a whacky Cold War satire that introduced British comedian Peter Sellers to international audiences. Carl followed it with *The Guns of Navarone* (1961), starring Gregory Peck, David Niven, and Anthony Quinn, a spirited adventure film set in the Greek islands during World War Two, in which a British commando team sets out to find and destroy a massive German gun emplacement. The action scenes were thrilling and the picture became an international hit. "On a technical level, at least, my script was the best I had written since *High Noon*," Carl would recall. "What emerged was a kind of tour de force of pure cinema in the genre of adventure."

Still, while *Navarone* earned him a small fortune and another Oscar nomination for best screenplay, he was strangely disappointed in the film's reception. He had set out to write a script that would depict the waste of human life even as it told a rousing war story, but critics and audiences mostly failed to notice the subtle characterizations and profound meanings. "It is galling to me that most of my ironies were swamped in the heroics, and sometimes appeared as little more than pauses for portentous and pretentious dialogue," recalled Carl, "and that there are undoubtedly some people who believe I deliberately made a film glorifying war for the sake of money."

One person who loved *The Guns of Navarone* was Winston Churchill, and it occurred to the former prime minister, now nearing eighty-eight, that Carl was the perfect choice to make a movie based on *My Early Life*, Churchill's coming-of-age book recounting his childhood and military adventures as a young cavalry officer in India and the Sudan and war correspondent during the Boer War in South Africa. The two men met at the statesman's office, and in the interest of full disclosure, Carl informed Churchill that he had been blacklisted in Hollywood for his former Communist connections. "Oh, I know all about you," Churchill replied. "But we don't like political blacklists in England. And speaking for myself, I don't care what a man believed in when he was a boy. My concern is whether or not he can do the job." The meeting became the basis for a deal that led eventually to the making of *Young Winston* (1972).

Carl had come to realize that the balance of creative power in filmmaking was shifting from producers to directors and stars, and that if he was going to make a movie that expressed his horror and hatred of war, he would have to direct it himself. Given his streak of success, Columbia allowed him total control over his next project, *The Victors* (1963), a nearly three-hour epic that Carl produced, wrote, and directed. It follows a small unit of American soldiers throughout the war in Europe and its aftermath. More than any other film, this one reflected his "personal vision," he declared. It was "a backward look at what we, the allies and the winners, won and lost, seventeen years ago, and raises the question of what we may win or lose in the future."

A series of grim vignettes, *The Victors* bombed both critically and financially. His old friend Bosley Crowther savaged the film as "specious, sentimental, and false . . . Mr. Foreman's direction is generally artless, highly romanticized, and there really is not one good performance—one strong characterization—in the whole film."

While Carl was deeply disappointed, he bounced back two years later with *Born Free* (1965), labeled "A Carl Foreman Presentation," an utter crowd-pleaser about a lion cub raised in captivity by game warden George Adamson and his wife, Joy, in Kenya and then set free. Helped by a stirring theme song that topped the charts for months—the same musical marketing strategy that had helped propel *High Noon* to success—it captivated children and parents alike and made big profits for Columbia and for Carl.

It also proved a major breakthrough for Lester Cole, one of the Hollywood Ten, whom Carl hired to write the screenplay. When the head of Columbia found out, Cole recalled, he ordered Carl to find a different writer. Carl refused, saying he would rather quit than fire Cole. "Carl laid his own job on the line," Cole recalled. Columbia backed down, but refused to allow Cole to use his own name. The screenplay is credited to "Gerald L. C. Copley." When the picture was finished, Carl invited Cole to go to Los Angeles for the studio preview. "Carl brought me down for a purpose," says Cole. "It was his determined way of subtly attempting to bring me out of the producer's closet."

After *Born Free*, Carl's filmmaking career began to head downhill. He wrote and produced *Mackenna's Gold* (1969), a star-studded Western, and *Young Winston*, the historical epic about Churchill, both of which failed critically and financially. Vincent Canby, Crowther's successor as the *New York Times* chief film critic, mocked *Mackenna's Gold* as "a Western of truly stunning absurdity." He wasn't much kinder to *Young Winston*, which he called "a big, balsa-wood monument to the Winston Churchill of pre-history" that lumbers "in that peculiar flatfooted gait peculiar to movies equipped with so much foresight."

Still, Carl was nominated for another screenwriting Oscar for *Young Winston*, but lost again—making five times he had been nominated without a win. The only screenplay that had won, ironically, was his script for *Kwai*, a movie for which he got no official recognition.

He had never intended to live in the United States again, even after he was cleared and had resumed working under his own name. But by the mid-1970s the British film industry was reeling from high costs, foreign competition, and confiscatory-level taxes from the new Labour government. When Universal offered him a three-picture deal, Carl felt he had no choice but to return to Hollywood.

He had always wanted to help aspiring young filmmakers get the training opportunities he himself had hungered for when he first arrived in Hollywood in the 1930s. Once he returned to the States, he gave lectures at the American Film Institute and also helped fund fellowships for film students at the University of Southern California. One program involved internships for four talented students to work on *Mackenna's Gold*. Each of the four worked on the set and each produced a short film about the making of the movie. Future director Michael Ritchie handled his project with aplomb, deftly turning out an accomplished piece of work that Carl admired for its professionalism. But another more cerebral and rebellious student immediately clashed with Carl.

George Lucas had no interest in mainstream commercial movies— he saw himself either as a documentarian or creator of avant-garde underground films—and he proposed making his short film about the desert where much of *Mackenna's Gold* was filmed. "Carl had a fit, he got so angry with me," Lucas would later recall. "And he said 'you can't do one about the desert, you're supposed to do it about the movie' . . .

"So we kind of butted heads . . . I just thought of him as some big Hollywood producer, you know, had tons of money and had connections . . . one of the establishment."

In the end, they worked it out. Carl recognized the powerful drive and talent in his young student and encouraged him to go his own way. "I still have very fond feelings for Carl," said Lucas in a 2001 interview, "and he was a very important significant person in my life as I was growing up because he was one of the first people who, from the professional community, took an interest in me."

Ultimately, what Lucas and Carl shared was an almost savage commitment to succeed as a filmmaker, no matter the cost. To another group of film students, Carl once described it this way: "Your whole life will change. You will neglect your wife, your children, and your friends. You'll go to bed at night numb and wake up exhausted. To make your film you will have to fight, beg, grovel, cajole, persuade, and fight again . . . And with it all, you may fail, because hard work and dedication and high purpose are no guarantee of successful films. But however it comes out, your film will have your hallmark, your signature. It will be yours."

WHILE CARL FOREMAN WAS reconstructing his life and career in London, Gary Cooper was also undergoing a self-imposed exile from the United States, but for much different reasons. After bowing to political pressure and cutting ties with Carl's attempt to become an independent film producer, Cooper had been welcomed back into the conservative fold. He'd even joined Hedda Hopper and other Hollywood establishment figures in attending the 1952 Republican convention in Chicago. But films were increasingly being made overseas to save on labor costs and taxes, and movie stars inevitably followed the cameras and the tax breaks. Cooper made four consecutive movies abroad, starting with *Return to Paradise* (1953) in Samoa, and *Blowing Wild* (1953), *Garden of Evil* (1954), and *Vera Cruz* (1954), all of which were filmed in Mexico. Legally separated from his wife Rocky since May 1951 and estranged from his passionate mistress Patricia Neal, he romanced beautiful young actresses such as Lorraine Chanel, a San Antonio–born model whom he met in Mexico, and Gisèle Pascal, a French starlet. By 1954, however, he and Rocky had reconciled and he moved back home, although stories of his love affairs—including a brief fling with Swedish bombshell Anita Ekberg—always trailed close behind him.

The surprising success of *High Noon* made him a highly bankable asset again and he took full advantage, making eight Westerns in the 1950s of widely varying quality. A few were mildly entertaining, such as *Vera Cruz*, in which he and Burt Lancaster teamed up as soldiers of fortune caught up in the Mexican revolution, with Cooper's fundamentally decent former Confederate army officer triumphing over Lancaster's avaricious gunslinger. Others, like *They Came to Cordura* (1959), written and directed by Robert Rossen, were more or less dreadful. What Cooper brought to all of these films, good or bad, was his personal authenticity. He was now playing the same role over and over again with dignity and stoicism. His body continued to visibly age and his mobility grew more and more restricted, but his power on the screen remained undiminished, even in films, such as *Man of the West* (1958) and *Cordura*, in which his characters were physically humiliated by younger, cruder men.

Throughout this period, he and Carl Foreman kept in close touch. "Carl absolutely adored Cooper," recalls Carl's widow, Eve, "and after he went to Europe, every screenplay he wrote he sent it first to Cooper."

"You know how much I have wanted to do another picture with you," Carl wrote to Cooper from London in June 1957. "I hope this will still be possible. I have some very exciting things coming up after [*The Key*], and it would be my dearest wish that one of them should be the means of our reunion."

"They really liked each other a hell of a lot and they really did want to work together again," says Cooper's daughter, Maria.

Cooper had two major operations in 1960, just five weeks apart. "When the carving was over," he told an interviewer for *McCall's* magazine, he had a lot of time in his hands while recuperating. "I took stock of myself."

He didn't much care for what he found. "I've been in the motion-picture business a long time . . . Yet nothing I've done lately, the past eight years or so, has been especially worthwhile. I've been coasting along. Some of the pictures I've made recently I'm genuinely sorry about. Either I did a sloppy job in them, or the story wasn't right . . . When I get talked into a project I don't believe in, I'm the one who's wrong.

"Lying there in bed or out on my terrace at home," Cooper added, "I began to feel much as I used to when I was just starting out in movies. Like a fraud."

Cooper wasn't finished with his critical self-assessment. He'd never really wanted to be an actor, he went on, and even now he rated himself as "barely adequate." Truth was, he said, "I am uncomfortable so much of the time when I am acting, that I find it hard to concentrate on doing what I am supposed to be doing." He recognized and appreciated good acting: he expressed the highest regard for younger performers like Marlon Brando, Paul Newman, Joanne Woodward, and Eva Marie Saint. They gave realistic performances, he said, "because they believe in what they are doing." Cooper added, "I wish I had studied acting, now that I've spent so many years fumbling around in it."

Although he acknowledged he had done a wide range of film parts, "The roles I feel most comfortable in are those in which I get up on a horse and, sooner or later, do some shooting." But Westerns too had become disappointing. He mocked the lack of realism in TV Westerns where everyone wears a six-shooter and men take to the streets "looking like a walking arsenal."

Even *High Noon* did not escape his critical eye. "I hate to disappoint a lot of customers, but *High Noon* wasn't new or especially genuine," he said. "There was nothing especially Western about it. It was a story about a phase of life, more current today, I suspect, than years ago— namely, how tough it is for a man to buck the apathy of the crowd even when he is trying to do something for their own protection . . . I suppose incidents like that happened in real life, but it's hard to believe that any man in the West was ever so completely alone as the marshal was in *High Noon*."

All in all, it was a stunning critique for a man who had risen to the pinnacle of the movie business and stayed there for nearly three decades, but he was keenly aware of its shortcomings and his own. The *McCall's* article, published in January 1961, was his last public reckoning of his own career, and it was a sad one.

He seemed not to appreciate his own qualities as an actor. Perhaps it had all been a conjurer's trick—some kind of cheap celluloid magic—but if so it had been a very good one. "I had worked with actors who were magnificent on the set, but somehow unsatisfactory when you saw the results in the projection room," writes screenwriter Philip Dunne, who worked with Cooper on *Ten North Frederick* (1958), one of his last films. "Gary Cooper was exactly the opposite. When you printed a take you wondered if the scene was really there, then you ran the dailies, it was perfection. Cooper had mastered the art of acting to the camera's lens, rather than to an audience."

In truth, he was only partly to blame for what had gone wrong. The collapse of the studio system meant limited choices and mediocre screenplays, and the best actors, writers, and directors were going out on their own. Under such circumstances, the market for aging stars was rapidly shrinking. It wasn't just Cooper. Bogart, Gable, Hepburn (Katharine, not Audrey), and Stanwyck were all being pushed aside. By the end of 1960, Bogart, Gable, Tyrone Power, and Errol Flynn were all dead from heart disease or cancer; none of them made it to age sixty.

When Cooper was in London that year to film *The Naked Edge* (1961), his last feature film, he stopped by Carl Foreman's office on Jermyn Street to see his old friend. Carl offered Cooper the lead role in *The Guns of Navarone*; Cooper said he loved the part but was too ill to consider it. It was the last time the two men ever met. Fred Zinnemann also maintained close personal ties with Cooper. Despite his growing illness, Cooper and Rocky helped arrange for Fred and his wife, Rene, to be remarried in a Catholic ceremony in Los Angeles in early April 1961 with Cooper serving as best man.

He never left the house again. He hadn't told *McCall's*, but those two operations he had undergone were because he had been diagnosed with prostate cancer. Despite the surgery, the malignancy rapidly spread. Later that same month he was to receive a third, honorary Oscar for lifetime achievement, but he was too sick to attend the ceremony, and his friend James Stewart broke down and wept as he spoke on Cooper's behalf.

Gary Cooper died at home on May 13, 1961, six days after turning sixty. Hundreds of movie stars and studio executives attended the funeral to mourn the fallen prince. From London, Carl hailed him as "one of the bravest men I have ever known." He compared Cooper to Abraham Lincoln, praising his "quiet nobility and steadfast integrity . . . He put his entire career on the block in the face of the McCarthyite witch-hunters who were terrorizing Hollywood at the time."

Cooper's last film was *The Real West*, a black-and-white television documentary shot in December 1960 for which he delivers the narration on camera. It begins with evocative photographs of frail old buildings decaying in a deserted frontier town. Then Cooper ambles onto a stage set. First you see just his laced-up boots and long thin legs. He's wearing an open-collar shirt, well-trimmed flannel jacket, and broad-brimmed tan hat. "This could be Elkhorn, Montana, just a few miles from where I was born and raised," he begins, and then rattles off a dozen more names of abandoned Western towns.

"The names don't matter, they're just epitaphs for places that died, ghost towns. And they're all part of the Old West that's been dead and gone for going on sixty years."

The narration is low-key but expressive. Cooper chuckles, raises his eyebrows, and occasionally suppresses a grin. He is playing himself playing a man of the Old West. Watching it now, you realize he's giving his own eulogy.

"They did what they set out to do," he says of the pioneers. "They made it a fit country to raise kids in, and when they did that the West was over."

There are images of settlers, families, gunslingers, cavalrymen, Native Americans, mounds of buffalo carcasses. Cooper narrates from diaries and from the speeches of vanquished Indian leaders. "I am tired of fighting," he quotes one as saying. "Our chiefs are all killed . . . the little children are freezing to death . . . I want to have time to look for my children. Maybe I shall find them among the dead."

Then the camera shifts back to Cooper himself, sitting on the edge of the small stage. "The Real West: it lasted only forty years and then it was finished. If it's a good land and grows good people it's because it's been irrigated by a lot of spit and sweat and blood."

Then he gets up and, like Will Kane in *High Noon*, Gary Cooper walks away.

EPILOGUE

The blacklist period was like a continuous earthquake, in the sense that almost everybody involved that I can think of lost their footing in it in some way or other.

CARL FOREMAN

Gary Cooper was gone, but *High Noon* not only endured as an important film, it made an extraordinary leap from the movie house to popular culture, where it has remained entrenched for more than sixty years. It is celebrated around the world.

Most famously, in the run-up to Poland's first free election in 1989 after four decades of one-party Communist rule, graphic designer Tomasz Sarnecki transformed a *High Noon* poster into a campaign poster for the Solidarity trade union movement. The image shows Marshal Will Kane with a folded ballot in his right hand and a Solidarity badge pinned to his vest. Below is the message: HIGH NOON: 4 JUNE 1989.

The poster was a huge hit, and it helped Solidarity win a landslide victory. "Cowboys in Western clothes had become a powerful symbol for Poles," Solidarity leader Lech Wałesa later wrote. "Cowboys fight for justice, fight against evil, and fight for freedom, both physical and spiritual." Fifteen years later, Wałesa said, people were still presenting copies of the poster to him for autographs.

In America *High Noon* has become part of the political-journalistic lexicon, a term that connotes a ritualistic confrontation between good and evil in a showdown in which good is often embodied by a solitary person. When President Obama announced he was planning executive action to tighten restrictions on gun sales in his last year in office, the

Arizona Republic's headline read OBAMA TO GO *HIGH NOON* ON NRA AND GUN LOBBY. "He may, like Cooper in the movie, wind up bloodied and disenchanted," wrote E. J. Montini. "But at least when the credits roll on his presidency, Obama will be able to drop his marshal's badge on the ground and limp off into the sunset with his head held high."

Every editorial headline writer seems to rely on *High Noon* for a metaphor whenever a beleaguered public official takes on a mob of opponents. When the health minister of the Canadian province of Alberta sought to crack down on bonuses to public executives, a headline in the *Edmonton Journal* asked, HIGH NOON AT ALBERTA HEALTH SERVICES? When congressional Republicans threatened to refuse to pass a continuing budget resolution in the fall of 2013, the *Daily Times* of Salisbury, Maryland, warned of a *HIGH NOON* FOR POSSIBLE SHUTDOWN, while former secretary of labor Robert Reich decreed it was OBAMA'S *HIGH NOON*. When the United States and Iran were negotiating a suspension of Tehran's nuclear weapons development, columnist Noga Tarnopolsky of *Global Post*, referring to the prime minister of Israel, said a deal would amount to NETANYAHU'S PERSONAL *HIGH NOON*. Even in southern Africa a headline writer for the *Mail & Guardian* detected a *HIGH NOON* FOR MUJURU, MNANGAGWA when the two Zimbabwean politicians squared off in a power struggle to become the heir apparent to elderly president Robert Mugabe. Meanwhile the *Kansas City Star* characterized Mayor James Sly as undergoing "something of a *High Noon* moment" when he led the city council in a seven to six vote to defy state law and ban drunken people from carrying firearms in public.

In fact, *High Noon* and firearms often go together in the American imagination. A Google search lists eight High Noon gun shops or firing ranges from Anchorage, Alaska, to Sarasota, Florida, plus a holster manufacturer in Tarpon Springs, Florida, and three saloons where, presumably, gunfire is discouraged.

American presidents have also been drawn to *High Noon*'s archetypal message and meaning. Dwight Eisenhower screened the film at least three times during his eight-year tenure. When Will Kane confronted Frank Miller and his three henchmen, Ike "bent forward in genuine anxiety," reported a magazine writer who watched the film with the president. "Run!" shouted Ike, when Kane leaped on a horse to escape the burning barn.

According to White House projectionists' logs, *High Noon* has been the film most requested by American presidents, led by Bill Clinton, who reportedly screened it some twenty times while in office. "*High Noon* has stayed with me over fifty years now and enriched my life," Clinton once told an interviewer, "and reminded me that courage is not the absence of fear, it is perseverance in the face of fear."

Clinton acknowledged that Will Kane's solitary struggle, after he has been forsaken by the people he believed were his friends and supporters, has great appeal to presidents, who tend to see themselves as lonely figures who make their decisions based upon principle rather than the crass calculations of their political allies and enemies. "This weary loner's brave posture of prescient and courageous certainty in the face of public cowardice is the American politician's ego ideal," writes film historian J. Hoberman. But it's Kane's vulnerability that has most stayed with Clinton. "The thing that makes it a great movie was that Cooper was like you and me and he rose above his fear," says the former president. "He was terrified and he did the right thing anyway."

ALTHOUGH FRED ZINNEMANN NEVER rose to the auteurist heights of John Ford, Orson Welles, or Alfred Hitchcock, his place seems secure alongside such outstanding directors as William Wyler, George Stevens, Billy Wilder, and John Huston. His best films—among them *High Noon*, *From Here to Eternity* (1953), *The Nun's Story* (1959), and *A Man for All Seasons* (1966)—are as artful, powerful, and distinctive as anything from that turbulent era of filmmaking.

High Noon, *From Here to Eternity*, and *A Man for All Seasons* won eighteen Oscars among them, including two for best picture and two more for best director. But the one project to which he was personally most devoted never got made. Fred set out to film *Man's Fate*, André Malraux's epic novel about a failed insurrection in Shanghai in the 1920s, and spent three years and $1.7 million of his own money in preparation. But the new president of MGM—James T. Aubrey Jr., an abrasive former TV network executive known as "the smiling cobra"— killed the project three days before shooting was to begin. Fred sued successfully to recover most of his own costs, but the sudden demise of the project was a bitter and heartbreaking blow.

Fred could be prickly and self-obsessed, and as the years went by he jealously guarded his film credits and royalties. He and Carl Foreman remained friends except for a brief but telling rupture in October 1965 when Carl published a piece about Western films in the *Sunday Observer* magazine that referred to "George Stevens' *Shane*," "John Ford's

Cheyenne Autumn," "John Sturges' *Magnificent Seven*"—and "Carl Foreman's *High Noon.*" It was as if Carl had not only written the film but directed it as well. When Carl saw an advance copy of the magazine, he immediately wrote a letter of apology that was published in the *Observer*'s news pages on the same day the magazine article appeared. But Fred was not appeased. "Carl Foreman's *High Noon* is in fact NOT Carl Foreman's *High Noon,*" he wrote to the editor. "This film is the result of a collective effort, initiated by Stanley Kramer and including Floyd Crosby's photography, Elmo Williams' editing, and Dimitri Tiomkin's music. It may be worth mentioning that I directed *High Noon*; every frame of it."

It was, in its way, Fred's summation of his view that *High Noon* had been a collaboration among several gifted people. The only major contributor he omits in this accounting is Gary Cooper, but elsewhere he unfailingly honors Cooper for his powerful yet understated performance. For himself, Fred insisted on due recognition, nothing more and nothing less, but he was willing to give the same to others as well.

After Fred died in London in March 1997 at the age of eighty-nine, his son Tim put together a reel of scenes from his father's most noteworthy films interspersed with commentary from Fred. He sounds proudest of the moments when he defied the studio bosses to stay true to his vision—most especially in *From Here to Eternity* when he insisted on casting the brilliant but scrawny Montgomery Clift as the former boxer Robert E. Lee Prewitt, even though Clift bore no physical resemblance to a real pugilist; and cast the elegant and demure Deborah Kerr as Karen Holmes, the sex-obsessed wife of a corrupt and adulterous Army captain. Fred also stood firm in insisting that Paul Scofield play Thomas More in *A Man for All Seasons*, a role the actor had originated on the London stage. The film's financial backers wanted a more recognizable movie star like Richard Burton or Laurence Olivier. But under Fred's direction, Scofield won an Oscar for best actor.

Fred Zinnemann loved to make movies about outsiders who face a crisis of conscience. Like Prewitt, who refuses to box after beating a man nearly to death in the ring, even though his commanding officer constantly harasses him; or Sister Luke in *The Nun's Story*, who quits the church after seventeen years of devoted service when she realizes she can no longer provide the unquestioning obedience it demands; or Thomas More, who for religious reasons refuses to bless King Henry VIII's decision to divorce one wife and marry another even though it ultimately costs him his life. More, said Fred, "is a spiritual cousin of the marshal in *High Noon* as a man who is prepared to honor his commitment and to stay in his convictions even if in the end his head rolls."

"There is a through line, a common theme, running through *High Noon, From Here to Eternity, Nun's Story*, and *A Man for All Seasons*: the outsider sticking to his guns no matter what happens to him, no matter the obstacles—and that's exactly how my father was," says Tim Zinnemann. "He was what he chose to make movies about."

MARTIN BERKELEY'S CAREER AS a professional Red hunter ultimately proved no more enduring than his screenwriting career. He blamed his lack of work after he turned informer in 1951 on the Reds and their sympathizers who purportedly backlisted him in retaliation for his prodigious act of name naming. By 1954 he was reduced to doing public relations work for Crown Opticians, a business he had invested in. "The Reds and their pals have practically run me from the industry, Hedda, and I need all the help I can get," he wrote to his old pal, Hedda Hopper. "My partner is a wonderful optician, our prices are right, and we'll do business if we get our people behind us . . . Do come and do bring some friends. I'm counting on you."

Berkeley still worked sporadically in television and movies, writing teleplays for TV Westerns and the screenplay for *Red Sundown* (1956), a B Western for Rory Calhoun at Universal International. "We have just finished the screenplay and are dickering for release and financing," he told Hopper. "A plug from you may make all the difference in the world to us!"

There's no record she gave him one.

Berkeley remained an FBI informant into the mid-1950s, reporting regularly to the bureau's L.A. office on purported Communist activities and rivalries inside the Motion Picture Alliance. In an October 1955 meeting with FBI agents, Berkeley was particularly scathing about Roy Brewer, his former ally and benefactor. According to Berkeley, Brewer had made a power grab to establish himself as the ultimate arbiter of which former Communists deserved clearance. After performing this public service, Brewer had left his union post and went to work as an executive for Allied Artists, where he helped the studio obtain clearances for troublesome liberals like John Huston, Billy Wilder, and William Wyler. Brewer, said Berkeley, remained "consistently and sincerely anti-Communist," but had "accumulated a great deal of self-esteem and importance." It was typical of Berkeley: praising Brewer on the one hand, yet accusing him of egotism and corruption on the other.

Brewer's power play had caused Ward Bond, George Sokolsky, and James O'Neil to quit the informal committee that vetted and cleared alleged leftists to work for the major studios. The result, claimed Berkeley, was that the process was now effectively left in the hands of the studios themselves, which had every incentive to "clear" the people they most wanted to hire.

The Hollywood blacklist died for many reasons. There was the rise of Senator Joseph McCarthy, a classic demagogue who wrested control of the Red Scare headlines and emotions away from HUAC, personalized it, and turned it against the federal bureaucracy that itself had sought to control and regulate the purging of alleged Communists within its ranks. McCarthy finally went too far, aiming at fellow Republicans and at hallowed institutions like the Army, inevitably turning the political establishment against him. His spectacular decline and fall invariably damaged HUAC's credibility as well.

The federal judiciary, awakening belatedly to the abuses of power inherent in HUAC's inquisition, also intervened. The courts not only undermined the State Department's power to curtail travel by those suspected of subversion, they also pared back HUAC's authority to conduct its investigations without legislative purpose or intent. "There is no general authority to expose the private affairs of individuals without justification in terms of the functions of Congress," the Supreme Court ruled in 1957, overturning the conviction for contempt of Congress of a labor union official who had refused to name names before the committee. "Nor is the Congress a law enforcement or trial agency. These are functions of the executive and judicial departments of government. No inquiry is an end in itself; it must be related to, and in furtherance of, a legitimate task of the Congress. Investigations conducted solely for the personal aggrandizement of the investigators or to 'punish' those investigated are indefensible."

Eight years of the Eisenhower administration calmed some of the nation's political anxieties, and the rise of John F. Kennedy and the New Frontier suggested that Americans were ready to turn the page on the Red Scare era. But optimism and anxiety still mixed uneasily. The beginnings of détente between the United States and the Soviet Union followed the near-miss of a nuclear exchange over Russian missiles in Cuba.

Stanley Kramer struck one of the blows that damaged the blacklist when he hired screenwriter Nedrick Young, working under the pseudonym "Nathan E. Douglas," to co-write with Harold B. Smith the screenplay for *The Defiant Ones* (1958), a drama about two escaped prisoners in the Jim Crow South, one white and the other black. "Kramer did not insist on coffee shop exchange of rewrites, credit fictions, or fronts," said Smith's son Joshua. Indeed, in the title sequence at the beginning of the film Young and Smith appear as prison guards as the writing credit for "Douglas" and Smith is screened. The following year the screenplay was nominated for an Oscar, but by then the *New York Times* had revealed the true co-writer. The governors of the Motion Picture Academy, faced with the embarrassing prospect of having to withdraw the nomination, instead voted to repeal its exclusion rule as "unworkable and impractical." When *The Defiant Ones* won, Nedrick Young joined his writing partner up on stage to receive the award, to an enthusiastic ovation.

Ward Bond, one of the founders of the Motion Picture Alliance, conceded defeat. "They're all working now, all the Fifth Amendment Communists," he told a radio interviewer. "There's no point at issue. We've lost the fight, and it's as simple as that."

Still, American Legion national commander Martin B. McKneally declared a new "war of information" against "a renewed invasion of American filmdom by Soviet-indoctrinated artists," and he singled out Stanley's hiring of Ned Young to co-write the screenplay for his next picture, *Inherit the Wind*. Stanley was also attacked in columns by Ed Sullivan and Walter Winchell, and in an editorial in the Hearst-owned *Los Angeles Examiner*, which denounced "the danger and folly of employing enemies of our society in a particularly susceptible area—the transmission of ideas." But he refused to back down. He denounced the campaign by the Legion and its supporters as "un-American and reprehensible."

"Those who set up their own yardsticks may do so for themselves," said Stanley. "But when they threaten economic retaliation on those who disagree with them, then they are as guilty of misconstruing democracy as were the people who blundered into the Communist Party in the thirties and forties."

Having blasted the American Legion, Stanley went on to describe Hollywood's major studios as the "most frightened and the most easily intimidated of any major industry in the United States." Two days later he debated McKneally on national television, insisting that he had the right to hire whoever he pleased "according to the dictates of my conscience."

Stanley was back in the role of rebel with a cause and enjoying it in his usual conflicted way. He was frequently lumped together in news media accounts with Otto Preminger, who announced in January 1960 that blacklisted writer Dalton Trumbo had written the screenplay for his new movie, *Exodus*; and Kirk Douglas, whose company announced later in the year that Trumbo had written his new film, *Spartacus*.

"Martyrdom comes hard," a somber and sardonic Stanley told the Society of Motion Picture and Television Engineers convention in May 1960. "What do I think will happen? Do I think the American Legion can hurt me or my picture? I think they can make life miserable."

He added, "How much pressure will I withstand? Don't ask me how I am involved in this, and don't ask me what I think will happen." It was classic Stanley Kramer—taking a principled position and acting more than a little annoyed at himself for doing so.

PRESIDENT KENNEDY HIMSELF THREW a small shovel of dirt on the blacklist soon after he took office in January 1961 when he slipped out of the White House on a Saturday evening to see *Spartacus*. His brother Robert, the new attorney general, had seen the movie the previous week and had recommended it. "It was fine," Kennedy told reporters when he came out. No one asked him about Dalton Trumbo and the political significance of an American president endorsing a film written by a former member of the Hollywood Ten. For the blacklist it was defeat by omission.

Still, the blacklist took a long time to expire. Ring Lardner Jr., Trumbo's good friend and another of the Hollywood Ten, reckons he went twelve years without being able to use his real name on screenplays. His wife, actress Frances Chaney, also couldn't find work because she was married to him. She had, Lardner writes, acquired "unemployability by marriage."

The intimacy of the damage was profound. Actress Lee Grant went a dozen years without work in Hollywood or on television. She eventually met with HUAC's lawyers in a vain attempt to clear herself. When she finally got an acting job in the fall of 1964, she received a telegram from her ex-husband, backlisted screenwriter Arnold Manoff. I KNOW YOU NAMED ME, it read, THAT'S WHY YOU'RE WORKING. Lucille Ball, just emerging as the star of TV's *I Love Lucy*, had to hold a humiliating press conference and swear that the only reason she had registered to vote as a Communist in 1936 was to assuage her senile grandfather.

Dore Schary lasted at MGM until 1956, when he was ousted as company president. Schary was supposed to have been the studio's savior, and for a while MGM made steady profits under his reign. But the studio system was in a state of rapid deterioration and Schary's commitment to the old order inevitably alienated the company's ownership in New York. After his firing, he moved back to New York and wrote and produced *Sunrise at Campobello*, a Tony Award–winning play about Franklin D. Roosevelt's triumph over polio. It was Schary's vision of the making of enlightened, liberal leadership. His own liberalism, at once deeply committed to civil liberties yet staunchly anti-Communist, had failed to defeat the Red Scare hysteria. Liberals had been trapped in the middle between the Red-baiting autocrats of HUAC and the intrepid but secretive and dogmatic Communists. Yet in the end, lacking a firm agenda of their own, well-meaning liberals like Schary and Philip Dunne had ended up functioning as enablers of the blacklist. But a hearty few, like Stanley Kramer, Kirk Douglas, and Otto Preminger, played significant roles in helping destroy it.

HUAC's power was fading, but its self-image as a warrior in the vanguard of the struggle against international Communism remained intact. Staff director Richard Arens left the committee under a cloud in 1960 after it was revealed he had been a paid consultant for a shadowy and racist pro-eugenics group known as the Pioneer Fund. But before he left HUAC, Arens gave an extraordinary address to the Pepperdine College Freedom Forum in California in which he warned that Communism was "moving relentlessly toward world domination." He painted a dark portrait of the state of world freedom. "Of the eighty-six nations of the world, only one, the United States, stands as a formidable obstacle" to Communism. "It is a total war, a political war, an economic war, a psychological war, a diplomatic war, a global war," he declared, "and it is a war which they and not us are winning internationally and domestically at an alarming rate." When Arens died of a heart attack ten years later at age fifty-six, he undoubtedly still believed he had been a noble soldier in a losing cause.

In 1969, the House of Representatives changed HUAC's name to the House Committee on Internal Security. Six years later the House abolished the committee altogether and transferred its functions to the House Judiciary Committee. The war against the shrunken American Communist Party—reduced to a mere five thousand members nationwide, one third of them estimated to be FBI informers—was officially over.

As for Martin Berkeley, he and his wife, Kate, eventually sold their suburban house and horses and moved to Marbella, Spain, near the Mediterranean coast, where their money went farther and Hollywood was a distant memory. Berkeley developed a heart condition and Parkinson's disease. While many of his former comrades wrote memoirs or made frequent public appearances, he languished in silence and obscurity. When Victor Navasky wrote to him in 1976 requesting an interview for Navasky's landmark study *Naming Names*, Berkeley regretfully said no, citing his failing health. "I know you will be disappointed to hear this, and I assure you that I am disappointed too," he told Navasky. He moved to Florida in the late 1970s for medical reasons and died there in 1979.

ON OCTOBER 27, 1997, the fiftieth anniversary of the Hollywood Ten hearings, the four major entertainment guilds sponsored jointly "Hollywood Remembers the Blacklist," a tribute to the Ten and the other blacklist victims, demonstrating the old dictum that when it comes to history, the writers always get the last word.

There were film clips, live commentary by some of those who had been blacklisted, and dramatizations of the HUAC hearings of 1947 and 1951. The actor Billy Crystal read from Larry Parks's tragic testimony, including the line, "I am probably the most completely ruined man you've ever seen." John Lithgow read a portion of Sterling Hayden's testimony, Kevin Spacey portrayed blacklisted screenwriter Paul Jarrico, and actress Alfre Woodard read a scathing letter that blacklisted actress Anne Revere wrote in 1953 demanding in vain that her fellow Screen Actors Guild colleagues abolish the loyalty oath they had imposed on all members. It turned out that the oath had remained intact as a requirement until members of the Grateful Dead rock band refused to sign it in 1967. "We regret that when courage and conviction were needed to oppose the blacklist, the poison of fear paralyzed our organization," declared Richard Masur, president of the Screen Actors Guild, whose former leader, Ronald Reagan, had been instrumental in enforcing the blacklist. Leaders of the Directors Guild, the Writers Guild of America, and the American Federation of Radio and Television Artists also expressed their regrets.

Over the years the Writers Guild has gone farther by restoring screen credits for blacklisted writers. As of the year 2000, the credits of eighty-two films had been corrected and more than one hundred others were under review.

Despite the recognition, many wounds had not healed. In March 1999 when eighty-nine-year-old Elia Kazan was given an honorary Oscar for his work as a director, some Motion Picture Academy members refused to stand and applaud as Kazan was embraced onstage by director Martin Scorsese and actor Robert De Niro. Outside, some 250 demonstrators protested the honor, including blacklisted screenwriters Bernard Gordon and Robert Lees, and a full-page ad in *Daily Variety* condemned Kazan for having testified against his former comrades forty-seven years earlier.

On November 30, 2012, sixty-five years after the 1947 HUAC hearings, the *Hollywood Reporter* published a detailed account of its own role in fomenting the Red Scare and blacklist. Included as a sidebar was an apology from W. R. Wilkerson III, Billy Wilkerson's son, who said his father had been driven less by anti-Communist ideology than by a burning desire to retaliate against the studio heads who had shunned him when he had first arrived in town and had sabotaged his plans to establish his own film studio. "In his maniacal quest to annihilate the studio owners, he realized that the most effective retaliation was to destroy their talent," W. R. Wilkerson III wrote. "The blacklist," he continued, "silenced the careers of some of the studios' greatest talent and ruined countless others merely standing on the sidelines."

Billy Wilkerson had died in 1962 at age seventy-one. "It's possible, had my father lived long enough, that he would have apologized for creating something that devastated so many careers," his son wrote. Since Billy couldn't do so himself, "on behalf of my family, and particularly my late father, I wish to convey my sincerest apologies and deepest regrets to those who were victimized by this unfortunate incident."

The sins of mainstream journalists had been less consciously malicious but no less damaging—a willingness to print the phony or exaggerated allegations of public officials and "friendly" witnesses without holding them up to scrutiny or challenging their assumptions. Not until a generation later, after the mistaken official judgments and outright falsehoods of the Vietnam War and the crimes of Watergate, would reporters hold the government, including Congress, more frequently accountable for its secrets and lies.

Beyond the suffering of hundreds of individuals was the impact that the blacklist had on American cinema. Dorothy B. Jones's study for the Fund for the Republic, published in 1956, concluded that the proportion of Hollywood films with social themes peaked at 21 percent in 1947, the year of the first HUAC public hearings, and then began a steep decline to 9 percent in 1950 and 1951, while the proportion of escapist entertainment rose accordingly. Some of the most successful movies of the 1950s critically and financially—including *High Noon, From Here to Eternity, On the Waterfront,* and *Giant*—had clear social content and meaning. Still, many of the great Hollywood filmmakers of the 1950s and early 1960s, including Alfred Hitchcock, Howard Hawks, John Ford, William Wyler, and Billy Wilder, steered clear of social issues and focused on cultural and psychological ones (Stanley Kramer being a notable exception). The return to productive film work in the 1960s of blacklisted writers and directors like Ring Lardner Jr., who won an Academy Award for his screenplay for *MASH* (1969), Waldo Salt, who won Oscars for *Midnight Cowboy* (1969) and *Coming Home* (1978), Abe Polonsky, Martin Ritt, Dalton Trumbo, and Walter Bernstein signaled a new era of social engagement in American cinema and paved the way for filmmakers like Warren Beatty, Hal Ashby, Norman Jewison, and Francis Ford Coppola to make movies with meaningful political messages.

The blacklistees had been sorely missed. "In *Naming Names,* I wrote about all the moral issues and constitutional violations of peoples' rights," says Victor Navasky. "What I did not write about was what we lost as a country and a culture by disqualifying people from participating in the national conversation for a decade or more."

AS TIME HAS PASSED, many of Gary Cooper's films have faded from public view. Unlike John Wayne, who had the good fortune of working with legendary director John Ford for much of his career, Cooper had bounced from studio to studio, often playing them off against each other, and from director to director, never forging a long-time partnership with a great filmmaker.

But one film that endures is *High Noon,* a movie that has both sustained Cooper's legend and benefited from it. If anything, the movie and the legend have been revitalized in recent decades as America's place in the world has come under increasing scrutiny. As portrayed in *High Noon,* Cooper's values—his decency, stoicism, and intuitive sense of right and wrong—have been recognized as sterling American characteristics worthy of celebration.

When three young Americans risked their lives to disarm a suspected jihadist about to launch a murderous rampage aboard an Amsterdam-to-Paris train in August 2015, a headline in the opinion section of the *Wall Street Journal* read: GARY COOPER IN EUROPE. The column praised the young men as representing "an admirable strain in American culture that doesn't shrink from individual acts of heroism for the larger good . . . The heroes on the French train showed the world the kind of men that America is still made of."

Even those who have never seen one of Cooper's films or who know nothing about his life still recognize the legend he represents. Maria Cooper Janis, in an ode to her father written on the sixtieth anniversary of the release of *High Noon*, says his rugged moral courage is embodied by the anonymous hero of the Tiananmen Square massacre who stood in the path of Chinese tanks; by Myanmar's Aung San Suu Kyi, who spent more than fifteen years under house arrest for her political activism; by South Africa's Nelson Mandela, who spent twenty-seven years in prison for his resistance to apartheid; and even by President George W. Bush when he appeared defiantly atop the rubble of the World Trade Center in New York after the September 11, 2001, attacks.

"It's too much to say that all of these people were knowingly moved by the lessons of *High Noon*," Janis writes. "But it's not too much to say that Will Kane provided a template for principle and courage that has seeped deeply into the global consciousness over the decades."

Maria helped arrange an extraordinary personal reconciliation between her mother and Patricia Neal, her father's most serious mistress. It began when Maria wrote a sympathy note to Neal after she had a massive, near-fatal stroke in 1965. Neal wound up having tea with Maria and many years later lunch with her and her mother. Rocky and Maria encouraged Neal's conversion to Catholicism and the writing of her exceptionally candid memoir. Neal's husband, author Roald Dahl, had left her for another woman, giving her and Rocky something else in common, along with, of course, their mutual love for the same extraordinary man. "We had shared a purgatory," Neal would write. "I felt that when she put her arms around me."

WHEN IT CAME TO *High Noon*, Stanley Kramer expressed several regrets. The first was financial: early on, he had decided to sell the rights to NTA Pictures, which later changed the name of its television and video distribution arm to Republic Pictures after buying the name and logo of the once-famous B-movie studio. *High Noon* was a huge success on television beginning in the late 1950s and later on videocassette and DVD, and it has been a steady earner for NTA and Republic. "At the time I sold my interest, it was impossible to imagine the magnitude of the profits I would have earned if I had kept it," Stanley wrote ruefully. "Television was not yet, in those days, the money machine it has become. But though I receive nothing from the recurring reruns of *High Noon*, I can enjoy the even greater satisfaction that my name will forever be associated with that picture."

Stanley's deal with Harry Cohn and Columbia Pictures turned out to be a disaster for both sides. None of the first ten movies the Kramer Company made for Columbia was a financial success, and with each successive failure the relationship between Stanley and his annoying, uncouth, and autocratic overseer worsened. Only the eleventh and last picture, *The Caine Mutiny* (1954), directed by Hollywood Ten member-turned-informer Edward Dmytryk, was a hit. Its success was big enough to make up for the losses of its ten predecessors, but by then Stanley felt deeply relieved to walk away from what he called "the unhappiest period of my career." Still, Stanley's deal with Columbia was the forerunner of the New Hollywood that emerged from the ashes of the old studio system. Old companies like MGM, Warners, and Paramount survived in name, but they were no longer integrated entities that produced and distributed movies and owned their own theater chains. They were, instead, financing and distribution companies that serviced packaged deals put together by independent talent agents and producers like Stanley. The Jewish film moguls who had invented and ruled the old system for four decades had survived the dangers to their institutions posed by the blacklist by caving to the political demands of HUAC and its allies. But their acquiescence could not prevent the system's economic demise. Many of the new rulers—the lawyers, agents, directors, financiers, and performers—were also Jews, but of a new generation that was more confident of its identity and far less fearful of anti-Semitism.

Stanley, who was desperate to direct as well as produce his own pictures, took full advantage of the new structure to create the next stage of his career. He went back to his independent status and proceeded to make the socially relevant dramas for which he became most famous: *The Defiant Ones* (1958), *On the Beach* (1959), *Inherit the Wind* (1960), *Judgment at Nuremburg* (1961), *Ship of Fools* (1965), and *Guess Who's*

Coming to Dinner (1967). Those six pictures established Stanley as the most consistently liberal filmmaker in Hollywood and garnered thirty-four Academy Award nominations and won six Oscars.

Once he returned to Hollywood, Carl Foreman occasionally ran into Stanley, but the two men never spoke. The first time occurred in an elevator at Columbia Pictures, Carl's widow Eve recalls, but neither man looked at the other. Carl could forgive his enemies; he could not forgive his former friend, and his judgment of Stanley remained harsh throughout the rest of his life. While others hailed Stanley as a great fighter for liberal causes, Carl saw him as "the apostle of the safely controversial," and a moral coward. "He had a chance then [in 1951] and he blew it," said Carl.

Even after both men had died, the bad blood flowed anew in 2002 with the release of *Darkness at High Noon: The Carl Foreman Documents*, a two-hour documentary film written and directed by Lionel Chetwynd—Carl's old friend from London days—and produced by him and Norman S. Powell for the Public Broadcasting Service. Relying heavily on Carl's unpublished August 1952 letter to Bosley Crowther, the film accused Stanley and his business associates of having cheated Carl out of his associate producer's credit for *High Noon*.

"It was taken from him, an act of apparent betrayal," intones the narrator. "The blacklist worked for the same reason that Vichy France worked. It was all too often something that we happily did to one another."

When she found out about the film, Karen, Stanley's third wife and widow, launched a vigorous campaign to refute its accusations. She called the documentary "a deliberate hatchet job on Stanley's character and reputation." Karen contends it was actually Carl who betrayed Stanley. "Carl lied to him and said 'I've never been a Communist,'" says Karen Kramer. "Stanley was very sad to lose Carl. But Carl lied."

After Karen Kramer raised objections, PBS attached an introductory advisory that the film offered "one point of view in the making of *High Noon*." The film was screened at the L.A. County Museum of Art in April 2002 and had one showing on PBS in September. It has had few public screenings since then.

The documentary makes no mention of Stanley's claim that Carl had misled him. Nor does it note that Carl waived his associate producer's credit as part of a written agreement in return for a sizable severance payment from the Kramer Company.

In the end what was most striking was the degree of bitterness and anger that had lingered for five decades and been passed on from the two principals to their families and friends. It underscored the sad truth that while the conflict between ideological enemies was intense, the blacklist era's deeper hurt was between former friends and intimates. Carl ultimately could make peace with John Wayne and Hedda Hopper; he could never reconcile with Stanley Kramer.

The distinguished blacklist historian Larry Ceplair, who examined the case made by both sides, concluded that "Stanley Kramer may not have behaved with exemplary steadfastness in 1951, but he did not blacklist Foreman and nothing Kramer could have done would have saved Foreman from the blacklist." In short, wrote Ceplair, "There were no heroes, no villains, simply two colleagues, decent men, confronted with indecent circumstances over which they had little control."

OVER THE YEARS, STANLEY expressed regret over the way Carl had been hounded from Hollywood, and in most of his interviews he took pains not to openly criticize Carl nor engage in an argument over who had betrayed whom. Still, he continued to take credit for having saved *High Noon* with his editing.

But in an untranscribed and never-before-published 1973 interview with Michael A. Hoey, a British-born film editor and producer, Stanley discusses *High Noon* in an open, self-critical, stream-of-consciousness manner.

"Why is it that some films [are] beautifully tooled . . . [but] you put the whole thing together, you see it and you couldn't care less?" he asks Hoey. "And then a film has a kind of driving spine to it all of a sudden that made everything fizz, wow. It terribly excites you. Now that kind of chemistry happened in *High Noon*."

Stanley goes on to praise Fred Zinnemann, Carl Foreman, Dimitri Tiomkin, Elmo Williams—and himself. "I think all of these people are the people who made it possible. Now I don't know whose chemistry made what fizz. I only know that we fooled around with it and that I fooled around with it forever and ever and a day."

"It's taken on an aura, and anybody who had to do with it who feels that aura probably should have his head examined because as soon as you feel the aura of what you've done yourself you're in great trouble. I must say I feel no aura . . . It was a picture job and I see no reason why in my whole life *The Defiant Ones* or *Judgment at Nuremburg* or *Inherit the Wind* or any other picture . . . why they didn't turn out that well."

But, Stanley concedes, "They didn't."

"None of them occupy the position that *High Noon* does. I'm sorry, I guess in the final analysis they aren't as good and they certainly didn't have as much impact. But I can't tell you why and that's as honest as I can be . . . Its chemistry happened and we're very happy it did."

It was the closest Stanley Kramer ever came to admitting that he was baffled by *High Noon*'s success and chagrined that the little Western that he didn't direct had exceeded all of his greatest pictures in terms of its stature and impact.

When Kevin Spacey won a Golden Globe in January 2015 for best actor in a television series for *House of Cards*, he recalled visiting Stanley at the Motion Picture and Television Home a few months before he died in February 2001 at age eighty-seven. Spacey said he took a moment to tell Stanley how much he admired his work: "The films you made, the subjects you tackled, the performances you got out of some of the greatest actors that have ever walked the face of the earth, the Oscars you won—your films will stand the test of time and will influence filmmakers for all time." Spacey couldn't tell if Stanley, who by then was suffering from Parkinson's disease and other ailments, had heard and understood him. But as he got up to leave, Stanley grabbed his hand. "Thank you so much for saying that—that means so much to me," he told Spacey.

Then he added a quintessentially self-critical Stanley Kramer observation: "I just wish my films had been better."

CARL FOREMAN'S RETURN TO Hollywood in 1975 was bittersweet. "A part of him wanted to come home, it was a vindication," his son Jonathan recalls. "But in my opinion it was a disaster. Unlike many Americans, he had never tried to become British. There was no pretension in him, but he'd actually grown to love the life in London."

Several big movie projects didn't get off the ground, including the filming of the life and martyrdom of Steve Biko, the black South Africa activist, for which Carl hoped to cast Sidney Poitier as Biko and Paul Newman and Jane Fonda as white journalist Donald Woods and his wife, Wendy.

After he moved back home, Carl made peace with several of his former antagonists, including John Wayne. He ran into Wayne at Dan

Tana's, the popular Los Angeles restaurant. After a wary greeting, the two men embraced as if they were old friends, and Carl introduced Wayne to Eve and their two children, Jonathan and Amanda, with a hearty, "Duke, I want you to meet my English son and my English daughter." It went without saying that Wayne and his friends in the Motion Picture Alliance were the reason Carl had an English family in the first place. After they sat down again, Carl explained to Dan Tana why he had been so conciliatory with Wayne. "You know, he was a patriot. He didn't do it to hurt me."

Carl and Universal Pictures announced a deal for three feature films plus two major multi-hour television projects for CBS, but none of them ever got made. Less than a year later, he announced he was leaving Universal for a long-term, nonexclusive pact with Warner Bros. At the same time, he started recording his memories with his old friend John Weaver for an autobiography he contracted with Simon & Schuster to write. But Carl was too busy on film projects to ever devote enough time on the actual writing.

And then he got sick. He dropped his tennis racquet on the court one day, then couldn't control his knife at dinner. In December 1983, he finally went to the doctor, got a CAT scan, and discovered he had a brain tumor. There were two operations, he got better for a spell, but then he began to decline rapidly.

Crushed by his old friend's illness, Weaver asked Carl if there was anything he could do. Carl mentioned the Oscar that he and the late Michael Wilson had never received for *The Bridge on the River Kwai.* Everyone knew they had written it but how could they prove it? The original manuscript of the screenplay had supposedly disappeared, but Weaver found a copy in Wilson's papers at UCLA. And there on the page was proof: three characters named Baker, Weaver, and Grogan, the same names of friends that Carl had used in every screenplay. The names were like a DNA marker. Weaver took the screenplay to Carl. "He was sitting in bed and he just put his arms around it, the tears came to his eyes," Weaver recalled.

On June 25, 1984, the board of the Writers Guild of America—successor to the Screen Writers Guild—unanimously agreed that credit for *Kwai* belonged to Carl Foreman and Michael Wilson. Weaver took the news to Carl in his sickbed at home. The next morning he died.

Eve Foreman and Michael Wilson's widow, Zelma, officially received the Oscars later that year. At the ceremony Zelma Wilson read from her late husband's remarks when he had received the Writers Guild Laurel

Award in 1976. "I trust that you younger men and women will shelter the mavericks and dissenters in your ranks and protect their right to work," Wilson had pleaded. "The Guild will have need of rebels and heretics if it is to survive as a union of free writers. The nation will have need of them if it is to survive as an open society."

In 1977, in an interview with Larry Ceplair, Carl had made a mental and moral tally of all that had happened to him because of the blacklist. The negative impact of that era still ate at him: the trauma of having been betrayed and excluded had cost him his self-esteem and many friendships and had made it hard for him to practice his craft for an extended period. "Every time I sat down at the typewriter, bitter and aggrieved feelings intruded and I wanted to write letters rather than the script," he told Ceplair. The blacklist had cost him his passport, his freedom to travel, and, ultimately, his marriage to Estelle. And it had pressured him to play a role he hated: that of the political martyr, the bitter expatriate, the transplanted misfit abroad. Plus, he conceded, "it hurt like hell" that other men had been given credit for work he himself had done, especially on *Kwai*.

At the same time, Carl had faced the ordeal on his own terms—not as a saint, nor a hero, just as a flawed but decent human being. He had remarried and created a new family with Eve. He had done good work in the field that he loved. His pride and his honor had remained intact.

All four of the principal creators of *High Noon*—Fred Zinnemann, Stanley Kramer, Gary Cooper, and Carl Foreman—had had fabulously successful careers, and together they had made an enduring American classic. Yet all four felt a sense of frustration and regret over their own supposed failures and the shortcomings of others. Fred never quite achieved the critical recognition he deserved, and never got to make *Man's Fate*, the film he hoped would be his ultimate statement about history and personal responsibility. Stanley was never satisfied with his own work, nor anyone else's. Cooper felt defeated by the collapse of the studio system and his own self-perceived limitations as an actor. And Carl was haunted by his restlessness and his anger.

Still, he told Larry Ceplair, he had been faithful to his own code. Like Will Kane, the character he had created, "I discovered that I could be scared and still come through a situation. I actually was the kind of person I thought I was." Carl Foreman had faced his personal High Noon, had confronted his enemies and his fears, and he had survived.

ACKNOWLEDGMENTS

The seeds for this book were planted in February 2013 when I attended a screening of *High Noon* at the University of Texas at Austin presided over by film studies professor Charles Ramírez Berg. One of the most knowledgeable scholars at UT's outstanding Department of Radio-Television-Film, Charles identified and analyzed various elements of the film that made it great—superb acting, storytelling, editing, music—and he placed it in the context of the blacklist era. Having recently completed my book on *The Searchers*, John Ford's classic Western, I was about to embark on a hunt for a new project. But by the time Charles had finished, I knew my search was over before it had begun.

Three years, eight cities, and fifteen thousand miles later, I've reached the end of a challenging and rewarding project. I've conducted research in Washington, D.C.; London; New York; Los Angeles; Salinas; Helena, Montana; and Carthage, Texas. I've met fascinating people and been immersed in one of the most troubled and compelling eras in modern American history.

Along the way I've benefited from the expertise of many who have studied and written about this subject with wisdom and grace. I am especially grateful to Larry Ceplair and Victor Navasky, whose books on the Hollywood blacklist remain the gold standard for understanding these events. Larry spent several hours with me at his home in Southern California discussing the era and offering paths for further research. Victor met with me twice and helped me gain quick access to his papers at New York University's Tamiment Library.

Gary Cooper, Carl Foreman, Stanley Kramer, and Fred Zinnemann, the four major figures in my story, have all passed away, but I was fortunate to meet close family members of each man who shared insights and materials. Maria Cooper Janis, Gary Cooper's daughter, granted me a long interview and several phone calls and offered much friendly guidance. Eve Williams-Jones, Carl Foreman's widow, and Jonathan Foreman, his son, were very generous with their time and memories, and Eve granted me permission to quote freely from Carl's extraordinary oral history transcripts. Karen Sharpe Kramer, Stanley Kramer's widow and passionate champion, provided documentary evidence of her late husband's role in making *High Noon*. And Tim Zinnemann, Fred Zinnemann's only child and himself a talented photographer and filmmaker, gave his frank and unvarnished memories of family life while vigorously defending his father's extraordinary skills as a director.

Bill Berkeley and Stephen Glass, whose fathers—Martin Berkeley and George Glass—played important but overlooked roles in the blacklist era, each submitted to phone interviews and email queries and helped me better understand the hard choices their fathers faced.

Documentary filmmaker Lionel Chetwynd and his associate, Shirin Amini, generously shared materials from their landmark 2002 documentary, *Darkness at High Noon: The Carl Foreman Documents*. They granted me access to transcripts of Carl's extensive interviews with his friend John Weaver and to the complete transcripts of their own interviews with Carl's friends and collaborators. They also shared papers from his personal files.

Tommie Ritter Smith gave me a personal tour of the Texas Country Music Hall of Fame and Tex Ritter Museum in Carthage, Texas, and allowed me access to the museum's files for her famous cousin. In Salinas, California, Joanne Taylor-Johnson spoke to me warmly about her father, Bruce Church, his life and involvement in financing Stanley Kramer's early films; Roger Powers and Carol Robles also contributed to my understanding.

My thanks for their insights and advice to Jeanine Basinger, Michael F. Blake, Scott Eyman, Mark Harris, J. Hoberman, Michael Kazin, Julie Kirgo, Sanford Levinson, Roberto Lovenheim, Joseph McBride, Susan R. Near, Geoffrey O'Brien, Johanna E. Rapf, Nick Redman, Steven J. Ross, Thomas Schatz, George Stevens Jr., and Eric Tarloff.

Kirk Douglas was ninety-eight years old when he agreed to see me at his Beverly Hills home. He was charming, energetic, and charismatic as he recalled memories of Carl, Stanley, and Patricia Neal. Marcia Newberger arranged for the interview. Master film critic Leonard Maltin not only offered his deep knowledge and insights into *High Noon* and the studio system but also helped me locate Roberta Haynes, a gifted actress and storyteller who is probably the last surviving member of the *High Noon* cast and crew. Roberta, whom I interviewed by phone, was utterly delightful to talk to, as was screenwriter Walter Bernstein, author of a superb memoir of his work and his years on the blacklist.

Librarians and archivists are a special breed whose mission is helping preserve and share their knowledge and resources with the world; my admiration of their work was boundless even before my *Searchers* book was honored with the 2014 Richard Wall Memorial Award for exceptional scholarship by the Theatre Library Association. The list of the archivists who helped me this time around is extensive.

The Margaret Herrick Library of the Motion Picture Academy of Arts and Sciences in Beverly Hills has a vast and exquisitely indexed collection of materials about Hollywood and its people. My thanks to Jenny Romero, Stacy Behlmer, Faye Thompson, Kristine Krueger, Elizabeth Cathcart, and all who work with them. Stacy was especially helpful in providing access to the research of her husband, popular film historian Rudy Behlmer, who has done groundbreaking work on the making of *High Noon*. Barbara Hall, who has left the library's employ, still saw it as her duty to point me to valuable materials from all over Los Angeles and online.

Others who helped me include Jonny Davies, special collections coordinator at the British Film Institute's National Archive in London; Joanne Lammers and Hilary Swett, archivists of the Writers Guild Foundation Library; Jenny Liu of the UCLA Oral History Research Center and Library Special Collections; Kevin B. Leonard, university archivist at Northwestern University in Chicago; and Sandra Garcia-Myers and Ned Comstock of the Cinematic Arts Library at the University of Southern California.

The records of the House Committee on Un-American Activities reside at the Center for Legislative Archives at the National Archives and Records Administration in Washington, D.C. Since 2001 the center has made public thousands of formerly confidential documents, including transcripts of HUAC's closed-door executive sessions. My thanks to Richard McCulley, the center's historian, and to archivists William Davis and Katherine Mollan. Carol Swain of NARA's Motion Picture, Sound, and Video Research Room in College Park, Maryland, guided me to vintage newsreels of HUAC's hearings.

I obtained FBI files on Cooper, Foreman, Kramer, and the Motion Picture Alliance for the Preservation of American Ideals via Freedom of Information Act requests to the FBI and NARA. Film scholar and author J. Hoberman loaned me copies of the FBI files he had obtained for his essential book, *An Army of Phantoms*. Daniel J. Leab's comprehensive microfilm collection of the FBI's surveillance files on Hollywood, 1942–58, was another essential resource.

The Library of Congress was an invaluable source of information. I viewed feature films and documentaries from the blacklist era at the Motion Picture and Television Reading Room headed by Zoran Sinobad and his capable staff. I was able to find virtually every book I needed at the library's Main Reading Room and read them under its majestic domed ceiling. I also used the facilities of the Microform and Electronic Resources Center just across the hallway and the Prints & Photographs Division.

In New York, John Calhoun at the New York Public Library for the Performing Arts helped me access clipping files and other materials on Gary Cooper and Grace Kelly. I used transcripts from the American Jewish Committee Oral History Collection at the NYPL's Dorot Jewish Division and from Columbia University's oral history collection, and accessed Victor Navasky's papers at the Tamiment Library at New York University. My special thanks go to the late Charles Silver, my friend and former colleague, who as film curator at the Museum of Modern Art guided me through MOMA's files on *High Noon* and Fred Zinnemann.

My researchers for this book were Meital Bloom, Alice Crites, Abra Frankel, Paul Hechinger, Susannah Jacob, Ashley Wood, and Benzamin Yi. My longtime friend and former *Washington Post* colleague Jennifer Beeson helped steer me to photo archive collections. Tamir Kalifa brought his keen eye and talent to redesigning my website.

Larry Ceplair, Jim Hoagland, David E. Hoffman, and Charles Ramirez Berg read the manuscript and caught numerous errors of fact and interpretation, as did Scott Eyman. Those that remain are my sole responsibility. I'm especially grateful to David, who contributed sympathetic guidance and critical insights to this book from conception to publication.

This is my third book with the Ross Yoon literary agency in Washington, D.C., and no one could be a better shepherd, negotiator, one-person support system, and champion than Gail Ross. I'm also grateful to my talented editor, Anton Mueller, and the hardworking crew at Bloomsbury, including Rachel Mannheimer, Callie Garnett, Sara Kitchen, Patti Ratchford, Lauren Hill, and Laura Keefe. Johanna Ramos Boyer provided important public relations help.

In Austin, R. B. Brenner, Wanda Cash, Stephen Harrigan, Bob Jensen, Jamie and Ruth Pennebaker, and Paul Stekler all provided companionship and sympathy and listened to me tell the same Gary Cooper stories over and over again. My friends Richard Cohen, Steve

Coll, Margaret Edds, Nadine Epstein, Blaine Harden, James Hohmann, Steve Luxenberg, Bob Thompson, and Sharon Waxman offered good advice and moral support.

In Montana, I benefited from visiting the Montana Historical Society and from an overnight stay at the Ranch at the Dearborn, run by Trudy and Rich Hayes, part of the Cooper family's original Seven Bar Nine Ranch. Writers always need places to stay, and longtime friends Rick Levine and Janet Gold in New York and Gregory Katz and Bea Sennewald in London provided accommodation.

My children and their spouses—Abra Frankel and Matt Ipri, Margo and Danny Brush, and Paul Frankel and Carolyn Schubert—were a great source of good cheer and encouragement. My five grandchildren— Milo and Tessa Ipri, and Sawyer, Owen, and Lydia Brush—manufacture joy by the ton. And finally, as always, there is Betsyellen Yeager, who has given me a lifetime of inexhaustible energy, happiness, and devotion.

Arlington, Virginia
August 2016

A NOTE ON THE SOURCES

This book uses a wide range of primary and secondary sources, including government records, interviews, oral histories, feature and documentary films, memoirs, scholarly works, and newspaper and magazine articles. The major archival collections that I used are listed in the Bibliography. The people whom I interviewed or consulted with are listed in the Acknowledgements.

The literature of the Hollywood blacklist is voluminous and constantly expanding, but the two most enduring books were originally published in 1980: *The Inquisition in Hollywood* by Larry Ceplair and Stephen Englund, a comprehensive account of the blacklist period; and *Naming Names* by Victor Navasky, his "moral detective story" about the meaning and consequences of testifying before the House Un-American Activities Committee. Since then several thousand documents have become public that have expanded and enriched our knowledge about HUAC, the FBI, and the blacklist. Since 2001 the National Archives and Records Administration in Washington has released ninety-four boxes of executive session transcripts, eighty-nine boxes of investigative materials, and 682 linear feet of File and Reference materials from HUAC's files. The National Archives is still in the process of processing and releasing thousands of FBI documents from that era. Meanwhile, many essential documents from the FBI's sixteen-year investigation into Communist infiltration of the motion picture industry are available on fourteen reels of microfilm compiled and indexed by Professor Daniel J. Leab of Seton Hall University. The materials helped me find more definitive answers to questions about the behind-closed-doors testimony of Carl Foreman, Martin Berkeley, and other HUAC witnesses and about the partnership between the FBI and HUAC in their separate but collaborative pursuit of those they targeted as subversive.

Larry Ceplair has gone on to write at least four more books and numerous articles on the blacklist, work that has established him as the era's most authoritative historian. Nancy Lynn Schwartz's *The Hollywood*

Writers' Wars, published in 1982, remains the most thorough account of the birth and life of the Screen Writers Guild and how its history and that of the blacklist are entwined. Rebecca Prime's *Hollywood Exiles in Europe* is a welcome recent addition to the literature. There are many memoirs by blacklisted writers and others whose lives were touched by events. My personal favorites are *Inside Out* by Walter Bernstein, and *Odd Man Out* by Edward Dmytryk, the former a backlistee and master storyteller, the latter one of those who named names; and *I Am Spartacus!*, a spirited reminiscence by Kirk Douglas. Betty Garrett's memoir, *Betty Garrett and Other Songs*, is an exuberant yet poignant remembrance of her life in show business and of her late husband, Larry Parks, and the personal and professional ordeal he went through. *A Very Dangerous Citizen* by Paul Buhle and Dave Wagner chronicles the life and times of Abe Polonsky, one of the most gifted writers and directors to be blacklisted.

Steven J. Ross's *Hollywood Left and Right* places the blacklist in the context of Hollywood's political history, while J. Hoberman's *An Army of Phantoms* captures the paranoia and anxieties of the era as reflected in its motion pictures. The documentary film *Red Hollywood* by Thom Andersen and Noël Burch explores the feature films of those who were blacklisted and punctures the myth that their work was inconsequential. Michael Kazin's *American Dreamers* and Ellen Schrecker's *Many Are the Crimes* strike a careful balance between criticism and sympathy for those who joined the American Communist Party in the 1930s and 40s, while the books of John Earl Haynes and Harvey Klehr, informed by the release of the Venona papers, offer an important counter-perspective. Athan Theoharis's *Chasing Spies* is a well-researched account of the FBI's egregious mistakes and misconduct in the pursuit of alleged Soviet spies and subversives. The memoirs of Dore Schary and Philip Dunne recount the dilemmas faced by two sincere liberals who tried and failed to thwart the blacklist.

Although they are largely available online, the most useful and evocative collection of Hedda Hopper's columns are in her scrapbooks donated to the Margaret Herrick Library; original, bound volumes of the *Hollywood Reporter* are available at the Main Reading Room and the Moving Image Research Center at the Library of Congress. Finally, no study of the era is complete without *Tender Comrades*, an extraordinarily resonant collection of oral histories edited by Buhle and Patrick McGilligan.

As my book makes clear, the controversy over who was responsible for the brilliance of *High Noon* remains as bitter as the ideological conflicts of the era. Stanley Kramer and Fred Zinnemann both wrote compelling memoirs of their life and work. Gary Cooper did not, but Jeffrey Meyers's *Gary Cooper: American Hero* is a well-researched biography. *Gary Cooper Off Camera* by his daughter, Maria Cooper Janis, is required reading for anyone wanting to understand the man and his work. The Gary Cooper online scrapbook at www. garycoopersscrapbook.proboards.com is an exhaustive compendium of articles and photographs from four decades of Cooper's professional life, and includes all six parts of the 1956 *Saturday Evening Post* series that Maria Cooper Janis says offers the most authentic version of her father's voice. Patricia Neal's brutally frank memoir, *As I Am*, is also essential reading. But nothing is more essential than watching Cooper's greatest and not-so-greatest films to see a cinematic artist and craftsman at work. Besides *High Noon*, my personal favorites are *Mr. Deeds Goes to Town* and *Meet John Doe*, in which Cooper embodies with passion and humor Frank Capra's vision of heroic populism.

Carl Foreman was never able to complete his autobiography, but he recorded several dozen hours of taped interviews conducted by his good friend John Weaver. Some of the transcripts are in the Foreman Collection at the British Film Institute library in London, as are transcripts of Foreman's four-part 1976 lecture at the American Film Institute on the making of *High Noon*. More complete copies of the interview transcripts are in the possession of the Foreman family and of Lionel Chetwynd, who used these materials in the making of his 2002 documentary, *Darkness at High Noon*. The transcripts I had access to were copies of copies, and many lack dates and page numbers. Chetwynd and his staff also conducted more than a dozen interviews with Foreman's friends and colleagues that are an invaluable resource for understanding the man and his times. Other revealing documentaries about the film and the blacklist are *Word Into Image: Writers on Screenwriting*, a thirty-minute session with Foreman, published in 1984; and Leonard Maltin's *The Making of High Noon*. The Maltin documentary, first issued in 1992, is included in the two-disc sixtieth anniversary DVD edition of *High Noon*, a trove of documentary features and nuggets.

As for the making of the movie itself, Phillip Drummond's *High Noon*, part of the British Film Institute's excellent series of film books, is a thorough account, as is John Byman's *Showdown at High Noon*, which covers the facts about the movie and the blacklist. Michael F. Blake's

Code of Honor also thoroughly recounts the details of the making of the film. Rudy Behlmer's *America's Favorite Movies* is a brisk but thoroughly researched account. Thomas Schatz's *The Genius of the System* and Jeanine Basinger's *The Star Machine* are deeply informed studies of the political economy of the studio system and its stars, and Neal Gabler's *An Empire of Their Own* is a highly original look at the Jewish moguls who invented Hollywood.

There are many interviews with Foreman, Kramer, and Zinnemann that briefly discuss their work together and their individual contributions to *High Noon*. Two of the best are George Stevens Jr.'s discussions with Kramer and Zinnemann published in his *Conversations with the Great Moviemakers of Hollywood's Golden Age*. But the most valuable concerning the making of *High Noon* are several audiotaped interviews from the 1970s that remain untranscribed in whole or part. These include film historian Rudy Behlmer's interviews with Carl Foreman and Elmo Williams, which can be accessed via an iPod at the Margaret Herrick Library in Beverly Hills; and screenwriter Michael A. Hoey's audio interviews with Stanley Kramer, Lloyd Bridges, and Floyd Crosby, which are stored on compact disk at the University of Southern California's Cinematic Arts Library.

NOTES

Abbreviations

AFI American Film Institute
BFI British Film Institute
CF Carl Foreman
COMPIC FBI investigation Communist Influence in the Motion Picture Industry
FZ Fred Zinnemann
HH Hedda Hopper
HR Hollywood Reporter
HUAC House Committee on Un-American Activities
LAT Los Angeles Times
LOC Library of Congress
MB Martin Berkeley
MPAPAI Motion Picture Alliance for the Preservation of American Ideals
MHL Margaret Herrick Library, Academy of Motion Picture Arts and Sciences
NARA National Archives and Records Administration
NYPL New York Public Library
NYT New York Times
NYU New York University
RB Rudy Belhmer
SEP Saturday Evening Post
SK Stanley Kramer
UCLA Special Collections Library, University of California at Los Angeles
USC Cinematic Arts Library, University of Southern California

Introduction

ix   *"A character is defined"*: Arthur Miller, *Timebends: A Life*, (New York: Grove Press, 1987), p.367.
x   *"What is a Communist?"*: Baarslag, "Know Your Enemy," National Americanism Commission, 1948, American Legion files, MHL.
xi   *"worse than . . . heart disease"*: in Ellen Schrecker, *Many Are the Crimes* (Boston: Little, Brown, 1998), p. 144.
xii   *"As I was writing the screenplay"*: CF, "Anatomy of a Classic, Series 1," p. 4, AFI.
xiv   *"A morality play"*: Maltin, *The Making of High Noon* documentary film.

1. The Natural

2   *"All I knew then":*   Cooper, as told to George Scullin, "Well, It Was This Way," Part 1, *SEP*, 2/18/56, p. 110. Cooper says he was nine or ten at the time, but Russell's mural was unveiled in 1912, when Cooper was in private school in England. He couldn't have seen it until his return a year later.

3   For accounts of Cooper's parents and his early life, see *SEP*, 2/18/56 and 3/3/56, and Jeffrey Meyers, *Gary Cooper: American Hero* (New York: Cooper Square Press, 2001), pp. 1–9.

3   *"swinging an ax at twenty below":* SEP, Part 3, 3/3/56, p. 56.

3   *the chinook:* Patricia Neal, *As I Am* (New York: Simon & Schuster, 1988), p. 89.

3   *learned to speak French, solve an equation:* Ibid., p. 90.

4   *"My wrists were too long . . .":* SEP, Part 3, 3/3/56, p. 56.

5   *"The more ferociously I scowled . . .":* SEP, Part 4, 3/10/56, p. 92.

6   *"did his own stunt work":* Homer Dickens, *The Complete Films of Gary Cooper* (New York: Citadel Press, 1970), pp. 6–7.

6   *It required only one take:* William Wellman Jr., *Wild Bill Wellman* (New York: Pantheon, 2015), pp. 194–5.

6   *Cooper "does something mysterious":* Hanks introduction in Maria Cooper Janis, *Gary Cooper Off Camera* (New York: Harry N. Abrams, 1999), p. 6.

7   *"I've come to Hollywood":* in Jane Ellen Wayne, *Cooper's Women* (New York: Prentice Hall, 1988), p. xiv.

7   *She saw the "terror in all their faces":* in Scott Eyman, *The Speed of Sound* (New York: Simon & Schuster, 1997), p. 160.

8   *"a slim young giant":* Owen Wister, *The Virginian* (New York: Grosset & Dunlap, 1929 edition), p. 4.

9   *the Norman Rockwell portrait:* Deborah Solomon, *American Mirror: The Life and Art of Norman Rockwell* (New York: Farrar, Straus and Giroux, 2013), p. 140.

9   *"I began to wonder who I was":* SEP, 3/24/56, p. 142.

10 *"Inwardly I was a scared young man":* Ibid., 3/31/56, p. 129.

10 *"There were departments for everything":* Jeanine Basinger, *The Star Machine* (New York: Knopf, 2007), pp. 13–14.

11 For an expert account of the studio system and its evolution, see Thomas Schatz, *The Genius of the System* (New York: Pantheon, 1988).

11 *"the absolute power of the tyrant":* Isherwood, *Prater Violet* (Minneapolis: University of Minnesota, 2001), p. 60.

11 *"Underneath is hostility":* Powdermaker, *Hollywood: The Dream Factory* (Boston: Little, Brown, 1950), p. 29.

12 *"Pretty young girls":* Ibid., p. 23. Other Powdermaker quotes are from pp. 37, 303, 254, and 44.

12 *"not a word of anyone else's":* Ring Lardner Jr., *I'd Hate Myself in the Morning* (New York: Nation Books, 2000), p. 85.

12 *Sometimes you have to fake it:* F. Scott Fitzgerald, *The Love of the Last Tycoon* (New York: Scribner, 1941, 1993 edition), pp. viii and 122.

13 *"These immigrants, these Jews":* in Jean Stein, *West of Eden* (New York: Random House, 2016), p. 43.

13 *"As soon as the Jews gained control"*: in Neal Gabler, *An Empire of Their Own* (New York: Crown, 1988), p. 277.

14 *"a rotten bunch of vile people"*: in Scott Eyman, *Lion of Hollywood* (New York: Simon & Schuster, 2005), pp. 342–3.

14 *most ignored . . . their Jewishness*: see Gabler, pp. 1–7.

15 *Ronald Reagan in his memoirs:* Ronald Reagan, *An American Life* (New York: Simon & Schuster, 1991), pp. 81–2.

15 *"We did everything for them"*: Basinger, p. 47.

15 *"It had restrictive clauses"*: Tino Balio, *Grand Design* (Berkeley: University of California, 1995), p. 145.

16 *stars were at the heart*: Ibid., p. 144.

16 *"actors are just a commodity"*: "Cooper is 'Too Busy' to Marry," *Chicago Herald*, 3/31/29, NYPL.

16 *"Kid, stay out of Hollywood"*: Meyers, p. 74.

17 *"Millions are to be grabbed"*: Ben Hecht, *A Child of the Century,* (New York: Simon & Schuster, 1954), p. 446.

2. The Elephant Man

18 *"There is no avoiding the fact"*: Lillian Ross, *Reporting Back: Notes on Journalism* (Washington: Counterpoint, 2002), p. 4.

19 *No room for Carl:* CF, "Wagons West," unpublished manuscript. Chetwynd Files.

19 *carried a torch for* A Midsummer Night's Dream*:* Reminiscences of CF (April 1959), Columbia Center for Oral History Collection, pp. 1664–5.

19 *It was an inauspicious beginning:* Details of CF's family and childhood in Chicago are from transcripts of CF Tapes, VIII-A and IX, 12/22-3/77, Chetwynd Files.

19 *Al Capone opened a soup kitchen:* http://www.chicagotribune.com/business/081024-great-depression-photogallery-photogallery.html

20 *"you couldn't walk three doors"*: in Studs Terkel, *Division Street: America* (New York: Pantheon, 1967), p. 130.

20 *he kept small bank accounts:* Jonathan Foreman, "Witch-hunt," *Index on Censorship*, June 1995, p. 97.

20 *"When I went home . . . I was a Communist"*: CF Tape 13, 1/3/78, pp. 2–3.

20 *"I am pleading for the future"*: CF, "Wagons West," draft, p. 3. Chetwynd Files.

21 *"the individual in conflict"*: CF, "Virtue and a Fast Gun," *Observer Magazine*, 10/10/65, p. 23.

21 *"the movies are the great mass art"*: CF, "For The Movies," *NYT Magazine*, 4/29/62.

21 *He made forty dollars a week:* CF Tape 15, 1/5/78.

22 *He'd exhaust himself:* CF Tape, 14-B, pp. 1–2.

22 *"The second coming of Foreman"*: CF Tape 13, 1/3/78, pp. 2–3.

22 *"You could hear the cars"*: CF Tape IV Side 1, 12/20/77, p. 8.

22 *such respected luminaries:* Nancy Lynn Schwartz, *The Hollywood Writers' War* (New York: Knopf, 1982), pp. 163–4.

23 *"Mr. Foreman, you're a writer"*: CF Tape IV, p. 2

23 *"I ate the salami"*: Ibid., p. 5.

23 For a comprehensive history of the founding of the Screen Writers Guild, see Larry Ceplair and Steven Englund, *The Inquisition in Hollywood* (Garden City, NY: Anchor Press, 1980), pp. 16–46; Schwartz, pp. 12–81.

25 *"a device of Communist radicals"*: in Ceplair and Englund, p. 37.

25 *"All you'll get from me is shit!"*: Dore Schary, *Heyday* (Boston: Little, Brown, 1979), p. 109.

26 *350 active party members:* Ceplair and Englund, p. 66.

26 *"The men were always working"*: *Tender Comrades*, Patrick McGilligan and Paul Buhle, eds. (Minneapolis: University of Minnesota Press, 2012), p. 164.

26 *"The people we met were very bright"*: CF Tape 23, 1/19/78, p. 2.

27 *"The greatest contribution"*: Irving Howe, *World of Our Fathers* (New York: Harcourt Brace Jovanovich, 1976), p. 345.

27 *Communism . . . "is the Americanism"*: Larry Ceplair and Christopher Trumbo, *Dalton Trumbo* (Lexington: University Press of Kentucky, 2015), p. 139.

27 *"The activities I engaged in"*: Collins HUAC testimony, Part 1, 4/12/51, p. 257.

27 *"When I joined the party"*: Schwartz, p. 88.

28 *"the best social club in Hollywood"*: *Tender Comrades*, p. 486.

28 *"because she was new in Hollywood"*: Philip Dunne, *Take Two* (New York: McGraw-Hill, 1980), p. 111.

28 *"it sounds silly"*: Norma Barzman, *The Red and the Blacklist* (New York: Nation Books, 2003), p. 29.

28 *the growth of mass culture:* Michael Kazin, *American Dreamers* (New York: Knopf, 2011), pp. 157–9.

28 *"We knew who we were"*: Nora Sayre, *Previous Convictions* (New Brunswick, NJ: Rutgers, 1995), p. 300.

29 *had "resorted to duplicity and conspiracy"*: "The Moscow Trials: A Statement by American Progressives," *New Masses*, 5/3/1938.

29 *"it was also a fatal flaw"*: Author's interview with Michael Kazin. See also Kazin, Chapter 5.

30 *"The Party tried very hard"*: *Tender Comrades*, p. 209.

30 *"We treated the Soviet Union"*: Steve Nelson, *American Radical* (Pittsburgh: University of Pittsburgh, 1981), pp. 249–50.

30 For an excellent account of the Schulberg incident, see Schwartz, pp. 168–70.

31 *"The Yanks are not coming"*: in John Cogley, *Report on Blacklisting* (Fund for the Republic, 1956), p. 39–40.

31 *"the industrious Communist tail"*: Dunne, p. 128.

31 *Dore Schary was stunned:* Schary, p. 107.

31 *"A Communist was an agent"*: Ceplair and England, p. 151.

32 *"If you left the Party"*: CF Tape 23, 1/19/1978, p. 8.

32 *"It was one of the happiest nights"*: Schwartz, p. 174.

32 *"the most excruciatingly exciting thing"*: Foreman, "Do It Yourself," draft article for *Screen Writers*, 4/12/61, pp. 1–2. CF Papers, BFI.

32 *It was only a slight improvement:* CF Tape 22, 1/18/78.

33 A compelling account of Hollywood's involvement with the U.S. Armed Forces during WWII is Mark Harris, *Five Came Back: A Story of Hollywood and the Second World War* (New York: Penguin, 2014).

33 *The Army had a dossier:* CF Tape 23, 1/19/78.

35 *"That picture was made"*: Jack L. Warner, HUAC, *Hearings Regarding the Communist Infiltration of the Motion Picture Industry*, 10/20/47, p. 152.

35 *"He had a brooding aura"*: CF Tape No. 23, 1/19/78.

3. The Icon

36 *"Charisma, the kind of natural power":* "The Oscars 2015: For the Birds," *New Yorker*, 2/23/15, http://www.newyorker.com/culture/richard-brody/oscars-2015-birds

36 *Cooper was thriving:* Ethan Mordden, *The Hollywood Studios* (New York: Knopf, 1988), p. 50.

37 *"All typing stopped":* Budd Schulberg, *Moving Pictures* (New York: Stein & Day, 1981), p. 266.

37 *"Gary kisses the way Charles Boyer looks":* Basinger, p. 8.

37 *"she was extremely shy":* Author's interview with Maria Cooper Janis.

38 *"There is not an actor alive":* Janis, p. 7.

39 *"Every line in his face":* Frank Capra, *The Name Above the Title* (New York: Macmillian, 1971), pp. 182–3.

39 *"the honest and forthright fellow":* NYT, 3/13/41.

40 *"The personality of this man":* David Thomson, *Gary Cooper* (Faber & Faber, 2010), p. 89.

40 *"Ingrid loved me more than any woman":* Wayne, p. 100.

40 *"His clothing is handsome":* Flair, July 1950, pp. 46–7.

40 *"with a paycheck of $482,820":* Associated Press, 8/2/41, Cooper Clip Files, NYPL for the Performing Arts.

41 *"It's astonishing to review":* Basinger, p. 78.

41 *"Words had to fit him":* Jesse Lasky Jr., *Whatever Happened to Hollywood?* (New York: Funk & Wagnalls, 1975), p. 200.

42 *"My screen character saw himself":* SEP, Part 8, 4/7/56, p. 36.

42 *"I was always conscious . . .":* SEP, Part 7, 3/31/57, p. 130.

42 *"As a persona he's just . . . perfect":* Author's interview with Jeanine Basinger.

43 *"the American Democrat, Nature's Nobleman":* Richard Schickel, *Schickel on Film* (New York, William Morrow, 1989), p. 181.

43 *"if you make me the hero":* Thomson, p. 11.

43 *He tried to avoid playing Sergeant Alvin York:* SEP, Part 8, 4/7/56, p. 120.

44 Cooper himself gives the best account of the Gehrig speech: Ibid., pp. 120–1.

46 *"They came to our land":* Gabler, pp. 345–6.

46 *"a slime mongering kike,"* Ibid., p. 355.

47 among the *"hard-nosed Red-baiters":* Schary, p. 86.

47 *"the biggest anti-Semite in Hollywood":* Hood Memo to Hoover, 3/22/44, FBI COMPIC, MPAPAI file, Leab Microfilm.

47 *"I'm gonna be one who rides":* in Schwartz, p. 63.

47 *"It' invariably transformed Dad":* Otto Friedrich, *City of Nets* (London: Headline, 1986), p. 168.

47 *"For ten years I've been sitting back:"* Hollywood Citizen-News, 2/8/44.

48 *"a subversive and dangerous organization":* "Double-Cross in Hollywood," *New Leader*, 7/15/44.

48 *"Motion pictures are inescapably":* MPAPAI 1944–55, f.288, HH papers, MHL.

48 *"Why is Hollywood so Red?":* The Vigil, published by the MPAPAI, March 49, vol. 3, no. 1, MHL.

48 *"the subversive minority has connived":* Los Angeles Examiner, 2/9/44, Part 1, p. 10.

49 Portrait of Wilkerson is from *HR*, 11/30/12; Marcia Borie, "Reporting on Hollywood for Sixty Years," *HR*, 9/28/90; and the W. R. Wilkerson Bio File, MHL Core Collection.

49 *"Dear Irving" letter*: Wilkerson to Thalberg, undated, Thalberg and Shearer Papers, f.2, MHL. There is no record of Thalberg's reply.

50 *"not only employing but actually pampering"*: "Tradeviews," *HR*, 12/3/46.

51 *"part of a gigantic, world-wide conspiracy"*: FBI, COMPIC, Internal Security Report, 2/18/43, Leab microfilm.

51 *fifty-six known Communist Party members*: Memo, COMPIC File 100-138754, 10/13/1944, Leab microfilm.

51 *"the strength of Communist influence"*: "Communist Infiltration of the MPI," COMPIC Bureau File No. 100-138754, 12/12/45, F. 8, Communist Activity in the Entertainment Industry bureau files, MHL.
See also memos in FBI File No. 100-15732, 12/12/1946 and 1/3/1947, Leab Microfilm.

51 FBI break-ins of CP offices in L.A.: Athan Theoharis, *Chasing Spies* (Chicago: Ivan R. Dee, 2009), p. 59.

52 Brewer profile is from "Roy M. Brewer," UCLA Oral History; and *LAT* obituary, 9/23/06.

52 *"That's Bob Rossen"*: Kirk Douglas, *I Am Spartacus* (New York: Open Road, 2012), p. 11.

53 *"There was no namby-pamby with me"*: Brewer, UCLA Oral History, p. 128.

53 Cooper's role with the Hollywood Hussars: Anthony Slide, "Hollywood's Fascist Follies," *Film Comment*, 27:4, 7/8/91, pp. 63–4.

53 *"The Hussars are not the social group"*: *Milwaukee Journal*, 1/9/35.

53 *"There's no question in my mind"*: Meyers, p. 206.

54 *"Terrible thing, civil war"*: in Alvah Bessie, *Inquisition in Eden*, (Berlin: Seven Seas, 1967), pp. 120–1.

54 *"lukewarm Americans"*: in Meyers, p. 206.

54 Cooper's role in the 1944 campaign: George Carpozi Jr., *The Gary Cooper Story* (New Rochelle, NY: Arlington House, 1970), pp. 167–9.

55 *"Despite the evidence before their eyes"*: "Attack!!! Why?" MPAPAI pamphlet, FBI File 100-271036-12.

4. The Boy Wonder

56 *"There is no substitute"*: Fitzgerald, p. 122.

56 *"trim and rugged-looking"*: Crowther, "Hollywood's Producer of Controversy," *NYT Magazine*, 12/10/1961.

56 *"I've never been close"*: "High Noon for Stanley Kramer," *LAT*, 2/24/78.

56 For SK profile, see Donald Spoto, *Stanley Kramer: Film Maker* (New York: Putnam, 1978; Stanley Kramer, *It's a Mad Mad Mad Mad World* (New York: Harcourt Brace, 1997), and Walter Wagner, *You Must Remember This* (New York: G.P. Putnam's Sons, 1975) p. 284.

57 *"Neither of us had a brother"*: CF Tape 23, 1/19/78.

58 *"I can't say we were ever close"*: SK, p. 18.

58 *"We saw things pretty much alike":* Ibid., p. 7.

58 *He ... formed a company:* SK, "The Independent Producer," *Films in Review* II:3, 3/51, p. 4.

58 George Glass profile: author's interview with Stephen Glass.

59 *"George is the most brilliant":* SK interview, Champlin Collection, f. 70, MHL.

59 *the system was creatively sterile:* SK audio interview with Michael Hoey, USC. 10/3/73.

60 *"The team of Kramer and Foreman":* Fleischer, *Just Tell Me When to Cry* (New York: Carroll & Graf, 1993), p. 35.

60 *"The walls were thin":* Dimitri Tiomkin, *Please Don't Hate Me* (Garden City, N.Y.: Doubleday, 1959), p. 226.

60 For studios and the rise of TV: Schatz, p. 412; and for statistics of the Radio, Electronics, and Television Manufacturers Association, www.earlytelevision.org/ us_tv_sets.html

60 *"euphoria steadily gave way":* Kinden, "SAG, HUAC, and Postwar Hollywood," in Thomas Schatz, *Boom and Bust: The American Cinema in the 1940s* (New York: Scribner's, 1997), p. 328.

61 *impact of the Supreme Court decision:* Ibid., pp. 329–32.

61 *"The war is not yet over":* Friedrich, p. 179.

62 *"He was frustrated":* Author's interview with Maria Cooper Janis

62 *he turned Hawks down:* Todd McCarthy, *Howard Hawks* (New York: Grove Press, 1997), p. 412.

63 *"We all rolled on the floor":* SK interview, Champlin Collection, MHL, f. 70.

64 *"He understood Midge Kelly":* CF Tape 24 (2), 1/20/78.

64 *"My agency was against it":* Author's interview with Kirk Douglas.

64 *"You mean Melvyn Douglas?":* in Wagner, p. 287.

65 Portrait of Bruce Church comes from author's interview with his daughter, Joanne Johnson Taylor, and from Roger Powers, "The Accidental Salinas Movie Magnate," www.rogerpowers.com/harv3.htm.

66 *a post-midnight meeting ... with Howard Hughes:* Kramer, pp. 30–31.

66 *"Many times I would hear Stanley:"* CF Tape 24 (2) 1/20/78.

66 *"Before he is through":* SK, "The Independent Producer," p. 2.

66 *"He could be stubborn":* Taradash Oral History, pp. 200 and 222, MHL.

66 *"Well, Boy Wonder":* SK interview, Champlin Collection, MHL, p. 23.

66 *Home of the Brave* preparation: see SK, pp. 33–43.

68 *"We rehearsed for two weeks":* NY Daily News, 4/6/1949.

69 Crowther review, *NYT,* 5/13/49.

70 For Schary profile, see Schary, p. 6; for *Crossfire,* see pp. 156–7.

71 *"It feels fine, hearing at last":* HR, 7/25/47, p. 6.

5. The Committee

72 *"The greatest dangers to liberty":* Olmstead v. United States, 1928.

72 For descriptions of Thomas, see Gabler, pp. 360–1, and Friedrich, p. 299–300.

72 "brilliantly trained, fanatically dedicated": Robert Stripling, *The Red Plot Against America* (Drexel Hill, Pa.: Bell Publishing, 1949), pp. 14 and 70.

73 *"Those who deny freedom ...":* Schrecker, p. 139.

73   *"a revival of the Red hysteria"*: Commager, "Who Is Loyal to America?" *Harper's* 195:4168, September 1947, p. 195.

73   *[Jack Warner] "made a mistake"*: HUAC Hearings. 10/20/1947, p. 14.

74   *"one of the main centers"*: Walter Goodman, *The Committee* (New York: Farrar, Strauss and Giroux, 1968) pp. 202–3.

74   *"hundreds of very prominent . . . people"*: in Friedrich, p. 300.

75   *"I do think it is long overdue"*: Hoover memo, 6/24/1947, FBI Files f.9, MHL.

75   Information on the FBI's COMPIC campaign in Hollywood is from Theoharis, pp. 151–63; as well as from Leab Microfilm collection.

75   *Reagan had been an FBI informant:* "Reagan acted as informant for FBI," *San Jose Mercury News*, 8/25/85.

75   *"He has no fear of anyone"*: "Ronald Reagan," Smith Report, 9/2/47, Reagan file, HUAC.

75   *"men like Cooper"*: "Gary Cooper," Smith Report, 9/2/47.

76   *"the hard cold facts"*: "Eternal Vigilance Is the Price of Liberty" full-page ad in *HR*, 10/1/47, p. 7.

76   The building was renamed the Cannon House Office Building in 1962.

76   *"shadow-less as an operating theater"*: J. Hoberman, *An Army of Phantoms* (New York: New Press, 2011), p. 53.

76   *"in love with a bullhorn"*: Edward Dmytryk, *Odd Man Out* (Carbondale: Southern Illinois University, Press, 1996), p. 40.

76   *"bigots, racists, reactionaries"*: David Halberstam, *The Fifties* (New York: Villard, 1993), p. 12.

76   *"Ideological hermits"*: HUAC Hearings, 10/20/47, p. 10.

77   *"You could see the sweat"*: Stein, p. 71.

77   *"I cannot prove it"*: Dmytryk, p. 45.

77   *"As a writer try to get five minutes"*: Lawson was likely referring to *The General Dies at Dawn* (1936), written by Clifford Odets. Cooper plays a freedom fighter working for a popular uprising against a Chinese warlord. "Your belief is in your own very limited self," he defiantly tells the warlord. "Mine is in people. One day they'll walk on earth straight, proud, men, not animals, but with no fear of hunger or poverty." Moffitt's HUAC testimony, 10/21/47, pp. 111.

78   *"the story of a boy and girl"*: Mayer, HUAC Hearings, 10/20/47, p. 74.

78   *"The mere presentation"*: Rand, Ibid., 10/20/47, p. 87.

78   *"If I were even suspicious"*: Taylor, Ibid., 10/22/47, p. 168.

78   *"I abhor their philosophy"*: Reagan, Ibid., 10/23/47, pp. 217–8.

79   *"I believe I have noticed some"*: Cooper, Ibid., pp. 219–221.

79   *"I didn't feel it was on the level"*: Ibid., p. 224.

80   *"actors haven't any business at all"*: Meyers, p. 213.

80   *"All our hotel rooms were bugged"*: Howard Koch, *As Time Goes By* (New York: Harcourt Brace Jovanovich, 1979), p. 167.

80   *"Tell the boys not to worry"*: in Stefan Kanfer, *A Journal of the Plague Years* (New York: Atheneum, 1973), pp. 41–2.

81   *Schary suggested a variation*: See Schary p. 162, and Ceplair and Trumbo, p. 203.

82   *"an illegal and indecent trial"*: Lawson, HUAC Hearings, 10/27/47, p. 291.

82   *"a parade of stool pigeons":* Alan H. Ryskind, *Hollywood Traitors* (Washington: Regnery, 2015), p. 214.

82   *"Kill him, kill him!":* Sayre, p. 365.

82   *"A damaging impression":* Johnston, HUAC Hearings, 10/27/47, pp. 306–8.

82   *"I could answer it":* Lardner, Ibid., 10/30/47, p. 481.

84   *"I want to tell you something":* Schary, HUAC Hearings, 10/29/47, p. 472. Schary's complete testimony is on pp. 469–78.

84   *Brecht as "a good example":* Brecht, Ibid., 10/30/47, p. 504.

84   *"We will resume the hearings":* Thomas, HUAC Hearings, Ibid., p. 522.

84   *"overtones of a broken record,":* Stripling, p. 75.

85   *"to clean its own house":* Thomas, Ibid., p. 522.

85   *Johnston wasted no time:* Ceplair and Englund, pp. 328–9.

86   *"Do it, maybe they won't go crazy":* Schary, pp. 164–5.

87   *"liars, hypocrites, and thieves":* Ceplair and Trumbo, p. 217.

87   *"I was clobbered":* Schary, p. 166.

87   *"I just came over to watch":* Kanfer, p. 99.

87   *the testimony would be "sensational":* XCIV, *HR*, 42, 7/31/47, p. 1.

88   *"somehow he had managed to disappear":* Dunne, p. 198.

88   *"One of the names":* Congressional Record, 93, 7, 11/24/47, p. 10792.

88   *Waldorf Statement:* Schary, pp. 369–70.

88   *"to view them as arrogant":* Gabler, pp. 373–4.

89   *"They were frightened to death":* Ibid., p. 385.

89   *"the actual decision had been made on Wall Street":* Dunne, p. 21–2.

89   *proceeded to summon talent agents:* Ceplair, "SAG and the Motion Picture Blacklist," *National Screen Actor*, 1/88. http://www.cobbles.com/simpp_archive/linkbackups/huac_blacklist.htm#Corey%20&%20Randolph

89   *"I'm No Communist":* Photoplay, May 1948, p. 54.

89   *"You fuckers sold me out!":* Schwartz, p. 281.

89   *"How the Reds made a sucker out of me:"* Robinson, *American Legion Magazine*, 10/52.

90   *Schary "acts dazed and looks sick":* Jennifer Langdon, *Caught in the Crossfire* (New York: Columbia University Press, 2009), p. 72.

90   *"behaved cowardly and cruelly":* Schary, p. 163.

90   *"That's all they had to do":* Lillian Ross, "Come in, Lassie!" *New Yorker*, 2/21/48 p. 48.

6. The Viennese Gentleman

91   *"It is odd how one finds":* Fred Zinnemann, *A Life in the Movies* (London: Bloomsbury, 1992), p. 220.

91   *The party was wrong to cling:* CF Tape XXXV, Feb. 1978.

92   *FZ portrait:* Zinnemann, pp. 7–16, and author's interview with Tim Zinnemann.

92   *"My contribution":* As I See It, documentary film by Tim Zinnemann.

92   *"A Jew was an outsider":* Zinnemann, p. 11.

93   *Flaherty "didn't know the meaning of compromise":* Ibid., p. 25.

93   *FZ at MGM's shorts department:* The Films of Fred Zinnemann, Arthur Nolletti Jr., ed. (Albany: State University of New York Press, 1999), p. 39.

94 *"They were speechless"*: Marsha Hunt Interview , Pt. 2, Film Noir Foundation, 7/3/12, https://www.youtube.com/watch?v=JfESD_XXg9c

94 *"a lean and wiry mountain climber"*: George Stevens Jr., *Conversations with the Great Moviemakers* (New York: Vintage, 2007), p. 409.

94 *"the only person"*: Nolletti, p. 12.

94 *"a gentleman and a dictator"*: J.E. Smyth, *Fred Zinnemann and the Cinema of Resistance* (Jackson: University of Mississippi Press, 2014), p. 23.

94 *"My father had this courtly manner"*: Author's interview with Tim Zinnemann.

94 *"it doesn't strike me very funny"*: FZ letter to Minnelli, 8/28/44, FZ Papers, 106.f-1555M, MHL.

95 *"a perfectly normal, charming little boy"*: Zinnemann, pp. 53–4.

95 *"MGM was happy"*: Ibid., p. 57.

95 *"We were as on an island"*: Ibid p. 55.

96 *"Where did you find a soldier"*: Ibid., p. 69.

96 *"a major revelation"*: *NYT*, 3/24/48.

97 *"the tiny little people"*: Zinnemann, pp. 71–3.

97 *"Working in a small rental studio"*: Ibid., p. 81.

97 *"I decided I had had enough"*: Ibid., p. 77.

97 Behind the story for *The Men*: Kramer, pp. 45–6.

97 *"The wonderful thing"*: in Stevens, p. 421.

98 *"I can walk!"*: Kramer, p. 48. Also "Preparing for Paraplegia," *Life*, 6/12/50, pp. 129–132.

100 *"The courage, resolution, and compassion"*: Houston, "Kramer and Company," *Films in Review*, 1952, p. 22.

100 *"the best story in town"*: Glass letter to HH, 4/13/50, HH Papers, f. 1994, MHL.

100 *a full-page ad: HR*, 3/1/51.

101 *"the marriage has turned unhappy"*: CF Tape XXVI, Side 1, 1/23/78.

101 *newspaper and subway ads:* Schoenfeld letter to FZ, 7/11 and 7/19/50; and FZ's letter to Schoenfeld, in FZ Papers, n.d., MHL.

101 *"Not only the nose"*: CF Tape XXVI, Side 1, 1/23/78.

102 *"They were three men"*: author's interview with George Stevens Jr.

102 *"Katz was a polished, well-groomed man"*: Schary, pp. 99–100.

102 *"Nobody can be as happy"*: Eyman, *Lion*, p. 238.

103 *They called the new enterprise:* Kramer, p. 75.

103 *"Thank you very much"*: CF Tape 25/1, 1/20/78, p. 13.

103 *"vulgar, domineering, semi-literate"*: Kramer, p. 74.

104 *Stanley authorized him:* Ibid., pp. 75–6.

104 *"the most important deal we've ever made."*: Bob Thomas, *King Cohn: The Life and Times of Harry Cohn* (New York: G.P. Putnam's Sons, 1967), p. 319

7. The Falling Star

105 *"His eyes were the most fabulous shade"*: Neal, p. 89.

105 *"an Ayn Rand character"*: Friedrich, p. 398.

106 *"Cooper seems slightly pathetic"*: *NYT*, 7/9/49.

106 *"She had an amazing ability"*: Author's interview with Maria Cooper Janis.

106 Neal portrait is from *As I Am.*

107 *"a worthy adversary"*: Ibid., p. 84.

107 *"Gary was famous"*: Ibid., p. 87.

107 *"He'd been taught"*: Ibid., p. 88.

107 *"No one else mattered"*: Ibid., p. 91.

107 *"Have had one hell of a rush"*: Patricia Neal Papers, Northwestern University.

108 *"Baby, I'm sorry"*: Neal, pp. 100–1.

108 *"She was black and blue"*: Author's interview with Kirk Douglas.

108 *"My mother said to me"*: Author's interview with Maria Cooper Janis.

108 *"If I had been older and wiser"*: Neal, pp. 118–9.

109 *"Gary Cooper has always talked very freely"*: HH column, 6/3/52.

109 *"My hands were calloused"*: Ibid., 8/28/47.

109 Hopper portrait is from Hedda Hopper, *The Whole Truth and Nothing But* (New York: Doubleday, 1963), pp. 60–63.

109 *22.8 million copies:* Jennifer Frost, *Hedda Hopper's Hollywood* (New York: New York University, 2011), p. 18.

110 *"The studios created both of them"*: Amy Fine Collins, "Idol Gossips," in *Vanity Fair's Hollywood*, Carter and Friend, eds. (New York: Viking Studio, 2000), p. 152.

110 HH's hats: Ibid., p. 154.

110 *"Hi, slaves!"*: Frost, p. 50.

110 *"Duel in the Sun is sex rampant"*: HH Columns 1947: 1/3; 3/7; 3/14, MHL.

110 *"To Victor Belong the Spoils"*: HH Columns, 1947: 4/20; 9/28; 12/7/47.

110 *"Hedda, you old hop toad,"*: HH Papers, f. 940, 11/15/40, MHL

111 *"Emphasizing the negative"*: HH column, 5/21/51, HH Scrapbook 19, MHL.

112 *"She'll have a hard time"*: "Telephone conversation between HH and Cooper, May 1951," HH Papers f.940, MHL.

112 *"He's looking for happiness"*: HH column, 5/24/51.

112 *"He was operated on once"*: HH column, 8/6/51.

113 *"He just wanted to hide"*: Tender Comrades, pp. 191–2.

8. The Committee Returns

114 *"The concept of loyalty"*: Commager, "Who Is Loyal to America?" *Harper's*, 195:4168, September 1947.

114 *he wanted no printed evidence:* Ceplair and Trumbo, pp. 211–2.

115 *"It'll ruin you"*: Schwartz, p. 265.

116 *"This is a coercive way"*: Zinnemann, p. 251.

116 *Rouben Mamoulian . . . rose to say:* Robert Parrish, *Growing Up in Hollywood*, (New York: Harcourt Brace Jovanovich, 1976) p. 208. Two of the best accounts of the Screen Directors Guild meeting can be found in Parrish, pp. 201–10, and Kenneth L. Geist, *Pictures Will Talk* (New York: Scribner's, 1978), pp. 173–206, plus the De Mille/SDG f. 1 file, MHL.

117 *Five days after the meeting:* Geist, p. 205.

117 *"I had contempt for that Congress"*: Hollywood on Trial documentary.

117 *"Hey, Bolshie!"*: Lester Cole, *Hollywood Red* (Palo Alto: Ramparts, 1981), p. 317.

118 *party leaders generally warned their members:* Cogley, p. 43.

118 *"The very nature of the . . . process":* Ibid., p. 197.

118 *"routine Hollywood fare":* Ibid., p. 206.

119 *"There was no plot":* Quoted in *Red Hollywood*, a documentary film written and directed by Thom Andersen and Noel Burch that offers a compelling analysis of the impact of leftist writers on the content of the films they helped make. My account relies heavily on their original work.

119 *"Joseph P. Kennedy . . . offered to pay":* Kazin, pp. 186–7.

120 *"As time went on":* See *Red Hollywood.*

120 *"the unthinking carelessness":* Screen Guide, p. 1, MPA file 303, MHL.

121 *"Don't tell people":* Ibid., pp. 7–8 and 12.

121 *"People got scared":* Poe file, interview with William Wyler, 5/17/55, MHL.

121 *"I now read scripts":* Ross, p. 46.

122 the shelving of Hiawatha: *NYT*, 9/13/50, p. 40.

122 *"The nation was ready,"* Halberstam, p. 9.

122 *"with the firing of 'The Ten'":* "Hollywood Meets Frankenstein," *Nation,* 6/28/52.

122 *A leaked FBI report:* "FBI report names Hollywood figures." 6/8/49, www.history.com/this-day-in-history/fibi-report-names-hollywood-figures-as-communists

123 *Robinson was "an active cooperator":* Box 14, Executive Session Transcripts, Budenz, 3/14/51, p. 4. HUAC files, NARA.

123 *"My name has been besmirched":* Robinson, Ibid., 12/21/50, pp. 7 and 10.

124 *Cold war paranoia was reflected:* See "Preview of the War We Do Not Want," *Collier's,* 10/27/51.

125 *"Where Communism is concerned":* Schrecker, p. 141.

125 *"You have to forget":* Ibid., p. 146.

125 *"The paranoid spokesman sees":* Hofstadter, "The Paranoid Style in American Politics," *Harper's,* Nov. 1964.

126 *"the grapevine has it":* HR, 1/10/51, p. 2.

126 *"Many of the 568 are innocent":* Billy Wilkerson, "TradeViews," *HR,* 1/25/51, p. 2.

126 *"we'd like to suggest":* Ibid., 3/12/51, p. 2

126 Characterization of HUAC members: Frank J. Donner, *The Un-Americans* (New York: Ballantine, 1961), p. 42.

127 *"I thought he was simply gorgeous":* Betty Garrett, *Betty Garrett and Other Songs* (Lanham, Md.: Madison, 1998), p. 70.

128 *"I feel I have done nothing wrong":* Parks' quotation and the ones that follow are from HUAC Hearings into Communist Infiltration of Hollywood Motion-Picture Industry, Part 1, 3/21/1951, pp. 78–111.

129 *Joyce O'Hara . . . announced:* Variety, 3/14/51, p. 1.

129 *Slaughter Trail scenes re-shot:* Kanfer, p. 128.

129 *"I tell you frankly":* Parks, HUAC Executive Session, 3/21/51, p. 7, NARA.

130 *"It is no comfort whatsoever":* Ibid., p. 18.

130 *"When any member":* Maurice Zolotow, *Shooting Star: A Biography of John Wayne* (New York: Simon & Schuster, 1974), p. 245.

130 *"The hell with Parks":* Hollywood Variety, 3/23/51.

130 *"Why so much emphasis?":* LAT, 3/26/51.

130 *"We do not want to associate":* L.A. Evening Herald Express, 3/23/51.

131 *"more than twelve Hollywood personages"*: "12 Reported Names as Film Reds; More Stars to Talk," International News Service, *L.A. Examiner*, 3/23/51.

131 *"by mutual consent"*: Associated Press, *L.A. Times Herald*, 5/8/51, p. 3.

131 *"By going first Larry had shown"*: Garrett, p. 140

131 *"They crucified Parks"*: Author's interview with Eve Williams-Jones.

132 *Gang wrote a letter:* Gang letter to Hoover, 7/31/50; Hoover reply 8/15/50. Hayden file, HUAC files, NARA.

132 *"I feel like a bear"*: Sterling Hayden, *Wanderer* (New York: Knopf, 1963), p. 375.

132 *"they want to put on a show"*: Ibid., p. 386.

132 *"displayed like a service flag"*: Ibid., p. 388.

132 *"the stupidest, most ignorant thing"*: Hayden testimony, Part 1, 4/10/51, p. 144.

133 *"Their boundless bigotry"*: Hayden executive session transcript, 4/4/1951, p. 43, HUAC Investigative Session, executive transcripts, Box 901, NARA.

133 *"courageous and forthright"*: Ibid., p. 149.

133 *"consigned himself to oblivion"*: Ibid., pp. 389–90.

133 *"That's the bad part"*: *NYT*, 4/15/1951.

134 *"a test of character"*: Victor Navasky, *Naming Names* (New York: Viking, 1980), p. ix.

134 *"the committee is more un-American"*: Donner, p. 36.

134 *"My life is an open book"*: Garfield HUAC testimony, Part 2, 4/23/51, p. 358

135 *Garfield "did his best"*: Goodman, p. 304.

135 *the FBI had opened a file:* Larry Swindell, *Body and Soul* (New York: Morrow, 1975), p. 254.

135 *"came on like a penitent fox"*: Kanfer, p. 140.

135 *a full-page ad:* HR, 3/7/51, p. 12.

135 *"Well, today, among other things"*: Ferrer testimony, HUAC Part 3, 5/22/51, p. 574.

135 *"Not that I know of"*: Ferrer HUAC interview, 4/17/51, p. 18, Box 1334–70, NARA.

136 *"I am just wondering"*: Gordon testimony, Part 4, 9/17/51, p. 1486.

136 *"I am a much older man"*: Schoen testimony, Part 5, 9/21/51, pp. 1172, 1714.

137 *"The press does not merely mirror"*: Donner, 148.

137 *"The tradition of objectivity"*: Alan Barth, *The Loyalty of Free Men* (New York: Cardinal, 1952), p. 12.

137 *"Wipe the mud off his face:"* Ibid., p. 82.

137 *"Politically Infantile Film Folk"*: *L.A. Times Herald*, 7/30/51, p. 2.

137 See Ceplair, "Reporting the Blacklist: Anti-Communist Challenges to Elizabeth Poe Kerby," *Historical Journal of Film, Radio, and Television*, 28:2, June 2008, pp. 135–51. DOI: 10.1080/01439680802077139

138 NYT firings: Sayre, p. 221; also Gay Talese, *The Kingdom and the Power* (New York: Dell, 1981, paperback) pp. 289–95.

138 *Bert Andrews of the* NY Herald Tribune: Richard Kluger, *The Paper* (New York: Knopf, 1986), pp. 407–10, and 472–4.

139 *"People's names have been mentioned"*: Willner testimony, HUAC Part 2, 4/24/51, p. 383.

139 *Collins later said he had assumed:* Navasky, pp. 229–30.

139 *rendered her an unfit mother:* Sayre, p. 277.

140 *"I could not conceive"*: CF Tapes, XXVIIa, 1/24/78.

140 *"You're feeling kind of low"*: Dmytryk letter, 7/25/50, Dmytryk File 2.24, MHL.

140 *"I was the only director"*: Dmytryk, *Odd Man Out*, p 94.

140 *"I had to purge myself"*: Ibid., p. 152.

140 *he gave them what they wanted:* Dmytryk testimony, HUAC Part 2, 4/25/51, p. 437.

141 *"I didn't want to be a martyr"*: *Hollywood on Trial* documentary.

9. The Screenplay

142 *"Of course, the whole story"*: SK letter to Rudy Behlmer, 3/23/78, f.35, RB Papers, MHL.

142 *A United Nations representative:* Rudy Behlmer, *America's Favorite Movies* (New York: Frederick Ungar, 1982), pp. 269–70; also CF audio interview, RB Papers, MHL.

142 *"It was these events"*: "Anatomy of a Classic: *High Noon*," Series 1, p. 10, AFI.

143 *they carpooled to the studio:* Fleischer interview for *Darkness at High Noon*, 12/15/00, pp. 2–3.

143 *A draft treatment:* "High Noon," An Original Story By Carl Foreman, 1/11/50, f.43, RB Papers.

144 In a 1978 oral memoir, CF said it was his agent, Henry Lewis, who had warned him about "The Tin Star." But the Sternad version is the one CF gave in a 1952 letter to Crowther and is more contemporaneous.

144 *"You risk your life"*: Cunningham, "The Tin Star," *Collier's*, 12/6/1947.

144 For a thoughtful discussion of the contrast between the short story and the film, see Phillip Drummond, *High Noon* (London: British Film Institute, 1997), pp. 60–1.

145 *he paid Cunningham eight hundred dollars:* CF letter to SK Productions, 5/31/51, Chetwynd Files.

146 *"nothing short of a masterpiece"*: FZ, p. 96.

146 *"I had grown up with the Western"*: "Anatomy of a Classic: 2," 2/27/76, p.10.

146 *"I was simply tired"*: CF, "Virtue and a Fast Gun," *Observer Magazine*, 10/10/65.

147 *"His films were . . . authentic"*: Ibid.

147 FZ's love of Karl May: Author's interview with Tim Zinnemann.

148 *"It's a picture of conscience"*: Nolletti, p. 15.

148 *High Noon* plot details: "Some Notes About This Story," *Film Scripts Two*, George P. Garrett, ed. (Milwaukee: Applause, 2013), pp. 40–1.

148 *"if I understand my characters"*: CF, "Anatomy: 2," pp. 3 and 9, AFI.

149 *"has enjoyed the prestige"*: Character studies of Doane, Amy, Helen, and Pell appear in "*High Noon*: First Draft Outline," 1/30/51, p. 1, RB Papers.

150 *"I was trying to write some women's parts"*: CF, "Anatomy: 2," p. 24.

150 Details of Warners contract: Meyers, p. 202.

150 *"The name of Gary Cooper"*: CF Tapes, XXVII. Chetwynd Files.

150 *"Everybody felt he was old"*: Hoey audio interview with SK, USC.

151 *"My concept"*: Meyers, p. 239.

151 Most previous accounts have put Cooper's salary at $65,000. But a 12/22/52 letter from the William Morris Agency to FZ reports "Star's Salary" at $100,000. B. 33. F.429, FZ Papers, MHL.

151 Photos from New Year's Eve, etc.: see Janis, *Gary Cooper Off Camera*.

151 Salary figures are from an Inter-Office Correspondence, CF to SK, 8/29/51, f. 14, Chetwynd Files.

152 Bridges profile and testimony: 10/22/51, HUAC B. 1.180–75, pp. 6 and 8.

152 *Bridges had been best man:* Garrett, p. 72.

153 *willingness to work for . . . $750 a week:* Donald Spoto, *High Society* (New York: Harmony, 2009), p. 68.

153 *"my life as a fairy tale":* Spoto, p. 7. Other details of Grace Kelly's childhood and education are from Spoto and Robert Lacey, *Grace* (London: Sedgwick and Jackson, 1994).

154 *"beautiful in a prim sort of way":* Zinnemann, p. 100.

154 *"She was too young":* in Spoto, p. 75.

154 *"miles of empty space":* Zinnemann, p. 101.

154 the location search: Behlmer, p. 274.

155 For Crosby bio see *American Cinematographer*, 12/85, and Crosby microfiche file, MHL.

156 Details of Williams's early career: Elmo Williams, *A Hollywood Memoir* (Jefferson, N.C.: McFarland, 2006), pp. 16–17, 67–8. His decision to work on *High Noon* is from his audio interview with Rudy Belhmer, RB Papers, MHL.

156 *High Noon was not a priority:* CF letter to Crowther, 8/7/52, Chetwynd Files.

10. The Informer

158 *"The so-called 'liberals' were stunned":* Victor Riesel column, *L.A. Daily News*, 8/2/52, HH Papers f. 742, MHL.

158 *"I AM NOT NOW":* MB, 4/12/51, HUAC B.1168–70, NARA.

159 *"The reckless bigwigs":* MB, "Do we want to see scenarists behind bars?" in Navasky Papers.

159 *"Be kind to your sister":* MB, *The Sparks Fly Upward*, Act 3, Scene 3, p. 42, MB Papers, UCLA.

159 *"It's been so empty":* MB, *Obsession*, pp. 10–11, MB Papers.

159 *"racing like the wind":* MB, *Will James' Sand*, 6/12/48, pp. 118, MB Papers.

159 *led . . . Lardner . . . to the observation:* Sayre, p. 333.

160 *"rather weakly handsome":* *Tender Comrades*, p. 122–3.

160 *"never written a great movie":* Author's interview with Bill Berkeley.

160 Collins's memories of MB: Collins Executive Session, HUAC, 4/13/1951. NARA.

161 *"Berkeley had asked Collins":* Wheeler memo, MB file, HUAC, 5/14/51, NARA.

161 *"The Committee has . . . strong evidence":* Tavenner HUAC memo, 7/9/51.

161 *"the most important witness":* Wheeler to Tavenner, HUAC, 8/6/51.

161 *"a group of marooned sailors":* Cogley, p. 92.

162 *Carl . . . decided to begin:* Behlmer, p. 279.

162 *"I honestly don't remember":* CF, "Anatomy: 1," p. 27, AFI.

162 *summary of* High Noon: Script with FZ's notes, FZ Papers, MHL.

168 *a pleasant young man:* CF Tape VI, Side 2, p. 4, Chetwynd Files.

168 *"Who do you suppose":* CF letter to Crowther, p. 4.

169 *"No hero me, and no saint":* Ibid.

169 *Glass revealed that he, too, had been subpoenaed:* CF Tape, XXVII-B. Also see CF letter, p. 5.

170 *"It was now happening to me":* CF audio interview with Behlmer, MHL.

171 *"I'm not leaving the picture":* CF Tape, XXVII-B.

171 *Do you have a lawyer?:* Ibid.

171 *his clients never initiated:* Navasky interview with Gang, p. 2, n.d., Navasky Papers, NYU.

171 *Martin Gang profile:* Oral History by Stephen Lesser, 7/28/75, p. 9, Dorot Collection, NYPL.

172 *"Even when the big studios":* Ibid., pp. 20–1.

172 *"Movie people are like everybody else":* Ibid., p. 89.

172 *"The industry expert":* Gabler, p. 376.

172 *"they're human beings":* Navasky interview, p. 12.

172 *Wheeler . . . was "a nice man":* Ibid., p. 37.

173 *"I didn't like the committee":* Gang Oral History, p. 80, Dorot, NYPL.

173 *"It was such a cowardly thing":* CF Tape XXVII-B, Side 2.

173 *"He had set out to frighten me":* CF Tape XXXVII-A.

174 *"one of the twelve most important":* Wheeler Memo, 4/11/51. HUAC file, NARA.

174 Rossen profile is from Alan Casty, *Robert Rossen* (Jefferson, N.C.: McFarland, 2013), and Paul Buhle and Dave Wagner, *A Very Dangerous Citizen* (Berkeley: University of California, 2001), pp. 110–11.

174 *"Now I had inherited Bob":* CF Tape 24 (2) 1/20/78) P. 6.

174 *Cohn . . . agreed to represent Carl:* CF Tape VI, 12/21/77, p. 9.

175 *"You will beat them":* Ibid., p. 2.

175 *diminished Fifth and "you can't win":* "Dialogue on Film: Carl Foreman," *American Film*, 4/79, p. 36.

175 *"Always bear in mind":* CF Tape VI, p. 5.

11. Citizen Kane

176 *"Morality, we are told":* Navasky, *Naming Names*, p. 427.

176 *"We worked together beautifully":* CF letter to Crowther, p. 5.

176 *"It soon became obvious":* Ibid., p. 4.

176 *problems with the location shoot:* Michael F. Blake, *Code of Honor* (Lanham, Md.: Taylor, 2003), has the best and most detailed description of the various sets.

177 Columbia Ranch history: Steven Bingen. *Warner Bros.: Hollywood's Ultimate Backlot* (Lanham, Md.: Taylor, 2014), p. 224.

177 *Guilty by Suspicion* set: Ibid., p.235.

178 *"We agreed . . . we would do nothing":* Interview with Crosby, f.43, RB Papers.

178 *"The makeup men were busy":* Blake, p. 20.

178 *time would finally stand still:* Zinnemann, p. 109.

179 FZ's personal script is in f.420 of FZ Papers, MHL.

180 *"Working fast is very helpful":* Nolletti, p. 29.

180 *Cooper attends rehearsals:* Behlmer, p. 277.

181 *"I was searching":* Hoey audio interview with Bridges, 1/15/74, USC.

181 *"It seemed that the odds":* CF, "Anatomy: 3," p. 28.

182 *"Everything was first take":* Crosby's memories are from Lawrence Suid interview, 7/22/78, pp. 13–15. SUID, 1974–78, Box 127, MHL.

182 *Lighting problems:* Suid interview: Crosby, p. 20. Hoey audio interview: SK.

183   *a huge Chapman crane:* http://www.chapman-leonard.com/history

183   *"It's a pull-back-and-up":* Suid interview: Crosby, p. 12, MHL.

183   *"You could be a pretty good director":* Zinnemann, p. 110.

184   *Stanley felt compelled to "hedgehop":* Hoey interview with SK at USC.

184   *a letter from [Stanley] to Carl:* Chetwynd Files, 9/14/51.

184   *"Floyd stood his ground":* Zinnemann, pp. 101–2.

184   *"It was supposed to be shot":* Hoey interview with SK, USC.

184   *"He seemed not to be acting":* Kramer, p. 70.

185   *"he was not my favorite":* Wagner, pp. 291, 294.

185   *"He made it so easy": The Making of High Noon* documentary.

185   *"She was miscast":* Spoto, p. 69.

185   *"From the very first day":* CF letter to Crowther, p. 6, Chetwynd Files.

186   *"We seemed to buck each other":* Ibid.

186   *"I think it stinks":* Glass's HUAC executive session testimony: 9/5/51, p.15, NARA.

186   *The atmosphere got colder:* CF Tape XXVIII-A.

187   *Carl was summoned to another meeting:* CF Letter, p. 6.

187   *"You are hereby further instructed":* SK letter, 9/12/51, Chetwynd Files.

187   *"This was not my idea":* CF Tape XXVIII-A.

187   *"Tomorrow . . . I want you to go":* Ibid.

188   *Stanley went to Zinnemann, Cooper, and Church:* Ibid. Also, CF Letter, p. 7.

188   *"neither we nor you":* SK letter to Foreman, 9/14/51, Chetwynd Files.

188   *"Well, you've won":* CF Tape XXVIII-A.

189   *"Let's fight as long as we can":* CF, "Anatomy: 1," p. 26.

189   *Stanley had reason to be anxious:* see "Announcement of Courses," Spring Term (1947), People's Educational Center, CF file, HUAC, NARA.

189   *"the Kramer outfit is Red":* M. A. Jones Memo, re: SK, 2/7/55, p. 4. FBI files.

189   *"there was this veil of unspoken ideas":* Navasky, pp. 159–160.

190   *"My only problem with his stand":* Kramer, p. 86.

190   *He and I had a sad parting":* Ibid., pp. 87.

12. "Bombshells"

191   *"I am not going to hang anybody":* LAT, 9/20/51, p. 8.

192   *"If you name any names":* Ibid., p. 1.

192   *"a moment of panic":* MB testimony, HUAC, Part 4, 9/19/51, p. 1577.

192   *"His job was so good":* Ibid., p. 1581.

192   *"I will not mention a name":* Ibid., p. 1582.

192   *"My dad was not cruel":* Author's interview with Bill Berkeley.

192   *Jerome . . . objectives:* MB testimony, p. 1584.

192   *"that very excellent playwright":* Ibid., p. 1586.

193   *"the grand Poo-Bah":* Ibid., p. 1590.

193   *And then Carl Foreman:* Ibid., 1599. Remaining quotes are from MB testimony, pp. 1595–1612.

194   *"What you have done":* MB Executive Session, 9/19/51, p. 7, NARA.

196   *He heard Cooper call after him:* CF letter to Crowther, p. 8.

196   *"Do what you have to do":* CF Tape XXVIII-B.

13. The Witness

197 *"I have already told you"*: CF testimony, HUAC: Part 5, p. 1756.

197 *Foreman had a persistent daydream*: CF Tape, XXVIII-B. Chetwynd Files.

197 *"We were together"*: Word Into Image: Carl Foreman documentary.

197 *"a very sincere tie"*: Ibid.

198 *"It is a suspense story"*: CF testimony, p. 1755.

199 *Wheeler was . . . whispering in his ear*: CF Tapes XXVIII-B, p. 27.

199 *"I hope you will believe this"*: CF testimony, p. 1765.

200 *"I personally will place no credence"*: Ibid., p. 1768. Other quotes are from CF Testimony.

201 *Katz had told Losey*: Ceplair, "Shedding Light on *Darkness at High Noon*," *Cineaste*, Fall 2002, p. 21.

202 *"There is a total disagreement"*: United Press report, *Washington Post*, 9/26/51.

202 *He called the office*: CF Tape, XXVIII-B.

202 *"They didn't wait the sixty days"*: CF "Anatomy: 1," p. 26. BFI.

202 *MPIC announced*: L.A. Mirror, 9/26/51.

202 *"it's obvious he's got to go"*: CF Tape, XXIX-A, p. 2.

203 *"The . . . countryside was ravishingly beautiful"*: FZ, p. 106.

203 *"the engine's brakes were failing"*: FZ, p. 102.

204 *"People go to a Western"*: CF, "Anatomy: 3," pp. 21–2.

204 *"Stanley liked it"*: Ibid., p. 22.

204 *Fred insisted that he had hated the sub-plot*: FZ, pp. 106 and 110.

204 *Carl supports Williams's claim*: 1982 letter from CF to Elmo Williams, p. 3. Chetwynd files.

205 *"My father did not tell me"*: Jordan Riefe, "The fabulous Bridges boys," 8/11/14, http://www.theguardian.com/film/filmblog/2014/aug/11/hollywood-celebrates-beau-and-jeff-bridges#img-1

205 *"He was a sweet man"*: The Making of High Noon documentary.

205 *"He was wonderful to work with"*: Author's interview with Roberta Haynes.

205 *"she was very serious"*: Cooper interview, 1955, HH Papers, f.980, MHL

205 *"She fills a much needed gap"*: Ibid., p. 12.

206 *"He's the one who taught me"*: George Scullin, "Grace Kelly: The Girl Who Dares to Do the Forbidden and Get Away with It!" Kelly File, NYPL.

206 *"Grace almost always laid the leading man"*: Gene Sheppard "Grace Kelly: Hollywood's Tarnished Princess," *Hollywood Studio Magazine*, 20:11, 11/87.

206 *"I was used to being snubbed"*: Neal, pp. 122–3.

206 *Grace's sister Lizanne tagged along*: Lacey, p. 118.

206 *"It's good to be skeptical"*: Author's interview with Jeanine Basinger.

207 *"I used to work with her a lot"*: CF: "Anatomy: 2," p. 68.

207 *"I wanted a Mexican gal"*: Hoey interview with SK, USC.

207 *Jurado profile*: "Jurado, Katy," *Latinas in the United States: A Historical Encyclopedia*. Vicki L. Ruiz and Virginia Sanchez Korrol, vol. 2. (Bloomington: Indiana University, 2006), p. 358.

207 *"You look into Gary Cooper's face"*: Spoto, p. 75.

208 *"All I do is use my instinct"*: Nolletti, p. 17.

208 Planning for the gunfight: "The Choreography of a Gunfight," *Sight and Sound*, 22:1, 7–9/52, pp. 16–17.

209 Comparative costs of *High Noon* and *Shane*: Blake, pp. 105–6.

209 *"One or two secretaries . . . dropped in"*: CF letter to Crowther, p. 9.

14. The Exile

210 *"I was convinced of Foreman's loyalty"*: in "Gary Cooper to Stay Out of Film Deal" by Hedda Hopper, *LAT*, 11/2/51.

210 *"differences of opinion"*: Agreement between Stanley Kramer Productions and Carl Foreman, 10/22/51, Chetwynd Files.

210 *Carl and Cohn later put the final figure*: CF Tape, XXIX-A, 1/27/78. Various accounts in earlier books have put the settlement amount at $250,000, but have presented no documentation.

211 *"what are you doing here, Bud?"*: CF Tape, XXVI, Side 2.

211 *Gang wrote letters:* Gang to Roy M. Brewer, 4/14/53, Navasky Papers, NYU.

212 *"Didn't work for several years"*: Maltin, *The Making of High Noon*.

212 *"they would certainly need the money"*: CF Tape XXVIII-B, pp. 16–17.

212 *Chamberlin got $750:* SK Co. Inter-Office Correspondence, 8/29/51, Chetwynd.

212 *"Both . . . had been named"*: 1943 Tenney Report, p. 150. LOC. See also "Information from the Files of the Committee on Un-American Activities . . . on Mary Virginia Farmer," Farmer HUAC file, NARA.

212 *"My present occupation is an actor"*: Chamberlin and Wood's exchange, HUAC Hearings, Part 4, 9/18/51, pp. 1505–7

213 *Wood cut her off:* HUAC Hearings, Part 5, 9/21/51, p. 1737.

213 *"Never have I felt . . . so deservedly"*: "Statement of Mary Virginia Farmer," www.eaglesweb.com/MVF-to-HUAC.htm

213 *"Hitherto I had been quite busy"*: Corey Testimony, HUAC Hearings, Part 5, 9/21/51, p. 1733.

213 *"All I had to do"*: Bob Thomas, "Jeff Corey Is Back from 10 Year Exile," Associated Press, published in the *LA Examiner*, 1/20/61.

214 *"I don't know if it was a blacklist"*: Lawrence H. Suid interview with Crosby, 7/22/78, p. 27, FZ Papers, b.127, MHL.

214 *"Crosby was . . . not a Communist"*: "Floyd Crosby," *Internet Encyclopedia of Cinematographers*, www.cinematographers.nl/GreatDoPh/crosby.htm

214 *Foreman . . . was forming his own production company: Daily Variety*, 10/25/51.

214 *"Use my name,"*: Meyers, p. 248.

215 *"It's not a gesture"*: CF Tape, XXIX-A.

215 *"You mustn't let him down"*: Meyers, p. 248.

215 *Chadwick and Trilling's warnings: Daily Variety*, 10/31/51.

215 *Jack Warner had called him:* CF Tape XXVI, Side 2.

215 *"Was Wayne pressuring him?"* Author's interview with Maria Cooper Janis.

215 *"I'm amazed to hear"*: HH Column, *LAT*, 10/30/51.

215 *"My only desire, Miss Hopper"*: CF Telegram, 10/30/51, HH Papers.

216 *"Okay, Mr. Foreman, that is $32 worth"*: HH Column, *LAT*, 11/1/51.

216 *"My opinion of Foreman has not changed,"*: *LAT*, 11/2/51.

216 *"Gary Cooper is the finest kind of an American":* Stuart Kaminsky, Coop (New York: St. Martin's Press, 1980), p. 175.

216 *"I don't care what Joe Ferrer says":* CF Tape XXXV, 2/6/78.

217 *Carl told Wayne:* CF Tape XXIX-A.

217 *"shoot the wounded":* Garry Wills, *John Wayne's America* (New York: Simon & Schuster, 1997), p. 197.

217 *Carl had one . . . meeting . . . with Martin Berkeley:* CF Tape, XXIX-B, 1/27/78.

218 *"Maybe you ought to go":* CF Tape VI, 12/21/77, p. 8.

219 *"My partners . . . saw their own futures":* CF interview, 4/59, p. 17, Columbia University Center for Oral History Collection.

219 *"If they'd taken a stand":* Author's interview with Walter Bernstein.

219 *"There's no underestimating":* Author's interview with George Stevens Jr.

219 *Carl booked a one-way passage:* CF Tapes, XXX-A and B.

220 *"I can write my own ticket here":* CF letter to FZ, 8/5/52, FZ Papers B.103.

220 *"I make terrible pictures":* CF Tape XXX-B.

220 *"every page was agony":* CF Tape XXXI-A.

221 *"I had it very bad":* "Dialogue on Film: Carl Foreman," *American Film*, 4/79.

221 *"I finally got tired":* CF letter to Crowther, 8/7/52, p. 10.

221 *"It's nice to be wanted":* Ibid., p. 11.

221 *"What's happening?":* CF Tape XXX-B.

221 *"The whole fabric of one's existence":* CF Tape XXIX-B, 1/27/78.

15. The Music Men

222 *the subplot with Toby:* FZ has implied that he did not include these scenes in his rough cut, but both Carl Foreman and Elmo Williams say he did.

222 *"I was terribly disappointed":* Kramer, p. 73.

222 *"He intimated to me":* Williams audio interview. RB Papers, MHL.

223 *"Every time you left Cooper":* Ibid.

223 *"I went out and shot":* Williams interview, *Darkness at High Noon*, 11/29/00, Tape 1. Williams in his memoirs, published in 2006 when he was 93, also claims CF flew to Washington to testify twice before a Senate committee and fled to London after his second appearance. These "facts" are wrong.

223 *"Stanley's talking to George":* audio interview with Williams, RB Papers, MHL.

223 Two of the more imaginative versions of Williams's tale can be found in Ronald L. Davis, *The Glamor Factory* (Dallas: Southern Methodist University, 1993), pp. 280–2; and Geraldine Fabrikant, "Grace on the Cutting Floor," *New Times*, 3/18/1977.

224 *"I hate to defend myself":* Williams interview for *Darkness at High Noon*.

224 *"Now Elmo was a very good editor":* Hoey audio interview with SK, USC.

224 *"I was certainly aghast":* Spoto, *Stanley Kramer*, p. 103.

224 *Stanley claims it was he, not Williams:* Ibid., p. 73.

224 *"Kramer did not cut . . . the picture":* Suid interview with Elmo Williams, 8/2/78, p. 1, B.127, FZ Papers, MHL.

225 *"He cut it brutally":* CF Letter to Crowther, p. 10.

225 *"Elmo Williams is . . . the most creative editor":* Ibid.

225 *In a 1982 letter:* Chetwynd Files.

225 *"the demon editor"*: CF letter to Arthur Knight, 7/12/82, Chetwynd Files.

225 *"wanting to avoid unpleasant . . . disputes"*: FZ letter to Maria Cooper Janis, 6/14/88, quoted in *Inside High Noon* documentary.

226 *"Music has always produced"*: Dimitri Tiomkin and Prosper Buranelli, *Please Don't Hate Me*, (Garden City, N.Y.: Doubleday, 1959) p. 10. Tiomkin profile and account that follows is based largely on the book.

226 *the Homeless Dog:* Ibid., p. 26.

227 *"like loving a beautiful woman"*: Ibid 121.

227 *"Walk like a man"*: Ibid., p. 122–3.

227 *When Tiomkin won an Oscar:* Christopher Palmer, *The Composer in Hollywood*, (London: T.E. Books, 1984), p. 118.

227 *"Having always been harassed"*: Ibid., p. 211.

228 *"I remember that he wept"*: Zinnemann, p. 85.

228 *compares Tiomkin's scores:* Palmer, pp. 120–1.

228 *"It isn't orgasm music"*: David Thomson, *Showman: The Life of David O. Selznick* (New York: Knopf, 1992,) p. 465.

229 Williams's use of temp tracks: See "The Relevance of Temp Tracks," http://www. epicsound.com/resources/temptracks/

229 *"I find in cutting"*: Behlmer audio interview with Williams, RB Papers..

229 *"I am not cowboy"*: in Williams, p. 84.

230 *"looked like the ugliest duckling"*: Tiomkin, p. 230. The account that follows: pp. 230–4.

230 *"Do Not Forsake Me"*: Lyrics by Ned Washington, Music by Dimitri Tiomkin, c. 1952 (renewed) Volta Music Corp. Catherine Hinen and Patti Washington Music. All Rights Reserved. Used by permission.

230 *"The song at first glance"*: Deborah Allison, "Do Not Forsake Me: The Ballad of High Noon and the Rise of the Movie Theme Song," *Cinema and Music*, October 2003. http://senseofcinema.com/2003/cinema-and-msuic/ballad_of_high_noon/

232 *profile of Tex Ritter:* see O'Neal, *Tex Ritter*. (Austin: Eakin Press, 1998).

232 Ibid., p. 34.

233 *"Tex and his cowboys nearly fell"*: Tiomkin, p. 270.

233 *"It wasn't supposed to be"*: O'Neal, p. 103.

233 *"The song . . . is the story line"*: "*High Noon* Theme Sets Mood and Tells Story," *Billboard*, 64:25, 6/21/52, p. 20. Author's italics.

234 *they summoned Ritter:* O'Neal, p. 103.

234 *"the only version . . . that ever rang true"*: Ibid.

234 *"Tiomkin was very irritated"*: Hoey interview with SK. This account matches Kramer's versions in *Mad Mad Mad Mad World*, pp. 71–2, and Spoto, pp. 103–4.

235 *"what does a European Jew know?"* Author's interview with Tim Zinnemann.

235 *"What are you upset about?"* Hoey interview with SK.

16. The Process

236 *"I can tell in five minutes"*: LAT, 9/23/06.

237 *"no talent whatever is hired"*: COMPIC memo, FBI LA Bureau, 100-15732, 11/30/54, p. 5, Leab microfilm.

237 *"I was blacklisted, I knew why"*: Dmytryk, pp. 179–180.

237 *The American Legion played an important role:* Cogley, pp. 124–7.

237 For an excellent account of how the blacklist and graylist functioned, see Ceplair, "SAG and the Motion Picture Blacklist," in *National Screen Actor*, 1/88.

238 *"I think Maltz hit the nail":* Hopper column, *LAT* 5/31/51.

238 *Berkeley met regularly:* FBI COMPIC memo, 12/12/52, p. 14. Leab Microfilm.

238 *"Reagan and I spent countless hours":* Brewer, "Hollywood Whitewash of the Cold War's Shameful Red Stain," *LAT*, 2/6/02.

239 *Reagan . . . met his future wife:* Reagan, *An American Life*, pp. 121–3.

239 *more than five hundred people:* See Ceplair, "SAG and the Motion Picture Blacklist."

239 *Sokolsky . . . personally had helped:* Daily Variety, 92, no. 26, 7/12/56.

239 *"Our work will never finish":* MB column, *LA Daily News*, 8/2/52.

239 *"I am back on Freedom Road":* MB letter to HH, 9/22/51, HH Papers.

239 *"Believe me I'll tell them":* MB letter to HH, 8/3/52.

239 Berkeley names 21 more: see MB Executive Session, 1/29/52, HUAC Box 19 NARA.

240 *"And it would do your hearts good":* Ibid, pp. 2–3.

240 *"I cannot get a job":* Ibid., p. 7.

240 *"Ask yourself how many":* "Berkeley Charges Blacklisting by Reds Against Anti-Commies" n.d. Chetwynd file.

240 *"Berkeley is disgusted":* Wheeler HUAC memo to Russell, 11/7/51, NARA.

241 *"handled the producers with kid gloves":* MB letter to Wheeler, 1/7/52, HUAC.

241 *"If the Navy is eliminating this boy":* Wheeler letter, 7/12/53, HUAC.

241 *accusing . . . congressmen:* MB "Red Congressmen?" *American Mercury*, 12/53.

241 *"The backbone of the Communist movement":* MB, "Reds in Your Living Room," *American Mercury*, 8/53.

241 *"shocked beyond words":* Huston letter to Hogan, 8/23/52, f. 1100, Huston Papers, MHL.

242 *"If I accepted his offer":* Dunne, p. 215.

242 *"Metro Goldwyn Moscow":* Schary, p. 209.

242 Hoover remained skeptical: FBI memo, SAC Los Angeles to Director, 1/2/51. FBI files, MHL.

242 *"What about Communists?"* HH, "Man with a Mission," *Chicago Sunday Tribune*, 7/27/52 Scrapbook 19, HH Papers, MHL.

242 *"a bitter and cynical hope":* The Hoaxters, LOC Motion Picture Collection.

243 *"A heavy cost in courage":* Schary, p. 241.

243 *"a vaporous and reckless romance":* NYT, 9/18/52.

244 *"it seethes with . . . emotionalism":* NYT, 4/9/52.

245 *"undoubtedly the greatest":* Hoberman, p. 195.

245 *"The answer is no":* Matthews, "Did the Movies Really Clean House?" *American Legion Magazine*, 12/51.

245 *"sickeningly accurate":* HH column, *LAT*, 11/28/51. In 1953 Matthews was named executive director of Senator Joseph McCarthy's investigating subcommittee, but he was forced to resign after it was revealed he had written an article claiming 7,000 Protestant ministers were "party members, fellow travelers, espionage agents, party-line adherents, and unwitting dupes." See Cogley, pp. 122–3.

245 *"You'll never work in films again":* Interview with Marsha Hunt, 6/13/55, in E. P. Kerby papers, f.6, MHL; see also *Tender Comrades*, pp. 319–20.

17. The Movie

247 *"I'm going to go back":* John Wayne on Oscar night, 1953.

247 *George J. Schaefer profile: NYT,* 8/11/81.

247 *"A basic Western formula": Variety,* 4/29/52.

248 *its leaders were desperate:* Behlmer, p. 288.

248 *"Every five years or so": NYT,* 7/25/52.

249 *"'Do you know how good this is?'":* Hoey audio interview with SK, 10/3/73.

249 *"an American movie achievement": New York Herald Tribune,* 12/28/52.

249 *"a taut, sense-making horse opera": Time,* 7/14/52.

249 *box office achievements:* Blake, p. 39.

249 *$2.5 million in eighteen weeks:* Drummond, pp. 41–43.

249 *It became the eighth biggest: Variety,* 1/7/53.

249 For Cooper's earnings, see Meyers, pp. 249–50.

249 *"It's a great movie":* Author's interview with Leonard Maltin.

251 *"Look, no one is there":* Lyman, "A Boy Shaped by *High Noon," NYT,* 3/30/01.

253 *"Cooper is not just . . . Will Kane":* in Janis, *Gary Cooper Off Camera,* p. 6.

253 *"Dear Freddy":* f.428, FZ Papers, MHL.

253 *"a subtle attack":* Gwendolyn Foster, "The Women in High Noon," *Film Criticism,* Spring/Fall 1994, p. 80.

254 *"The close-up is how":* Author's interview with Charles Ramirez Berg.

254 *"What surprises us in retrospect":* Foster, p. 80.

255 *"It is the women who control":* Joanna E. Rapf, "Myth, Ideology, and Feminism in *High Noon," Journal of Popular Culture,* Spring 1990, p. 79.

255 *"As lines of age have come":* Robert Warshow, *The Immediate Experience* (Garden City, N.Y.: Doubleday, 1962), p. 143.

255 *"a pathetic rather than a tragic figure":* Ibid., p. 149.

256 *"I don't think a good sheriff":* McCarthy, *Howard Hawks* (New York: Grove Press, 1997), pp. 548–9.

256 *"runner-up" . . . "most overrated Western":* Andrew Sarris, "Western," *American Heritage,* 50, no.3, 5/99, p71. Sarris's most overrated Western was *Cimarron* (1931), the first to win an Oscar for best picture.

256 *"external and shallow": Howard Hawks: American Artist,* Hillier and Wollen, eds. (London: BFI, 1996), p. 33.

256 "High Noon *is not a Western":* Zinnemann, p. 67.

257 *"There was little regard":* Charles Silver, "Fred Zinnemann's *High Noon,"* www. moma.org/explore/inside_out/2012/05/15/fred-zinnemanns-high-noon

257 *"an expression of the genre":* Michael Selig, *"High Noon," Cinema Texas Program Notes,* 16, no. 2, 2/28/79.

257 For an entertaining summation of *High Noon's* bastard cinematic children, see David Thomson, "The Winding Road of the Western Hero," *NYT,* 8/20/00.

258 *"I saw no parallel":* Gavin Barrie interview with FZ, THE MOVIES, Museum of Modern Art, Job No. 5627/0188, p. 21.

259 *"a drama of one man's bravery": NYT,* 8/3/1952.

259 *"There must be times":* "Darkness at *High Noon," The Nation,* 176:2, 1/10/53.

259 *Pravda's* dismissal of *High Noon:* Jeremy Byman, *Showdown at High Noon* (Lanham, Md.: Scarecrow Press, 2004), p. 22.

259 an "inflated archetype": NYT, 5/22/07, p. E3.

259 "What convinces in High Noon": NYT, 7/13/12.

260 Variety, 3/18/53, quoted in Byman, p. 24.

260 "People were not really talking": NYT, 3/30/01.

260 "Looks to Sweep": Variety, 3/18/53.

260 "This is a rather stupid argument": HR, 3/16/53.

261 "We feel that the continued employment": Tino Balio, United Artists (Madison: University of Wisconsin, 1987), p. 55.

261 written reports to "Owen": David N. Eldridge, "'Dear Owen': The CIA, Luigi Luraschi, and Hollywood, 1953," Historical Journal of Film, Radio, and Television, 20:2, 2000.

262 "none of the Kramer boys": HR, 3/20/53.

262 "spectacular but old-fashioned": NYT, 3/29/53.

262 "I still believe High Noon was the best": Kramer, p. 73.

263 "I'm over here in London": CF Tape IV, p. 7.

18. Writer's Block

264 "Carl couldn't get home": Estelle Foreman interview, Darkness at High Noon, 1/17/01, p. 25. Chetwynd Files.

265 "Carl was kind of a different man": Ibid., p. 28.

265 "It's a cowardly business": Author's interview with Jonathan Foreman.

265 By the end of the night: CF Tape 1, Part Two, BFI.

265 "I felt it was important": Ibid.

265 "Carl changed completely": Navasky interview with Estelle Foreman, 2/24/74.

266 Dealings with the Rank Organisation: CF Tape, XXXI-A.

266 An FBI memo: Memo 100-35625, 5/22/53, CF FBI file.

266 "It was obvious": CF Tape XXXI-A.

266 Levy, Roberts, Shor, and Lang: See Memo from SAC, FBI LA bureau, to Hoover, 7/23/53, CF FBI file.

266 "I felt terribly guilty": CF Tape VI, p. 11.

266 "He couldn't live with the fact": CF Tape XXX-B.

266 "He was a very lucid": CF Tape XXXI-A.

267 "Carl, I'm your friend": Author's interview with Kirk Douglas.

267 For a colorful and affectionate portrait of salon life at the Stewart-Wynter house, see Sayre, Previous Convictions, pp. 303–27.

267 "The English assumed": Ibid., p. 325.

267 "I didn't want to be part": CF Tape 1, Part Two, BFI.

267 "He handled himself magnificently": Sidney Cohn Interview, CF Tape 1, BFI.

268 Carl "was extraordinarily warm": Michel Ciment, Conversations with Losey (London: Methuen, 1985), p. 133.

268 "That kept me alive": Ibid., p. 107.

268 Evading Lela and Ginger Rogers: David Caute, Joseph Losey, (London: Faber and Faber, 1994), pp. 121–2.

269 Barrymore had been pressured: Ibid., p. 107.

269 "The English market wanted": Ciment, p. 134.

269 one of . . . Walter's favorite films: Cohn, CF Tape 1, 2/17/77, Part 3, p. 5.

269 *"reason to believe"*: David Caute, *The Great Fear* (New York: Simon & Schuster, 1978), p. 245.

270 *The panel relied on confidential information*: Ibid., p. 245–6.

270 *the appeals board upheld the decision*: "Memo for Case of Carl Nathan Foreman and Estelle Barr Foreman," Passport Security Program, 10/4/56, HUAC Individual Name Files, Box 19. NARA.

270 *turn down . . .* War and Peace*: Rebecca Prime, *Hollywood Exiles in Europe* (New Brunswick: Rutgers, 2014), p. 70.

270 *"self-pity and rage"*: CF Tape, XXX-B.

270 *A civil servant listened carefully:* CF Tape VI, pp. 20–1.

271 *A judge ruled:* "Film Writer Wins Battle," *NYT*, p. 4, 1/14/56.

271 *"Paris was worth a mass"*: CF Tape V-A, 12/20/77, pp. 10–11.

271 *Williams said he would charge:* Evan Thomas, *The Man to See* (New York: Simon & Schuster, 1992), p. 73.

271 *Cohn set up a meeting:* CF Tape 1, Part 3, pp. 3–4.

272 *"He'll tell you all about it"*: Ibid.

19. The Return

273 *"I had and have strong convictions"*: "Testimony of Carl Nathan Foreman," HUAC Executive Sessions, 8/8/56, p. 3, NARA.

273 *"a very unimportant little fellow"*: Ibid p. 10.

274 *"I entered the party"*: Ibid., p. 16. Subsequent quotes are from pp. 16–32.

274 Cohn would later claim that the comittee had drastically edited the transcript. CF Tape 1, Part 3.

274 *eventually Cohn received a transcript:* CF Tape 1, 12/17/77, Part 4, p. 1.

276 *"The artfully worded statement"*: *NYT*, 3/11/57; see also Paul Jacobs, "Good Guys, Bad Guys, and Congressman Walter," *The Reporter*, 5/15/58.

276 *a glittering party:* Prime, p. 205.

276 *"to probe a report"*: HR, 3/14/57, p. 2.

276 *"If Foreman can get away with it"*: "Anti-Communist Front Is Crumbling in the Entertainment World," *Guardpost for Freedom*, VFW, 4:4, 4/1/57, pp. 1–2.

276 *"until he testifies"*: *American Legion Firing Line*, VI:14, 7/15/57.

277 *"not a formal hearing"*: "Statement by Rep. Francis E. Walter," 6/12/57, HUAC.

277 *"I wasn't interested"*: Jacobs, p. 31.

277 *"Nobody in the world"*: *LA Examiner*, 6/3/57.

277 *"There was no proof"*: Walter Bernstein, *Inside Out* (New York: Knopf, 1996), p. 261.

277 *"he made statements,"*: in Navasky, p. 164.

277 *"Obviously there was corruption"*: Ibid, p. 393.

278 *His old friend Hy Kraft:* Hy Kraft, *On My Way to the Theater* (New York: Macmillan, 1971), p. 173.

278 *"he stooled"*: Author's (brief) telephone interview with Norma Barzman.

278 *"They were both island races"*: CF, "Dialogue on Film," *American Film*, April 1979.

278 *He bought a six-month option:* CF Tape XXXI-A.

279 *"To me the ending is confusing"*: Ibid., pp. 37–8.

279 *"The consequence of these hearings"*: Joseph McBride, "A Very Good American," *Written By*, February 2002.

280 *"Now that's the sixty-four-thousand-dollar question"*: Kevin Brownlow, *David Lean: A Biography* (New York: St. Martin's Press, 1996), p. 388.

280 *Carl announced . . . in London:* "Kwai His Script, Says CF," United Press, 3/26/57.

280 *the Academy "had added a new trick"*: "My Life on the Blacklist," *SEP*, 10/14/61.

281 *"our bloody Oscar"*: Miranda J. Banks, *The Writers* (New Brunswick, N.J.: Rutgers University, 2015), p. 115.

281 *"a custody arrangement"*: Anthony Holden, *The Oscars* (London: Warner Books, 1994), p. 214.

281 $250,000 for Carl, $10,000 for Wilson: Brownlow, pp. 387–8.

281 *a one-on-one session with Hedda Hopper:* CF Tape XXXI-A.

282 *"the most un-American thing"*: *Playboy*, May 1971, p. 82.

282 *"Wayne's . . . senile maunderings"*: *Today's Cinema*, 5/16/71, Item 42. Personal Clippings, CF Collection, BFI.

282 *"I was in the counting house" and subsequent quotes:* CF, "On the Wayne," *Punch*, 8/14/74, pp. 240–42.

283 *"He decided we should move back"*: Navasky interview with Estelle Foreman, 2/24/74, Navasky Papers.

284 *"He was very acerbic"*: Author's interview with Eve Williams-Jones.

284 *"I am indeed very happy"*: CF letter to Claude Inverdane, 9/24/65, Part 6, Articles and Correspondence 1965, CF Collection, BFI.

284 *"That's London"*: "Carl Foreman's London," *Saturday Review*, 8/16/69.

284 *"It took me a long, long time"*: "My Land of Hope and Glory," John London interview with CF, *Evening News*, 5/27/72.

284 *"He recovered but the damage"*: Author's interview with Jonathan Foreman.

284 *"He was a mordant man"*: Author's interview with Lionel Chetwynd.

285 *" it was the opposite of* High Noon*"*: *Word Into Image: Carl Foreman*.

285 *"On a technical level"*: "The Road to The Victors," *Films & Filming*, 9:12, 9/63.

285 *"It is galling to me"*: Ibid.

286 CF meeting with Churchill: Amanda and Jonathan Foreman, "Our Dad Was No Commie," *New Statesman*, 3/26/99.

286 *"a backward look"*: CF, "Road to the Victors."

286 *"specious, sentimental, and false"*: *NYT*, 12/20/63.

287 *"Carl laid his own job on the line"*: Cole, pp. 382 and 390.

287 *"A Western of truly stunning absurdity"*: *NYT*, 6/19/69.

287 *"a big balsa-wood monument"*: *NYT*, 10/11/72.

288 *"Carl had a fit"*: George Lucas interview, *Darkness at High Noon*, 2/12/01.

288 *"Your whole life will change"*: CF, "Do It Yourself," 4/12/61, draft for *Screen Writers* magazine, p. 4, Item 3: Articles 1961–2, CF Collection 2, BFI.

289 *"Carl absolutely adored Cooper"*: Author's interview with Eve Williams-Jones.

289 *"You know how much I have wanted"*: Meyer, pp. 248–9.

289 *"They really liked each other"*: Author's interview with Maria Cooper Janis.

289 *"When the carving was over"*: Cooper, "I Took a Good Look at Myself and This Is What I Saw," as told to Leonard Slater, *McCall's*, 1/61, p. 62.

290 *"I am uncomfortable"*: Ibid., p. 138.

290 "High Noon *wasn't new*": Ibid., p. 140.

290 *"I had worked with actors"*: Dunne, p. 287.

291 *he stopped by Carl Foreman's office*: Author's interview with Eve Williams-Jones.

291 Arranging Fred Zinnemann's remarriage: Janis, p. 98.

291 Cooper's declining health: Meyers, p. 314.

291 *"one of the bravest"*: Draft piece by CF, Item 3, Articles 1961–2, BFI.

291 *Cooper's last film: The Real West* documentary, 1961.

Epilogue

293 *"like a continuous earthquake"*: CF Tape, XXIX-B, 1/27/78.

293 *"Cowboys fight for justice"*: Lech Wałesa, "In Solidarity," *Wall Street Journal*, 6/11/04.

294 Articles and headlines are from: *Arizona Republic*, 1/4/16; *Edmonton Journal*, 12/9/13; *Chicago Daily Herald*, 2/3/13; *Salisbury (Maryland) Daily Times*, 9/30/13; www. fryingpannews.org, 10/16/13; www.globalpost.com, 9/30/13; *Mail & Guardian* (Johannesburg, South Africa), 11/29/13; *Kansas City Star*, 3/7/14.

294 "'Run!' shouted Ike": Hoberman, "It's Always *High Noon* at the White House," *NYT*, 4/25/04.

295 *"High Noon has stayed with me"*: Clinton quotes from *Inside High Noon* documentary.

295 *"This weary loner's brave posture"*: *NYT*, 4/25/04.

295 *Man's Fate* project: see FZ, pp. 208–9.

296 *"Carl Foreman's* High Noon *is in fact NOT"*: Unpublished letter, FZ to the Editor, *The Observer*, 10/12/65, b.103, FZ Papers, MHL.

297 *"a spiritual cousin:"* "Fred Zinnemann: As I See It," documentary by Tim Zinnemann.

297 *"There is a through line"*: Author's interview with Tim Zinnemann.

297 *"The Reds and their pals"*: MB letter to Hopper, 10/31/53, HH Collection, MHL.

297 *"A plug from you"*: MB to Hopper, 10/20/55.

298 *"self-esteem and importance"*: FBI COMPIC Memo, 100-15732, 11/30/54, p. 30 Leab Microfilm.

298 *"There is no general authority"*: Watkins v US, 6/17/57.

299 *"Kramer did not insist"*: Joshua Smith, "The True Story of the Breaking of the Hollywood Blacklist," press release, n.d.

299 *"We've lost the fight:"* in Larry M. Wertheim, "Nedrick Young et al v. MPAA et al: The Fight Against the Hollywood Blacklist," *Southern California Quarterly*, 57:4, Winter 1975, p. 389.

299 *"the danger and folly"*: LA Examiner, 2/17/60.

299 *"un-American and reprehensible"*: Independent Film Journal, 2/13/60.

299 *he debated McKneally*: "Kramer Debates Legion Head," *NYT*, 2/15/60.

300 *"Martyrdom comes hard"*: Film Daily, 117: 85, 5/3/60.

300 *"It was fine"*: "Kennedy Attends Movie in Capitol," *NYT*, 2/5/61, p. 39.

300 *"unemployability by marriage"*: Lardner, I'd Hate Myself, p. 139.

300 *"I know you named me"*: Lee Grant, *I Said Yes to Everything* (New York: Blue Rider Press, 2014), p. 199.

300 *Lucille Ball: LAT,* 11/24/76.

301 *Arens left the committee under a cloud: The Nation,* May 14, 1960. 190:2.

301 *"moving relentlessly"*: Richard Arens, "Dangers to U.S. Internal Security," 6/22/59. National Education Program, p. 5, Arens file, HUAC Box 1487–76.

302 *"I know you will be disappointed"*: MB letter to Navasky, 6/25/76, B.19, f.34.

302 *fiftieth anniversary of the Hollywood Ten:* Greg Kritzman, "Hollywood Remembers the Blacklist," *Screen Actor*, January 1998.

303 *members failed to stand: NYT*, 3/21/99.

303 *"In his maniacal quest"*: *HR*, 11/30/12.

304 *Dorothy B. Jones's study:* Cogley pp. 231–2.

304 See Karina Longworth's discussion of political movies, *You Must Remember This* podcast.

304 *"What I did not write about"*: Author's interview with Victor Navasky.

305 *"Gary Cooper in Europe"*: *Wall Street Journal*, 8/23/15.

305 *"It's too much to say"*: Maria Cooper Janis, "The Tao of Cooper: Why *High Noon* Still Matters," *Time*, 7/24/12.

305 *"We had shared a purgatory"*: Neal, p. 358.

305 The enduring economics of *High Noon*: "The Republic Pictures Film Library," *Film Score Monthly*, 6/15/13. http://filmscoremonthly.com/board/posts.cfm?threadID=96880&forumID=1&archive=0

306 *"At the time I sold"*: Kramer, p. 67.

306 *"the unhappiest period"*: Ibid., p. 89.

306 For the remaking of the studio system, see Schatz, *Genius*, pp. 4–5.

307 *"the apostle of the safely controversial"*: CF, "Anatomy of a Classic", 1, p. 27.

307 *"a deliberate hatchet job"*: Author's interview with Karen Kramer.

308 *"There were no heroes"*: Ceplair, "Shedding Light on *Darkness at High Noon*," *Cineaste*, Fall 2002, p. 22.

308 *"Why is it that some films"*: This and subsequent quotes are from Hoey audio interview with SK, 10/3/73, USC.

309 *"The films you made"*: David Robb, "Golden Globes' Most Touching Moment." *Deadline Hollywood*, 1/12/15.

309 *"A part of him wanted to come home"*: Author's interview with Jonathan Foreman.

309 The Biko project was finally filmed in 1986 by Richard Attenborough as *Cry Freedom*, starring Kevin Kline, Denzel Washington, and Penelope Wilton.

310 *"Duke, I want you to meet"*: *Darkness at High Noon* documentary.

310 *announced a deal:* See "CF to Make Three Features, Two Major TV Projects, for Universal," Universal Pictures Press Release, 7/17/78, Chetwynd Files.

310 *nonexclusive pact with Warner Bros.:* "CF to WB in Spring," *Variety*, 5/23/79.

310 *Weaver found a copy:* John D. Weaver, *Darkness at High Noon* interview, 12/6/00, p. 8, Chetwynd Files.

310 *Weaver took the news: NYT*, 3/16/85, p. 11.

311 *"I trust that you"*: Dmohowski, "Under the Table: Michael Wilson and the Screenplay for *The Bridge on the River Kwai*," *Cineaste*, Spring 2009, p. 21.

311 *"Every time I sat down"*: CF interview with Ceplair, 5/19/77, Ceplair Files.

SELECT BIBLIOGRAPHY

Archives and Collections

British Film Institute, London:
Carl Foreman Papers
Fred Zinnemann Papers

Columbia University Oral History Collection, New York:
Edward Dmytryk
Carl Foreman

Library of Congress, Washington, D.C.:
Main Reading Room
Microfilm and Electronic Research Center:
    Communist Activity in the Entertainment Industry FBI Files (Leab Microfilm)
Moving Image Research Center:
    Body and Soul, Cornered, Force of Evil, The Hoaxters, I Was a Communist for the FBI,
        The Sniper, Till the End of Time
Performing Arts Reading Room
Prints and Photographs Division

Margaret Herrick Library of the Academy of Motion Picture Arts and Sciences, Los
    Angeles:
American Legion anti-Communist Material
Rudy Behlmer Papers
Charles Champlin Collection
Communist Activity in the Entertainment Industry FBI Files
Hedda Hopper Papers
Elizabeth Poe Kerby Papers
Joseph L. Mankiewicz Papers
Lawrence H. Suid File
Fred Zinnemann Collection

National Archives and Record Administration, Washington, D.C.:
House Committee on Un-American Activities Files
FBI Files on Gary Cooper, Carl Foreman, and Stanley Kramer

National Archives Motion Picture, Sound and Video Branch at College Park, Md.:
Paramount News newsreels

Museum of Modern Art, Film Study Center, New York:
High Noon, Gary Cooper, and Fred Zinnemann Clipping Files

New York Public Library, Dorot Jewish Division:
American Jewish Committee Oral Histories: Martin Gang

NYPL Performing Arts Library:
Clipping files for Gary Cooper and Grace Kelly

New York University Tamiment Library, New York:
Victor Navasky Papers

Northwestern University, Chicago:
Patricia Neal Papers

UCLA Special Collections Library, Los Angeles:
Martin Berkeley Papers
Stanley Kramer Papers
Michael Wilson Papers

UCLA Oral History Collection:
Roy M. Brewer
Ben Margolies
Elizabeth Poe Kerby
Zelma Wilson

University of Southern California Cinematic Arts Library:
Michael A. Hoey audio interviews
Warner Bros. Archives

Writers Guild Foundation, Los Angeles:
Screen Writers Guild files

Private Holdings

Larry Ceplair:
Interviews and articles

Lionel Chetwynd:
Carl Foreman Papers and CF Tape transcripts
Darkness at High Noon interview transcripts

J. Hoberman:
Select copies of FBI files

Joanne Taylor-Johnson:
Bruce Church letters, memos, and photographs

Karen Kramer:
Stanley Kramer letters and clippings

Tim Zinnemann:
Letters to Fred Zinnemann

Blacklist Books

Banks, Miranda J. *The Writers: A History of American Screenwriters and Their Guild*. New Brunswick, N.J.: Rutgers University, 2015.

Barth, Alan. *The Loyalty of Free Men*. New York: Cardinal, 1952 (paperback).

Barzman, Norma. *The Red and the Blacklist: The Intimate Memoir of a Hollywood Expatriate*. New York: Nation Books, 2003.

Bentley, Eric. *Thirty Years of Treason: Excerpts from Hearings Before the House Committee on Un-American Activities, 1938–68*. New York: Nation Books, 2001.

Bernstein, Carl. *Loyalties: A Son's Memoir*. New York: Simon and Schuster, 1989.

Bernstein, Walter. *Inside Out: A Memoir of the Blacklist*. New York: Knopf, 1996.

Bessie, Alvah. *Inquisition in Eden*. Berlin: Seven Seas, 1967.

Buhle, Paul and Dave Wagner. *Radical Hollywood: The Untold Story Behind America's Favorite Movies*. New York: New Press, 2002.

——*A Very Dangerous Citizen: Abraham Lincoln Polonsky and the Hollywood Left*. Berkeley: University of California Press, 2001.

Casty, Alan. *Communism in Hollywood: The Moral Paradoxes of Testimony, Silence, and Betrayal*. Lanham, MD: Scarecrow Press, 2009.

——*Robert Rossen: The Films and Politics of a Blacklisted Idealist*. Jefferson, N.C.: McFarland, 2013.

Caute, David. *The Great Fear: The Anti-Communist Purge Under Truman and Eisenhower*. New York: Simon & Schuster, 1978.

——*Joseph Losey: A Revenge on Life*. London: Faber and Faber, 1994.

Ceplair, Larry and Steven Englund. *The Inquisition in Hollywood: Politics in the Film Community 1930–1960*. Garden City, NY: Anchor Press, 1980.

——and Christopher Trumbo. *Dalton Trumbo: Blacklisted Hollywood Radical*. Lexington: University Press of Kentucky, 2015.

Ciment, Michel. *Conversations with Losey*. London: Methuen, 1985.

Cogley, John. *Report on Blacklisting: I. Movies*. The Fund for the Republic, 1956.

Cole, Lester. *Hollywood Red: The Autobiography of Lester Cole*. Palo Alto: Ramparts Press, 1981.

Critchlow, Donald T. *When Hollywood Was Right: How Movie Stars, Studio Moguls,* and *Big Business Remade American Politics*. Cambridge, UK: Cambridge University, 2013.

Dmytryk, Edward. *Odd Man Out: A Memoir of the Hollywood Ten.* Carbondale: Southern Illinois University Press, 1996.

Donner, Frank J. *The Un-Americans.* New York: Ballantine, 1961.

Douglas, Kirk. *I Am Spartacus!* New York: Open Road, 2012.

Dunne, Philip. *Take Two: A Life in Movies and Politics.* New York: McGraw-Hill, 1980.

Eyman, Scott. *John Wayne: The Life and the Legend.* New York: Simon & Schuster, 2014.

FBI Confidential Files. *Communist Activity in the Entertainment Industry. FBI Surveillance Files on Hollywood 1942–58* [microfilm]. Daniel J. Leab, ed. Bethesda: University Publications of America, 1991.

Forster, Arnold. *Square One.* New York: Donald I. Fine, 1988.

Fourth Report: Un-American Activities in California, Communist Front Organizations. Joint Fact-Finding Committee to the 1948 Regular California Legislature, Sacramento 1948.

Gabler, Neal. *An Empire of Their Own: How the Jews Invented Hollywood.* New York: Crown, 1988.

Garrett, Betty with Ron Rapoport. *Betty Garrett and Other Songs: A Life on Stage and Screen.* Lanham, Md.: Madison, 1998.

Grant, Lee. *I Said Yes to Everything.* New York: Blue Rider Press, 2014.

Goodman, Walter. *The Committee.* New York: Farrar, Strauss and Giroux, 1968.

Hayden, Sterling. *Wanderer.* New York: Knopf, 1963.

Haynes, John Earl and Harvey Klehr. *In Denial: Historians, Communism & Espionage.* San Francisco: Encounter, 2003.

——and Fidrikh Firsov. *The Secret World of American Communism.* New Haven: Yale University, 1996.

Hellman, Lillian. *Scoundrel Time.* New York: Little, Brown, 1976.

Hoberman, J. *An Army of Phantoms: American Movies and the Making of the Cold War.* New York: New Press, 2011.

Horne, Gerald. *The Final Victim of the Blacklist: John Howard Lawson, Dean of the Hollywood Ten.* Berkeley: University of California, 2006.

House Committee on Un-American Activities. *Communist Infiltration of the Motion-Picture Industry, Hearings.* 82nd Congress, 1951–2, Parts. I-X. Washington: Government Printing Office, 1951–2.

——*Hearings Regarding the Communist Infiltration of the Motion Picture Industry*, 80th Congress, October 1947. Washington, GPO, 1947.

Kanfer, Stefan. *A Journal of the Plague Years.* New York: Atheneum, 1973.

Kazan, Elia. *A Life.* New York: Knopf, 1988.

Kazin, Michael. *American Dreamers: How the Left Changed a Nation.* New York: Knopf, 2011.

Koch, Howard. *As Time Goes By: Memories of a Writer.* New York: Harcourt Brace Jovanovich, 1979.

Kraft, Hy. *On My Way to the Theater.* New York: Macmillan, 1971.

Langdon, Jennifer. *Caught in the Crossfire: Adrian Scott and the Politics of Americanism in 1940s Hollywood.* New York: Columbia University, 2009.

Lardner Jr., Ring. *I'd Hate Myself in the Morning: A Memoir.* New York: Nation Books, 2000.

McWilliams, Carey. *The Education of Carey McWilliams.* New York: Simon & Schuster, 1978.

Miller, Arthur. *Timebends: A Life*. New York: Grove Press, 1987.

Navasky, Victor S. *Naming Names*. New York: Viking, 1980.

Nelson, Steve, and James B. Barrett and Bob Peck. *American Radical*. Pittsburgh: University of Pittsburgh, 1981.

Prime, Rebecca. *Hollywood Exiles in Europe: The Blacklist and Cold War Film Culture*. New Brunswick, N.J.: Rutgers University, 2014.

Radosh, Ronald and Allis. *Red Star Over Hollywood: The Film Colony's Long Romance with the Left*. San Francisco: Encounter, 2005.

Ross, Steven J. *Hollywood Left and Right: How Movie Stars Shaped American Politics*. Oxford: Oxford University, 2011.

Ryskind, Alan H. *Hollywood Traitors: Blacklisted Screenwriters, Agents of Stalin, Allies of Hitler*. Washington: Regnery, 2015.

Sayre, Nora. *Previous Convictions: A Journey Through the 1950s*. New Brunswick, N.J.: Rutgers University, 1995.

——*Running Time: Films of the Cold War*. New York: Doubleday, 1982.

Schrecker, Ellen. *Many Are the Crimes: McCarthyism in America*. Boston: Little, Brown, 1998.

Schwartz, Nancy Lynn. *The Hollywood Writers' Wars*. New York: Knopf, 1982.

Swindell, Larry. *Body and Soul: The Story of John Garfield*. New York: Morrow, 1975.

Tender Comrades: A Backstory of the Hollywood Backlist. Patrick McGilligan and Paul Buhle, eds. New York: St. Martin's Press, 1997.

Theoharos, Athan. *Chasing Spies*. Chicago: Ivan R. Dee, 2002.

"Un-American" Hollywood: Politics and Film in the Blacklist Era. Peter Stanfield, et al, eds. New Brunswick, N.J.: Rutgers University, 2007.

Vaughn, Robert. *Only Victims: A Study of Show Business Blacklisting*. New York: Putnam's, 1972.

Wills, Garry. *John Wayne's America: The Politics of Celebrity*. New York: Simon & Schuster, 1997.

Hollywood and High Noon *Books*

Balio, Tino. *Grand Design: Hollywood as a Modern Business Enterprise, 1930–1939. History of the American Cinema 5*. Berkeley: University of California, 1995.

——*United Artists: The Company That Changed the Film Industry*. Madison: University of Wisconsin, 1987.

Basinger, Jeanine. *The Star Machine*. New York: Knopf, 2007.

Behlmer, Rudy. *America's Favorite Movies: Behind the Scenes*. New York: Frederick Ungar, 1982.

BFI Companion to the Western, The. Edward Buscombe, ed. London: Andre Deutsch, 1993.

Bingen, Steven. *Warner Bros.: Hollywood's Ultimate Backlot*. Lanham, Md.: Taylor, 2014.

Blake, Michael F. *Code of Honor: The Making of Three Great American Westerns*. Lanham, Md.: Taylor, 2003.

Byman, Jeremy. *Showdown at High Noon: Witch-Hunts, Critics and the End of the Western*. Lanham, Md.: Scarecrow Press, 2004.

Capra, Frank. *The Name Above the Title*. New York: Macmillan, 1971.

Dickens, Homer. *The Complete Films of Gary Cooper*. New York: Citadel Press, 1970.

Drummond, Phillip. *High Noon*. London: British Film Institute, 1997.

Englund, Steven. *Grace of Monaco: An Interpretive Biography*. Garden City, N.Y.: Doubleday, 1984.

Eyman, Scott. *Lion of Hollywood: The Life and Legend of Louis B. Mayer*. New York: Simon & Schuster, 2005.

——*The Speed of Sound: Hollywood and the Talkie Revolution 1926–1930*. New York: Simon & Schuster, 1997.

Film Scripts Two: High Noon, Twelve Angry Men and the Defiant Ones. George P. Garrett, O. P. Hardison Jr., Jane R. Gelfman, eds. Milwaukee: Applause, 2013.

The Films of Fred Zinnemann: Critical Perspectives. Arthur Nolletti Jr., ed. Albany: State University of New York, 1999.

Fitzgerald, F. Scott. *The Love of the Last Tycoon*. New York: Scribner's, 1993 edition.

Friedrich, Otto. *City of Nets: A Portrait of Hollywood in the 1940s*. London: Headline, 1986.

Frost, Jennifer. *Hedda Hopper's Hollywood: Celebrity Gossip and American Conservatism*. New York: New York University, 2011.

Geist, Kenneth L. *Pictures Will Talk: The Life and Films of Joseph L. Mankiewicz*. New York: Scribner's, 1978.

Holden, Anthony. *The Oscars: The Secret History of Hollywood's Academy Awards*. London: Warner Books, 1994.

Hopper, Hedda and James Brough. *The Whole Truth and Nothing But*. New York: Doubleday, 1963.

Isherwood, Christopher. *Prater Violet*. Minneapolis: University of Minnesota, 2001.

Janis, Maria Cooper. *Gary Cooper Off Camera: A Daughter Remembers*. New York: Harry N. Abrams, 1999.

——*Gary Cooper: Enduring Style*. Text by G. Bruce Boyer. Brooklyn: Powerhouse, 2011.

Kaminsky, Stuart. *Coop: The Life and Legend of Gary Cooper*. New York: St. Martin's Press, 1980.

Kramer, Stanley. *A Mad, Mad, Mad, Mad World*. New York: Harcourt Brace, 1997.

Lacey, Robert. *Grace*. London: Sedgwick and Jackson, 1994.

Lasky Jr., Jesse. *Whatever Happened to Hollywood?* New York: Funk & Wagnalls, 1975.

McCarthy, Todd. *Howard Hawks: The Grey Fox of Hollywood*. New York: Grove Press, 1997.

Meyers, Jeffrey. *Gary Cooper: American Hero*. New York: Cooper Square Press, 2001.

Neal, Patricia. *As I Am: An Autobiography*. New York: Simon & Schuster, 1988.

O'Neal, Bill. *Tex Ritter: America's Most Beloved Cowboy*. Austin: Eakin Press, 1998.

Palmer, Christopher. *Dimitri Tiomkin: A Portrait*. London: TE Books, 1984.

Parrish, Robert. *Growing Up in Hollywood*. New York: Harcourt Brace Jovanovich, 1976.

Picker, David V. *Musts, Maybes, and Nevers: A Book About the Movies*. North Charleston, S.C.: CreateSpace, 2013.

Powdermaker, Hortense. *Hollywood: The Dream Factory*. Boston: Little, Brown, 1950. Reprinted 2013 by Martino Publishing.

Reagan, Ronald. *An American Life*. New York: Simon & Schuster, 1991.

Schary, Dore. *Heyday: An Autobiography*. Boston: Little, Brown, 1979.

Schatz, Thomas. *Boom and Bust: The American Cinema in the 1940s. History of the American Cinema 6*. New York: Charles Scribner's Sons, 1997.

——*The Genius of the System: Hollywood Filmmaking in the Studio Era*. New York: Pantheon, 1988.

Schickel, Richard. *Schickel on Film*. New York: William Morrow, 1989.

Schulberg, Budd. *Moving Pictures: Memories of a Hollywood Prince*. New York: Stein & Day, 1981.

——*What Makes Sammy Run?* New York: Random House, 1941.

Slotkin, Richard. *Gunfighter Nation: The Myth of the Frontier in Twentieth-Century America*. New York: Atheneum, 1992.

Smyth, J. E. *Fred Zinnemann and the Cinema of Resistance*. Jackson: University of Mississippi, 2014.

Spoto, Donald. *High Society: The Life of Grace Kelly*. New York: Harmony, 2009.

——*Stanley Kramer: Filmmaker*. New York: Putnam, 1978.

Stein, Jean. *West of Eden: An American Place*. New York: Random House, 2016.

Stevens Jr., George. *Conversations with the Great Moviemakers of Hollywood's Golden Era at the American Film Institute*. New York: Vintage, 2007.

Swindell, Larry. *The Last Hero: A Biography of Gary Cooper*. New York: Doubleday, 1980.

Thomson, David. *Gary Cooper* (Great Stars series). Faber & Faber, 2010.

Tiomkin, Dimitri and Prosper Buranelli. *Please Don't Hate Me*. Garden City, NY: Doubleday, 1959.

Wagner, Walter. *You Must Remember This*. New York: G.P. Putnam's Sons, 1975.

Walker, Alexander. *Hollywood England: The British Film Industry in the Sixties*. London: Michael Joseph, 1974.

Warshow, Robert. *The Immediate Experience: Movies, Comics, Theatre and Other Aspects of Popular Culture*. Garden City, NY: Doubleday, 1962.

Wayne, Jane Ellen. *Cooper's Women*. New York: Prentice Hall, 1988.

Williams, Elmo. *A Hollywood Memoir*. Jefferson, N.C.: McFarland, 2006.

Wister, Owen. *The Virginian*. New York: Grosset & Dunlap edition, 1929.

Zinnemann, Fred. *A Life in the Movies: An Autobiography*. London: Bloomsbury, 1992.

Select Articles

Berkeley, Martin, "Red Congressmen," *American Mercury*, Dec., 1953, pp. 93–6.

——"Reds in Your Living Room," *American Mercury*, August, 1953, pp. 55–62.

Bogart, Humphrey, "I'm No Communist," *Photoplay*, May, 1948, p. 53–4.

Commager, Henry Steele, "Who Is Loyal to America?" *Harper's*, 195:1168, September, 1947, pp. 193–9.

Cooper, Gary (as told to George Scullin), "Well, It Was This Way," *Saturday Evening Post*, Eight-Part Series, 2/18 thru 4/7/56.

——(as told to Leonard Slater), "I Took a Good Look at Myself, and This Is What I Saw," *McCall's*, January 1961, pp. 62, 138–42.

Cunningham, J. W., "The Tin Star," *Collier's*, 12/6/1947.

English, Richard, "We Almost Lost Hawaii to the Reds," *Saturday Evening Post*, 2/2/1952.

——"What Makes a Hollywood Communist?" *Saturday Evening Post*, 5/10/1951.

Foreman, Amanda and Jonathan Foreman, "Our Dad Was No Commie," *New Statesman*, 3/26/1999.

Foreman, Carl, "*High Noon* Revisited," *Punch*, 4/25/1972, pp. 448–50.

——"Dialogue on Film," *American Film*, 4 (April 1979), pp. 35–46.

Foreman, Jonathan, "Exile on Jermyn Street," *Standpoint*, July/August 2009, http://standpointmag.co.uk/node/1697/full

——"Witch-hunt," *Index on Censorship*, June 1995, pp. 96–9.

Foster, Gwendolyn, "The Women in *High Noon*: A Metanarrative of Difference," *Film Criticism*, c. 18/19, 1, Spring/Fall 1994, pp. 72–81.

Hofstadter, Richard, "The Paranoid Style in American Politics," *Harper's*, Nov. 1964.

Kramer, Hilton, "The Blacklist & the Cold War," *The New York Times*, 10/3/1976.

Jacobs, Paul, "Good Guys, Bad Guys, and Congressman Walter," *The Reporter*, 5/15/58, pp. 29–31.

Lardner Jr., Ring, "My Life on the Blacklist," *Saturday Evening Post*, 10/14/61, pp. 38–44.

Maltz, Albert, "What Shall We Ask of Writers?" *New Masses*, 2/12/1946, pp. 19–22.

Mathews, J. B., "Did the Movies Really Clean House?" *American Legion Magazine*, Dec. 1951.

"Preview of the War We Do Not Want," *Collier's* (special issue), 10/27/51.

Rapf, Joanna E., "Myth, Ideology, and Feminism in High Noon," *Journal of Popular Culture*, Spring 1990: 23, pp. 75–80.

Robinson, Edward G., "How the reds made a sucker out of me," *American Legion Magazine*, Oct. 1952, pp. 11, 61–70.

Ross, Lillian, "Come in, Lassie!" *New Yorker*, 2/21/48, pp. 32–48.

Yacowar, Maurice, "Cyrano de HUAC," *Journal of Popular Film*, 5:1, 1976, pp. 68–75.

Zinnemann, Fred, "Choreography of a Gun Fight," *Sight and Sound*, 6:1, Jan. 1966, pp. 14–15.

Documentary Films

Cooper & Hemingway: The True Gen. Written and directed by John Mulholland. New York: Passion River, 2013.

Darkness at High Noon: The Carl Foreman Documents. Written and directed by Lionel Chetwynd. Whidbey Island Films, 2001.

High Noon: 2 -Disc Ultimate Collector's Edition, 2008.

Hollywood on Trial. Directed by David Helpern, written by Arnie Reisman. Cinema Associates, 1976.

The Making of High Noon. Written by Leonard Maltin. Moda Entertainment, 2006.

Marsha Hunt Interview—Pt. 2, Film Noir Foundation, 7/3/12. https://www.youtube.com/watch?v=JfESD_XXg9c

The Real West, Written by Phillip Reisman Jr., produced and directed by Donald B. Hyatt. Project Twenty NBC News, 1961.

Red Hollywood. Written and directed by Thom Andersen and Noel Burch. Cinema Guild, 2014.

Word Into Image: Screenwriter Carl Foreman. Sanders, Terry and Frieda Lee Mock. Santa Monica, Ca.: American Film Foundation, 1981.

Websites

http://www.cinematographers.nl/GreatDoPh/crosby.htm
"Great Cinematographers: Floyd Crosby"
www.garycooperscrapbook.proboards.com online collection of articles, photographs,
    and other memorabilia gathered and maintained by Coopsgirl.
www.youmustrememberthispodcast.com Karina Longworth's stories of Hollywood's
    first century, including a sixteen-part series on the Hollywood blacklist.

INDEX

A NOTE ON THE AUTHOR

Glenn Frankel is a Pulitzer Prize–winning journalist and bestselling author of *The Searchers: The Making of an American Legend*, as well as critically acclaimed books on Israel and South Africa. He spent twenty-seven years at the *Washington Post*, serving as bureau chief in southern Africa, Jerusalem, and London, and as editor of the *Washington Post Magazine*. He won a Pulitzer Prize for International Reporting for "balanced and sensitive reporting" of Israelis and Palestinians. He has taught journalism at Stanford University and the University of Texas at Austin, where he also served as Director of the School of Journalism. He and his wife live in Arlington, Virginia.